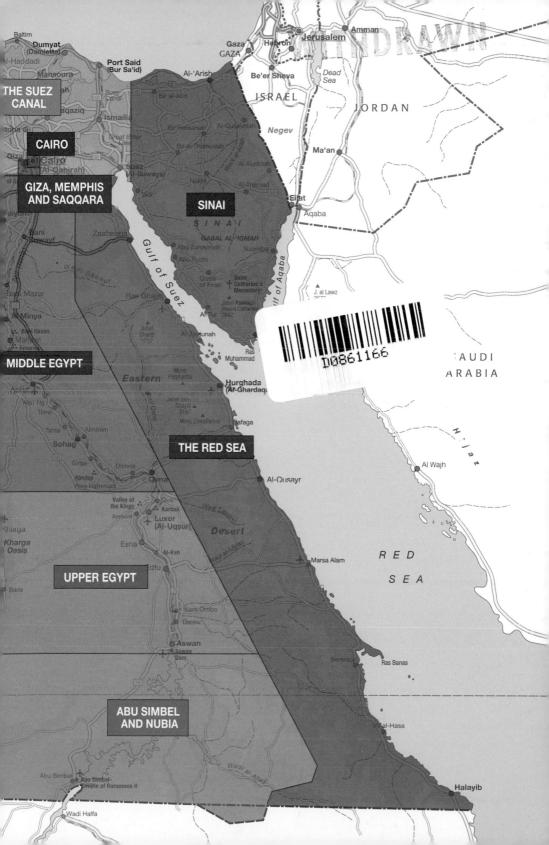

INSIGHT GUIDES
EGYPT

PLAN & BOOK
YOUR TAILOR-MADE TRIP

BRAZIL CHILE ECUADOR

TAILOR-MADE TRIPS & UNIQUE EXPERIENCES CREATED BY LOCAL TRAVEL EXPERTS AT INSIGHTGUIDES.COM/HOLIDAYS

Insight Guides has been inspiring travellers with high-quality travel content for over 45 years. As well as our popular guidebooks, we now offer the opportunity to book tailor-made private trips completely personalised to your needs and interests. By connecting with one of our local experts, you will directly benefit from their expertise and local know-how, helping you create memories that will last a lifetime.

HOW INSIGHTGUIDES.COM/HOLIDAYS WORKS

STEP 1

Pick your dream destination and submit an enquiry, or modify an existing itinerary if you prefer.

STEP 2

Fill in a short form, sharing details of your travel plans and preferences with a local expert.

STEP 3

Your local expert will create your personalised itinerary, which you can amend until you are completely satisfied.

STEP 4

Book securely online. Pack your bags and enjoy your holiday! Your local expert will be available to answer questions during your trip.

BENEFITS OF PLANNING & BOOKING AT INSIGHTGUIDES.COM/HOLIDAYS

PLANNED BY LOCAL EXPERTS

The Insight Guides local experts are hand-picked, based on their experience in the travel industry and their impeccable standards of customer service.

SAVE TIME & MONEY

When a local expert plans your trip, you save time and money when you book, even during high season. You won't be charged for using a credit card either.

TAILOR-MADE TRIPS

Book with Insight Guides, and you will be in complete control of the planning process, from the initial selections to amending your final itinerary.

BOOK & TRAVEL STRESS-FREE

Enjoy stress-free travel when you use the Insight Guides secure online booking platform. All bookings come with a money-back guarantee.

WHAT OTHER TRAVELLERS THINK ABOUT TRIPS BOOKED AT INSIGHTGUIDES.COM/HOLIDAYS

Trip to Portugal

Every step of the planning process and the trip itself was effortless and exceptional. Our special interests, preferences and requests were accommodated resulting in a trip that exceeded our expectations.

Corinne, USA   ★★★★★

Trip to Vietnam

The organization was superb, the drivers professional, and accommodation quite comfortable. I was well taken care of! My thanks to your colleagues who helped make my trip to Vietnam such a great experience. My only regret is that I couldn't spend more time in the country.

Heather   ★★★★★

DON'T MISS OUT BOOK NOW AT
INSIGHTGUIDES.COM/HOLIDAYS

CONTENTS

LEGEND

◯ Insight on
◉ Photo story

THE BEST OF EGYPT: TOP ATTRACTIONS

△ **Temple of Karnak**. This fine temple at Luxor was developed over many centuries. Its massive Hypostyle Hall is the largest hall of any temple in the world, and its columns are carved with scenes of the pharaohs who built it. See page 209.

▽ **Egyptian Museum**. Crammed with Pharaonic treasures, statues, mummies and tomb goods. Highly recommended if you want to learn more about ancient Egypt. See page 134.

△ **Abu Simbel**. On the shores of Lake Nasser. With its smaller temples dedicated to Ramesses II and his Queen, Nefertari, Abu Simbel is one of Egypt's most impressive sights. See page 247.

△ **Pyramids of Giza**. One of the original Seven Wonders of the Ancient World, on the edge of the desert plain, west of Cairo. See page 166.

△ **Cairo**. The capital's historic mosques, madrasas and bazaars nestle below the domes and minarets of the Citadel. See pages 131–63.

◁ **Red Sea**. The Red Sea's coral reefs offer some of the best diving and snorkelling in the world. If you don't dive, you can unwind on white-sand beaches. See page 295.

▷ **Nile cruise**. There are many ways to enjoy the Nile, but it is hard to beat a cruise, on a modern cruise boat, a *dahabeeyah* or a simple felucca. See page 310.

△ **Thebes Necropolis**. Thebes Necropolis, on the west bank of the Nile at Luxor, is riddled with ancient royal tombs. In the Valley of the Kings you'll find the tomb of boy-king Tutankhamun, but don't miss the wonderfully decorated Tombs of the Nobles. See pages 220 and 222.

▽ **Aswan**. This slow-paced city in Upper Egypt is situated on the picturesque First Cataract, where the Nile is scattered with islands such as Elephantine. It is a great place to relax, with a superb winter climate. See page 228.

△ **The Temple of Isis**. One of the finest Ptolemaic temples is located at Philae. Spectacularly set on Agilkia Island, it is approached by boat from Aswan. See page 244.

THE BEST OF EGYPT: EDITOR'S CHOICE

Inside the Temple of Horus, Edfu.

PHARAONIC HIGHLIGHTS

The Pyramids of Giza. One of the Seven Wonders of the Ancient World, the Pyramids are on the edge of Cairo. Also here are the Sphinx and the Solar Boat Museum. See page 166.

Saqqara. A day-trip from Cairo, Saqqara is well worth visiting. Its Step Pyramid is the earliest of all the pyramids, and its tombs are among the most finely decorated. See page 171.

Thebes Necropolis, Luxor. Comprising the Valley of the Kings, the Valley of the Queens and the Valley of the Nobles, as well as the various mortuary temples, this vast necropolis on the west coast of the Nile has the greatest concentration of ancient tombs in Egypt. See page 215.

Karnak, Luxor. The splendid Temple of Amun-Ra at Karnak was one of the most important religious and intellectual centres for more than 13 centuries. See page 209.

Abu Simbel. The Temple of Ramesses II on Lake Nasser, south of Aswan, is all the more awe-inspiring for being cut into the cliff face. Nearby is the Temple of Queen Nefertari. See page 247.

Edfu. This Ptolemaic temple south of Luxor is dedicated to the falcon god Horus and is one of the best-preserved temples. See page 226.

Kom Ombo. This temple dedicated to Sobek the crocodile god and Horus the falcon god is set on a sweeping bend in the Nile 40km (25 miles) north of Aswan. See page 227.

Philae. Set on Agilkia Island, this Ptolemaic temple was moved here stone by stone to escape the waters of Lake Nasser after the creation of the Aswan Dam. See page 243.

Kom Ombo at night.

MOSQUES AND MADRASAS

Mosque of Ibn Tulun, Cairo. This mosque dates from 905 and is built in the imperial style of the Abbasid court in Samarra in Iraq. See page 146.

The Mosque-Madrasa of Sultan Hassan, Cairo. This 14th-century madrasa is the greatest of the Bahri monuments. Its neighbour, the Al-Rifa'i Mosque, is also worth seeing. See pages 148–9.

Muhammad Ali Mosque, Cairo. Built in the Ottoman style, this mosque with its slender minarets and dome forms an evocative silhouette on the city's eastern skyline. See page 150.

Al-Ghouri Complex, Cairo. The beautiful madrasa and mausoleum of one of the last Mamluk sultans. See page 154.

Mosque of Aqsunqur, Cairo. This mosque, built in 1347, is adorned with Damascene tiles and is often known as the Blue Mosque. See page 152.

Al-Azhar Mosque and University, Cairo. Built in 988, the Al-Azhar was one of the first universities in the world. See page 155.

The beautiful Al-Azhar Mosque.

BEST VIEWS

The Pyramids, Giza. Nothing quite matches the view of the Pyramids, even if it is somewhat marred by the proximity of Cairo's sprawling suburbs. See page 166.

The Nile at Aswan. The views across the First Cataract at Aswan are among the loveliest in Egypt, especially when a felucca or two is floating past. See page 230.

Jebel Musa. Popularly known as Mount Sinai, a climb to the top offers far-reaching views of the Sinai Desert that haven't changed since biblical times. See page 291.

View from Cairo's Citadel. Great views of Cairo can be had from the Citadel. Darb al-Ahmar, leading north from the Citadel, offers evocative views of the city's medieval architecture. See page 149.

IMPORTANT CHRISTIAN SIGHTS

Churches of Misr al Qadima, Cairo. Confusingly called "Old Cairo", this area contains the remains of Roman and early Christian Cairo, including several churches dating from the 4th century. See page 143.

Coptic Museum, Cairo. This museum in Old Cairo contains items from early churches all over Egypt. See page 142.

St Catherine's Monastery, Sinai. This fortress monastery in the Sinai was constructed on the orders of the Roman emperor Justinian and contains 6th-century mosaics, silver chests inlaid with precious stones and ancient icons. See page 289.

The Monasteries of Wadi El Natrun. This handful of ancient monasteries in the Western Desert once numbered 50. See page 270.

Wall painting of Christ at the Coptic Museum, Cairo.

Pilgrims atop Mount Sinai.

Camel on a Sharm El Sheikh beach.

REST AND RELAXATION

Red Sea. The coral reefs of the Red Sea are among the world's top diving sites. Sharm El Sheikh on the coast of the Sinai and Hurghada on the coast of the Eastern Desert are the best-known resorts. See pages 292 and 298.

Aswan. Built on the banks of the First Cataract, Aswan enjoys one of the loveliest settings in Egypt. Experience it from the terrace of the Old Cataract Hotel or take a felucca cruise to Kitchener's Island. See page 228.

Luxor. With its wealth of Pharaonic tombs and temples, Luxor offers most for active, culture-loving visitors. But it also has a lovely setting, good hotels and a superb winter climate. See page 209.

Nile cruise. Sit on the sun-deck and watch the spectacle of Egypt slide past. Also consider a cruise on a *dahabeeyah*, a 19th-century sailing boat equipped with mod-cons that offers a more intimate and romantic experience than the floating hotels. See page 310.

Exhibit at the Museum of Islamic Art, Cairo.

BEST MUSEUMS

Egyptian Museum, Cairo. This huge collection of Egyptian artefacts is one of Egypt's must-see attractions. Watch out, too, for the Grand Egyptian Museum in Giza, which will show the treasures of Tutankhamun when it opens in 2020. See pages 134 and 170.

Museum of Islamic Art, Cairo. One of the world's finest collections of Islamic applied arts, from giant carved wooden doors to tiny, intricate copper sculptures. See page 153.

Coptic Museum, Cairo. Treasures and relics from churches all over Europe, including the Nag Hammadi codices, a leather-bound 1,200-page collection of 4th-century Christian texts on papyrus. See page 142.

Alexandria National Museum. State-of-the-art setting for a superb collection of Pharaonic and Graeco-Roman artefacts. See page 260.

Luxor Museum. Contains a small but high-quality collection of antiquities that is well displayed. See page 214.

Solar Boat Museum, Giza. This intriguing museum near the Great Pyramid contains the reconstructed cedar-wood funerary boat of Khufu, excavated in 1954. See page 168.

Nile cruise.

BEST SOUQS AND BEST BUYS

Khan El Khalili Bazaar, Cairo. This labyrinthine bazaar remains the best place to buy copperware, silver, gold and amber jewellery, and other souvenirs. See page 155.

Shari al-Muski, Cairo. To get away from tourist-oriented goods and to immerse yourself in local commerce join the throng along this market street near the Khan El Khalili. See page 155.

Pharaonic replicas. Alabaster statuettes, sphinxes and cats abound, but for top quality visit the shop in the Egyptian Museum, Cairo. See page 134.

Papyrus. You will find hand-painted papyrus, often replicating tomb paintings, in any souvenir shop. Original ones are made by using high-quality Ink and papyrus paper grown in the Nile Delta.

Cotton. Egypt is renowned for its exquisite cotton, but much of it is exported. For good quality *galabiyas* and kaftans, visit the more up-market shops of Cairo, Luxor and the Red Sea resorts.

Wall-hangings and tapestries. For brightly coloured textiles called *khayamiyas*, which used to decorate the interior of tents and can now be used as cushion covers, bedspreads and wall-hangings, visit Sharia al-Khayamiya (Tentmaker's Street) in Khan El Khalili. See page 155.

Khan El Khalili Bazaar in Cairo.

BEST ATMOSPHERE

Cairo's coffee houses. Café culture is especially vibrant in Cairo. Among the more atmospheric venues try Café Riche on Tala'at Harb where Gamal Abdel Nasser plotted the revolution. See page 136.

Historic hotels. The Old Cataract in Aswan and the Winter Palace in Luxor have bags of character. Even if you don't stay in them, visit their terraces for afternoon tea – perhaps travelling along the corniches by calèche, a horse-drawn carriage.

Sound and light shows. These take place at Karnak in Luxor, Edfu, Philae, Abu Simbel and at the Pyramids. In spite of the hammy actorial voices, dramatic use of music and lighting do bring the monuments to life in a unique way.

Felucca trips. A late afternoon felucca cruise in Luxor or Aswan is one of the best ways of experiencing the magic of the Nile. Lean back on the cushions, enjoy the breeze and sip a glass of mint tea brewed by the captain's mate. See page 311.

TRAVELLERS' TIPS

Visas. One-month tourist visas are issued on the spot upon arrival in Cairo, Luxor or Sharm El Sheikh. Tourist visas granted using the e-visa system are also valid for a maximum of 30 days.

Taxis. City taxis are very cheap and readily available and are usually the best way to get around. However, the taxis that congregate outside hotels tend to charge more, so it is best to walk a few blocks and hire one on the street.

Sleeper trains. These run between Cairo and Upper Egypt. The first-class deluxe sleeper is the best bet, but it should be booked at least a few days in advance, and even longer if you are travelling on a national holiday. Go in person to the railway station on Midan Ramesses in Cairo or book through the website of the Egyptian National Railway.

Evening visiting. Some monuments, especially in Upper Egypt, are open until quite late in the evening, when temperatures are cooler, there are fewer tour groups and the sites are much quieter.

Leafy boat on its way to Aswan.

A romantic dusk at a twinkling Bahariya Oasis ecolodge.

Stunning architecture near the Khan El Khalili Bazaar in Cairo.

THE SPELL OF EGYPT

Egypt is the Nile, and the Nile is Egypt, or so the saying goes. But there is much more to this ancient land than that...

Nubian village.

Egypt has long exercised a potent spell over ordinary people. It has inspired poetry and literature, and styles in everything from Western architecture to paper packaging.

It has even influenced Western ways in matters of life and death, often grotesquely so. Interest in mummified flesh, for example, arose when word spread in medieval times about the therapeutic value of powdered *mumia* in the treatment of ailments. By the 16th century, mummies so fascinated visitors to Egypt that an active trade in their desiccated flesh began.

Descriptive accounts and attractive sketches of Egypt made in the 18th century, joined with a trickle of small objects – scarabs, amulets and a multitude of fakes – excited interest in Egypt as a source of the "primitive", a search for which was one of the century's preoccupations.

One event that particularly captured English imagination was the opening of the Egyptian Hall in London in 1821 as a museum of "natural curiosities". On display were the latest finds by Italian Giovanni Belzoni, who had cleared the Temple of Abu Simbel and shipped tonnes of treasures back to England.

The event that attracted world attention, however, was Howard Carter's discovery of Tutankhamun's tomb in 1922. The 5,000 works of art discovered in the tomb were widely publicised. Thousands of sightseers flocked to Egypt and made their way to the Valley of the Kings. When the treasures toured the world in the 60s and 70s, the number of people wanting to visit Egypt skyrocketed. By 1976, some 12 percent of government budget was allocated to upgrading state-owned lodgings, providing loans for private hotels and improving infrastructure. Several new colleges opened to teach courses in hospitality and tourism management, while tour companies began devising affordable package tours; Nile cruises were no longer the preserve of the rich and cultured. The tourist inflow increased to 1.8 million by 1981 and 5.5 million by 2000, reaching an all-time high of 14.7 million by 2010.

Over the last decade, however, Egypt's tourist industry has faced some serious challenges. Hampered by social and civil unrest, as well as a series of terrorist attacks and threats targeting foreign visitors, in 2016 tourist numbers dropped to 5.26 million. Things have improved greatly since then and in 2017 the United Nations World Tourism Organization (UNWTO) revealed Egypt as one of the world's fast-growing tourist destinations. The allure of Egypt – from vibrant Cairo to the mighty Nile, the Pyramids of Giza to the Suez and the Red Sea – is bringing visitors back once more.

Egyptian men in the Temple of Horus, Edfu.

THE EGYPTIANS

The people of every region in Egypt have their own characteristics, which have been defined by thousands of years of history. But all Egyptians are generally thought to be humble, pious, mischievous and extremely hospitable. They also bear both riches and poverty with good grace, while hoping for a better future for their children.

When God created the nations, so Arab wisdom has it, he endowed each with two counter-balanced qualities: to the intelligence of the Syrians he thus added fatuousness; to Iraq he gave pride, but tempered it with hypocrisy; while for the desert Arabs he compensated hardship with good health. And Egypt he blessed with abundance at the cost of humility.

It does not require a deep understanding of the past to feel that, as far as Egypt is concerned, God has withdrawn the first half of his covenant – or that, at any rate, he has made a

> *Naguib Mahfouz encapsulated the Egyptians' tragic sense of life when he wrote: "Life is wise to deceive us, for had it told us from the start what it had in store for us, we would refuse to be born."*

Bedouin woman in Upper Egypt.

new deal with the desert dwellers. As any Egyptian will explain, it is not many generations since Egyptian donations fed the poor of the holy cities of Mecca and Medina, in what is now Saudi Arabia. To the desert Arabs, however, God has given abundance, in the form of oil, while Egypt, formerly the land of plenty, has suffered unaccustomed hardship, in the forms of wars, droughts and chronic over-population.

Egyptian humility takes many forms. One is a tragic sense of life, arising from a tragic view of history. While the West embraces the idea of progress as a solution to all man's ills, the Egyptians have an impulse to turn towards a utopian past, perhaps to a time when Muhammad's successors, the four Rightly Guided Caliphs,

brought justice, prosperity and true belief to the land.

The humiliating defeat suffered by Egypt in the 1967 war would have brought on a revolution in another country. Yet when President Nasser, in an emotional speech, offered to resign, the response was dramatic: millions of Egyptians poured into the streets demanding that he stay. His willingness to share their humiliation brought forth instant sympathy from the masses, who saw it as more important that his intentions had been morally right than that he had failed to realise them.

ISLAM AND POPULAR PIETY

Any visitor to Egypt will be struck by the piety of its people. Humility is inherent in the very word Islam, the religion of roughly 90 percent of Egyptians. Islam (from the Arabic roots *salima*, to be safe; *aslama*, to surrender and *salaam*, peace) means "submission", whether it be to God, fate or the social system framed by the Qur'an.

Many Egyptian Muslims do not go to the mosque or pray five times a day, but the majority believe in a supreme deity and it is commonly presumed that without the just guidance of Islam, society would fall apart. The dawn-to-dusk fast during Ramadan is officially observed by almost the entire country, a sign of Islam's pervasiveness, and many Egyptian tastes, habits and preferences are referred directly back to the Qur'an. Religious expressions of a kind like "God willing" (*In shā' Allāh* in Arabic) are as common as the word "Goodbye" is in English. Apart from piety, however, this exchange also reflects a point of etiquette – any greeting must be followed by a response that outdoes the other in politeness. The Qur'an says: "When

Muslim school girls.

Coptic monk at the Monastery of St Anthony.

⊘ THE POWER OF THE WORD

Many Westerners find the continuing dominance of Islam perplexing in what purports to be an age of reason. The important thing to recognise is that Muslims believe the Qur'an – literally, a "recitation" – is the word of God as directly transmitted by the Prophet Muhammad. The power of the Word thus has a strength in Islam that is unmatched by the literature of any other "revealed" religion; and the beauty of the Qur'an, which is by definition "inimitable", is cited as a miracle in its own right. For this reason translations of the Qur'an are considered vastly inferior and all Muslims are urged to read the Qur'an in Arabic.

you are greeted with a greeting, greet in return with what is better than it, or (at least) return it equally." As such, the proper response to this greeting is *"Salam aleikum"* (Peace be upon you) or *"Wa alaykumu s-salam"* (And unto you peace). The Coptic Christians, too, standing at between 10 and 15 percent of Egypt's population, are conscious of being members of one of the earliest Christian sects, and maintain a degree of devoutness. As a denomination they originated in Alexandria, one of the most faithful, respected and fruitful cities during the Apostolic Period, sometime between AD 42 and AD 62. They acknowledge and herald John Mark (author of the Gospel of Mark) as their founder and first bishop.

JESTS, GIBES AND PRACTICAL JOKES

Egyptian piety is balanced by a deep love of mischief. If anything can compete in public esteem with holiness, it is wit; Egyptian humour holds nothing sacred. Political jokes are particularly sharp and irreverent, but the smallest incident can provoke laughter. In a café or bar, wisecracks are fired back and forth with increasing hilarity until the whole company falls off its chair.

Some intellectuals have remarked that, while the condition that formulates much of

For many, belief in the supernatural extends beyond orthodoxy to a world of genies and spirits of the dead. Fertility rites are still held in Upper Egyptian temples, and magicians, witches and fortune-tellers do a brisk trade in spells and potions.

"That which dominates in the character of the Egyptians is the love of pleasure... They are extremely inclined to cunning and deceit."

Old friends enjoying the simple life in Aswan.

Western behaviour is a sense of guilt, arising from an individual "conscience", in the East it is shame, arising from a sense of public disapproval or contempt. Egyptian children, raised with the idea that whatever you can get away with socially is morally permissible, must rank among the world's naughtiest. Historically, Egyptian mischievousness has its roots in the legacy of centuries of repressive government. Numerous are the stories that celebrate the victory, through a mix of cunning and trickery, of the poor *fellah* (peasant) over pashas or foreigners.

This love of trickery has its drawbacks, as the 15th-century Egyptian historian Al Maqrizi noted in an unflattering portrayal of his countrymen:

Maqrizi notes, among other things, that the Egyptians of his time showed a distinct disdain for study. Examples of this indifference can still be found today, and some Egyptians attempt to achieve goals by means other than hard labour and careful planning. Although much of it can be attributed to overcrowding and a faulty educational system, the degree of cheating in Egyptian schools and universities is scandalous.

FAMILY LIFE

Attitudes to sex are fairly open and discussed freely, and it is generally believed that both men and women cannot resist the temptations of sex. The Arabic language itself is full of sexual innuendoes, so its richness lends a wonderful bawdiness to Egyptian talk. Marriage, however, is deemed an absolute prerequisite for sex, as well as for full adulthood and respectability. Among women, whose freedom is still very much limited by rigid social norms, finding and keeping the right husband is the major focus of life. Since the 1920s, substantial progress towards equality of the sexes has been made, but it is still the rule for a girl to remain in the care of her father until the day she is passed into the care of her husband.

Father and son at Daraw Camel Market.

Respect for parents and elders is so strongly ingrained that it is uncommon for even a male child to leave home before marriage. Things have gradually changed in Cairo, but few urban males can afford to marry much before the age of 30. Despite Islam's flexibility on the subject – easy divorce and polygamy are both sanctioned – marriage is regarded as a binding agreement, made more absolute by economics. For this reason, couples are expected to work out every detail of their future life together before signing the contract.

"Money and children," the Qur'an says, "are the embellishments of life," and Egyptians adore children. The Ancient Egyptians considered their children to be a blessing from the gods and so they took exceptional care of them and the tradition continues today. The family is more important than the individual as a social unit, and large families are the norm, extending not only over several generations but also to distant cousins.

In the cities, political and business alliances are often reinforced through marriage. Because numerous children enlarge a family's potential for wealth and influence, and also because it is considered healthier for children to grow up with lots of siblings, the family planners have had a hard time bringing down the birth rates.

Egyptian mothers are notoriously soft on their children. Centuries of high infant mortality, sexual roles that give housebound wives complete responsibility for children, and lingering belief in the power of the evil eye mean that mothers are inclined to cater to their child's every whim for fear that some harm may befall him or her. This is particularly true in the case of boys. It is not uncommon, in fact, for a woman's strongest emotional tie to be with her eldest son rather than her husband. As infants, children are swaddled and doted upon. By the time they can walk, however, they are often left to spend time as they wish, with plenty of opportunity to play and socialise. As they become teenagers, parents generally introduce their children to their own ideas about the world, their religious outlook, ethical principles and modes of behaviour. This combination of coddling, freedom and education is often cited as a reason for the self-confidence and even obstinacy of the Egyptian character.

LIFE-SUPPORT SYSTEMS

Beyond the family, Egyptians have a strong attachment to their immediate community. In the big towns, the *hara* (alley) is the main unit of neighbourly social bonding and solidarity is very strong. An old Arab adage serves to illustrate this: "I and my brothers against my cousins, I and my cousins against my tribe, and I and my tribe against the world".

Regional loyalties persist, too. Each major town and province has its acknowledged characteristic, from Alexandria in the north to Aswan in the south. Alexandrians are known chiefly for their toughness and willingness to fight, but are also noted for their cosmopolitan outlook and business acumen. The farmers of Lower Egypt and the Delta are regarded as hardworking, thrifty and serious. Rashidis, from Rosetta, are supposed to be kind-hearted, while Dumyatis, from Damietta at the Nile's eastern mouth, are said to be untrustworthy.

Cairenes, like New Yorkers or cockneys, are seen as slick, fast-talking and often immoral. Simply being from the capital allows them to sneer at less sophisticated compatriots, a Cairene habit that their country cousins dislike.

The Saidi people of Upper Egypt are considered to be simple-minded and impulsive and will even joke about these traits themselves. On the positive side, Saidis are noted for their generosity, courage, virility and sense of honour.

The dark-skinned Nubians of the far south, an ancient people with their own languages, are considered to be the most gentle and peaceful of Egyptians. Long isolated by the cataracts that made the Nile above Aswan impassable, Nubian life, relaxed and carefree, had a unique charm. Nubian villages are spotlessly clean, the spacious mud-brick houses always freshly painted, and both men and women are apt to be more enterprising than their Egyptian neighbours.

The desert Bedu have not given up their ancient occupation of smuggling, and fierce tribal loyalty is still maintained. The Bedu are feared, scorned and envied for their aristocratic wilfulness. The old rivalry between these free-wheeling bandits of the desert and the hard-working peasants of the valley has all but died out, but their pure Arab blood and the beauty of their women are still admired.

Nonetheless and across all regions, money, in particular, causes endless anxieties; feeding, educating and underwriting the marriages of children are not cheap, especially when respectability must be maintained. While families and neighbourhoods provide a degree of support, they can also eliminate privacy, so sometimes even the smallest problems become everybody's business.

PRIDE AND PREJUDICE

This catalogue of accepted regional differences obscures an essential homogeneity of attitudes and feelings, however. Despite differences and despite the bitter legacy of imperialism – of defeat, occupation and dependence – pride in Egypt and "the Egyptian way" is fervent. The purpose of all allegiances, from the family to the neighbourhood to the region to the nation and even beyond, is to prevent being pushed around.

It is characteristic of the Egyptians that they prefer compromise to conflict. By inclination, habit and training, Egyptians are tactful and diplomatic, on occasion to the point of obsequiousness. Forms of address are complex and varied, as befits a highly stratified society. A taxi driver

Smoking shisha in a Nubian Village.

may be addressed as "O Chief Engineer" or "O Foreman". (Note that, when sitting in a taxi, one is a temporary guest, not merely a fare, so it is insulting for a lone male passenger to sit in the back seat by himself.) A person of high social standing should be addressed as "Your Presence", while a person of respectable but indeterminate standing is "O President" or "O Professor". An older person is "O Teacher" or "O Pilgrim", the latter referring of course to someone who has made the pilgrimage to Mecca. Even Turkish titles – bey, pasha, hanem – survive, though they have no legal standing, and are used for courtesy's sake.

This diversity underlines the cohesiveness of the society rather than its disparateness:

Egyptians see all men as equals, but allots to each a specific status and with it a role.

MAKING DO

As in many other countries with middle-income economies, sharp disparities of wealth exist. In 2017, estimates suggested that Cairo was home to 8,900 millionaires, 480 of whom were multimillionaires – the second-largest number of high net-worth individuals in Africa after South Africa's Johannesburg. For a time in the late 1970s, poverty-stricken Egypt was importing more Mercedes cars than any other country in the world, and by 2016, 140 Egyptian multimillionaires owned their own private jets. However, also by 2016, it was recorded that 27.8 percent of the Egyptian population was living in poverty, considered the highest rate recorded since 2000. Of this percentage, and as one of the most heavily populated regions in the country, Greater Cairo (*El Qāhira El Kobrā*) made up a colossal 18 percent. The contrast between the elegance of imported luxury in the shops, homes and vehicles, and the vast rolling slums,

Nile fishermen.

⊘ INSTANT PRESTIGE

The ostentatious display of wealth in Egypt can seem vulgar. But the flaunting of riches only confirms that, in a society forced to count its pennies, money carries a special prestige. As a wealthy merchant, whose lifestyle is otherwise modest, commented, "Yes, I would rather have spent my money on something other than a Mercedes. But you wouldn't believe how much it saves me. I don't have to waste time – or money – proving myself. I get instant respect."

Likewise, extravagant weddings are also a symbol of prestige. Wealthy families will blow vast sums on a binge in a five-star hotel, with a fanfare of trumpets, video crews, DJs, singers and belly dancers.

packed buses and frenetic street life in Cairo today particularly highlights the wide social and economic gaps.

OPENING DOORS

Materialist ostentation became rife after the mid-1970s, when President Sadat reversed 20 years of socialist legislation with his Open Door policy of 1974 to 1986. Before him, Nasser had worked to redistribute the country's wealth, parcelling out the great feudal estates, seizing the property of the richest families and reinvesting it in new state industries. Nasser's policies brought dignity to the majority at the expense of the few, but also frightened off private initiative. Not many landlords bothered even to paint their houses, for fear of attracting the tax man. With the Open Door policy, the lid was abruptly removed; luxury imports boomed as money came out of Swiss banks or from under the floorboards.

Allowing people who were underpaid at home to work profitably abroad, the Open Door policy brought improved living standards in the form of more cars, better clothing and a richer diet. But it also inflated expectations and undermined social cohesiveness, something that was later exacerbated by President Mubarak's economic reforms from 1981, which stressed reducing the

Green-fingered farmer near Qena.

size of the public sector and expanding the role of the private sector.

Today's present government under Abdel Fattah el-Sisi is now implementing bold reforms to address these deep-seated issues and achieve the twin goals of eliminating extreme poverty and promoting shared prosperity. Driven by public investments, private consumption and exports of goods and services, these reforms have seen some progress to date, with GDP growing by 5.3 percent in 2018, compared to an average of 4.3 percent in the three years before.

NEWER ANXIETIES

While reforms are underway, given that nearly 30 percent of Egyptians still live in poverty, the primary condition of Egypt – too many people – doesn't help. The population continues to grow rapidly – after Nigeria and Ethiopia, Egypt is the most populated country in Africa. Between 1970 and 2010, a population boom was facilitated by advancements in agriculture and medicine; by 2019, the United Nations estimated the number of people at 100.8 million (up from the last official census figure of 72.7 million in 2006), of which almost 40 million live in urban areas. There are some districts of Greater Cairo where the population density is thought to be more than 19,000 people per square kilometre, making it the third largest urban area in the Islamic world behind the massive capitals of Jakarta, Indonesia, and Karachi, Pakistan.

Low pay and a general loathing for the bureaucracy and government since the Arab Spring of 2011 (see page 96) has meant that government jobs have lost most of their prestige. Increasingly one finds university graduates working as taxi drivers, plumbers, mechanics and the like. The money is better and tradesmen stand a likelier chance of saving in order to get married, though with inflation and the limited availability of decent apartments, many are obliged to scrimp for years before they can establish a household.

COMPENSATION

An atmosphere of melancholy pervades life but, strangely enough, the salient characteristic of the Egyptians is their cheerfulness. They are past masters at coping. All problems and situations are so endlessly discussed and analysed that they end by becoming mere topics of amusement. The tales of intrigue, frustrated love, good fortune or catastrophe that even the simplest people in this country relate in connection with their own personal lives retain a quality of wonder reminiscent of *One Thousand and One Nights*. Everyone has a story.

The protective structure of society, based on the strength of family ties, allows Egyptian men and women to give free rein to their emotions. Families, neighbours and countrymen at large can all be relied on for compassion, commiseration or help. This solidarity makes Egypt one of the safest countries in the world. When someone shouts "Thief!" on the street, every shop empties as all and sundry help to chase the culprit, who is almost invariably caught and hauled off to the nearest police station by a gesticulating mob. Throughout Egypt fewer murders are committed in a year than take place annually in any typical large city in America – a comparison reflecting the fact that Egyptian society allows fewer people to be marginalised. Every person has his recognised place in the scheme of things.

Meanwhile, as of 2019, a staggering 52 percent of the population is under the age of 25.

Men aged 19–30 who do not go on to university or manage to obtain an exemption must face between 12 and 36 months of military service. In the bigger cities, many women in the same age group find jobs before marriage, but the majority stay at home – often wanting to find a husband to provide for them so that they can start a family.

On a positive note, today's Egypt has an extensive education system that outstrips all others in the Middle East and North Africa, and even tertiary education is free. Better

Football fans support the Egyptian national team in Cairo.

⊘ FOOTBALL FEVER

Cairo is home to the two biggest football teams in Egypt, Al Ahly and El Zamalek, whose success or failure is passionately followed throughout the autumn and winter season. Matches between these two giants are great occasions, and afterwards the city's streets are crowded with flag-waving jubilant fans hanging out of car windows and blowing their horns.

Al Ahly (www.alahlyegypt.com) was originally formed by Englishman Mitchell Ince in 1907, and they soon became an Egyptian club for Egyptians and have won the Egyptian Premier League more than any other team. Their name means "national" and they are nicknamed the Red Devils.

Al Ahly's great rival is their fellow Cairo-based club, El Zamalek (www.el-zamalek.com), a team founded by a Belgian lawyer in 1911 and originally called Kasr el-Nil. After the 1952 Revolution they took the name Zamalek Sporting Club and are nicknamed the White Knights.

The Egypt national football team, also known under the nickname of The Pharaohs, takes players from both clubs and has won the African Cup of Nations a record seven times. However, despite their respectable African record, Egypt has so far made only three appearances in the FIFA World Cup: in 1934, 1990 and – most recently – 2018.

prospects await young Egyptians of both sexes who attend universities, technical institutes and further-education colleges. About 30 percent of all Egyptians go on to higher education beyond the age of 17, and presently there are around 50 public and private universities, as well as hundreds of other colleges and institutions.

TAKING TIME OUT

Egypt's true carnivals, in the form of *mouled* or saints' days, offer a glimpse of the country's assorted tests of strength. However, *mouleds* have attracted considerably fewer believers in recent years, under pressure from Muslim fundamentalist groups, which claim they are un-Islamic.

DVDs and television, with its melodramatic soap operas and trashy foreign serials, now provide the entertainment of the majority. These appurtenances of modern life have a powerful effect in a traditional society. Glorifying the bourgeois and "liberal" attitudes of the city and thus homogenising Egyptian life,

Egyptians shop in preparation for Mawlid al-Nabi (the Prophet's birthday).

street energy in concentrated form. Almost every village – and every district in the big cities – has its saint, and their festivals are celebrated once a year, mostly by Muslims, although some Coptic Christian saints are also honoured in similar celebrations. The most important *mouled* is that of Sayyidna Husayn, the martyred nephew of the Prophet. Up to 2 million people flock from the rural areas to Cairo for the occasion. Pushcarts hawking everything from plastic guns to chickpeas sprout up overnight, vying for space with the tents and sleeping bodies of country pilgrims. On the Big Night, while dervishes dance to exhaustion to the *dhikr* rhythms (chanting in remembrance of God), local children try out the swings, shooting galleries and

television has also deprived it of much of its vitality. Visiting shopping malls is also a popular pastime, particularly for the young, who find them a convivial arena in which to meet the opposite sex. Mobile phones and Wi-fi have given them much more freedom than their parents ever had.

In spite of the many changes, it will be a long time yet before the Egyptian people lose their special appeal. Sensitivity and kindness still abound. Solicitous for the welfare of their fellows, Egyptians are invariably helpful, friendly and hospitable. The warmth of human relations brings a soft sweetness, even extended to visitors, which has always been the best part of Egypt's charm.

The Great Temple of Ab.

DECISIVE DATES

EARLY DYNASTIC PERIOD

3150–2686 BC

First and 2nd dynasties: Memphis founded as the capital of Egypt. The rulers are buried in tombs at Saqqara, where the first pyramids were built.

Old Kingdom pyramid.

OLD KINGDOM (2686–2181 BC)

2686–2613 BC

Third Dynasty. Zoser complex at Saqqara built.

2613–2498 BC

Fourth Dynasty. Centralised government; pyramids at Dahshur, Giza and Abu Ruwash built.

2498–2181 BC

Fifth and 6th dynasties. Pyramids and sun temples at Abu Sir and Saqqara built. Tomb reliefs at Saqqara and Giza, and Pyramid texts executed.

FIRST INTERMEDIATE PERIOD

2181–2040 BC

Seventh–Tenth dynasties. Country divided among local rulers; famine and poverty.

MIDDLE KINGDOM

2040–1782 BC

11th–12th dynasties. Reunification by Theban rulers; powerful central government. Pyramids at Dahshur and Hawarah built by Amenemhet III (1842–1797). Pyramids at Al-Lisht, Mazghunah and south Saqqara built.

SECOND INTERMEDIATE PERIOD

1782–1550 BC

13th–17th dynasties. Country divided again. Asiatics ("Hyksos") rule in Delta.

NEW KINGDOM (1550–1070 BC)

1550–1292 BC

18th Dynasty. Reunification under Theban kings; expulsion of Asiatics in north and annexation of Nubia. Period of greatest prosperity, with Thebes (Luxor) as main royal residence. Pharaohs include Akhenaten (1349–1334) and Tutankhamun (1334–1325).

1292–1185 BC

19th Dynasty. Ramesses II (1278–1212) embodies ideal kingship and builds many monuments.

1185–1070 BC

20th Dynasty. Invasions by Libyans and "Sea Peoples". Weak kings rule from the Delta.

THIRD INTERMEDIATE PERIOD

1070–525 BC

21st–26th dynasties. Tanis, in the northeastern Delta, is

capital, but is displaced as Egypt is divided among several rulers.

712–656 BC

25th Dynasty from Kush (Sudan) unites country. Assyrian invasions in 667 and 663.

664–525 BC

26th Dynasty rules from Sais in western Delta. First settlement of Greeks at Memphis.

LATE PERIOD (525–332 BC)

525–404 BC

27th Dynasty (Persian). A canal linking the Nile with the Red Sea is completed under Darius I. A fortress called "Perhapemon" (Babylon in Greek) is built at the Nile end of the canal on future site of Cairo.

404–342

28th–30th dynasties. Slow decline.

342–332

31st Dynasty (Persian).

PTOLEMAIC EMPIRE (332–30 BC)

332–30 BC

Alexander the Great conquers Egypt and founds Alexandria. Ptolemy I rules as governor after Alexander's death in 323 BC, then after 304 BC as first king of dynasty.

ROMAN PERIOD

30 BC–AD 324

Rule from Rome. Fortress rebuilt at Babylon in AD 116 under Trajan (98–117). Visits to Egypt by Vespasian, Trajan,

Hadrian (twice), Septimus Severus and Caracalla. High taxes, poverty and revolt. Spread of Christianity, despite persecution from AD 251.

BYZANTINE PERIOD
AD 324–642
Rule from Constantinople (Byzantium).

324–619
Christianity made state religion in 379. Coptic Church separates from Catholic Church in 451. Last pagan temple (Philae) converted into church in 527.

Egyptian depiction of Trajan.

619–29
Third Persian occupation.

629–39
Re-establishment of Byzantine rule.

639–42
Arab conquest under Amr ibn al-As, who founds new capital, Fustat, next to Babylon.

ARAB EMPIRE
AD 642–868
Rule by governors on behalf of caliph.

642–58
The Rashidun ("Orthodox") caliphs.

658–750
The Umayyad caliphs rule from Damascus.

750–878
The Abbasid caliphs rule from Baghdad. Al-Askar built. First Turkish governor appointed, 856.

TULUNID EMPIRE
AD 878–905
Ahmad Ibn Tulun, the Turkish governor, declares independence, founds Al-Qatai and builds the great mosque that carries his name, 876–9.

ABBASID INTERIM
905–935
Rule from Baghdad reasserted.

FATIMID EMPIRE (969–1171) GOLDEN AGE.
969
Al-Qahirah, royal enclosure, founded.

970–2
Al-Azhar built.

996–1021
Reign of Al-Hakim, known as "The Mad Caliph".

1085–92
Mosque of al-Guyushi, walls of Al-Qahirah, Bab al-Futuh, Bab an-Nasr and Bab Zuwaylah built.

1168
Frankish invasion; Fustat destroyed.

AYYUBID EMPIRE (1171–1250)
Saladin (Salah ad-Din) and his successors conduct campaigns against Franks and other invaders.

1174
Crusader invasion repelled. Jerusalem and most of Palestine retaken 1187–92.

1219–21
Frankish invasion by sea; occupation of Damietta. Advance on Cairo ends in Muslim victory at Mansura ("The Victorious") in the Delta.

1249
Frankish invasion under St Louis culminates in second Muslim victory at Mansura.

BAHRI MAMLUK EMPIRE (1250–1382)
Era of expansion and prosperity.

1260–79
Reign of Baybars al-Bunduqdari. Defeat of the Mongols, reduction of Frankish states to vassalage, extension of empire.

Al Hakim.

Suez Canal opening.

1279–90
Reign of Qalawun.

1293–1340
Three reigns of An-Nasir Muhammad ibn Qalawun. Period of architectural splendour in Cairo.

1340–82
Reign of the descendants of An-Nasir Muhammad.

BURGI (CIRCASSIAN) MAMLUK EMPIRE (1382–1517)

Continuation of building works under the rule of 23 sultans.

OTTOMAN PERIOD (1517–1914)

1517–1798
Ottoman rule through 106 governors. Cultural decline, commercial prosperity.

1798–1805
French invasion and occupation.

1805–48
Muhammad Ali Pasha. Massive programme of modernisation and creation of new empire.

1848
Ibrahim Pasha is viceregent for just 11 months and predeceases his father.

1849–54
Abbas Pasha expels French advisors, grants railway concession to the British. He is murdered by two bodyguards.

1854–63
Said Pasha rules. Suez Canal concession granted. Cairo–Alexandria rail link and Nile steamship service begins.

1863–79
Ismail the Magnificent reigns. Programme of modernisation. Chamber of Deputies established (1866), principle of primogeniture accepted by sultan. Title of "Khedive" (sovereign) granted (1867). Suez Canal opens (1869).

1879–92
Khedive Tawfik. British Occupation begins (1882).

1892–1914
Khedive Abbas Hilmi II.

POST-1914: PROTECTORATE-REPUBLIC

1914–17
Sultan Husayn Kamel. British Protectorate declared, martial law instituted.

1917–22
Sultan Fuad. Revolution of 1919.

1922–36
King Fuad I rules. Monarchy established.

1936–52
King Farouk. Saad Wafd party formed. During World War II

Egypt is neutral, but is reoccupied by Britain, which installs its own candidate as prime minister. Rioting and fires of Black Saturday (1952) lead to a bloodless military coup, engineered by Nasser.

1952–53
The July Revolution deposes King Farouk in favour of his infant son, Ahmad Fuad, then declares Egypt a republic. Gamal Abdel Nasser becomes leader and negotiates a new Anglo-Egyptian treaty.

1956
Suez Canal nationalised. Tripartite attack on Egypt by Britain, France and Israel. US and USSR force the aggressors' withdrawal. Egypt, Syria and Yemen form the United Arab Republic.

1967
The Six-Day War against Israel.

1970
Nasser is succeeded by Anwar Sadat. He expels Soviet teachers and advisors.

1973
The October War against Israel.

1974–77
Open Door Policy, political liberalisation. Sadat visits Israel (1977) and addresses the Knesset.

1979
Camp David accords lead to peace treaty with Israel. Egypt is then boycotted by the rest of the Arab world, which denounces the accords as treachery.

1981
President Anwar Sadat assassinated. Vice President Hosni Mubarak succeeds him as fourth president of Egypt.

MUBARAK TO THE EGYPTIAN REVOLUTION

1987
Mubarak first tries to promote a more democratic government but gradually becomes more repressive. In 1987 he wins a second six-year term.

Hosni Mubarak.

1991
As a member of the Allied coalition during the Gulf War, Egyptian troops are some of the first to remove Iraqi forces from Kuwait.

1996–7
Spate of terrorist attacks on tourists. Perpetrators are executed.

2000
Egyptian government proclaims the Islamists completely crushed after a campaign of mass arrests.

2004
Al-Qaeda carries out three bombings in the Sinai Peninsula, targeting tourists and resulting in 34 deaths.

2005
Bombs in Sharm El Sheikh on the Red Sea kill 88 people in July. Mubarak asks his parliament to amend the constitution to permit the first free presidential elections, but restrictions on serious opposition candidates result in a landslide victory for Mubarak.

2006
Further bomb attacks in Red Sea resort of Dahab kill more than 20 people.

2008
In April, riots in protest at the soaring cost of food and low wages culminate in a general strike.

2011
In January, protests against Mubarak and his regime erupt in Cairo and other cities. In February Mubarak steps down and hands power to the military; protests continue until November in Cairo's Tahrir Square over slow pace of political change. Parliamentary elections are held in November and the Muslim Brotherhood's Freedom and Justice Party wins.

2012
Muslim Brotherhood leader Mohammed Morsi wins presidential elections. The now Islamist-led parliament approves new constitution that emphasises Islamism, and Morsi issues a declaration granting him unlimited power to legislate without review.

2013
Demonstrations erupt again demanding Morsi steps down and hundreds are killed. In July the military, led by General Abdul Fattah el-Sisi, overthrows Morsi in a coup d'état.

2014
A new constitution is implemented in January, and elections are held in June. Retiring from the military, Abdel Fattah el-Sisi becomes President by a decisive 96.1 percent of the vote.

2015
The Islamic State launches a wave of attacks in North Sinai and on Coptic churches nationwide, and also claims responsibility for bombing and bringing down a Russian tourist aircraft over the Sinai in October.

2016
Islamic State carries out attack at Giza, killing nine, and is suspected of being behind another attack in Hurghada, where three European tourists were wounded.

2017
In April, suicide bombers kill dozens at two churches where worshippers are celebrating Palm Sunday, and in November, Jihadists attack a mosque in North Sinai killing 305.

2018
In March, el-Sisi is elected to a second term with virtually no competition and wins by 97 percent of the vote.

2019
Thirty wooden coffins dating from 945–715 BC are discovered in Luxor.

David Roberts lithograph from 1845 depicting the splendid Temple of Amun-Ra at Karnak.

ANCIENT EGYPT

Egypt's ancient civilisation saw the rise of the great pharaohs but also witnessed their fall, which opened the floodgates to centuries of foreign rule.

Egypt produced one of the earliest and most magnificent civilisations the world has ever witnessed. Five thousand years ago, when Mesopotamia was still the scene of petty squabbling between city-states and while Europe, America and most of western Asia were inhabited by Stone-Age hunters, the ancient Egyptians had learned how to make bread, brew beer and mix paint. They could smell and cast copper, drill beads, mix mineral compounds for cosmetics, and glaze stone and pottery surfaces. They had invented the hoe, the most ancient of agricultural implements, and had carried out experiments in plant and animal breeding.

Egypt is a land of unusual geographic isolation, with well-defined boundaries. To the east and west are vast deserts. To the north is the Mediterranean Sea. To the south there was, before the construction of the High Dam at Aswan, a formidable barrier of igneous rock, beyond which lay the barren land of Nubia.

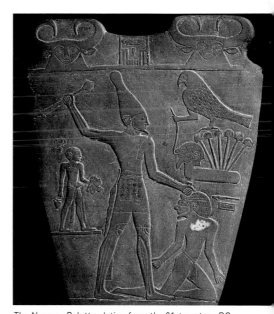

The Narmer Palette, dating from the 31st century BC.

Were it not for the Nile, Egypt would not exist. It would be one of the most barren places on earth. This becomes obvious when seen from the air today: a green strip borders the river; the rest is desert.

Within these recognisable boundaries, however, was a land divided; Upper Egypt extended from Aswan to a point just south of modern Cairo and was largely barren, apart from a narrow strip of land flanking the river; the Delta, or Lower Egypt, spread from the point where the Nile fanned into a fertile triangle some 200km (125 miles) before reaching the Mediterranean Sea. Linking Upper and Lower Egypt was the vital artery, the River Nile.

Before the Nile was harnessed by technology, the annual flood, a result of the monsoon rains on the Ethiopian tableland, spilled into the flood plain, leaving a thick layer of alluvial soil. Since rainfall in Egypt is almost nil, the people depended on the river for their crops; and it was ultimately on the fertility of the soil that ancient Egyptian civilisation was based.

The earliest human inhabitants of the Nile Valley were hunters who tracked game across northern Africa and the eastern Sudan, later joined by nomadic tribes of Asiatic origin who filtered into Egypt in sporadic migrations across the Sinai Peninsula and the Red Sea.

Late Palaeolithic settlements (c.12000–8000 BC) reveal that both these newcomers and the indigenous inhabitants had a hunting and gathering economy. As time went by, their lives became bound to the ebb and flow of the annual flood. As the water rose each year in July, the inhabitants were obliged to draw back from the banks. By August, when the waters swept across the lowlands, they took to the highlands and pursued hunting activities, tracking antelope,

hunting activity was at a minimum. From January to March seasonal pools dried out and fishing was limited, but in the swampy areas near the river there were turtles, rodents and clams. At low Nile, from April to June, game scattered, food became scarce and hunting was pursued once more.

Despite their diverse origins, therefore, there was a natural tendency for the people to group together during the "season of abundance", when there was plenty of food to eat, and then to split up into smaller groups or communities

Scene from the Tomb of Nakht, depicting him and his family hunting wildfowl.

> It is probable that Palaeolithic people had no means – or no concept – of preserving the rich bounty that nature offered them. They may have dried meat in the heat of the sun and smoked fish over fires, although we have no evidence of this.

hartebeest, wild ass and gazelle with lances, bows and arrows. In the first half of October the river attained its highest level, and thereafter began to subside, leaving lagoons and streams that became natural reservoirs for fish.

A variety of plants grew in the fertile, uniform deposit of silt. During this season of plenty,

during the low-flood season or during periods of drought.

RELIGION AND AGRICULTURE

As a certain rhythm formed in their lives, people observed that the gifts of their naturally irrigated valley depended on a dual force: the sun and the river, both of which had creative and destructive powers. The life-giving rays of the sun that caused a crop to grow could also cause it to shrivel and die. And the river that invigorated the soil with its mineral-rich deposits could destroy whatever lay in its path or, if it failed to rise sufficiently, bring famine. These two phenomena, moreover, shared in the pattern of death and rebirth that left a profound impression: the sun that "died" in the western horizon each evening was "reborn" in the eastern sky the following morning; and the river was responsible for the germination or "rebirth" of the crops after the "death" of the land each year.

Agriculture was introduced into the Nile Valley about 5000 BC. Once grain (a variety of domesticated barley from Asia) could be cultivated and stored, the people could be assured of a regular food supply, an important factor in the movement away from primitive society towards civilisation. Agriculture freed up time and economic resources, which resulted in population increase and craft specialisation. Polished stone axes, well-made knives and a variety of pottery

When life became less of a struggle for day-to-day survival, craft work flourished and items of adornment as well as domestic tools were produced.

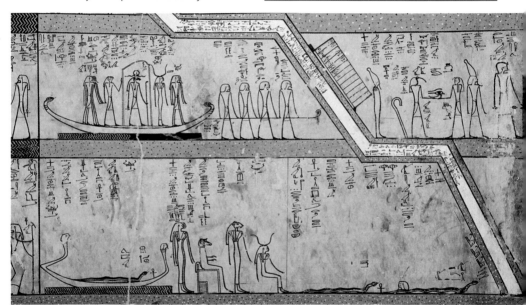

Tomb decoration showing the descent into the realm of the dead

⊘ RESURRECTION MYTH

Some form of resurrection myth has been central to the beliefs and customs of most societies throughout the ancient world. Universally, this myth was connected to the reappearance in spring of foliage on trees and plants that had seemed withered and dead and, as in Egypt, to the nightly death and daily rebirth of the life-giving sun (represented in Egyptian tomb paintings by the goddess Nut; stretched over the earth, she was thought to swallow the setting sun and give birth to it each morning). Among the people of the Nile Valley this belief would have been intensified by the annual flooding of the river, and the bounty that this unfailingly brought in its wake.

vessels were produced, as well as ivory combs and slate palettes, on which paint for body decoration was prepared.

Slowly, assimilation took place. Some villages may have merged as their boundaries expanded; or small groups of people may have gravitated towards larger ones and started to trade and barter with them. The affairs of the various communities became tied to major settlements, which undoubtedly represented the richest and most powerful. This tendency towards political unity occurred in both Upper and Lower Egypt. In Upper Egypt, the chief settlement was Nekhen, where the leader wore a conical White Crown and took the sedge plant as his emblem. In the Delta or Lower Egypt, the capital was Buto; the leader wore the characteristic Red Crown and adopted the bee as his symbol.

THE OLD KINGDOM

Unification of Upper and Lower Egypt has been ascribed to Narmer (Menes), around 3100 BC. He set up his capital at Memphis, at the apex of the Delta, and was the first king to be portrayed wearing both the White and Red Crown. He stands at the beginning of Egypt's ancient history, which was divided by Manetho, an Egyptian historian (c.280 BC), into 30 royal dynasties starting at Menes and ending with Alexander the Great.

The dynasties were subsequently combined and grouped into three main periods: the Old Kingdom or Pyramid Age, the Middle Kingdom and the New Kingdom. Although further divided by modern historians, these periods remain the basis of ancient Egyptian chronology.

The Old Kingdom, from the 3rd to 6th Dynasties (2686–2181 BC), is considered by many

Engraving of the Sphinx and the Great Pyramid, Giza.

⊙ A LOVE OF BEAUTY

Most of the buildings of ancient Egypt, including the royal palaces, were built of perishable materials such as brick, wood and bundles of reeds, while tombs were built of stone, designed to last for eternity. This distinction gives the erroneous impression that the ancient Egyptians were preoccupied with thoughts of death, but evidence to the contrary is abundant.

Wishing to ensure bounty in the afterlife similar to that enjoyed on earth, the ancients decorated their tombs with a wide variety of farming scenes and manufacturing processes as well as leisure activities such as hunting parties and musical gatherings, along with scenes from their own personal lives.

The Old Kingdom tombs at Saqqara, south of Giza, are adorned with painted relics of the deceased, his wife and children, overseers of his estates, supervisors of his factories, scribes, artisans and peasants. The graphic portrayals of everyday life are clear evidence that the ancient Egyptians took great pride in beautiful possessions: chairs and beds (which often had leather or rope-weave seats or mattresses fastened to the frame with leather thongs) had legs carved in the form of the powerful hind limbs of an ox or lion; the handle of a spoon was fashioned to resemble a lotus blossom. The Egyptians may have been very aware of death, but they surrounded themselves with things of beauty while they were alive.

historians as the high-water mark of achievement. A series of vigorous and able monarchs established a highly organised, centralised government. The Great Pyramids of Giza, on the western bank of the Nile southwest of Cairo, have secured undying fame for Khufu (Cheops), Khafre (Chephren) and Menkaure (Mycerinus).

These kings ruled during a period of great refinement, an aristocratic era, which saw rising productivity in all fields. Cattle and raw materials, including gold and copper, were

Fishing scene in the mastaba of Kagemni.

taken in donkey caravans from the Sudan and Nubia. Sinai was exploited for mineral wealth and a fleet of ships sailed to Byblos (on the coast of Lebanon) to import cedar wood. The "Great House", *peraha*, from which the word pharaoh is derived, controlled all trade routes throughout the land, as well as all the markets.

THE END OF THE OLD KINGDOM

In the Old Kingdom the power of the pharaoh was supreme and he took an active part in all affairs of state, which ranged from determining the height of the Nile during the annual inundation, to recruiting a labour force from the provinces, to leading mining and exploratory expeditions. Naturally, such responsibility was too much for one person and he therefore delegated power to the provincial lords, who were often members of the royal family. The provincial nobility became wealthier, began to exert power, and the result was an inevitable weakening of centralised authority. At the end of the 6th Dynasty some of the provinces shook themselves free from the central government and established independence. The monarchy collapsed, and the Old Kingdom came to an end.

The era known as the First Intermediate Period, between the 7th and 10th dynasties, saw anarchy, bloodshed and a restructuring of society. The provincial lords who had gained power and prestige under the great monarchs began to reflect on the traditional beliefs of their forefathers. It was a time of soul-searching; and great contempt was voiced for the law and order of the past.

A powerful family of provincial lords from Herakleopolis Magna (Middle Egypt) achieved prominence in the 9th and 10th dynasties and restored order. In Upper Egypt, meanwhile, in the Theban area (near Luxor), a confederation had gathered around the strong Intef and Mentuhotep family, who extended their authority northwards until there was a clash with the family from Herakleopolis. A civil war resulted in triumph for the Thebans.

THE MIDDLE KINGDOM

The Middle Kingdom covers the 11th and 12th dynasties (c.2040–1782 BC). Amenemhet I, whose rule heralded a revival in architecture and the arts, as well as a breakthrough in literature, established the 12th Dynasty, one of the most peaceful and prosperous eras known to Egypt. Political stability was soon reflected in material prosperity. Building operations were undertaken throughout the whole country. Amenemhet III constructed his tomb at Hawarah (in the Fayyum, now called Faiyum) with a funerary monument later described by classical writers as "The Labyrinth" and declared by Herodotus to be more wonderful than the Pyramids of Giza. Goldsmiths, jewellers and sculptors perfected their skills, as Egyptian political and cultural influence extended to Nubia and Kush in the south, around the Eastern Mediterranean to Libya, Palestine, Syria and even to Crete, the Aegean Islands and the mainland of Greece.

THE OSIRIS LEGEND

According to legend (of which several variations exist), Osiris was a just and much-loved ruler who taught his people how to make farm implements, rotate crops and control the waters of the Nile. He also showed them how to adapt to a wheat diet and make bread, wine and beer. Isis, his devoted wife, was also popular. She taught the people how to grind wheat and weave linen with a loom.

Osiris had a brother, Seth, who was jealous of his popularity. He tricked Osiris into climbing into a chest, had it sealed, then cast it into the Nile. Broken-hearted, Isis went in search of the body of her husband, eventually found it, and hid it. But Seth discovered the body and tore it into 14 pieces, which he scattered over the land. Isis again went in search of Osiris, collected the pieces, bound them together with bandages and breathed life back into the body. Isis then descended on her husband in the form of a winged bird, received his seed and brought

The invasion of the Hyksos at the end of the 12th Dynasty led to foreign occupation.

⊘ MOTHER OF POTSHERDS

In the Middle Kingdom an increasingly wealthy middle class led the ordinary man to aspire to what only members of the aristocracy had had before: elaborate funerary equipment to ensure a comfortable afterlife. To pay homage to their legendary ancestor, Osiris, thousands of pilgrims from all walks of life made their way to the holy city of Abydos each year, leaving so many offerings in pottery vessels that two low mounds developed consisting entirely of broken votive pots, and the site acquired the name of Umm al-Gaab, meaning "Mother of Potsherds".

Abydos continued to be a place of pilgrimage right up to the end of the Pharaonic period.

forth an heir, Horus. She raised her son in the marshes of the Delta until he grew strong enough to avenge his father's death by slaying Seth. Horus then took over the earthly throne and the resurrected Osiris became king of the underworld.

The cult of Osiris captured the popular imagination. It became desirable to have a stele erected at Abydos, so the spirit of the deceased could join in the annual dramatisation of his resurrection, enacted by the temple priests. During the New Kingdom, when Thebes became capital, deceased noblemen were borne to Abydos and placed in the temple precinct before being interred at Thebes. If for some reason this posthumous pilgrimage could not be made, it was done symbolically, their tombs decorated with handsome reliefs of boats bearing their mummified bodies to Abydos.

Hyksos is a Manethonian term corrupted from Hekakhasut, which means simply "rulers of foreign countries" – perhaps an appropriate name for those who challenged Egyptian authority.

they "restored what was ruined" and "raised what had gone to pieces", but the almost total absence of contemporary documents during the Hyksos occupation leaves scant evidence of what actually took place.

The humiliation of foreign occupation came to an end when Ahmose, father of the New Kingdom (18th–20th dynasties, 1570–1070 BC) started a war of liberation and finally expelled the hated invaders from the land.

This first unhappy exposure to foreign domination left a lasting mark on the Egyptian

Carving of Asiatic prisoners of war at Abu Simel.

END OF THE MIDDLE KINGDOM

At the end of the 12th Dynasty the provincial rulers once again rose against the crown. During this period of instability the Hyksos, who are believed to have come from the direction of Syria, challenged Egyptian authority. With the assistance of horses and chariots (which were hitherto unknown in Egypt, and must have had a devastating effect), they swept across the northern Sinai, fortified a stronghold at Tel ad-Deba, south of Tanis in the northeastern Delta, then moved towards the apex of the Delta, from where they surged southwards.

The damage done to Egypt's great cities can only be guessed at. Pharaohs of later times inscribed self-aggrandising declarations that

character. The seemingly inviolable land of Egypt had proved vulnerable, and now had to be protected from invasion. To do so meant not only to rid the country of enemies, but to pursue them into western Asia. Out of the desire for national security was born the spirit of military expansion characteristic of the New Kingdom.

THE NEW KINGDOM

The New Kingdom (1570–1070 BC) was the period of empire. The military conquests of Thutmosis III, in no fewer than 17 campaigns, resulted in the establishment of Egyptian power throughout Syria and northern Mesopotamia, as well as in Nubia and Libya. Great wealth from conquered nations and vassal states poured into Thebes (Luxor). The caravans were laden with gold, silver, ivory, spices and rare flora and fauna.

The greater part of the wealth was bestowed upon the god Amun who, with the aid of an influential priesthood, was established as Amun-Ra, "King of Gods". Thebes flourished, and some of Egypt's most extravagant monuments were built during this period.

The 18th Dynasty was a period of transition. Old values were passing and new ones emerging. The spirit of the age was based on wealth and power. But grave discontent, especially among the upper classes, was apparent in criticism of the national god Amun and the materialism of the priests who promoted his cult.

AKHENATEN'S REVOLUTION

It was in this atmosphere that Amenhotep IV (Akhenaten) grew up. He was the pharaoh who would revolt against the priests and order temple reliefs to be defaced, shrines to be

Block from a temple relief showing Akhenaten sacrificing a duck.

⊘ A REVOLUTION IN ART

Certain innovations had already begun to transform the character of Egyptian art in the early years of Akhenaten's reign. By the time of his move from Thebes to Al-Amarnah, these slight innovations had become radical reforms. For many centuries portrayals of the pharaohs had been highly stylised; they were always depicted as being strong and powerful, and artists were not permitted to divert from this image in any way.

Now, with the consent, it seems, of Akhenaten, figures in a variety of movements and postures were sculptured in exquisite low relief. Akhenaten himself wished to exaggerate his physical imperfections in order to create the impression of a pharaoh who was mortal – a stark contrast with the representations of earlier pharaohs, which had portrayed them as physically perfect god-kings.

Artistic representations of Akhenaten make him look quite strange, with an unusually long, prominent chin, a protruding belly, and hips that are unnaturally wide for a man. Some scholars have suggested that he suffered from a disease that was responsible for these attributes, but it is more likely that the depictions were some form of religious symbolism. His mummy has never been discovered so it is impossible to know if the sculpted representations were realistic.

destroyed, and the image of the god Amun to be erased. Akhenaten transferred the royal residence to Al-Amarnah, in Middle Egypt (see page 193), and promoted the worship of one god, the Aten, the life-giving sun. The city was called Akhetaten ("The Horizon of the Aten").

Unfortunately, the ideal needs of a religious community and the practical requirements of governing an extensive empire were to prove incompatible demands. After the deaths of Akhenaten and his half-brother Smenkare, the boy-king Tutankhamun (famous today as one of the few pharaohs whose remains escaped the early tomb-robbers) came to the throne. Tutankhamun abandoned Al-Amarnah and returned to Memphis and Thebes. The priests of Amun were able to make a spectacular return to power.

EMPIRE-BUILDERS

Horemheb, the general who seized the throne at the end of the 18th Dynasty, was an excellent administrator. He re-established a strong government and started a programme of restoration, which continued into the 19th Dynasty, when the pharaohs channelled their boundless energies into reorganising Akhenaten's rule. Seti I, builder of a famous mortuary temple at Abydos, fought battles against the Libyans, Syrians and Hittites; Ramesses II, hero of a war against the Hittites, with whom he signed a famous peace treaty, was also celebrated as a builder of great monuments, including the famous temples at Abu Simbel; and Ramesses III not only conquered the Libyans, but also successfully protected his country from the "People of the Sea".

All these warrior kings of the 19th Dynasty raised magnificent temples in honour of Amun. It was considered both a duty and a privilege to serve the state god, who granted them military success; and successive pharaohs systematically tried to outdo their predecessors in the magnificence of their architectural and artistic endeavours, especially in the great Temple of Amun at Karnak. It became a temple within a temple, shrine within shrine, where almost all the pharaohs wished to record their names and deeds for posterity.

As new pylons, colonnades and shrines were built, valuable blocks of inscribed stone from earlier periods were often used. The sun temples of Akhenaten suffered this fate: thousands of their distinctly uniform, decorated sand-stone blocks, known as *talatat*, were buried in various places in Karnak, such as beneath the flagstones of the great Hypostyle Hall.

RAMESSES III

Ramesses III (1182–1151 BC) was the last of the great pharaohs. His ever-weakening successors fell more and more under the yoke of

Statue of Horemheb.

the priests of Amun who controlled enormous wealth. According to a text known as the Harris Papyrus, written in the reign of Ramesses III, they possessed more than 5,000 divine statues, more than 81,000 slaves, vassals and servants, well over 421,000 cattle, 433 gardens, 690,000 acres (279,000 hectares) of land, 83 ships, 46 building yards and 65 cities.

Naturally, such a priesthood wielded enormous power and gradually the priests came to regard themselves as the ruling power of the state. At the end of the 20th Dynasty, around 1085 BC, the high priests of Amun overthrew the dynasty. In theory, the country was still united, but in fact, the government became synonymous with corruption. Anarchy flourished and occupation by successive foreign military powers ensued.

CENTURIES OF FOREIGN RULE

In 945 BC, Sheshonk, who was from a family of Libyan descent but had become completely Egyptianised, took over the leadership. His Libyan followers were probably descendants of mercenary troops who had earlier been granted land in return for military service. The Libyan monarchs proceeded to conduct themselves as pharaohs and their rule lasted for two centuries.

Ramses III and his son.

⊙ KARNAK'S GLORY

The Hypostyle Hall at Karnak is the largest single chamber of any temple in the world, covering an area of 4,983 sq metres (53,318 sq ft), with the roof supported by 134 immense columns, arranged in 16 rows. The columns were intended to recreate the papyrus forests of the sacred island from which all life sprang. According to Napoleon's savants, who examined the hall in 1798, the whole of Notre Dame cathedral would fit within its walls. Seti I was responsible for the northern half of the hall and Ramesses II for the southern portion, but other 19th-Dynasty pharaohs also recorded their names there, honouring Amun.

In 748 BC a military leader, Piankhi, from the region of Kush (northern Sudan), marched northward. Because his people had absorbed Egyptian culture during a long period of Egyptian rule he did not view himself as a conqueror, but as a champion freeing Egypt from the barbarism that had engulfed it.

The Egyptians did not regard Piankhi and the Kushites as liberators and it was only after a military clash at Memphis, when the foreign invaders surged over the ramparts, that they surrendered. Like the Libyans before them, the Kushites established themselves as pharaohs, restored ancient temples and were sympathetic to local customs.

The Assyrians, who were reputedly the most ruthless of ancient peoples, conquered Egypt in 667 and 663 BC. With a disciplined, well-trained army they moved southward from province to province, assuring the local population of a speedy liberation from oppressive rule.

During these centuries of foreign rule Egypt had one short respite. This was the Saite Period, which ensued after an Egyptian named Psamtik liberated the country from Assyrian occupation. He immediately turned his attention to reuniting Egypt, establishing order and promoting tradition.

The unflagging efforts of this great leader, and the Saite rulers who followed him, to restore former greatness led them to pattern their government and society on the Old Kingdom, a model 2,000 years old. Instead of channelling their energies into creating new forms, they fell back on the past.

Egypt's revival came to an end when the Persian King Cambyses occupied the land in 525 BC and turned it into a Persian province. The new rulers, like the Libyans and the Kushites before them, at first showed respect for the religion and customs of the country in an effort to gain support. But the Egyptians were not deceived and as soon as an opportunity arose they routed their invaders. Unfortunately, they were able to maintain independence for only about 60 years before another Persian army invaded.

When Alexander the Great marched on Egypt in 332 BC, he and his army were welcomed by the Egyptians as liberators.

Hieroglyphs (shown here at Karnak) combined alphabetic signs, pictures (ideograms) and symbols representing sounds (phonograms).

A PARADE OF THE MORE IMPORTANT GODS

The ancient Egyptians explained the mysteries of nature and the world through myths concerning the origins and powers of their gods.

The movement of the sun was one of the most significant forces in the ancients' world and, according to his myth, the sun-god Ra created himself from the primeval waters where everything was dark and chaotic. His eyes became the moon and the sun and, mating with his own shadow, he created Shu, god of the air, and Tefnut, goddess of mist. At this point, Ra wept and his tears fell as men and women. Shu and Tefnut then gave birth to Geb, god of the earth, and Nut, goddess of the sky, which completed the creation of the universe. Isis and Osiris, Seth and his sister-wife Nephtys were created through the union of Geb and Nut.

RISE AND FALL OF THE GODS

Through the centuries, different gods gained importance as the capital moved from city to city. In Memphis, Ptah was considered the supreme god and creator of the universe. He was usually depicted as a bald man with a mummiform body and false beard. His consort Sekhmet, a woman with a lion's head, was goddess of war and represented the harmful powers of the sun. Imhotep, architect of the step pyramid at Saqqara, was later deified as their son and the god of medicine (and equated with Asklepios by the Greeks). Amun was the supreme god of Thebes, depicted as a ram with curved horns.

The life-bringing Nile was also personified as the god Hapi, while fertility was represented by Min, depicted with an erect phallus and celebrated in the important Feast of Min.

Represented as an ibis or a baboon, Thoth was the god of wisdom, science and medicine. He invented hieroglyphics and the art of writing and became the scribe in the Hall of Judgement.

One of the most important gods, falcon-headed god Horus was a sun-god (he often has a sun disk on his head), god of the sky, a protector of kings and a guide to the dead in the underworld. Every pharaoh was considered an incarnation of Horus.

Depicted as a jackal, or a man with a jackal head, Anubis greeted the dead in the underworld and protected their bodies from decay.

Amun-Ra, a composite god of Ra, sun-god of Heliopolis, and Amun, god of the wind, became a national deity during the Middle Kingdom.

Goddesses Isis (right) and Nephthys (left), identified by the hieroglyphs on their heads.

The murder of Osiris

The myth of the murder of Osiris and his sister-wife's hunt for his body clearly illustrates the Egyptian belief in the afterlife. There are a number of variants of this myth; one is described below.

Osiris was born a god but grew up as a man who became the king of Egypt. His brother Seth was so jealous of his popularity and success that he locked him in a coffin, which he threw into the Nile. Isis, mourning her husband's death, went looking for the coffin and eventually found it near Byblos (modern Lebanon) where it had been surrounded by a tree.

Having recovered the body, Isis took the form of a bird (symbol of the spirit) to revive Osiris, but only managed to stir him long enough to impregnate herself with a son, Horus the Younger. While Isis was giving birth to her son, Seth was cutting Osiris's body into 14 pieces, which he scattered across Egypt. Isis later recovered all of them except his penis, which had been eaten by Nile fish. She reassembled the parts and made a mould of the missing organ, while Horus, having fought a battle with Seth, brought the eye of his father's murderer and placed it in Osiris' mouth, ensuring his eternal life.

Osiris, depicted as a mummified king, with a false beard, was the god of the underworld.

A David Roberts engraving of the Ptolemaic Temple of Philae showing traces of the original colours.

THE PTOLEMAIC PERIOD

Under Ptolemaic rule, Egypt became the seat of a powerful empire and Alexandria, its capital, a centre of learning. But internal rivalry, during the reign of Cleopatra, reduced the country to a province of the Roman Empire.

When Alexander the Great marched on Egypt, the Egyptians had no reason to fear that this would mark the end of their status as an independent nation. He first made his way to thickly populated Memphis, the ancient capital, where he made an offering at the Temple of Ptah, then lost no time in travelling to Siwa Oasis to consult the famous oracle of Amun-Ra (see page 209). When he emerged from the sanctuary he announced that the sacred statue had recognised him, and the priests of Amun greeted him as the son of the god.

GOVERNING EGYPT

Before he left Egypt, Alexander laid down the basic plans for its government. In the important provinces (*nomes* in Greek), he appointed local governors from among Egyptian nobles; he made provision for the collection of taxes and he laid out the plans for his great city and seaport, Alexandria, so situated as to facilitate the flow of Egypt's surplus resources to Greece and to intercept all trade with Africa and Asia.

> The finest Ptolemaic temples can be seen in Upper Egypt, at Dendarah north of Luxor, between Luxor and Aswan (Esna, Edfu and Kom Ombo) and Philae just south of Aswan.

When Alexander died from a fever at Babylon, his conquests fell to lesser heirs. Egypt was held by a general named Ptolemy, who took over leadership as King Ptolemy I. During the three centuries of Ptolemaic rule that followed, Egypt became the seat of a brilliant empire once more.

Eighth-century mosaic showing Alexandria.

THE FIRST OF THE PTOLEMIES

Ptolemy did not continue Alexander's practice of founding independent cities. With the exception of Ptolemais, on the western bank of the Nile in Middle Egypt, and the old Greek city of Naucratis in the Delta, only Alexandria represented a traditional Greek city-state. Ptolemy chose instead to settle his troops (Greeks, Macedonians, Persians and Hellenised Asiatics) among the Egyptian population in towns near the capitals of the provinces into which Egypt was divided. Many settlers married Egyptians and by the second and third generations, their children bore both Greek and Egyptian names.

In Alexandria Greeks formed the bulk of the population, followed in number by the Jews.

But there was also a large Egyptian population, which lived west of the city, in the old quarter of Rhacotis. Alexandria occupied the strip of sandy soil between Lake Mareotis and the sea, where the island of Pharos stood, surmounted by its famous lighthouse, one of the Seven Wonders of the Ancient World (see page 272).

ALEXANDRIA, SEAT OF LEARNING

Alexandria became capital in place of Memphis and was soon to become the major seat of learning in the Mediterranean world, replacing Athens as the centre of culture. Ptolemy II commissioned Egyptians to translate their literature into Greek; and a priest, Manetho, wrote the history of his country. Research was also fostered; and distinguished astronomers, mathematicians, geographers, historians, poets and philosophers gravitated to the *Mouseion* or museum attached to the Library in Alexandria, which was a research institution.

Alexandrian astronomers revised the Egyptian calendar, then, some two centuries later, the Roman one, creating the Julian calendar

Woodcut depicting the Mouseion Library of Alexandria, founded by Ptolemy II.

⊙ THE APIS BULL

Ptolemy I introduced a cult designed to provide a link between his Greek and Egyptian subjects. He observed that the Apis bull was worshipped at Memphis and assumed that the cult was popular and widespread, although this was not the case. Apis was at first a fertility god concerned with good harvests and herds. The deceased Apis was known as Osiris-Apis or "Oserapis", from which the name Serapis was derived. Ptolemy supplied Serapis with anthropomorphic features and declared him to be a national god.

To slot the new deity deftly into the path of his own career, Ptolemy announced that he had dreamt that a colossal statue was revealed to him. No sooner had he communicated his revelation to the people than a statue of Serapis, closely resembling his vision, was put on view.

The cult of Serapis was to have some success throughout Greece and Asia Minor, in Sicily, and especially in Rome where, as the patron god of the Ptolemaic Empire, its presence enhanced the empire's prestige.

In Egypt Serapis was worshipped in every major town, but especially in Alexandria and in Memphis, where the Serapeum, the Temple of Serapis and the catacomb of the Apis bull, in the necropolis of Saqqara (see page 171), became a famous site.

that was used throughout Europe until the end of the Renaissance. Literary critics and scholars edited classical texts, giving them the editions we now know. Many living poets such as The-

> The resemblance between Biblical and Egyptian expression and imagery is not surprising in view of the centuries of contact between Egyptians and Jews in Egypt.

kings in the manner of the ancient pharaohs. Like the ancient pharaohs, the kings fulfilled religious duties and made ceremonial journeys up the Nile, enjoying the public worship of political leadership that was a feature of life in Egypt.

THE GREEK LANGUAGE

Bilingual Egyptians realised long before the conquest by Alexander that if they transcribed their own language into the Greek alphabet, which was well known among the middle classes and was simpler to read, communication would be easier. Scribes

Relief at Kom Ombo depicting an offering being made to the crocodile-headed god, Sobek, and to Hathor.

ocritus, Callimachus and Apollonius Rhodius received generous financial support.

The Ptolemies regarded Egypt as their land and they consequently played a dual role in it, conducting themselves simultaneously as bearers of Greek culture and as guardians of Egyptian culture. Although they resided in Alexandria, as pharaohs they lavished revenues on local priesthoods for the upkeep of temples, or at least exempted them from taxes.

One aspect of the power of the pharaoh was his capacity to uphold religious order; and the Ptolemies thus continued an ancient tradition. Ptolemaic temples were built on traditional lines, often on the sites of more ancient temples. The walls were adorned with scenes depicting Ptolemaic

started the transliteration, adding seven extra letters from the Egyptian alphabet to accommodate sounds for which there were no Greek letters, and created a new script, now known as Coptic.

Greek also became the mother-tongue of the Jews in Egypt, who constituted the second-largest foreign community. Many had been imported as soldiers, even before the arrival of the Ptolemies. When Palestine fell under the control of Ptolemy I in 301 BC, he brought back Jewish mercenaries, who joined the established communities. Unable to speak Hebrew, which had already disappeared as a living language, the Egyptian Jews soon felt a need to translate their sacred books into Greek, which resulted in the version of the Old Testament known as the Septuagint.

The Ptolemies encouraged other foreigners to come to live in Egypt, including Syrians and Persians, as well as Greeks. There was a strong anti-Egyptian feeling among the sophisticated Greeks, who did not encourage Egyptians to become citizens of Alexandria and the Greek cities. Although they held Egyptian culture in reverence in many ways, they did not learn the Egyptian language or writing. Even the Greek masses, although they were fascinated by the "sacred mysteries" and "divine oracles" of the Land of Wonders, nevertheless held the Egyptians in contempt. There were reciprocal anti-Greek sentiments among the Egyptians, who had a strong sense of cultural superiority towards anyone who did not speak their language.

Although there is evidence that Egyptian priests and officials collaborated with the Ptolemies, there are also indications that they rebelled frequently, resentful of the fact that they were being treated as a conquered race. Prophetic writings were widely circulated among the Egyptian people, promising the expulsion of the foreigners.

"Cleopatra Testing Poisons on Condemned Prisoners" by French artist Alexandre Cabanel.

⊘ THE REAL CLEOPATRA

Cleopatra's contemporaries were entranced by her seductive voice and witty repartee. It seems she was an accomplished linguist, capable of conversing with Egyptians, Ethiopians, Hebrews, Arabs, Syrians, Medes and Parthians. We cannot really know what she looked like because her adversary, Octavian, destroyed most of the statues and portraits of her after her death. But, despite her reputation as a beauty, there has been plenty of uncomplimentary conjecture about the size of her nose. "All that we can feel certain about," wrote a Victorian historian, "is that she had not a short nose."

An exhibition devoted to Cleopatra at the British Museum in London brought to light 10 previously unrecognised Egyptian-style images of this endlessly fascinating queen. In depictions on coins and statues sculpted during her lifetime, she is shown with a very long neck and the sharp features of a bird of prey – more of a wicked witch than a seductive beauty. In the view of Plutarch, it was quite possible to gaze upon her without being bowled over, which suggests that, even then, her reputation for beauty exceeded the reality. But big noses are said to represent strength of character, and this is probably what the 17th-century French philosopher Pascal had in mind when he wrote: "If Cleopatra's nose were shorter, the shape of the world would have been different."

THE LAST OF THE PTOLEMIES

Towards the end of the 2nd century BC, Egypt experienced economic problems and political unrest, along with a decline in foreign trade. The court, rich in material wealth and lax in morals, became the scene of decadence and anarchy.

By the last century of Ptolemaic rule, the Egyptians had acquired a position that was somewhat closer in equality to the Greeks than they had endured under the earlier Ptolemies. This era saw the emergence of a landed, wealthy Egyptian population, who were ardently nationalistic and

on the throne. Soon afterwards Cleopatra bore his only son, Caesarion.

A little over five years later, she met Mark Antony at Tarsus. Their legendary love affair brought her

When her son Caesarion was only four years old, Cleopatra made him her coregent. As Ptolemy XV, he retained this role until he was assassinated, probably on the orders of Octavian, in 30 BC.

Octavian defeating Antony and Cleopatra at Actium.

had little respect for the settlers. It was from their ranks that the great spiritual leaders of Coptic Christianity (see page 64) were to arise.

FAMOUS QUEEN

Cleopatra VII, the most famous of the Ptolemies, came to the throne at the age of about 18, as coregent with her even younger brother Ptolemy XII. They were at that time under the guardianship of the Roman Senate and Romans interfered in the rivalry between them, which led Ptolemy to banish his 21-year-old sister from Egypt. Cleopatra sought refuge in Syria, with a view to raising an army and recovering the throne by force. When Julius Caesar arrived in Alexandria in 47 BC, he took the side of the banished queen and set her

three more children, but succeeded in alienating Antony from his supporters in Rome. His purported will, stating his wishes to be buried at Alexandria, angered many Romans, and gave Octavian (later known as Emperor Augustus) the excuse he was looking for to declare war on Antony. Octavian marched against him, defeating him at Actium and capturing Alexandria. Antony committed suicide and Cleopatra is recorded as having caused her own death with the bite of an asp. Caesarion, who had been coregent since 43 BC, was murdered, and Octavian became sole ruler in 30 BC.

Egypt thenceforth was a province of the Roman Empire, subject to the rule of the emperor in Rome and his viceroys or prefects, who were represented as successors of the ancient pharaohs.

THE ROMAN PERIOD AND EARLY CHRISTIANITY

Early Christians were brutally persecuted under the Romans, until the conversion of Emperor Constantine. Once Christianity was established, dogmatic differences within the new religion led to fierce factional disputes.

The Roman occupation of Egypt, ostensibly a mere extension of Ptolemaic rule, was, in fact, markedly different. While a mutual hostility towards the Persians and a long history of commercial relations bound Egyptians and Greeks together, no such affinity existed between Egyptians and Romans. Alexander the Great had entered Egypt without striking a blow; Roman troops fought battles with Egyptians almost immediately. The Ptolemaic kings had lived in Egypt; the Roman emperors governed from Rome and their prefects took over the position formerly held in the scheme of government by the kings.

> The burning of the esteemed Mouseion Library in Alexandria resulted in the loss of some 490,000 rolls of papyrus.

Sunset over sacred Mount Sinai.

To the Egyptians the prefect, not the emperor, was therefore the royal personage. And the prefect did not perform the ceremonial functions of divine kingship, which was by tradition highly personal. There was thus a drastic change in the climate of leadership throughout this period.

THE SEEDS OF STRIFE

The Emperor Augustus made the mistake of arousing the ire of the Greeks when he abolished the Greek Senate in Alexandria and took administrative powers from Greek officials. Further, in response to an appeal by Herod, king of Judaea, he not only agreed to restore to him the land that had been bestowed on Cleopatra during her short refuge in Syria, but also agreed to grant self-government to the Hellenised Jews of Alexandria.

All this caused great consternation among the Greeks. Fighting soon broke out, first between Greeks and Jews, then with the Romans when they tried to separate the two. The unrest that marks the beginning of the Christian era in Alexandria had already begun. Ships in the harbour were set on fire, the flames spread and the Mouseion Library was burned.

The Romans thenceforth stationed garrisons at Alexandria, which remained the capital; at Babylon (Old Cairo), which was the key to communications with Asia and with Lower Egypt; and at Syene (Aswan), which was Egypt's southern boundary. They controlled Egypt by force, and an enormous burden of taxation was placed not on the productivity of the land, but on the number of men in a village.

Those Egyptians who had enjoyed certain privileges under the later Ptolemies and acquired considerable wealth received no special consideration by the Romans, but had their problems compounded when the Emperor Trajan declared that peasant farmers should be recruited for the Roman Army. Hadrian reduced rentals on imperial lands and exempted citizens of Greek cities and Greek settlers in the Fayyum from taxation, but the Egyptian rural population

Well-preserved artwork at Dendarah.

> The Romans regarded Egypt, like other parts of North Africa, as no more than a granary, supplying wheat to Rome, and as a pleasure-ground for the Roman upper classes.

on the people of the Nile Valley. A census was imposed on villages throughout the land and house-to-house registration of the number of residents was made, which might have been considered normal procedure in Rome, but was regarded as an infringement of privacy by Egyptians. Calculation of the wheat quota was based was assessed at a flat rate, without regard for income, age or capacity for work. Hardship followed. There are records of men having "fled leaving no property", 43 in number, then 60, then 100 from a single village. Some took refuge in remote areas of the desert, while others hid in caves and ancient tombs flanking the Nile Valley. When men fled or hid, their families suffered the penalties.

STRATEGIC PLANNING

The Romans made an overt show of respect for Egyptian priesthoods by constructing new temples or completing older ones built by the Ptolemies. The temple to the goddess Hathor at Dendarah, for example, which was started under the later Ptolemies, was completed some 185 years later under the Emperor Tiberius; and temples in the traditional style were completed at Esna, Kom Ombo and Philae. It is worth noting, however, that these sites were chosen for their strategic position as well as the sake of ancient tradition. Esna had been a centre for local commerce from earliest times; Kom Ombo, situated on a hill, commanded the trade routes to Nubia in the south; and Philae was situated on Egypt's southern border.

Ancient sphinx and Pompey's Pillar, Alexandria.

⊘ THE NAG HAMMADI CODICES

The 12 Nag Hammadi codices were collected by Egyptians and translated into Coptic, the Egyptian language of the time. They vary widely in content, presenting a spectrum of heritages that range from Egyptian folklore, Hermeticism, Greek philosophy and Persian mysticism to the Old and New Testaments. The codices include a "a gospel of Thomas", a compilation of sayings attributed to Jesus; extracts from Plato's *Republic*; and apocrypha ("secret books") related to Zoroastrianism and Manichaeism. With such diversity, it is perhaps little wonder that the Gnostics came under attack from orthodox Christians, who eventually destroyed the majority of their writings.

Temple lands elsewhere, however, were annexed and placed under the control of the Roman Government. Local priests were allotted only a small part of sacred property and their own material wealth was curbed. The produce of vineyards, palm groves and fig plantations owned by temples was collected by Roman officials, and taxes were levied on sheep, oxen, horses and donkeys. A Roman official held the title of "High Priest of Alexandria and all Egypt".

EARLY CHRISTIANITY

Such were the conditions in Egypt during the 1st century of the Christian era, when the apostle Mark preached in Alexandria. Remains from the period showing the diffusion of Christianity in Egypt are scant, but New Testament writings found in Bahnasa in Middle Egypt date from around AD 200, and a fragment of the gospel of St John, written in Coptic and found in Upper Egypt, can be dated even earlier. They testify to the spread of Christianity in Egypt within a century of St Mark's arrival.

The Catechetical School of Alexandria was the first important institution of religious learning in Christian antiquity. It was founded in 190 by Pantanaeus, a scholar who is believed to have come to Alexandria approximately 10 years earlier. Significantly, the emergence of the school coincides with the first direct attacks by the Romans on the Christians of Alexandria.

Clement (160–215), a convert from paganism who succeeded Pantanaeus, is regarded as an early apostle of Christian liberalism and taught in Alexandria for more than 20 years. He was succeeded by Origen (185–253), the theologian and writer who is considered as the greatest of the early Christian apologists. Like Clement, he was highly critical of the Gnostic movement (from the Greek *gnosis* or "knowledge").

GNOSTICISM

The origin of the Gnostic communities is obscure, and until recently not much was known about them: the Gnostics were hounded into silence, in the name of orthodox Christianity, from the 4th century onwards and their writings were burned. Fortunately, however, a collection of manuscripts was discovered in Nag Hammadi in Upper Egypt in 1945. These texts, which have raised some important questions about the development of Christianity in Egypt, are copied from original writings that may date from the second half of the 1st century AD (see page 59).

NEOPLATONISM'S EGYPTIAN ROOTS

A more formidable rival to Christianity in the long run came directly from pagan thought: Neoplatonism. Coalescing in Alexandria during the 3rd century, this philosophical school revived the metaphysical and mystical side of Platonic doctrine, explaining the universe as a hierarchy rising from matter to soul, soul to reason and reason to God, conceived as pure being without matter or form. Neoplatonists understood reality as the spiritual world contemplated by reason and allowed the material world only a formal existence. Ascetic disciplines were part of their ethical code, which urged them to ascend from the bonds of matter to the spiritual world, in order to become ecstatically united with the divine.

The first Neoplatonist, Ammonius Saccas, had been the teacher of Origen and was a lapsed Christian, while his famous successors – Plotinus, Porphyry, Iamblichus, Hypatia and Proclus – were all pagans. Plotinus, born in Asyut, was the most influential, making many converts at the imperial court in Rome. Porphyry, who was his student, came to be regarded by the Christian bishops as their greatest enemy – they burned his books in public – and the last important work of the school was Proclus' defence of the pagan philosophical tradition against Christianity. More than one Christian was a student of Neoplatonism, nevertheless, and even Porphyry found Christian readers and translators, by whom Neoplatonic ideas were coopted into the teachings of the early Church.

RELIGIOUS PERSECUTION

The first systematic attempt to put an end to Christianity by depriving the Church of both its leaders and followers took place under the emperor Decius (249–251), who ordered Egyptians to participate in pagan worship in the presence of Roman officers and to submit certificates of sacrifice. Those who refused were declared to be self-avowed Christians and were tortured. Some Christians sent in false certificates; others managed to escape to the solitude of the desert. Many, however, were willing to die rather than

abjure their faith, and their martyrdom further accelerated the Christian movement.

BEGINNINGS OF MONASTICISM

St Paul the Theban, orphaned as a youth, and St Anthony, who came from a wealthy family of landowners, were two of Egypt's earliest and greatest spiritual leaders. Both lived lives of meditation and prayer at about this time; each, unknown to the other, had chosen a retreat in the Eastern Desert in a range of mountains near the Gulf of Suez. St Paul, older than St Anthony

Fresco at the Monastery of St Paul.

Thousands of ascetics, whose original models may be traced to pre-Christian times in Egypt, were living either alone or in small groups during the 3rd and 4th centuries.

and with the gift of healing, is believed to have retired to the desert at the age of 16 to escape the persecutions of Decius. St Anthony, after visionary inspiration, sold his inheritance, gave his money to the poor, then retreated to the cliffs flanking the Nile Valley, later settling beneath a range of mountains known today as the South Qalala.

These two men became regarded as having special powers and a special relationship with the divine, attracting other eremites to draw near them looking for guidance and instruction in an atmosphere of security and spirituality.

As with most great movements that spread beyond the borders of the country in which they took root, contradictory beliefs as to the origins of Monasticism have emerged. St Jerome credits St Paul the Theban with being the first hermit. In both Coptic and Western tradition, however, St Anthony holds a more prominent position, and Copts regard him as the prototype of the Egyptian anchorite.

A TURNING POINT

In 284 the Roman army elected Diocletian emperor and his reforms mark a turning point in the history of Christianity. The appalling social and economic conditions throughout the Roman Empire led him to reorganise it along military lines. He divided Egypt into three major provinces, separated civic and military powers, then imposed new methods of tax assessment based on units of

The Thebaid by Ucello Paolo (1397–1475), depicting the valley of the Nile under Roman domination.

⊘ NEOPLATONIC LEGACY

Many major Neoplatonic works survived intact, and by the end of the Middle Ages, a handful of Europeans could read them in the original. As knowledge of Greek began to extend outside the clergy, aristocratic study-groups sprang up, most notably in Florence, and Neoplatonism rapidly became first a fashion, then a movement. The 15th-century humanist philosopher, Marsilio Ficino, founder of the Florentine Academy, was particularly influential in spreading Neoplatonist ideals. Within a few years its influence had spread from northern Italy throughout Western Europe, largely creating that cultural consensus we call the Renaissance.

Thus a common element in the paintings of Botticelli or Titian, the engravings of Dürer, the sculpture of Michelangelo or the poetry of Shakespeare, which distinguishes them from earlier European art, is their rootedness in Neoplatonic images and ideas. For two centuries or so, while a 1,000-year-old Christian orthodoxy came increasingly into question, these images and ideas were to be the conceptual currency of every educated European, although they were not regarded as being in opposition to Christianity.

They were also modern man's first key to an understanding of the ancient pagan culture that the early Church, in Egypt and elsewhere, had conscientiously set out to destroy.

productivity. Under these reforms Egyptians were forced into public service and, to facilitate control, Latin was introduced as the official language.

Unification of the Roman Empire was undoubtedly the reason for these reforms, but Egyptians had had enough. They rebelled so violently that Diocletian decided that if they could not be subjugated, they should be eliminated. They were dismissed from government service, their property was confiscated, and their houses levelled. Searches were made for Christian literature, and copies of the scriptures, when found,

large numbers of ascetics. Pachom drew them together and introduced a schedule of activities for every hour of the day and night, emphasising

> *All Christian monasticism stems from Pachomian monasticism: St Basil, organiser of monasticism in Asia Minor, visited Egypt around 357; St Jerome made it known to the West; and St Benedict used the model of St Pachom in a stricter form.*

The Council of Nicea.

were burned. Though thousands of people died during the terrible persecutions of Diocletian, unknown numbers escaped to find refuge in the deserts, taking their zeal for Christianity with them, to create new converts.

EARLY MONASTIC REFORM

St Pachom (Pachomius in Latin, Anba Bakhum in Arabic), born about 285, first saw the benefits of organising the widespread anchoritic communities, and became the founder of a form of monasticism that took his name. A native Egyptian who learned Greek only late in life in order to communicate with strangers, Pachom established a community near Akhmin, where the caves in the hills flanking the Nile floodplain were populated with

that a healthy body provided a healthy spirit, and stressing that there should be no excesses of any kind, even in spiritual meditation.

Pachom's aim was to establish a pious, enlightened and self-sufficient community that would set an example to others. An applicant for admission did not have to exhibit spectacular feats of mortification of the flesh – this would have contradicted Pachom's dislike of excess. Although there are numerous examples of physical self-torture in the lives of the Desert Fathers, a candidate for Pachomian monasticism merely had to undergo a period of probation, after which he was clothed in the habit of a monk and officially became part of the community.

Pachom's first monastery was so successful that he moved on to found a second similar institution and yet another, until he had established no fewer than 11 monasteries in Upper Egypt, including two convents for women, although not all the ascetic communities adopted St Pachom's rule.

CONVERSION AND CONTROVERSY

The famous revelation of the Emperor Constantine in 312, which resulted in his conversion to Christianity, was followed by the Edict of Milan,

St Pachom, father of monasticism in Egypt.

⊘ ST PACHOM'S MONKS

Leading healthy, disciplined lives, St Pachom's monks brought productivity to the soil, revived crafts and, more importantly, were in communication with non-Christian neighbouring communities. There is much evidence in the surviving records of various monasteries that the monks aided the people economically by providing them with their crop surpluses and with products from their craft industries. They dispensed medication to the sick and even acted as mediators in grievances, whether between members of a family or in disputes over land or water rights between neighbours. Their monasteries were usually fairly close to settlements, which made communication easier.

which established Christianity as the favoured religion throughout the Roman Empire. It was at last safe to admit to being a Christian in Egypt. Unfortunately, the theological disputes that had plagued the early Christian movement became even fiercer in the 4th and following centuries. The controversies centred on the attempt to define the Incarnation: if Jesus was both God and Man, had He two natures? If so, what was their relationship? Defining the nature of Jesus was of crucial importance to a new religion that attracted people from many backgrounds, with different traditions, concepts of godliness, and styles of worship. It concerned such definitions as "Father", "Son", "begotten" and "unbegotten".

The chief antagonists were the Arians, named after Arius, an elderly Alexandrian presbyter, and the Monophysites, led by Alexander, bishop of Alexandria. The former held that "a time there was when He was not" – in other words that Jesus did not have the same nature as God the Father. The Monophysites regarded this doctrine as recognition of two gods and a reversion to polytheism. They believed that Father and Son were intrinsically of one nature, and that Jesus was therefore both divine and human.

The dispute was discussed in a highly charged atmosphere and reached such an impasse that Constantine felt impelled to define a dogma to unify Christian belief. The Council of Nicea, convened in Asia Minor in 325 for this purpose, was the earliest and most important church council, the first meeting between the Church and the State. Bishop Alexander officially led Egypt's delegation but his deacon, Athanasius, was his chief spokesman. It says a great deal for his eloquence, reasoning and persistence that the Nicene Creed, to the effect that Father and Son are of the same nature, was sanctioned and remains part of the Christian liturgy. Constantine formally accepted the decision of the bishops, and issued a decree of banishment against those who refused to subscribe to it.

THE DECLINE OF ALEXANDRIA

Soon after the Council of Nicea, Constantine moved his capital to the ancient Greek town of Byzantium, which became Constantinople (Constantine's city), and gained much of the prestige that once belonged to Alexandria. The new metropolis was embellished with great monuments from many ancient cities, including an obelisk over 30 metres (98ft) high shipped from Egypt. Known as "New Rome", Constantinople became a storehouse of Christian and pagan art and science. It rapidly usurped Alexandria's reputation as a seat of learning, held since Ptolemaic times.

Thus began an era when ecclesiastical dignitaries excommunicated one another in Egypt and mobs sacked churches of opposing factions. Athanasius was driven into exile five times and sought shelter with hermits in their isolated caves.

Monastery of St Anthony.

⊘ PILGRIM CENTRE

Pilgrims came from all over the Christian world to visit the famed collection of monasteries in Egypt. The bishop of Bahnasa estimated there were a significant 10,000 monks and 20,000 nuns in Middle Egypt. A huge 4th-century monastic settlement has been revealed in Al-Khargah Oasis, in the Western Desert, with a necropolis at Bagawat containing more than 200 chapels. In the biography of St Macrufus (6th century), the Ishnin an-Nasarah is reported to have had "as many churches as there were days in the year." Today, there are still more than 30 monasteries in Egypt, many with splendid icons.

Under Theodosius I, Christianity was formally declared the religion of the empire and the Arians were again declared heretics. The Monophysite bishops of Alexandria were reinstated but, as a result of the partition of the empire between the emperor Honorius of Rome and the emperor Arcadius of Constantinople, their power was limited. Egypt fell under the jurisdiction of the latter and the so-called Byzantine rule of Egypt began.

BYZANTINE PERIOD

Theophilus was made patriarch of Alexandria and displayed tremendous zeal in destroying heathen temples. A wave of destruction swept over the land of Egypt. Tombs were ravaged, walls of ancient monuments scraped, and statues toppled. In Alexandria the famous statue of Serapis was burned and the Serapeum destroyed, along with its library, which had replaced the Mouseion as a centre of learning. It was a folly of fanaticism in the name of orthodoxy not, ironically, so different from that which had earlier opposed Christianity. In 415, under Theodosius II, Patriarch Cyril expelled the Jews of Alexandria from the city.

Despite the growth of the Christian movement, factional disputes continued, especially when the see of Alexandria officially lost precedence to the see of Constantinople at the Council of Constantinople in 381. There had been riots so violent that the Catechetical School, a central force in intellectual life at Alexandria for nearly two centuries, had been destroyed.

THE COPTIC ORTHODOX CHURCH

Convened in 451, the Council of Chalcedon showed Byzantine determination to exert authority throughout Egypt. A new statement of dogma declared that Christ had two natures "concurring" in one person. When the Egyptians refused to endorse this revisionist doctrine, their patriarch was excommunicated. In the struggle that followed, several Egyptian leaders were killed, and Alexandria was pillaged by imperial troops. From then on, Egypt generally had two patriarchs, one representing the orthodoxy of Constantinople, the other upholding the "one person" beliefs of the majority of Egyptian Christians, embodied in the Coptic Orthodox Church, the national Church of Egypt, which emerged as a separate entity.

The English word Copt, meaning "Egyptian Christian", is derived from the Arabic *qibt*, which is derived in turn from *Kyptaios*, the Coptic form of the Greek word *Aigyptios*. It also designates not only the last stages of the ancient Egyptian language and script, but also the distinctive art and architecture that developed everywhere in Egypt except Alexandria – which remained attached to cosmopolitan forms – during the country's Christian era. It is used, finally, to refer to most of modern Egypt's Christian minority, who officially con-

Theodora, his wife. After her death, however, Justinian sent Alexandria a patriarch-prefect determinedly armed with both civil and religious powers. Greeted by a mob, which stoned him when he attempted to speak in church, the new bishop retaliated with force by ordering the troops under his command to carry out a general slaughter. This act effectively quelled immediate resistance, but completed the alienation of the Copts, who henceforth simply ignored any ecclesiastical representatives sent from Constantinople.

Image of Jesus and St Bishoi at St Bishoi's Monastery.

stitute about 9 percent of the population and who continue to be identified with the same intense patriotism that distinguished their forebears.

The Emperor Zeno's attempt in 482 to mend the breach between Churches was unsuccessful, but after strengthening his garrison and deporting the more obstreperous Copts to Constantinople, he let matters rest. There were no more significant disturbances involving the Christians until the reign of Justinian (528–565).

THE END OF BYZANTINE RULE

Under Justinian, the Copts were saved from persecution only by the interest of the Empress

PLACES OF WORSHIP

In the 4th and 5th centuries many ancient temples were converted into monastic centres – Deir al-Medinah and Deir al-Bahri, both in the Theban necropolis, are two well-known examples – or churches, as in the second court of the Mortuary Temple of Ramesses III at Medinat Habu and the Court of Amenhotep III in Luxor Temple. One of the earliest Christian buildings in Egypt was constructed between the Birth House and the Coronation House of the Temple of Hathor at Dendarah. It is possible that this church was the famous Christian centre somewhere in the neighbourhood of Dendarah that St Jerome alludes to as sheltering an assembly of 50,000 monks to celebrate Easter.

The prayer hall of the Muhammed Ali Mosque in Cairo's Citadel.

EGYPT UNDER ISLAM

The Fatimid caliphs claimed direct descent from the Prophet Muhammad and believed themselves the rightful rulers of the Arab world. After their overthrow in 1171, Egypt was ruled from Turkey until the mid-20th century.

In the early 7th century, while the great rival Byzantine and Sasanian empires were exhausting themselves in a futile and costly struggle for supremacy, the Arabs were being spiritually and politically united by the Prophet Muhammad. His call for the creation of a Muslim community (the Ummah) obedient to the commands of God, as revealed in the Holy Qur'an, cut across tribal conflicts and forged the Arabs into a single nation.

Under the leadership of his successors, the caliphs, the energy of the Arabs was directed outward against the contending empires of the north, who were too weak to resist an invasion from the heart of the Arabian Peninsula. Inspired by both the duty of waging jihad (holy war) against nonbelievers and the promise of rich booty, the Muslim armies conquered all of Persia and half of the Byzantine Empire between 636 and 649.

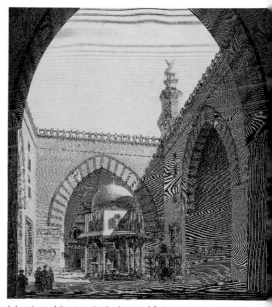

Islamic architecture in the heart of Cairo.

> *The Muslim general Amr ibn al-As justified his actions by saying that the people of Egypt were sheep, that its land was gold, and that it belonged to whoever was strong enough to take it.*

FALL OF THE BYZANTINES

The Byzantine province of Egypt was invaded in 639 by Amr ibn al-As, one of the ablest of the early Muslim generals, who had visited Alexandria in his youth and had never forgotten the Egyptian capital's obvious wealth. Acting on his own initiative, he was a master of hit-and-run tactics, and his horsemen easily defeated a Byzantine army near the ancient ruins of Heliopolis

in 640. He then set about besieging both the fortress of Babylon, at the head of the Delta, and Alexandria itself. Paralysed by internal problems and foreign wars, the Byzantines were unable to reinforce their army in Egypt. Babylon fell in 641 and the rest of the country was formally surrendered soon after.

COPTIC ALLIES

The Arabs were aided in their conquest by the indifference of the native Egyptians, the Copts, whose political and religious disputes with Constantinople had made them deeply hostile to Byzantine rule. Not yet interested in converting subject peoples to Islam, which they still viewed as a purely Arab religion, the Muslim conquerors favoured the Coptic Church over the Byzantine establishment and allowed it autonomy, using it to assist them in collecting the poll tax levied on all non-Muslims.

During the siege of Babylon, the Muslims had camped to the north of the fortress and it was here that Amr founded Fustat, a garrison city, for the control of the Nile Valley.

THE ABBASID CALIPHS

The rapid growth of the new Islamic Empire brought in its wake a host of problems. Tribal

Engraving in the mosque of Ibn Tulun.

differences among the Arabs began to reassert themselves as various factions fought over the spoils of conquest and the leadership of the Ummah. These conflicts, usually expressed in religious terms, deeply divided the Arabs and resulted in more than 100 years of rebellions and civil wars.

A semblance of Muslim unity was eventually re-established in 750 when the Abbasid family seized control of the empire. Brought to power by a coalition of Arab and Iranian forces, the Abbasids established a more international state, which was centred on Baghdad and which drew upon the services of all Muslims.

In Egypt a new administrative capital was built to the north of the former capital Fustat.

Known as Al-Askar or "the Cantonments", this military suburb became the official residence of the provincial governor, his attendant army and the large bureaucracy.

Arabic began to replace Greek as the language of government, culture and commerce in the city and in time filtered down to the rural population, causing the Coptic language to be forgotten.

During the first 200 years of Muslim rule, Egypt was a pawn rather than a true participant in the wider political issues that dominated the affairs of the Islamic Empire. Controlled by a series of military governors appointed by the caliphs in the east, most of the country's great agricultural wealth was channelled into the coffers of the central treasury. The power of these governors was severely curtailed by short terms of office and by restrictions placed upon their internal authority to prevent the establishment of an independent state in Egypt.

The result was oppressive taxation and widespread official corruption, which brought Egypt to the verge of economic collapse in the early 9th century. This state of affairs also reflected the progressive decline of Abbasid authority throughout the empire, which was simply too large to be effectively ruled by one man.

In order to hold their state together, the caliphs in Baghdad began to employ Turkish slave armies to act as a counterbalance to their turbulent Arab and Iranian subjects. Far from being slaves in the Western sense of the word, these Turks were groomed as a ruling caste, loyal only to the Abbasids. The power of the Turkish generals became so great and the upkeep of their armies so expensive that the caliphs were compelled to distribute whole provinces to them in lieu of pay. In this manner Egypt became a private fief of the new Muslim military elite in 832. Unwilling to leave the political nerve centre of Iraq, which might result in a loss of influence, the generals appointed their own governors for Egypt, who acted independently rather than as agents of the caliphs.

INDEPENDENCE UNDER IBN TULUN

The most famous Turkish governor was Ahmad Ibn Tulun. The son of a Turkish slave, he had been raised and educated in the Abbasid court and was posted to Egypt in 868 at the age of 33. Taking advantage of rivalry among the Abbasid family and its Turkish armies, Ibn Tulun was able to gain total control of the provincial government, establishing the first autonomous Muslim state in Egypt. By drastically reducing the imperial tribute to Iraq and by reinvesting the country's wealth in his new domain, Ibn Tulun brought about a period of prosperity. One of his first actions as independent sovereign was the creation of a strong army made up of Turkish, Greek and Sudanese slaves, with which he conquered all of Syria in 878.

In order to celebrate his independence, Ibn Tulun built a new royal city to the north of Al-Askar called Al-Qatai or "the Wards" after its division into separate districts, each housing a different contingent of his multiracial army.

Ibu Tulun died in 884 and was succeeded by his 20-year-old son Khumarawayh. With his father's army he extended the borders of the Tulunid state to the Euphrates, forcing the Abbasids to recognise his sovereignty. In 896 Khumarawayh was murdered by slaves from his harem and was succeeded by his two sons and a brother, notable for the extravagance of their lifestyle and incompetence of their rule. After exhausting the state treasury and alienating the army, they were deposed and murdered, leaving Egypt too weak to resist the re-establishment of direct Abbasid rule in 905.

For the next 30 years Egypt was again ruled by a series of oppressive and ineffectual provincial governors, appointed from Iraq. The growing threat of the Shi'a Fatimid dynasty, centred in Tunisia, however, demanded a more effective form of government in the Nile Valley. The Abbasids were therefore compelled to allow the establishment in 935 of a new semi-autonomous state in Egypt, founded by Muhammad Ibn Tuglij, known as "the Ikhshid". His main task was the creation of a strong Egyptian buffer state to prevent further Fatimid eastern expansion.

On his death in 946, he was nominally succeeded by his young sons, but the real power was held by their regent, the Nubian eunuch Kafur. Kafur's strong rule held the Ikhshid state together, but on his death it fell when faced by the Fatimid invasion of 969.

THE ORIGINS OF THE FATIMIDS

The Fatimids were a radical Shi'a sect that believed their imams (leaders) were the only rightful rulers of the Muslim world. Basing their claim on their direct descent from the Prophet Muhammad through his daughter Fatima, they viewed the Abbasids as usurpers, and dreamed of uniting all of Islam under the joint banner of Shi'a Islam.

The Fatimid period gave rise to many splendid buildings.

⊘ ABBASIDS VERSUS FATIMIDS

The Abbasid–Fatimid rivalry dates back to the start of the Islamic era, when the early Muslims were divided over who was to succeed Muhammad on his death in 632. The majority of his followers, who became the Sunnis, favoured the election of one of them as caliph, while a minority, who became the Shi'a, supported a hereditary principle that would preserve the caliphate within the Prophet's family. Among the most extreme of the various Shi'a sects that grew out of this conflict were the Isma'ilis, of whom the Fatimids were the most successful members, and who believed their imams were the only men capable of leading the Ummah to perfection.

The conversion of the Kutama Berbers of Algeria by an Isma'ili agent in the early 10th century supplied the Fatimids with an army and a North African kingdom, but their dreams were set on Egypt. The death of Kafur and the consequent downfall of the Ikhshid state supplied the Fatimid caliph Al-Mu'izz with the chance he had been waiting for.

THE FOUNDING OF AL-QAHIRAH

In 969 Egypt fell to General Jawhar, a military slave of European origin, whose first action was the construction of a new royal enclosure to house the victorious Al-Mu'izz and his Shi'a government. The new Fatimid capital was named Al-Qahirah, "The Subduer", later corrupted by Italian merchants into Cairo.

Plans for the conquest of the Abbasid Empire were postponed indefinitely and little effort was made to convert the Christian and Sunni Muslim native population to Shi'a Islam. As a minority sect in Egypt, unconcerned with proselytising, the Fatimids were extremely tolerant, employing Sunnis, Christians and Jews equally.

Twelfth-century depiction of the Fatimid cavalry attacking a Crusader fortress.

⊘ INSIDE THE ROYAL ENCLOSURE

Separated from the predominantly Sunni population of Fustat by a mile of wasteland, Al-Qahirah's high walls could be penetrated only by the Isma'ili elite. Within were two great palaces, the home of the imam and his court bureaucracy. Its religious and intellectual centre was the mosque of Al-Azhar, the headquarters of the Da'wa and the main congregational mosque of the city. The rest of Al-Qahirah's 120 hectares (300 acres) were filled with gardens.

Secluded in the luxury of their fortress city, the Fatimid imams underwent a dramatic change and the more radical aspects of their esoteric teachings were toned down.

The Fatimid imams controlled a mammoth secret organisation, the Da'wa, which sent highly trained agents throughout the Muslim world, winning converts and duly preparing the way for the eventual takeover of the Isma'ili caliphs. But the initial military success of the Fatimids was short-lived. After gaining control of Palestine and the holy cities of Mecca and Medina, they encountered impressive Byzantine resistance in northern Syria. To offset their military failure the Fatimids turned instead to the realm of trade. Fustat became a major trade emporium and Fatimid Egypt prospered, collecting a vast amount of wealth.

THE MAD CALIPH

The shift to a conservative and materialistic state deeply concerned the third Fatimid caliph, Al-Hakim (996–1021). Described as insane by medieval Arab historians, he was preoccupied with revitalising the spiritual mission of the Isma'ili movement and with the maintenance of his personal power in the face of governmental opposition. His fervour resulted in measures that were both extreme and brutal, but rarely without a purpose.

Decrees aimed against women, forbidding them from leaving their houses or possessing independent wealth, besides being a concession to public morality, were probably directed against his sister, Sitt al-Mulk, who was an influential opponent of his policies. When he allowed a group of extremist Iranian Isma'ilis to proclaim his divinity in 1017, he was only carrying the spiritual pretensions of his family to their ultimate limits.

The Fatimid hierarchy eventually decided the imam had to go. While he was riding his donkey alone in the Muqattam Hills at night, Al-Hakim mysteriously disappeared, almost certainly murdered on the orders of his sister and the Fatimid elite, who now took over the reins of government.

FAMINE AND THREATS

During the reign of Al-Mustansir (1036–94), Fustat reached the peak of its prosperity. With a population of almost half a million people living in five-storey buildings, with running water and sophisticated sewer systems, it was one of the great cities of its age.

Despite its wealth, the Fatimid state rapidly began to decline. The Turkish troops, who had largely replaced their Berber rivals, were unruly and a constant threat to internal security. A series of seven low Niles between 1066 and 1072 plunged the country into further chaos. Famine and plague spread throughout the Nile Valley, reducing the people of Fustat to cannibalism. The Turkish soldiers looted the Fatimid palaces on the pretext of arrears of pay, and Al-Mustansir secretly called in Badr al-Jamali, the Fatimid's Armenian governor at Acre in Palestine, to restore order.

A surprise attack on Al-Qahirah in 1072 crushed all opposition and won Badr al-Jamali full dictatorial powers. He now had to face an impending invasion by the Seljuk Turks and the enclosing walls of Al-Qahirah were rebuilt,

> The followers of Al-Hakim were eventually driven out of Egypt and forced to flee to Lebanon, where they founded the Druze religion, a sect that still believes Al-Hakim to have been the incarnation of God.

Minaret of the historic Al-Hakim Mosque.

incorporating massive new gates, to withstand the expected siege. The sudden break-up of the Seljuk Empire after 1092 saved the Fatimids from certain defeat, but left the Middle East crowded with petty Muslim states. Their lack of unity facilitated the victories of the first Crusade of 1099, launched in response to the Seljuk conquest of Jerusalem a few years earlier. The crusaders were themselves divided into four, often hostile, principalities, more concerned with their individual short-term needs than with the establishment of a single, strong Christian kingdom.

The rise of the Zangids of Mosul, who began absorbing their Muslim neighbours and preaching jihad in the first half of the 12th century, meant it was just a matter of time before the Christians were encircled and picked off one by one.

SALADIN

The Fatimids tried to play one side against the other, but in 1169 were compelled to submit to the Zangid general Salah ad-Din (Saladin), who abolished the Fatimid caliphate in 1171, re-establishing Sunni Islam in Egypt. The Fatimids were the last Arab dynasty to rule Egypt. From this point on the country would be under the control of Turks and related peoples from the eastern Islamic world, a situation that would continue until the 1952 revolution.

In theory Egypt was now a part of the Zangid Empire, ruled by Nur ad-Din, a man dedicated to jihad against the crusaders; in reality it was firmly in the hands of his Kurdish general, Saladin. Refusing to leave Egypt until it was secure from crusader attack and Fatimid resurgence, Saladin fell out with his master, who wanted Egypt's resources for his own war effort.

> Though weakened by dynastic and military rivalries, Egypt was incredibly wealthy. The key to victory in the various power struggles was that whoever controlled its vast resources could dominate the whole region.

Sending only apologies and excuses, Saladin set about building a power base. His enlarged army was stationed in the newly constructed Citadel, situated about halfway between Al-Qahirah and Fustat. The two urban centres were linked to the new fortress by a series of walls to facilitate the defence of the Egyptian capital, setting the stage for the future development of one unified city.

RESISTING THE CRUSADES

The death of Nur ad-Din in 1174 and the subsequent break-up of this empire left Saladin undisputed master of Egypt. He spent the next 13 years conquering the divided Zangid principalities of Syria and placing them under the control of his family, the Ayyubids. With Egypt and Syria once again united, Saladin turned his attention to the crusaders, who were decisively defeated in 1187.

The capture of Jerusalem and Palestine established Saladin as a champion of Islam, but also triggered the Third Crusade. Led by Richard the Lionheart of England and Philippe II of France, the Christians retook Acre, but were unable to advance further. The peace settlement of 1192 recognised Saladin's gains, leaving the crusaders in possession of a small coastal strip of Palestine. Saladin died the following year a satisfied man.

Saladin (1138–93) depicted by Cristoforo dell'Altissimo.

The Ayyubid Empire created by Saladin was a federation of sovereign city-states, loosely held together by family solidarity. The rulers of Egypt, the wealthiest and most centralised of the provinces, exercised a vague suzerainty over their kinsmen, which they used to try to limit the endless intrigues and power struggles that dominated Ayyubid politics. As the head of the family, the sultans of Egypt had the right to demand military aid from their brothers and cousins in Syria, but this was often reluctantly given, the minor princes being more afraid of their Ayyubid neighbours than of an external enemy. The sultans, as a result, were hesitant about engaging in serious warfare, preferring to use diplomacy to achieve their aims.

The Sultan Al-Kamil (1218–38) was able to defeat a Christian invasion of the Nile Delta in 1221, but to avoid a repetition of the experience, came to a peaceful agreement with the Holy Roman Emperor Frederick II in 1229, whereby Jerusalem was declared an open city, accessible to Muslims and Christians alike. This solution to the crusading problem proved unpopular with religious fanatics on both sides and hostilities were soon resumed.

The last major Ayyubid sultan, As-Salih (1240–9), whose ruthless rise to power had by the growing power of the Bahris, the new sultan began to replace them with his own men. But the Mamluks were not to be ousted so easily. Instead, they murdered Turan Shah and seized control of Egypt.

THE BAHRI MAMLUKS

To legitimise their coup, the Mamluks proclaimed Shagar Ad-Durr (As-Salih's widow) as sultan. The Ayyubid princes of Syria, refusing to accept the loss of the richest province of their empire to a woman, prepared for war. Needing

The Battle of Hattin, 1187, in which Muslim forces under the command of Saladin vanquish the crusaders.

alienated most of his relatives, could no longer rely on the support of his Syrian kinsmen. Faced with the threat of a Mongol invasion from the east, As-Salih began building a Turkish slave army, loyal only to him, to defend the Ayyubid state.

The fighting abilities of As-Salih's new military slaves, or Mamluks, were put to the test in 1249, when the Sixth Crusade of St Louis IX of France invaded Egypt. During the course of hostilities As-Salih died, but news of his death was concealed by his wife and the Mamluk emirs to allow his son, Turan Shah, to reach Egypt and claim the sultanate. Turan Shah arrived in time to witness the defeat of the French king by the Mamluks in 1250. Alarmed

a man to lead her army, Shagar Ad-Durr married the Mamluk commander, Aybek, who ruled with her as sultan. The Ayyubids were defeated in 1250 and Aybek, encouraged by his victory, conquered Palestine.

To strengthen his position, in 1257 Aybek began negotiating a second marriage with a princess of Mosul. Unwilling to share her power with another woman, Shagar Ad-Durr had her husband murdered. Aybek's Mamluks, enraged by the death of their master, seized his queen and handed her over to the former wife of Aybek, whom he had been compelled to divorce by Shagar Ad-Durr upon becoming sultan. Egypt's only woman sultan was beaten to death in front of her rival.

The Mamluks had proved their military prowess against the crusaders and the Ayyubids, but were now called upon to face a far greater threat: the heathen Mongols, who in

> The Mamluks' Maristan hospital was ahead of its time. There were wards for all known diseases, baths, kitchens, laboratories and a lecture hall for interns.

Mamluk of the Ottoman Imperial Guard.

1257 swept through Iraq into Syria, crushing all Muslim resistance. Undefeated in battle, the Central Asian hordes seemed on the verge of extinguishing Muslim civilisation in the Middle East. Only the Mamluks remained to stop them and at the battle of Ayn Jalut in 1260 they did, becoming the saviours of Islam.

Under the sway of their first great sultans, Baybars al-Bunduqdari (1260–79) and then Qalawun (1279–90), the Mamluks emerged as the foremost military power of their age. Kept in top fighting shape by the constant threat of the Mongols, now centred in Iran, the Mamluks recaptured Syria and expelled the last of the crusaders from the Palestinian coast.

THE MAMLUK SYSTEM

The political system created by Baybars was based on a military slave oligarchy. Young Qipchaq Turks would be brought to Egypt as slaves, converted to Islam and given a military training. On completion of their education they would be freed and enrolled in the private army of one of the great Mamluk emirs, who collectively controlled all of Egypt's resources and governmental positions. The most powerful emir would be chosen as the sultan.

The foundation of the system was the intense loyalty the individual Mamluk felt for his military house (*bayt*). His political fortunes were linked to those of his emir. If his *bayt* was successful, the common Mamluk could expect to be promoted to the rank of emir and even to the sultanate. The political environment was therefore dominated by intrigue and constant striving for power among the *bayts*. The sultan tried to manipulate these conflicts to maintain his position but if he was unsuccessful he would be destroyed by his emirs' ambitions.

THE REIGN OF AN-NASIR MUHAMMAD

The one exception to this rule was that the son of a sultan often succeeded his father as a stopgap ruler without power, allowing the emirs time to determine who was the strongest without resorting to civil war. In this manner Qalawun's son An-Nasir Muhammad was made nominal sultan in 1293, at the age of nine. After ruling for a year he was deposed, but then reinstated in 1299, when the emirs fell out amongst themselves.

> Position within the Mamluk hierarchy depended on slave origins. The sons of Mamluks were not allowed to follow their fathers' military careers so a steady flow of new slaves was required to replenish army ranks.

Having been raised in an atmosphere of intrigue and double-dealing, An-Nasir emerged at the age of 25 as a ruthless, suspicious and absolutely despotic sultan. Resolving to rule alone after enduring the miseries of his youth, he murdered the emirs of his father one by one, replacing them with his own men. Unwilling to trust even the emirs of his own *bayt*, An-Nasir inaugurated an era of peace to prevent arming a potential rival with the command of an army. A period of trade and great prosperity ensued, the apex of Muslim civilisation in Egypt.

An-Nasir's success in mastering the Mamluk system brought about the beginning of its decline. So firmly did he grip the reins of power that, on his death in 1340, none of the emirs was strong enough to replace him. Instead he was succeeded by a series of ineffective sons and grandsons.

An-Nasir's policy of peace filled the state's treasury but caused the Mamluks to neglect their military training. A whole generation grew up without having fought a major war, a serious deficiency for a state founded on martial superiority.

THE CIRCASSIAN MAMLUKS

For 41 years after the death of An-Nasir, 12 of his direct descendants ruled Egypt as nominal sultans. But in 1382 the emir Barquq (1382–99) seized control and distributed all positions of power to his fellow Circassians. This second Mamluk dynasty maintained the same political system as the Qipchaq predecessors. An important difference, however, was that the Circassians were brought to Egypt not as boys, but as young men. Instead of being moulded by the rigours of a Mamluk education, they arrived in Cairo with clear ideas of how to manipulate the system to their own benefit. Ambitious, unruly and deficient in their military training, they were a terror to the inhabitants of Egypt, but proved to be poor soldiers.

Unable to defeat the invading Tamerlane in 1400, the Circassians watched helplessly as the new central Asian conqueror devastated their Syrian province. Repeated outbreaks of plague during the 15th century reduced the ranks of the Mamluks, whose replacement was both costly and difficult. The threat of strong neighbours and the chronic outbreak of factional fighting at home further drained the treasury, forcing the sultans to adopt the short-sighted economic policies of excessive taxation, debasement of the currency and the introduction of state-owned monopolies.

The chief failing of the Circassians, however, was their refusal to adopt modern military methods. Bred to be a cavalry elite, they despised gunpowder as unmanly. Their major rivals in the early 16th century, the Ottoman Turks, had no such snobbish qualms. When the two forces finally clashed at the battle of Marj Dabiq in 1517, the Mamluks were blown off the field by superior cannon fire. Following this victory, the Ottoman Sultan Selim the Grim conquered the Mamluk sultanate and Cairo became the provincial capital of a new Muslim empire centred in Istanbul.

Interior of the al-Ghuri Mosque.

⊘ THE BLACK DEATH

The reign of the Mamluk sultan Hasan (1347–61) saw the outbreak of the Black Death, which rocked the economic foundations of Egypt by drastically reducing its population. Whole districts of Cairo were completely wiped out, indirectly benefiting the sultan, who inherited the property and valuables of the plague's numerous victims. With this unexpected windfall Hasan financed his great mosque, which was completed in 1362 and considered the grandest of all Cairo's Mamluk buildings. This was no small distinction: the Mamluk sultans' lust for political power was matched only by their love of luxury and the number and splendour of their grand buildings.

EGYPT AS AN OTTOMAN PROVINCE

The Ottomans, engaged in continual warfare with Iran and the Christian West, could not afford to spare the necessary men to uproot the Mamluks from Egypt completely. Instead the Mamluks were incorporated into the Ottoman ruling elite and held in check by a provincial governor and a garrison of crack Ottoman troops, the Janissaries.

In the 17th century, military defeats brought steady decline to the Ottoman Empire. Rampant inflation, caused by the flood of Spanish silver from the New World, upset the balance of power in Egypt. The office of governor was sold to the highest bidder, then resold at the first opportunity, to supply the central treasury with a steady flow of cash. The governors, rarely ruling for more than three years, could never establish effective control over Egypt. The Janissaries, forced into local trade by the steady devaluation of their salaries, became little more than armed shopkeepers and artisans.

The rise of Ali Bey al Kabir (1760–72) saw the re-emergence of the Mamluks as an international

The Battle of the Pyramids.

Ⓞ NAPOLEON'S SAVANTS

A scientific mission consisting of 60 savants accompanied the French expedition up the Nile in 1798. Their task was to compile a complete dossier on Egypt's antiquities, people, topography, flora and fauna, producing a massive *Description de l'Egypte*, which became a runaway success when it was published between 1809 and 1813.

The task of the savants, who comprised intellectuals and scholars, was to learn and record as much about Egypt and its ancient monuments as they possibly could. Their number included specialists in every conceivable discipline from astronomy to zoology, and none of them was more colourful – or destined for

greater fame – than Dominique Vivant Denon, an impoverished minor aristocrat, failed lawyer, temporary diplomat, antiques dealer, archaeologist and interior decorator. Among his friends he included Voltaire and – more relevant to his inclusion in the party – Josephine, Napoleon's wife.

The military did their best to accommodate the group in their attempt to absorb and record the sights, and sometimes provided a squad of soldiers to protect Denon when he fell behind the French column to make sketches. On 1 February 1799 the French reached Aswan, from where Denon returned to Cairo loaded with drawings and notes.

power. By destroying the rival *bayts*, the governor and the Janissaries, Ali Bey became master of Egypt. He was on the verge of re-establishing the Mamluk Empire when he was betrayed by his

> The French conquest of Egypt was ostensibly carried out in order to threaten Britain's Indian trade from a Middle Eastern stronghold. In fact, it was largely inspired by irrational factors, not least of which was Bonaparte's own pursuit of glory.

lieutenant, Abu'l-Dhahab. Deprived of its strong leadership, the Mamluk *bayt* of Ali Bey fragmented and Egypt was plunged into a devastating civil war that lasted until 1791. Although order was restored by the victory of Murad Bey and Ibrahim Bey, the economy of the country was in ruins. In this unsettled state, Egypt was invaded in 1798 by the French under Napoleon Bonaparte.

THE FRENCH EXPEDITION

On the morning of 21 July 1798, the combined musketry and artillery of 29,000 French troops smashed an onslaught of Mamluk cavalry. This, known as the Battle of the Pyramids, marked a turning of the tide against the East. It also roused Egypt from the slumber of 300 years as an Ottoman province.

Bonaparte's expedition was doomed right from the start. Within seven days of raising the *tricolore* over Saladin's citadel, the British had sunk the French fleet off Abu Qir and the Mamluks under Murad Bey had fallen back to Upper Egypt, from where they continued to conduct a successful guerrilla war.

Hoping to regain momentum and impress his constituency in France, Bonaparte embarked on a campaign in Palestine. Again, superior French artillery brought quick victories. These efforts to terrorise their opponents into submission failed, however, and at the fortress of Acre in northern Palestine the French were brought to an abrupt halt. Reinforced from the sea by a British fleet, the Turkish garrison managed to hold out for two months, while Bonaparte's army was depleted by malaria and dysentery.

Despite the propaganda churned out in Arabic by his printing press – the first in modern

Egypt – his attempt to portray the Palestine debacle as a victory was not greeted with enthusiasm in Cairo. With communications to Paris cut by the marauding British and his own troops disillusioned, he concluded that his personal ambitions were unlikely to be served by lingering. Fourteen months after his arrival, Bonaparte slipped home in such haste that General Kléber, his second-in-command, received news of his appointment as the new General-in-Chief scrawled on a scrap of paper.

Napoleon roused Egypt from its slumbers.

Although the French remained in Egypt for two more years, defeating two Turkish attempts to dislodge them, the hopelessness of their mission finally forced them to succumb. Kléber was assassinated at Azbakiyyah in June 1800 and the task of negotiating with an Anglo-Ottoman force that landed in the Delta in the autumn of 1801 was left to his successor. The French, now numbering only 7,000, were allowed to return to France. In three years of occupation, they had failed to meet any of their strategic objectives. Britain still dominated the seas, the Ottomans had reinforced their hold on the Levant, and the Egyptians, though impressed by the power of European science, technology and military organisation, had rejected what little they saw of the infidel's civilisation.

An 1840 portrait of the great Muhammad Ali (1769–1849).

MUHAMMAD ALI AND MODERNISATION

The history of modern Egypt dates from the emergence of Muhammad Ali's rule in the early 19th century and his launching of Egypt's modernisation project. His dynasty would last until the Egyptian Revolution of 1952.

Muhammad Ali Pasha, who ruled for nearly half a century, is credited with having laid the foundations of modern Egypt. In addition to building an empire, he carried out reforms aimed at modernising the country and founded the dynasty that was to rule for a period of almost 150 years.

Muhammad Ali was born in 1769 in Kavalla, Macedonia, in what is now part of modern Greece but then belonged to the Ottoman Empire. He entered Egypt as second-in-command of an Ottoman army sent to join the British in expelling the French, who had occupied the country since 1798. After the French and British troops left Egypt, the Ottoman troops stayed on to reassert the sultan's authority.

During the four ensuing years, however, Egypt was reduced to a state of anarchy, with Mamluk beys fighting against one another and against the Ottomans, who were themselves divided along ethnic lines. In 1805, having had enough of chaos, the people of Cairo finally turned to Muhammad Ali to restore order, naming him the new viceroy. Such an appointment was the prerogative of the sultan in Constantinople, but the sultan, presented with the *fait accompli*, confirmed the Cairenes' choice.

Nevertheless, Muhammad Ali's position as viceroy was tenuous. Defeating a British force at Rosetta in 1807 consolidated his power, but bold steps were still required. Boldest and bloodiest was his extirpation of the rebellious Mamluk beys (officers). In March 1811, he invited 470 Mamluks to a ceremony in the Citadel. Assembled to take their leave, the departing Mamluks had to pass through a narrow passageway to a locked gate, where the pasha had arranged

Muhammad Ali with his retinue.

for their massacre. For the next 37 years his authority was absolute in Egypt.

Among Muhammad Ali's best-known exploits are his military conquests. In 1811, at the request of the Turkish sultan Mahmud II, he sent troops into the Arabian province of the Hijaz to combat the Wahhabi movement, a fundamentalist sect of Islam that threatened the sultan's authority. In 1816 Egyptian troops entered the Nejd, the Wahhabi's homeland, and by 1818 all of western and central Arabia was under Egyptian control.

After the Arabian campaigns, Muhammad Ali sent an expedition under one of his sons up the Nile to gain control of the Sudan's mineral resources and its active slave trade, which he saw as a possible source of military manpower. Next came campaigns in Greece. At the request of the sultan, an army commanded by his son Ibrahim was sent to Crete in 1822 to quell an uprising against Ottoman control.

In 1824 a second expedition, again commanded by Ibrahim, sailed from Alexandria for the Morea, now known as the Peloponnese. This reassertion of Ottoman power provoked the major European states, Britain, France and Russia. An allied fleet sent to mediate ended up sinking the entire Egyptian fleet at Navarino in 1827.

SYRIA GAINED

Muhammad Ali's last successful expansionist venture was his Syrian expedition of 1831. Using a quarrel with a governor as a pretext, he sent in Ibrahim with an army of peasant conscripts. At the end of 10 months all Syria had acknowledged him as overlord. In 1832 Ibrahim pushed on into Anatolia, defeating the Ottomans at Konya. Before he could occupy Constantinople, however, Russian intervention again brought European interests into play; and in 1833 an agreement was signed between the sultan and his unruly vassal,

Equestrian statue of Ibrahim Pasha (1789–1848), Muhammad Ali's adopted son, Azbakiyyah Garden, Cairo.

⊘ HEALTH OF THE NATION

Muhammad Ali was fanatical about public health. Swamps were drained, cemeteries were moved, hospitals, infirmaries and asylums were built, a school for midwives was established, and French-trained physicians were appointed as public-health officers in all provinces. In Cairo, accumulated rubbish was cleared and seasonal ponds were filled, while a start was made on a street system that would allow the use of wheeled vehicles. Additionally, by 1840 Muhammad Ali had planted more than 16 million trees. This was extremely far-sighted at a time when the links between sanitation, dirt and disease were only just being recognised and addressed in Europe.

by which Egypt was formally accorded rule over Crete and Syria in return for an annual tribute.

With the Sudan, the Hijaz and these new acquisitions, the Egyptian Empire rivalled the Ottoman in size, although Egypt itself was still nominally a part of the Ottoman Empire and Muhammad Ali still only a pasha, the sultan's viceroy. In 1839 the sultan attempted to regain Syria by force.

Ibrahim's own crushing victory over an Ottoman army at Nezib was followed by the desertion of the Ottoman Navy to Alexandria – these two events led to a European crisis. Britain, Russia and Austria sided with the sultan, while France supported Muhammad Ali. A catastrophe was averted when Muhammad Ali signed an agreement by which his rule was to be made hereditary, but which also confirmed the sultan's suzerainty, the terms of which were agreed under European pressure in 1841.

MODERNISING ON ALL FRONTS

Shorn of his acquisitions abroad, the pasha turned his remaining energies back to the task of modernising Egypt. The benefits to his country were enormous. They include the massive upgrading and extension of Egypt's irrigation system and the introduction of a multitude of

was to avoid dependence upon Europe, the infant textile industry was protected by embargoes and subsidies, but this step toward economic independence was foiled, like his foreign policy, by European interests: the provisions of 1841 made Egypt subject to the tariffs that prevailed through the Ottoman Empire, allowing cheaper imports, mainly from Britain, to flood into Egypt.

In other respects, his efforts were more successful. The Bulaq Press was to become the most distinguished publisher in the Arab world. Its production of printed books was an essential

Grand Cairo, painted by the orientalist David Roberts.

exotic plants. Rice, indigo and sugar cane were massively encouraged, as well as the cultivation of longtime staple Egyptian cotton, which later became the country's principal export.

Land tenure and tax systems were reformed by nationalising all property, making Muhammad Ali titular owner of all land and eliminating the iniquitous tax-farming system that had prevailed earlier.

Muhammad Ali also created modern industries in Egypt. Beginning with an industrial complex at Bulaq, the Nile port of Cairo, where the famous Bulaq Press was set up, he built shipyards, foundries and armament factories. Textile mills, the basis of the European Industrial Revolution, soon followed. Since a primary aim

element in the creation of a new intellectual elite, which would gradually replace the European experts recruited during his early years in power.

In Alexandria Muhammad Ali established a Quarantine Commission, thus identifying the city once again as the country's main port of entry. And it was here that the pasha died in 1849, a ripe 80 years old, but predeceased by his son, the gallant Ibrahim, to whom he had given the viceregal throne 11 months before.

MUHAMMAD ALI'S SUCCESSORS

Ibrahim had shown himself to be a good leader but his nephew, Abbas, the only son of Muhammad Ali's second son, Tussun, became viceroy and immediately rejected all his policies. While

Muhammad Ali had been eager for Western agricultural and technical ideas, particularly those of the French, Abbas was xenophobic, disliking the French in particular and favouring the British, to whom he granted a railway concession. He summarily expelled all the French advisors upon whom his grandfather had depended, closed all secular or European schools, and turned for support to religious leaders. He was as autocratic as his grandfather, but earned the gratitude of the Egyptian peasants by his negligence, which left them in comparative peace. Apart from the Brit-

later, Said managed to renegotiate and got somewhat more favourable terms, but only at the cost of an indemnity of more than 3 million Egyptian pounds. To pay this sum he was forced to take Egypt's first foreign loan, thus not only setting a dangerous precedent, but planting a time bomb under Ismail, the third of Ibrahim's four sons, who became viceroy on Said's death in 1863.

ISMAIL THE MAGNIFICENT (1863–79)

Under Ismail's rule the modernisation begun by Muhammad Ali moved forward with new

Khedive Ismail's country drive, 1879 engraving.

ish railway completed after his death, the sole positive relic of his six-year rule was that he left full coffers and no foreign debt.

When Abbas was murdered in 1854 by two of his personal bodyguards, his uncle Said succeeded him. Said again reversed the direction of the government, favouring a return to his father's programmes and to abandoned projects in irrigation, agriculture and education.

Open to European influences, Said is perhaps best known for his friendship with Ferdinand de Lesseps, to whom he granted a concession for the Suez Canal. As originally granted in 1854, this concession was one of the great swindles of all time, with terms extremely disadvantageous to Egypt. Recognising the enormity of his error

dynamism. Reviving his grandfather's policy of independence from the sultan, Ismail sought to transform Egypt into a country Europe would respect. In 1866, through payments to the sultan and an increase in tribute, he secured a change in the hereditary principle from seniority to primogeniture, thus guaranteeing the throne to his own line, and permission to maintain a standing army of 30,000. The same year he summoned the first Chamber of Deputies, a move that pleased the Europeans as representing a step towards constitutionality. The following year he obtained the Persian title of khedive (sovereign), borne by his heirs down to 1914, as well as the right to create institutions, issue regulations and conclude administrative agreements with foreign powers without consulting Constantinople. His new independence was signalised in June 1867 by Egypt's autonomous participation in the Exposition Universelle in Paris.

FOREIGN DEBTS COME HOME

The sultan's response to the festivities at the canal opening was to send Ismail a decree forbidding him to undertake foreign loans without approval. A massive bribe secured confirmation in 1873 of all rights obtained earlier, as well as permission to raise a large army.

The American Civil War had brought wealth to Egypt by raising the price of cotton, enriching the new class of landowners that Said and Ismail had created. This was not enough, however, even coupled with Egypt's tax revenues, to keep pace with Ismael's ambitions. In the confusion of public and private exchequers, colossal debts had been run up, prompting alarm in Paris and London, where Ismail's independence was already regarded as a threat to the status quo.

Most of the debt was the result of swindles perpetrated by European adventurers. The

The opening of the Suez Canal.

⊘ TRANSFORMING THE COUNTRY

Ismail had been sent as a student to Paris by Muhammad Ali in 1844. He was one of a delegation of 70 that also included a young man named Ali Mubarak, who would later serve Ismail as minister of education, director general of the state railways, minister of endowments and minister of public works. Ismail and Mubarak had thus known Paris as it was before the Second Empire: an essentially medieval city, largely consisting of slums and only partially touched by modernisation under Bonaparte.

When Ismail saw the transformation wrought by Haussmann – the new city, with its parks and broad tree-lined boulevards – he was dazzled; and on his return to Egypt he sent Mubarak to Paris to see for himself, and appointed him minister of public works in the meantime. The result was the transformation of Cairo.

The changes made in Cairo during the few months leading up to the opening of the Suez Canal, in 1869, were the culmination of five years of feverish modernisation not just in Cairo but throughout the country. Two other major canals had already been completed. Municipal water and gas companies had been set up in 1865, telegraph linked all parts of the country and Cairo's main railway station had been inaugurated in 1867, the same year that Ismail opened the Egyptian exhibition at the Exposition Universelle in Paris.

largest of these, like the first of the debts, was an inheritance from Said: the Suez Canal, built using the corvée, at Egyptian expense. In 1875, Ismail was forced to sell his shares in the canal company to Britain. An Anglo-French dual control set up to oversee his finances began creaming off three-quarters of the annual revenues of Egypt to pay European creditors.

Ismail was forced to liquidate his personal estates and to accept British and French ministers in his cabinet. Playing the few cards left to him, he evaded a complete takeover of his

provided the final excuse for intervention. Over the sultan's protests, British warships bombarded Alexandria on 11 July 1882. Hoping to regain status after repeated humiliations through the instrument of these invaders, Tawfiq abandoned his own government and put himself under their protection. Support for a provisional government also melted away. Near the end of August, 20,000 redcoats were landed on the supposedly sacrosanct banks of the new Suez Canal and two weeks later the Egyptian Army under 'a was crushingly defeated at Tell al-Kabir.

The Bombardment of Alexandria in 1882.

government until finally the Europeans lost patience. Putting pressure on the sultan, they had Ismail deposed.

FOREIGN OCCUPATION

His son Tawfiq, whom Ismail himself described as having "neither head nor heart nor courage", was no match for the adversaries who had defeated his father. But the army made a stand. The chief spokesman, a senior officer named Ahmad 'Urabi, was appointed minister of war and thus found himself at the forefront of resistance to further European intrusion.

Presented abroad first as a military dictatorship, then as a danger not only to European interests, but also to the sultan's, this situation

Thus came to an end 19th-century Egypt's experiments with modernisation, twice halted by European displays of power. The many cultural, social and even physical marks left on the country by Muhammad Ali and Ismail have, however, so far proved indelible.

BRITISH RULE

Evelyn Baring, who became Lord Cromer in 1891, first came to Egypt in 1879 as the British financial controller during the dual control of France and Britain, but later returned in 1882 as the consul-general. In 1882, the British government promised an early evacuation of its troops, but they lingered on and, since the British refused to formalise their presence, the British consul-general became the de facto ruler of Egypt, with absolute authority in both its internal and foreign affairs.

Cromer discouraged both industrialisation and higher education, putting an end to the kind of

> *Egypt's role within the British Empire was essentially to supply raw materials and a market for manufactured items, like any other colony or possession.*

response was to seek out the young nationalist leaders and provide them with financial support.

Secular nationalism drew growing strength between 1890 and 1906 from the country's enormous prosperity, derived almost exclusively from cotton. The landowning class created by Said and Ismail grew even richer, merging with the old and new elites. Greeks and Italians chiefly, but also Britons, French, Swiss, Germans and Belgians, all received privileges under the Ottoman capitulations that granted them immunity from Egyptian laws and taxes.

British Army marching band watched by pedestrians and street vendors in Cairo, 1890.

autonomous development that before the occupation had made Egypt, with Japan, unique among countries of the non-Western world. It is therefore not surprising that the British occupation helped to solidify nationalist awareness in Egypt.

This awareness received added stimulus after 1892, when Abbas Hilmi Tawfiq's 18-year-old son succeeded as khedive. Educated at a Swiss school and at the celebrated Theresianum in Vienna, Abbas II was typical of the new Egyptian elite that had been created by Muhammad Ali's and Ismail's educational designs. In Egypt under Cromer, however, there was no real role for this elite or even for Abbas himself, as the consul-general made humiliatingly clear to the young khedive at the earliest opportunity. Abbas'

> *The khedive and his family owned around one-fifth of the cultivable land, and as the price of cotton rose on international markets much of the new wealth came his way.*

THE DINSHAWAI INCIDENT

As Cromer approached retirement from Egyptian service in 1906, he contemplated changes to allow for more self-government, but his autocratic rule had left him few friends in the country. In that year the Dinshawai Incident occurred when a group of British officers were casually shooting domestic pigeons that belonged to peasants in the Delta village of Dinshawai. The villagers tried to stop them, and in the skirmish a woman and four men were wounded. Outraged villagers surrounded the officers, beat them and held them until the police arrived. One officer escaped and ran through the noon-day heat to a British army camp, but died of sunstroke just outside the camp entrance. A peasant who had tried to help him was beaten to death by British soldiers. This murder was subsequently forgotten. To consider charges against the villagers of Dinshawai, however, a special tribunal was set up.

policy. He cultivated a friendship with the khedive, whom he permitted to wield increased power, and undertook several reforms. Egypt's first secular university was allowed to open in 1908 and the provincial councils were encouraged towards more autonomy. Unfortunately, Gorst's arrival coincided with a worldwide economic slump. Blamed for the ensuing crash, his policies were resented by British civil servants in Egypt and misinterpreted as weakness by the Egyptian population. In 1910, recognising their failure, he resigned and Lord Kitchener succeeded.

Egyptian camel ambulances attached to the Imperial Camel Corps at Rafa during World War I.

The tribunal met in Dinshawai for 30 minutes then sentenced eight villagers to lashes, 11 to periods of penal servitude ranging from one year to life, and four – including a 17-year-old boy and a 60-year-old man – to hanging. Though public executions had been outlawed in Egypt two years earlier, the villagers of Dinshawai were forced to witness these sentences being carried out.

Nobody connected with this incident – to which Egyptians could only respond with helpless grief – was ever forgiven.

CHANGE AT THE TOP

Cromer's successor as consul-general, Sir Eldon Gorst, spoke Arabic, having lived many years in Egypt, and was ready to effect change in British

There was little enthusiasm in Egypt for either side in World War I, but much resentment of the arrogance of British power. During the war, opposition to British rule crystallised among Egypt's elite.

Kitchener had served as commander-in-chief of the Egyptian army and knew Egypt well. He introduced regulations for censorship, school discipline and the suppression of conspiracy. Once again the khedive came under the consul-general's strict authority. In 1913, however, he introduced what seemed to be a liberal reform: a new constitution that provided for a Legislative Assembly. It had met on only one occasion before World War I broke out.

THE PROTECTORATE (1914–22)

The outbreak of the war was the catalyst for a series of important events. Severing the 400-year-old Ottoman connection, Britain declared Egypt a protectorate, thereby finally formalising the authority it had had for the past 32 years. Abbas Hilmi, who had been in Con-

until the Protectorate was declared in 1914 that Zaghlul joined the nationalist ranks, angered by Kitchener's treachery to the constitution he had supported in 1913.

EMERGENCE OF THE WAFD

As soon as the armistice was signed, Zaghlul asked the British Government to be allowed to go to London to present Egypt's case for independence, but London refused. This uncompromising position only hardened nationalist sentiment, and by early 1919 the demands were

Women in Cairo urge patriotism during the Revolution of 1919.

stantinople when the war started, was forbidden to return, then declared a traitor and deposed. His two young sons were excluded from succession, and his uncle, 60-year-old Husayn Kamel, was made ruler, with the title of sultan, by the British.

At the end of the war, the nationalist movement was stronger than ever, and a dynamic leader had emerged to direct its efforts. Saad Zaghlul was an Al-Azhar-educated lawyer of Egyptian peasant ancestry. Imprisoned briefly for participation in the 1882 resistance, Zaghlul later practised law. During this period, he married the daughter of a pro-British prime minister, and was shown favour by Cromer, who appointed him minister of education. It was not

⊘ THE REVOLUTION OF 1919

The uprising known in Egypt as the Revolution of 1919, provoked by the exile to Malta of Zaghlul and three of his colleagues, was a short-lived but bloody affair. Violence in Cairo, the Delta and the Nile Valley, especially around Asyut, was accompanied by a general strike. Many upper-class women also came out on to the streets to demonstrate, led by Safia Zaghlul, wife of Saad.

Several hundred Cairo citizens were killed in confrontations with British and Australian troops who had been unnerved, it is said, by delays in the demobilisation process. Forty British soldiers and civilians also died during the uprising.

for nothing less than complete independence, with representation at the Peace Conference in Paris. Following demonstrations in Cairo, Zaghlul and three other nationalists were exiled to Malta.

This provoked the successful uprising that Egyptians refer to as the Revolution of 1919 (see page 87). A field-marshal, Lord Allenby, was sent to replace Wingate, recalled because of his support for the Egyptians' demands. After appraising the situation, however, Allenby promptly brought Zaghlul home from exile, and

day that the Treaty of Versailles was signed, Allenby issued a proclamation reaffirming the Protectorate.

In November 1919, the British Government sent a mission to Egypt to study and make recommendations on the form of a constitution for the Protectorate. The mission's report recommended that, although Britain should maintain military forces in Egypt and control over foreign relations, the protection of foreign interests and the Sudan, Egypt should be declared an independent country. But the

English Egyptologist Howard Carter with the golden sarcophagus of Tutankhamun in 1923.

The Wafd spoke for the whole country during the interwar years. Its ranks consisted mostly of Egyptian professionals, businessmen and landowners, whose interests the Wafd represented until all the political parties were outlawed under Nasser.

gave him permission to go to Paris. With other members of the Wafd, as his followers had come to be called (wafd means "delegation" in Arabic), Zaghlul attended the conference, but failed to secure his major objective. On the same

report was not published until the end of 1921, and meanwhile Zaghlul was arrested and exiled again.

For his part, Allenby had privately made conclusions similar to those of the mission. In February 1922, upon his return from a visit to England, he bore a proclamation that unilaterally ended the Protectorate, but reserved four areas of British control. Three weeks later, Egypt's independence was officially declared; and Sultan Fuad – who had been chosen by the British from among several candidates to succeed his brother, Husayn Kamel, upon the latter's death in 1917 – became King Fuad. A constitution based on that of Belgium was adopted in 1923.

FUAD AS KING (1922-36)

The Wafdists at first rejected this declaration of independence, with its four "reserved points". When Zaghlul was finally allowed to return, however, they sought to participate actively in the forthcoming elections, which they won by an overwhelming majority. And so Zaghlul became Egypt's prime minister in early 1924.

As prime minister, Zaghlul gave up none of his demands connected with completing independence, which included the evacuation of all British troops and Egyptian sovereignty over Sudan.

only resign, leaving it to a successor to accept all the British conditions.

During this crisis, in December 1924, King Fuad took the opportunity to dissolve the Wafdist Parliament and rule by decree. Elections were held in March 1925 and the Wafd won by an overwhelming margin, so the king again dissolved parliament. A third set of elections in May 1926 also gave the Wafd a majority, but the British vetoed Zaghlul's reinstatement as prime minister. Already shattered by Stack's murder, Zaghlul's health deteriorated further and he died a few months later.

Egyptian politicians in 1928.

His hopes for their fulfilment were raised when a Labour government came to power in Britain. Less than a year after the Wafd's landslide victory, however, the assassination of Sir Lee Stack, the British commander-in-chief *(sirdar)* of the Egyptian Army and governor-general of the Sudan, put an end to such optimism.

Allenby delivered an ultimatum to the Egyptian Government, though it had clearly not been responsible for the murder, making punitive demands. Badly shocked, Zaghlul accepted most of them, but refused withdrawal of Egyptian troops from the Sudan, the right of Britain to protect foreign interests in Egypt, and the suppression of political demonstrations. Defiance seemed impossible, however, and he could

Population pressure in the rural areas encouraged large numbers of rural poor to migrate to the city. Beginning during the interwar period, this population shift has since made Cairo one of the most densely packed cities in the world.

ROYAL DICTATORSHIP

Mustafa An-Nahhas succeeded Zaghlul as the leader of the Wafd, and during the following four years the struggle between the Wafd and King Fuad took the same pattern, with the Wafd winning general elections and the king dissolving the Parliament to appoint his own ministers. In 1930, Fuad appointed Ismail Sidqi Pasha as prime minister and replaced the 1923 constitution with his own royally decreed one. Two successors managed to maintain Fuad's constitution until 1935, when combined nationalist, popular and British pressure finally forced him to restore the constitution of 1923.

Negotiations for an Anglo-Egyptian treaty concerning the status of Britain in Egypt and

In 1928, Hassan Al-Banna had founded the Muslim Brotherhood, the stated aim of which was to purify and revitalise Islam. But the brotherhood had political aspirations as well and began to take an active part in politics in the late 1930s. It has since been a force with which every Egyptian government has had to contend.

During the interwar period, agriculture remained the backbone of the economy, but the Egyptian middle class started to invest in factories. The process of industrialisation began again, in a modest way initially, but

British troops advancing during the Battle of El Alamein, 1942.

the Sudan had long been underway. It was finally signed in August 1936 and became the basis of the two countries' relations for the next 18 years.

KING FAROUK

After 1936, political leadership and the internal political situation deteriorated. Fuad died in April 1936 and his son, Farouk, still a minor, succeeded him. The Wafd split, and a new party, the Saad Wafd, was formed. Extremist organisations also emerged, such as Misr Al-Fatat, an ultra-nationalist pro-royalist group that combined elements of religious fanaticism, militarism and a deep admiration for Nazi Germany and Fascist Italy.

⊘ DECADENT RULER

Farouk epitomised the decadence of the final years of Egypt's monarchy. He was only 16 years old when he came to the throne, and had always been a spoiled child, indulged by his doting parents and several sisters. At the age of just 14 he was sent to the Royal Military Academy in London, as what was known as a "gentleman cadet", but this attempt to instil discipline in him failed.

Throughout his life Farouk was partial to practical jokes (including picking pockets), a childish trait he combined with playboy vices such as gluttony, womanising, gambling and a passion for cars, including, it is said, 10 Rolls Royces.

greatly stepped up after the end of World War II. Along with industrialisation inevitably came urbanisation.

WORLD WAR II AND ITS AFTERMATH

When World War II broke out, in accordance with the terms of the Treaty of 1936, Britain took control of all Egyptian military facilities, although Egypt itself remained officially neutral for most of the war. The government necessarily supported the British, but many Egyptians did not, while clandestine army groups and Al-Banna's Muslim Brotherhood not only rejected the idea of co-operation but secretly plotted the government's overthrow. In February 1942, with tanks drawn up in front of Abdin Palace, the British installed – at gunpoint – their own candidate, the Wafdist An-Nahhas, as prime minister. This not only poisoned Anglo-Egyptian relations for more than a decade, but also discredited the Wafd itself.

At the end of the war, Egypt was in a precarious situation. Prime ministers and cabinets changed often; the Wafd, the Saadist party and the king were mutually hostile, and communist elements were gaining strength. In addition, a new political force had appeared, the Free Officer movement in the army, led by Gamal Abdel Nasser. Fiercely nationalistic, completely disillusioned with the government, it denounced what it saw as Britain's humiliating occupation of Egyptian soil. The leaders of the Free Officers were in contact with the Muslim Brotherhood and, although some of the two groups' aims coincided, the Free Officers refused Al-Banna's offer to join forces.

The disastrous defeat of the Arabs – the Egyptian Army at their forefront – in Palestine in 1948–9 fuelled the Muslim Brotherhood, whose volunteers had fought bravely, and its membership rapidly increased. The defeat also increased the disaffection of the army with both the palace and the government, which it accused of complicity in a scandal involving defective arms. Both the Muslim Brotherhood and the Free Officers plotted to take power; and to this end the Brotherhood carried out a series of terrorist operations, including the assassination of the prime minister, Noqrashy Pasha, in December 1948. Aware of the danger that the Muslim Brotherhood represented, the government retaliated with massive arrests of its members and Al-Banna himself was assassinated in February 1949.

BLACK SATURDAY

In 1950, riddled with corruption and bad leadership, the Wafd was again elected to power. It instituted disastrous economic policies, but sought to hold onto popularity by releasing many members of the brotherhood, abrogating the 1936 Treaty and calling for the evacuation of British troops from the Canal Zone. Resistance to the British troops in the canal area took the form of guerrilla action with the tacit approval of the government. In January 1952, a second Dinshawai occurred when the British besieged and overran a post manned

King Farouk with his second wife and children in exile.

by Egyptian auxiliary police, who fought to the last man. Rioting broke out in Cairo, which the authorities either would not or could not control. On 26 January, the day known as Black Saturday, foreign shops, bars and nightclubs were burned and British land-marks such as Shepheard's Hotel and the Turf Club disappeared for ever.

The climax came in the night of 22 July, when the Free Officers took over key positions in a bloodless coup d'état engineered by Nasser and other members of his organisation. On the morning of 23 July, the people were informed that the army, commanded by General Neguib, had seized power. Disillusioned by their corrupt government and dissolute king, the Egyptians greeted the news with joy.

President Nasser revels in the crowd.

INTO THE PRESENT

Since the army's coup d'état of 1952, six presidents have taken office and shaped the Egypt we know today.

When Nasser and his Free Officers seized power in a bloodless coup in July 1952, most Egyptians were optimistic. The young officers moved quickly to consolidate their power. On 26 July, King Farouk was forced to abdicate in favour of his son, who was only six months old. The constitution was repealed, and all Egypt's political parties were suspended. In June 1953, the monarchy was formally ended, and a republic was declared.

THE NASSER ERA (1952–70)

General Neguib, brought late into the Free Officers' plans to serve as a figurehead, was declared president and prime minister of the new republic. Other Free Officers were installed as his ministers, Nasser becoming deputy prime minister and minister of the interior. Neguib tried to assert the authority he nominally held, but by May 1954 Nasser was prime minister and virtual dictator.

Nasser's first important public act as prime minister was the amicable negotiation of a new Anglo-Egyptian treaty that provided for the gradual evacuation of British troops from the Canal Zone. The agreement was signed in October 1954 after six months of negotiations. Although his opponents grumbled that it was not favourable enough to Egypt, since it provided that the British could use the canal base in times of war, Nasser was generally hailed as the leader who finally ended foreign occupation in Egypt.

In April 1955, Nasser attended the Bandung Conference of Afro-Asian states. Soon afterwards he announced Egypt's commitment to positive neutrality, or nonalignment, and its refusal to join the Baghdad Pact, a military alliance including Iraq and Turkey, which the United States and Britain hoped to establish in the Middle East as a way of maintaining Western influence. With

Bedouin woman voting in the 2018 elections.

⊘ THE SUEZ CRISIS

The turning point in political orientation away from the West came in June 1956, after the United States withdrew its financial backing for the High Dam at Aswan. Nasser nationalised the Suez Canal and announced that he would use the revenues from it to build the dam. This provoked the fury of France and Britain, whose nationals owned the Canal, and together with Israel they launched a tripartite attack on Egypt. The invasion was ended by the intervention of the United States and the Soviet Union, which forced the three aggressors to withdraw. Nasser had won an important victory with very little effort and came to symbolise the defiance of imperialist domination.

Nehru, prime minister of India, and Yugoslavian leader Tito, Nasser became one of the founding leaders of the Non-Aligned Movement.

ARAB SOCIALISM

It was not until July 1961, five years after the Suez Crisis (see pages 93 and 276), that Nasser adopted a comprehensive programme of rapid industrialisation, to be financed in part by nationalisation of all manufacturing firms, financial institutions and public utilities. Created to further the new programme decreed that

Israeli tanks in the Sinai during the Six-Day War.

⊘ REDISTRIBUTION OF WEALTH

One of Nasser's first policies was the institution of radical land reform. At the time, Egypt's farmland was in the hands of a tiny landowning elite. Under his new laws, ownership of land was limited to 80 hectares (200 acres), and holdings beyond this limit were subsequently reduced many times and redistributed among the dispossessed peasants (*fellaheen*).

In addition, private property was confiscated from foreigners, members of the royal family and the rich in general. Bank accounts, land, houses and personal effects were all seized in an effort to deprive the upper classes of their capital assets, political influence and the culture that had set them apart.

year, the Arab Socialist Union was to remain the only legal avenue for political activity open to the Egyptian people for more than a decade.

As Nasser built respect for Egypt abroad, he began to wave the banner of Arab unity. This led in 1958 to a union between Egypt and Syria, later joined by Yemen, called the United Arab Republic.

Nasser's next unfortunate undertaking in the name of Arab unity was his five-year embroilment in Yemen. He sent troops to help out the republican forces there in 1962, while Saudi Arabia aided the royalists. But both countries remained put until 1967, when they were forced to come to an agreement in order to face a common enemy: Israel.

THE SIX-DAY WAR

The Arab-Israeli war of June 1967 was a blow from which Nasser never really recovered. Following growing tension in the area, in May 1967 he demanded that UN troops stationed in the Sinai be withdrawn and announced a blockade of the Straits of Tiran. Probably only bluff on Nasser's part, these moves were quickly taken advantage of by Israel. On 5 June, it launched a sneak attack on Jordan, Syria and Egypt, wiped out the entire Egyptian Air Force on the ground, and in six days had occupied the Golan Heights, Gaza, Jerusalem, the West Bank and the Sinai. Israeli troops crossed the Suez Canal and were ready to march to Cairo. Only a ceasefire quickly worked out by the United States and the USSR prevented further disaster. After the Six-Day War Nasser resigned, but he resumed his post the next day following mass demonstrations for his return.

However popular he remained, the old charisma was gone, and Nasser was a broken man. Efforts to salvage a wrecked economy, no longer even agriculturally self-sufficient, proved fruitless. His last important act was an attempt to reconcile King Hussein and the Palestinians after the bloody events of Black September 1970, when the king tried to crush the PLO in Jordan. Later that month he helped negotiate an accord by which Hussein, Arafat and other Arab leaders agreed to end the fighting. He died of a heart attack the day after the signing of the accord.

THE SADAT ERA

On Nasser's death, Anwar Sadat, his vice president, succeeded to the presidency. No one expected him to last long in this position, but he proved more skilful than his opponents. In May 1971, in what he called a "corrective movement", he consolidated his power by dismissing high-ranking government officials who opposed him. The following year he expelled Soviet teachers and advisors, who had been in Egypt for more than a decade. After a long period of close relations with the Eastern bloc, Egypt was turning toward the West.

Sadat's boldest initiative was his launching of the fourth Arab-Israeli war in October 1973. The outcome of this was by no means a total victory, but it did allow Egypt to regain its pride and gave Sadat enough prestige to ignore Arab unity and seek a separate peace with Israel (see box).

Sadat's economic policies, encouraging foreign investment and private enterprise, created high inflation and widened differences between the new rich and older salaried classes, as well as the poor. The drain of Egyptian brains and brawn to oil-rich countries meanwhile became a torrent. Remittances from abroad emerged as the most important factor in the economy. Property prices soared as returning Egyptians sought to invest in something safe. The impact of these revenues was ignored by government planners, whose economic models were geared solely to public-sector revenues.

The high-handed style of Sadat's government, in an atmosphere of corruption and crony capitalism, alienated many. Overt opposition gathered around the new political parties, including a revived Wafd, while less public hostility crystallised in Islamic revivalism. The Muslim Brotherhood had regained most of its freedom of action, but there were other more radical groupings, one of which was responsible for Sadat's assassination on 6 October 1981 during a ceremony commemorating the crossing of the Suez Canal.

THE MUBARAK YEARS

About a week after Sadat's assassination, then vice president Hosni Mubarak, a former air-force commander, took office as president, an action that was approved through a People's Assembly referendum. He tried at first to promote more democratic government, and although he initially made an attempt to curtail the corruption of the Sadat years, it became a feature of his own regime, causing discontent among the masses.

At the same time, the freeing of exchange rates, easing of import controls, creation of an Egyptian stock exchange and the repatriation of large sums privately invested abroad helped the middle class.

But his greatest challenge came from the Islamic Group (Al-Gama'a al-Islamiyya), who embarked on a campaign of violence aimed at turning Egypt into a fundamentalist Islamic state. They attacked foreigners and various tourist sites in the 1990s – the worst of which came in November 1997, when 62 people were killed at the Temple of Hatshepsut in Luxor. Their activi-

Anwar Sadat in 1981.

ties caused tourism to plummet, and at times, travel by foreigners in parts of Upper Egypt was deemed dangerous and severely restricted. Serious damage was done to the largest sector of Egypt's economy, further increasing unemployment and discontent. During this period, Al-Gama'a al-Islamiyya was given support by the governments of Iran and Sudan, as well as al-Qaeda. The Egyptian government reacted with a harsh crackdown, and hangings of convicted terrorists – the first since the aftermath of Sadat's assassination – resumed in 1993.

Security was tightened even further a decade later, following the bomb attack on the Taba Hilton in 2004 which killed more than 30 Israelis on holiday in the Sinai resort. And in July 2005 bombs planted at the Red Sea resort of Sharm El Sheikh killed 88 people and injured some 200 more – an attack for which two separate organisations claimed responsibility.

In 2005, amid growing discontent and pressure from the US, President Mubarak called for a constitutional amendment to introduce contested presidential elections. However, restrictions prevented serious opposition candidates from running, and in the summer election Mubarak won a landslide victory. But the political ferment, stirred by sometimes violent cam-

Anti-Morsi protesters in Tahrir Square in 2013.

paigning, made the process towards democracy more likely. One of the strongest opposition voices belonged to a new party, Kifaya ("Enough" in Arabic), which staged hundreds of protests demanding change. The other force was the Muslim Brotherhood, which organised street protests across the country.

REVOLUTION IN THE 21ST CENTURY

Many Egyptians were unhappy with Mubarak's 30-year autocratic rule, and discontent finally came to a head in January 2011. A series of public protests and uprisings erupted across Egypt in events now referred to as the Egyptian Revolution of 2011 or the January 25 Revolution. In part, the revolution was spurred on by the Arab Spring, a series of anti-government protests, uprisings and armed rebellions that spread across North Africa and the Middle East in late 2010 in response to oppressive regimes and low standards of living – starting with protests in Tunisia.

From 25 January and lasting for 18 days, hundreds of thousands of Egyptians took to a number of public spaces across Egypt, and there were demonstrations, marches, strikes and occupations of plazas, including Cairo's Tahrir Square. Grievances included police brutality, state-of-emergency laws, lack of political freedom, corruption, high unemployment, food-price inflation and low wages. The message was simple, and the protesters, from a range of socio-economic and religious backgrounds, demanded that Mubarak step down. While the majority of demonstrations were non-violent civil resistance, a later government fact-finding mission reported that over the 18 days, at least 846 civilians were killed and more than 6,400 were injured during clashes with security forces. As the protests showed no sign of abating, particularly in Tahrir Square, the police retreated on 28 January, and by the 29th, it was becoming clear that Mubarak's government had lost control when a curfew order was ignored.

On 11 February, Mubarak resigned, and celebrations broke out across Egypt. The Egyptian Supreme Council of the Armed Forces assumed control and both the constitution and parliament were dissolved. A civilian, Essam Sharaf, was appointed as temporary prime minister on 4 March to widespread approval among Egyptians, though sporadic protests continued to the end of 2011 as many people expressed concern about the Supreme Council of the Armed Forces' perceived sluggishness in instituting reforms and relaxing their grip on power. Mubarak, meanwhile, was ordered to stand trial in May 2011 on charges of premeditated murder of peaceful protesters during the revolution. He was sentenced and imprisoned but was later acquitted in 2017.

On 28 November 2011, Egypt held a parliamentary election. The Muslim Brotherhood's Freedom and Justice Party (FJP) took 44 percent of the seats and the Al-Noor Party 25 percent of the seats, resulting in an Islamist domination of more than 69 percent of parliament. The Muslim Brotherhood's Mohamed Morsi was elected as president in June 2012, which marked the end of the Supreme Council of the Armed Forces transition period.

Morsi's government, however, was short-lived. He immediately encountered fierce opposition after his attempt to pass an Islamic-leaning constitution, and also because he issued a declaration in November 2012 that granted him unlimited power to legislate without review. In effect, the declaration made all constitutional laws and decrees that had been made since Morsi assumed power immune to appeal. This enraged liberal and secular groups, as well as the military and various human-rights groups. A number of other issues came into play including his condemnation of Israel's policies toward the Palestinians and his staunch support for the opposition forces in the Syrian Civil War.

On 30 June 2013, on the first anniversary of Morsi's election, hundreds of thousands of protesters took to the streets once again and massed in Tahrir Square and outside the main presidential palace in the Heliopolis suburb demanding his resignation. The demonstrations resulted in violent clashes between Morsi supporters and anti-Morsi protesters, and later Human Rights Watch reported that at least 1,150 people had been killed in five incidents in which security officials had opened fire on demonstrators. Morsi was heavily criticised for tolerating the security force's excessive use of force.

On 1 July, the Supreme Council of the Armed Forces issued a 48-hour ultimatum to the government, stating that it must meet the demands of the people by 3 July. Morsi rejected the ultimatum, vowing that his government would pursue their own plans to resolve the political crisis. The Supreme Council condemned Morsi's response, who was widely perceived to be a conservative authoritarian who was putting the Islamist Muslim Brotherhood before the good of his country. On 3 July, in a coup d'état now frequently known as the "Second Revolution", General Abdel Fattah el-Sisi, head of the Supreme Council of the Armed Forces, announced that he had removed Morsi from power, suspended the constitution and named the Supreme Constitutional Court's leader, Adly Mansour, as acting president.

Military officials arrested Morsi, who faced trial in September 2013 on charges of inciting deadly violence and later for espionage relating to suspected contacts with Hamas. Morsi was sentenced to 20 years in prison; on 17 June 2019, he died of ill-health. Thousands of Morsi's supporters were also arrested. Egypt has now banned the Muslim Brotherhood, which it considers a terrorist organisation.

A new constitution took effect in January 2014, and presidential and parliamentary elections were held in June of that year. El-Sisi retired from his military career and stood as candidate; he emerged victorious with more than 96 per-

Abdel Fattah el-Sisi.

cent of the vote. In the 2018 presidential election, El-Sisi faced only nominal opposition and won with 97 percent, retaining his position as the sixth president of Egypt.

However in September 2019 new scattered demonstrations flared up, again centring on Cairo's Midan al-Tahir, demanding El-Sisi's resignation and challenging his authoritarian rule. The rare protests were in response to corruption allegations implicating El-Sisi and the government – particularly unpalatable given millions of Egyptians still live in poverty. Security officers dispersed the protests, although many people were arrested, and El-Sisi repeatedly made it clear that dissent would not be tolerated.

Mohamed Salah street art outside a Cairo coffee shop.

POPULAR CULTURE

Egypt has long been regarded as the hub of popular culture in the Arab world, and from films to fiction, and soaps to song, it has led the way across the region. Traditional Arabic literature and music has accommodated Western influences in recent years and a newer visual-arts scene is flourishing.

In *The One Thousand and One Nights*, Cairo is called "the mother of the world", a phrase that Egyptians nowadays tend to modify to "Mother of the Arab World". Although in politics that may no longer be true, Egypt can still claim to be in the forefront as far as popular culture is concerned: from Damascus to Casablanca, Egyptian films and television are screened, books by Egyptian writers are read and its singers and musicians are given radio and internet airtime.

THE WRITTEN WORD

In 1914, Muhammad Husayn Haykal (1888–1956) published *Zaynab*, a story about romantic and marital relationships and the interactions between labouring cotton workers and plantation owners in the Egyptian countryside. It is considered the first contemporary Egyptian novel, and was also the first to feature dialogue in the Egyptian vernacular language rather than written Arabic.

But it was the year 1988 that was one of celebration for modern Egyptian writers when Naguib Mahfouz (1911–2006) became the first (and to date, only) Egyptian to win the Nobel Prize for Literature. Over a 70-year career, he published 34 novels, more than 350 short stories and several plays. More than half of his books have been made into films, which have circulated throughout the Arabic-speaking world.

Another literacy milestone came in 2008, when Bahaa Taher (1935–) was awarded the inaugural Booker International Prize for Arab Fiction with *Sunset Oasis*. Published in Cairo in 2007, the novel is set in 19th-century Egypt at the beginning of British rule and explores themes of occupation and subjugation. During the 1980s and 1990s Taher lived in Switzerland,

Egyptian author Alaa al-Aswany.

where he worked as a translator for the United Nations.

Other central figures in the development of modern Egyptian literature include academic Taha Hussein (1889–1973), who wrote more than 60 books (of which six were novels); although he never won, Hussein was nominated for the Nobel Prize for Literature no fewer than 14 times. Meanwhile, the hundreds of poems by Alexandrian-Greek poet Constantine P. Cavafy (1863–1933) that explore sexuality, memory and history still have a universal appeal, and Tawfiq al-Hakim (1898–1997), who wrote novels, poems and essays, is best remembered as a prolific playwright who played a key role in the development of Arabic drama.

These brilliant minds and their younger contemporaries created a tradition of modern storytelling, rich in folklore and heavy in allegory (a necessity given the variable censorship laws in more recent decades). Most wrote in Arabic, but works have been translated into English and/or French, too. Notable 20th- and 21st-century writers with arguably their most respected works include: Waguih Ghali (1928–1969; *Beer in the Snooker Club*); Yahya Taher Abdullah (1938–1981; *The Mountain of Green Tea*); Abdel Rahman al Sharqawi (1920–1987; *Egyptian Earth*); Yusuf Idris (1927–1991; *The Cheapest Nights*); Edwar al-Kharrat (1926–2015; *Girls of Alexandria*); Gamal al Ghitani (1945–2015: *Zayni Barakat*); Nawal al Saadawi (1931–; *Woman at Point Zero*); Sonallah Ibrahim (1937–; *Zaat: The Tale of One Woman's Life in Egypt During the Last Fifty Years*); Ibrahim Abdel Meguid (1946–; *No One Sleeps in Alexandria*); and Youssef Ziedan (1958–; *Azazeel*). The 1990s in particular witnessed the rise of many fine women writers, facilitated in part by the ease of modern, privatised publishing. Prominent female authors include Somayya Ramadan (1951–; *Leaves of*

Adhaf Soueif, novelist and journalist.

⊘ THE YACOUBIAN BUILDING

One of the most successful Egyptian authors in recent years is Alaa al-Aswany (1957–), who famously was a dentist before turning to full-time writing. *The Yacoubian Building* (2002) brings to life a Cairo where only the corrupted and the corruptible can succeed. The novel focuses mainly on the residents of the Yacoubian Building, a once-chic but now run-down edifice that's home to all strata of Egyptian society – it was actually inspired by the real Yacoubian Building, containing al-Aswany's dental surgery. The building is still located at the same address: 34 Talaat Harb Street (referred to by its old name of Suleiman Pasha Street in the novel). Through the prism of this building, the story touches on several taboo subjects and is an engrossing metaphor for the social problems in Egypt under then-President Mubarak. The novel has been translated into 23 languages, was made into a star-studded film in 2006, directed by Marwan Hamid with Adel Imam (see opposite) playing the lead role, and then a television series in 2007. In fact, many commentators believe that this work played a crucial role in triggering revolutionary sentiments among Egyptians, and even al-Aswany claims that during the Egyptian Revolution of 2011, many protesters approached him with sentiments along the lines of "We are here because of what you wrote".

Narcissus); Ahdaf Soueif (1950–; *The Map of Love*); and Miral al-Tahawy (1970–; *The Tent*).

CAIRO, CINEMA CITY

Much of Egypt's claim to cultural supremacy in the Arab world has been due to the phenomenal success of its film industry in the 20th century, when it was the most productive country in the Middle East for movie-making. However, the bulk of Egypt's output is low-grade melodrama and weak romantic comedy. Directors tread the fine line between titillating the audience and

with the actor Farid al-Atrash, who, like her, combined a talent for acting with an exceptional voice.

> So important was the musical in the development of Egyptian cinema that critic Samir Farid noted, "The Egyptian cinema only became talking in order to sing, without which it would be silent today."

Still from "The Yacoubian Building", based on Alaa al-Aswany's novel and starring Adel Imam.

not offending the government's censors, who mostly succeed in keeping nudity, overt political criticism and religious slurs off their cinema screens.

In 1927, *Qublah fel Sahara* ("Kiss in the Desert"), directed by Ibrahim Lama, was the first full-length silent feature film produced in Egypt, and was followed later in the same year by *Laila*, directed by Wedad Orfi. The first sound movie, *Unshudat al-Fuad* ("Song of the Heart"), arrived in 1931. The first musical was *Al Wardah al-Baida* ("The White Rose") in 1933, directed by Muhammad Karim, after which musicals dominated in the 1940s with a generation of famous Arab singer stars such as Umm Kulthum (see page 106). Her most successful partnership was

Salah Abou Seif (1915–1996) made some of Egypt's most important post-revolution films, and won the Critics' Prize at the 1956 Cannes Film Festival with *La Sangsue*. Abou Seif directed the leading stars of his day, including the legendary belly dancer Tahiya Karioka, Hind Rostom, Omar Sharif and his wife Faten Hamama. Abu Seif's films very much reflected the mood of the time – political, questioning, fiercely pro-Arab and anti-royalist.

Youssef Chahine (1926–2008) began directing films in the 1940s and perhaps did more than anyone to bring credibility to Egyptian cinema. He created a broad body of work, from the realism of the black-and-white *Cairo Station* (1958), in which the director took a key role as a station porter, to *The Emigrant* (1994), an allegory about corruption, ignorance and injustice, set in ancient Egypt. Part of Chahine's success was due to his ability to convince European film bodies to provide money or facilities, which also guaranteed him an international audience. His work was recognised by a Lifetime Achievement Award at the 1997 Cannes Film Festival. Few other Egyptian directors have achieved anything like Chahine's stature, with the exception perhaps of Yousri Nassallah (1952–), who was formerly Chahine's assistant and whose 2012 film

After the Battle competed for the Palme d'Or at the Cannes Film Festival.

The Egyptian film industry was nationalised back in the early 1960s, when a new film was released almost every day. Subjects ranged from historical epics to back-alley melodramas and plots were often copied from Hollywood. In the 1970s, the film industry was denationalised, and a more profit-driven and commercial period arrived. By the 1990s, rising costs, a lack of good cinemas, failure to control video piracy and the spread of satellite television saw film production

Scene from "The Night of Counting the Years" (1969).

⊘ ICONIC FILM

One of the most important films to come out of Egypt was made by Shadi Abdel Salam (1930–1986). *The Night of Counting the Years* (1969), for which he also wrote the screenplay, is unique among films about Egypt or directed by Egyptians. Telling the story of the discovery of the cache of royal mummies in the Theban hills in 1881, it is a political and topical allegory for the underlying tensions of the last years of President Nasser. Foreign experts, pashas from Cairo, dignified peasants and a good man who can do no right all have their roles to play. Although spoken of as "the spearhead of the Egyptian cinema", Abdel Salam never produced another major film.

dwindle further. Today, smaller art films attract some international attention, but have limited appeal in Egypt itself, while cheaply made popular films, often comedies, battle to hold audiences drawn to Hollywood or other international movies. However, the annual Cairo International Film Festival, which was established in 1976, goes a long way to promote the local industry and is the oldest and only internationally accredited cultural feature-film festival in the Arab world.

TELEVISION'S REVOLUTION

It would be hard to overestimate the impact television has had on the lives of rural Egyptians. The promise Nasser and Sadat made to link every village in the country to the national electricity grid had an unforeseen effect and changed rural life for ever. With electricity came television and with TV came late-night viewing and that, in turn, put an end to farmers getting into their fields before dawn. Egyptians especially enjoy crowding around their TVs to watch big-budget mini-series starring the country's top actors, including weepy melodramas and soap operas, police procedurals and sweeping historical epics. The best of these are exported across the Middle East.

Egypt launched its first broadcasts in 1960 and for the first few decades state-run channels held

Mohammad Abdel Wahab, Abdel Halim Hafez and Farid al-Atrash. These musicians still have a large audience among the older generation, but with just over half of the almost 1.1-million population aged under 25, the biggest slice of Egypt's music market today is taken by modern musicians.

Among the sounds to be heard is *shaabi* ("of the people") music, developed by singer Ahmed Adawiya in the 1970s, mixing protest lyrics with a strong back beat. After more than a decade of phenomenal sales, Adawiya began singing about God, relinquishing his place as king of *shaabi* to Hakim

Festival-type venues are becoming increasingly popular in Egypt.

a monopoly on terrestrial TV. But today, like most places in the world, satellite TV is widespread, and the overwhelming number of private stations has changed the Egyptian TV production market drastically. Additionally, the introduction of dubbed TV shows – mostly from Turkey and India – has made the market even more competitive, and television talk shows, once a ferment of raucous debate, have become so predictably progovernment that many Egyptians are tuning out.

THE SOUND OF MUSIC

Egypt's domination of the Arab music scene until the 1970s was facilitated by the classical Arabic music of the Egyptian singer Umm Kulthum (see page 106) and her contemporaries, including

and the hugely popular Shaaban Abdel-Rahim.

In contrast, and also developed in the 1970s, *al-jeel* ("the generation") music is a fusion of disco and local rhythms; with a background rhythm similar to reggae, its lyrics are generally confined to enduring themes of love and nostalgia. Mohammad Foad and Hisham Abbas are two names to listen out for, but Amr Diab is the most popular and in 1992, he became the first Egyptian and Middle Eastern artist to make music videos.

The sound of Egypt that has reached the West is an eclectic mix of Arab, Egyptian, Turkish and Indian sounds, produced by musicians such as George Kazazian, Natacha Atlas and the popular Les Musiciens du Nil ("The Musicians of the Nile"), a group of Upper Egyptian musicians led by the folk singer Metqal, himself a mix of Suda-nese, Nubian and Egyptian roots.

Other genres have emerged more recently, popularised by groups such as Arabian Knightz, a hip-hop trio from Cairo known for releasing *Rebel*, a protest rap that was one of the first songs released after internet censorship laws were relaxed following the Egyptian Revolution of 2011.

BELLY DANCING

Egyptian belly dancing – or *raqs sharqi*, mean-ing "oriental dancing" in Egyptian Arabic – is noted for its controlled and precise movements, and opens another window into the country's colourful culture. But it also poses a question: how can a conservative, Islamic society tolerate, much less adulate, curvaceous women making provocative gestures and emphasising complex movements of the torso in public? The answer is less and less. While belly dancing is native, traditional and entertaining in Egypt, deeply reli-gious people consider the display of bodies in public as unrespectable.

The origins of *raqs sharqi* are debatable. Tomb

Belly dancing for tourists in Hurghada.

paintings suggest that ancient Egyptians liked to dance, and the legend of Salome, who danced so beautifully that she was granted a wish by the king and asked for the head of John the Baptist, con-firms that dance was a court entertainment and that dancers have long commanded high fees.

Nineteenth-century writers, from Edward Lane to Flaubert, refer to the reputation of pub-lic dancers; Lane with disapproval, Flaubert with pleasure, having slept with one. Flaubert's line won out as far as foreign expectations go: both orientalist painters and the 20th-century Egyp-tian (and Hollywood) cinema industry (see page 103) made this sort of dancing universally rec-ognised and helped promote the popularity of public performances in Egypt, especially in

Cairo's nightclubs. For a dancer's reputation to survive, she had to mix regular club appearances with screen roles.

These days, however, Egyptians generally don't consider it a respectable profession, and despite employing belly dancers for wedding receptions and other celebratory events, the dancers do not display bare midriffs and excessive skin; it's more common for them to wear long, figure-hugging one-piece gowns. Those performing for tourists in Egypt, dressed in sequin-covered bikinis, are generally foreigners from Europe and elsewhere in the Arab world.

THE VISUAL ARTS

Because the Prophet Muhammad denounced "image-makers", visual art in Egypt cannot claim an ancient tradition. However, contacts with Western culture in the 19th century stimulated a debate, with the pro-independence nationalists being keen to promote a recognisable Egyptian style. Little advance was made until the early 20th century, when the mufti of Egypt suggested the Prophet's comment should be seen in context, having been made in an age of idolatry, and Prince Yusuf Kamal founded the School of Fine Arts in Cairo in 1908.

Egyptian artists started by confronting their ancient traditions. As sculptor Mahmoud Mukhtar (1881–1934) said, "When I was a child, there had been no sculpture in my country for more than 700 years." The Neo-Pharaonists, as they were called, believed that a new Egyptian identity would emerge by examining the past. The work of Modernist artists like Mukhtar, Mahmoud Sa'id (1897–1964) and Mohamed Nagy (1888–1956) reflected this.

Today, Mukhtar's sculptures can be seen in the Mahmoud Mukhtar Museum (see page 138) on Cairo's Gezira Island. Nearby, the Museum of Egyptian Modern Art (see page 138), also known as the Gezira Center for Modern Art, has been on Gezira Island since 1986, although it's moved a number of times since being established in 1931. It currently displays more than 10,000 paintings and sculptures that show the development of the Egyptian art movement from the early 20th century (visitors can also visit the adjacent National Museum of Egyptian Civilization, which contains numerous displays from ancient Egypt).

The contemporary art scene is now blossoming in Cairo. The acclaimed Townhouse Gallery opened in 1998 as the first independ-

> The Prophet Muhammad said, "Those who will be most tormented on Judgement Day will be image-makers." Consequently, Muslims have traditionally frowned on the representation of living creatures.

Graffiti in Cairo.

ent art space in the country and today works on a nonprofit basis to assist in raising the profile of gifted artists by hosting exhibitions, educational platforms and outreach programmes. Numerous other galleries and initiatives have started up since then, and art media includes everything from traditional oil paintings and sculptures to modern calligraphy and video installations.

Meanwhile, since the Egyptian Revolution of 2011, graffiti has grown in popularity in both formal art and on street walls. Graffiti in fact dates back to the Pharaonic period, when the ancient Egyptians used to document their daily life on temple walls. Today, it's used as a powerful visual-arts tool to reflect political debates.

Making falafel in Luxor.

A LOVE OF FOOD

Though not a bastion of haute cuisine, Egypt offers many tasty experiences, including memorable mezes, great street food, succulent fruit and oriental pastries.

In the Middle Ages, Egyptian cuisine enjoyed a high reputation all over the Islamic empire, but few now travel to Egypt in search of a culinary experience. Those looking for the best of Middle Eastern cuisine will undoubtedly choose countries like Lebanon or Turkey. Nevertheless, Egyptians love to eat – and to share a meal – and will endlessly discuss the delight of the dishes served, simple as they may be. As in most Arab countries, the best food is found at home. Restaurants usually serve only the more common Egyptian dishes such as kebabs, meze and perhaps stuffed pigeon or *meloukhia* (a thick soup made of a deep-green leaf, similar to spinach). Over the past few years, trendy restaurants in Cairo have rediscovered typical Egyptian dishes, including *fatta* (a mix of rice, bread and garlic).

FOOD FOR THE PHARAOHS

The Egyptians' sense of hospitality and their love of food goes back a long way, according to the

Sharing a meal in Daraw.

> Egyptian cuisine shows signs of a long history of occupation: the Persians, Greeks, Romans, Arabs and Ottomans have all left their mark. More recently, European influences have also been added.

evidence of many well-preserved wall paintings and carvings in tombs and temples around the country, which depict large banquets and a wide variety of foods. Such images also provide proof that many of the dishes enjoyed in Egyptian households today were also on the menu

in antiquity. *Meloukhia* soup, roast goose and salted dried fish (*fasieekh*) are examples.

A POOR MAN'S TABLE

However elaborate the cuisine enjoyed by Egypt's former kings and sultans, the majority of today's *fellaheen* (peasants) are far too poor to make the most of gastronomic opportunities. As in other Arab countries, their diet consists mainly of locally grown vegetables, lentils and beans, with meat at weekends or on special occasions. With the huge influx of people from the countryside to towns and cities, this vegetable-based peasant cuisine has become common and most middle-class families will now elaborate on these basic recipes, adding more expensive ingredients when they can afford them. Even in Cairo's most up-market quarters, colourful carts can be found on street corners early in the morning, where they serve steaming *fuul* (broad or fava beans) for breakfast.

A WARM WELCOME

"If people are standing at the door of your house, don't shut it before them" and "Give the guest food to eat even though you are starving yourself" are two of the many proverbs that insist that hospitality is a duty and that all guests should be offered food and drink. Whatever their social standing,

Enjoying fried fish in Dahab.

⊘ BEAN FEAST

First published in 1968, in her *Book of Middle Eastern Food*, Egyptian-born writer Claudia Roden reminisces about *fuul medames* (stewed broad or fava beans mashed with onions, tomatoes and spices): "Ceremoniously, we sprinkled the beans with olive oil, squeezed a little lemon over them, seasoned them with salt and pepper, and placed a hot, hard-boiled egg in their midst... Silently, we ate the beans, whole and firm at first; then we squashed them with our forks and combined their floury texture and earthy taste with the acid tang of lemon, mellowed by the olive oil."

Beans are a staple food for Egyptians and they make their way into many different street foods.

---

an Egyptian family will always serve guests several salads and a few vegetable and meat dishes. Guests will always be handed the best morsels of fish or the finest cut of meat from the central serving dish or platter. Guests also have a well-prescribed role to play: they must, at first, refuse the offer but then relent after some pressure. They are expected to praise every aspect of the food, without inspecting it too closely.

FUUL ABOVE ALL

Fuul (broad or fava beans), stewed and eaten with bread, form Egypt's staple diet. Usually eaten for breakfast or as a sandwich between meals, *fuul* can just as well be served as lunch or dinner in some households. Some people who can't afford any other food will eat it several times a day. At first the brown muddy stew may not look or smell

> The evening air is often scented by the warm smell of roasting maize (corn on the cob), libb (melon seeds) and tirmis (lupin seeds), sold from street carts, in little paper cones.

particularly appetising, but with familiarity the earthy dish can become quite addictive.

Broad (fava) beans are also used in another of Egypt's favourite dishes, *taameya* (deep-fried broad-bean balls, rather like falafels, which use chickpeas instead), which are often served with *fuul*. Another staple dish, usually sold as street food (which makes a delicious, inexpensive lunch), is *kushari*, a mixture of macaroni, lentils, rice and chickpeas, served with fried onions and topped with a generous dollop of hot tomato sauce. A familiar-sounding dish is *makarona* – pasta accompanied by a variety of sauces – which is also usually sold from a cart as lunch-time street food.

MAKE A MEAL OF MEZE

Of all the dishes on offer in Egypt it is a table full of meze, dips and salads that best reflects the Egyptian and Middle Eastern character. Meze are served with drinks as light snacks or as appetisers before a meal. Egyptians love to sit and relax at home, on a terrace or in a café, chatting and laughing with friends and savouring a few salads and small dishes. These can be anything from a plate of hummous, pickled vegetables or elaborate *mahshi* (stuffed vegetables), to little meat pies. With such a variety of dishes, meze can easily turn out to be a pleasurable and leisurely meal on their own.

CELEBRATIONS

Meat has always been considered a food for the rich and aristocratic. Poorer Egyptians rely on a diet of wheat, beans and lentils and there is only one day in the year when they are sure to get a taste of meat: Id al-Kebir, the 10th day of the last

was only sheep or lamb, and occasionally camel, goat or gazelle. Islam prohibits pork, but beef and veal are now widely available in Egypt. Meat is usually grilled as kebab or kofta (minced lamb) or used in a stew. Offal – particularly liver, kidneys and testicles – is considered a delicacy.

SWEET TREATS

The traditional end to a meal at home is a bowl of seasonal fruit, but Western-style ice cream and crème caramel will also be offered as a dessert in most restaurants. Even though they are not

Siwa street bakery.

month of the Muslim calendar. In commemoration of Abraham's sacrifice of his son Ismail, rural families who can afford it will sacrifice a sheep or a lamb. The animal, which should be fat and young, is ritually slaughtered and roasted whole on a spit, and usually some of its meat is distributed to the poor, according to the tenets of Islam. Sheep are also slaughtered to mark other important occasions such as death, birth or marriage.

Ramadan, the month of fasting from sunset to sunrise, is another occasion when more meat is consumed than usual. Families visit each other in the evenings and celebrate the end of another day of fasting with a rich display of foods and sweets.

Many Egyptian recipes won't stipulate what sort of meat is to be used, as traditionally there

usually eaten as a dessert, there are some delicious Egyptian puddings, including *muhallabia*, a milk cream thickened by cornflour and ground rice, and *roz bi-laban*, a creamy rice pudding, both topped with chopped almonds and pistachio nuts. More elaborate is *umm ali*, a warm, comforting bread pudding with coconut, raisins, nuts and cream. According to some sources, *umm ali* was introduced into Egypt by Miss O'Malley, the Irish mistress of the khedive Ismail.

Pastries are more likely to be served at parties and special, happy occasions such as weddings and births, than as a dessert. Baklava is the most famous oriental pastry, a filo wrapping stuffed with a mixture of nuts or almonds and covered with an orange-blossom syrup. More common are *basbousa*, a semolina cake of syrup and nuts, and the drier *kunafa*, angel hair filled with thick cream, ricotta cheese or chopped nuts and syrup. A woman who prides herself on making the best baklava or *kunafa* will often keep her recipe secret and only pass it on to her daughters.

JUICY DRINKS

Egyptians will tell you that "Once you drink water from the Nile, you will always come back to Egypt". A nice sentiment, but Nile water is more likely to curse than bless; stick to mineral water

Cairo erqsusi.

or fresh juices. Brightly coloured juice bars with their picturesque pyramids of strawberries and oranges and baskets of mangoes attract thirsty customers. Freshly squeezed *asir* (juice) is excellent and very cheap. The most widely available juice is *asir laymun* (fresh lemon or lime), usually served sweetened unless you say otherwise.

Usually there will also be a choice of *asir burtuqan* (freshly squeezed winter or summer oranges), *moz* (banana), *gazar* (carrot) and *gawafa* (sweet guava). Depending on the season there could also be deep-red *asir ruman* (pomegranate juice), *farawla* (strawberry) and thick *manga* (mango). Some stalls also offer *asab* or *gasab*, the sweet juice pressed out of sugar-cane sticks.

ALCOHOLIC PLEASURES

According to the Qur'an Muslims should not drink alcohol and, with religious tensions rising, much of Egypt is dry. But that doesn't mean that all Egyptians are teetotal, and there are bars to be found – although these usually close during the month of Ramadan, when no alcohol is served to Egyptians, even if they are Copts. Nevertheless, foreigners can get alcohol in tourist hotels and Western-style bars and restaurants, although imported brands are always considerably more expensive than the local varieties.

Perhaps surprisingly, for an Islamic nation, there is a good deal of alcohol production in Egypt itself. Al Ahram Beverages Company produces a lot of fine beers, wines and spirits, products that are exported to even European countries. Their locally brewed Stella beer has been brewed in Egypt since 1897 and is quite enjoyable, while the

> *Street vendors carry enormous glass containers from which they dispense drinks of laymun (lemon), tamar hindi (tamarind) and ersoos (liquorice). The latter concoction has given its name to the vendor, who is called an erqsusi.*

more expensive Stella Export and Stella Premium are stronger, as is the better Sakkara.

Wine has been drunk in Egypt since the time of the pharaohs and was even provided to the deceased and stored in their tombs. The quality of the local wine used to range from drinkable to downright dangerous, but these days quality has much improved. In particular, the Gianaclis Winery (first established in 1882 and now also owned by Al Ahram) produces a number of good labels. Cru des Ptolémées is a white wine made from pinot blanc; Leila is a fruity rosé; Valmont is a light and refreshing sparkling wine in both white and rosé; while Omar Khayyam and Grand Marquis are deep reds made from cabernet sauvignon grapes. The latter are very palatable and considered by many as the best in Egypt.

Zibeeb, or *arak*, the Egyptian version of ouzo, is reliable, as are Al Ahram's Auld Stag Whiskey and Butler's Gin. On the flip side, local spirits with inspiring names such as Dry Din, Marcel Horse, Ricardo and Johnny Talker are best avoided.

Fruit seller in Luxor.

Egyptian men drinking tea at Khan Al Khalili Bazaar.

EGYPTIAN COFFEE HOUSES

The coffee house is an essential part of urban Egyptian life, but coffee has had a chequered history in Egypt. Although now integral to the lives of millions, it once invoked the wrath of the clergy who saw it as a dangerous drug.

In crowded Egypt, Allah can be counted on for two great mercies: endless sunshine and abundant free time. Small wonder, then, that the street café, where much of these two great resources is spent, is so ubiquitous an institution. Few men let a day pass without spending time in their local, drinking coffee, exchanging jokes or discussing the events of the day.

DIFFERENT ATMOSPHERES

The *qahwa* – Arabic for both "coffee" and "café" – is defined loosely. It can be anything from a bench, a patch of charcoal, a tin pot and three glasses to a cavernous saloon reverberating with the clack of dominoes, the slap of cards and the crackling of dice.

In Cairo, a café may serve as the headquarters of a street gang, the meeting place for homesick provincials, or the rendezvous of intellectuals. There are cafés for couples, musicians, black marketeers, leftists, Muslim extremists, the LGBTQ community, retired generals and pimps.

Waiter in Café Riche, which opened in 1908.

In Edward Lane's *Manners and Customs of the Modern Egyptians*, he judged the number of cafés in Cairo in the 1830s to be over 1,000. Given a similar ratio of one café per 400 people, Cairo today would contain more than 48,000 cafés.

The ideal café adjoins a small square in the backstreets of a popular quarter. The simple decor of its exterior will reveal the sense of style its patronage demands. The few outdoor tables will be shaded by a tree or vine, while the ground will have been sprinkled with water to keep down the dust. A pungent sweetness emanates from the interior, where sawdust covers the floor.

An elaborate brass *sarabantina*, which resembles a cross between a steam locomotive and a samovar, occupies pride of place on the counter at the back of the room, behind which striped glass jugs for smokers' water pipes line the walls. The patron will puff judiciously as he takes in the crime column of the morning paper, while the *qahwagi*, or waiter, keeps up a continuous banter with customers, between forceful shouts to the tea boy.

LIQUID INCIDENTALS

Atmosphere is only one of the pleasures the café offers. There is also the pleasure of indulging in a hot drink. Tea, introduced in the 19th century, has replaced coffee as the staple. The powerful Egyptian version of the brew takes some getting used to. Since cheap tea dust is the preferred variety, don't anticipate a delicate flavour. Tea is drunk as a fix, as strong and sweet as possible. It is best to make no compromises with local taste: sugarless Egyptian tea is unpalatable. Some connoisseurs say that the truly classic glass of tea should be only faintly translucent, with a mild aroma of kerosene from extended boiling on a Primus stove.

Arabic coffee is still prepared and served in centuries-old style, without the fancy gadgetry of European invention. Sugar, then powdered coffee, is added to hot water and brought to the boil in a brass *kanaka*. The *qahwagi* brings the *kanaka* and cup on a tin tray and pours the liquid with solicitude, preserving the *wish* – the "face" or thick mud that sits on the surface before settling. In the better cafés, a dark blend spiced with cardamom is used. In all establishments, customers must specify how they want their coffee: *saada* (sugarless), 'arr-

El Fishawi's coffee house in Khan El Khalili Bazaar.

☉ A HEADY BREW

The first recorded mention of the coffee plant was by an Arab physician in the 9th century. Embraced by the Bedu, to whom it is a vital part of welcoming friends and strangers, it gradually spread all over the Arab world, and was introduced to the inhabitants of Cairo by Sufi mystics in the 16th century. The dervishes' adoption of the stimulant to prolong their ecstatic trances angered the orthodox clergy, who saw it as inspiring deviant behaviour, and in 1532 the coffee bean was outlawed. As with tobacco, controversy raged for years before the weight of popular taste concluded the debate, and coffee became a respectable part of social intercourse.

iha (with a dash of sugar), *mazbut* (medium), or *ziyada* (with extra sugar). In some "European cafés", *qahwa Faransawi* or French coffee is served, and newer, modern cafés have Italian espresso machines.

More traditional are the hot medicinal infusions still found in many cafés. The bases of these potations range from ginger, *ganzabeel*, which is recommended for coughs, *erfa* (cinnamon) and *yansun* (aniseed) for the throat, to *helba* (fenugreek) for stomach complaints. *Karkadé*, the scarlet tea of a hibiscus flower, is a speciality of Aswan. Packed with vitamin C, it is delicious hot or cold. *Sahlib*, a steaming cream, concocted from dried orchids and topped with chopped nuts, is a winter favourite. In summer, cafés serve cooler drinks, ranging from *laymun* (lemon), *tamar hindi* (tamarind), *ersoos* (liquorice) and *farawla* (strawberry), to the ever more pervasive Kukula, Bibsi and Shwibs, the commercially bottled soft drinks that have run old local brands off the market.

The formula of the traditional *qahwa* (coffee house) is increasingly popular with young, fashionable Cairenes. Several cafés, often open-air, have opened along the Nile or on ex-cruise boats, providing coffee, tea and shishas, or *sheeshas*, as well as snacks and alcoholic drinks.

(tuffah), or sticky cherry, strawberry and even cappuccino flavours. *Tumbak*, another variety, is loose, dry tobacco wrapped into a cone with a whole leaf. While *ma'assil* is easy to smoke, a cone of dry *tumbak* may take up to an hour to exhaust.

LIVE ENTERTAINMENT

Every café offers diversion in the form of cards *(kutshina)*, backgammon *(tawla)* and dominoes. But it is good conversation and companionship that draw regular crowds. Despite the mass

Shisha smokers in Old Cairo.

A SMOKER'S PARADISE

The Egyptian café is a paradise for the serious smoker and has perfected the ultimate tobacco tool. The shisha, or water pipe, cools, sweetens and lightens the taste of the burning leaves, makes a soothing gurgle and provides a pleasant distraction for idle hands. It is an instrument of meditation to be savoured serenely, and is often undertaken as a sociable group activity.

The tobacco comes in an assortment of flavours. Most popular is *ma'assil*, a sticky blend of chopped leaf fermented with molasses. It is pressed in small clay bowls that are fitted into the shisha and lit with charcoal. This tobacco is also sold with a smoother apple flavour

media and the smart phone, people still find that the best source of news – not to mention gossip, rumour, slander and fantasy – is found at the local café.

With the nation's characteristic penchant for nostalgia, aficionados will affirm that cafés are not what they used to be. Like the introduction of radio in the 1930s, which signalled the decline of storytellers, television has led to a decline in public entertainment. Luckily, most café owners leave their sets off except during major sports events.

The best time for dropping in on a café is the late afternoon, when the sun's dying rays turn dun-coloured buildings to gold, and smoke drifts skyward from the shisha.

NINETEENTH-CENTURY TRAVELLERS ON THE NILE

Tourists had been visiting since the time of the Greeks and Romans, but there was a sense of rediscovery when 19th-century Westerners arrived in Egypt alongside the rise of Egyptology as an academic and amateur pursuit.

It is hard for us to imagine the shock of arriving in Egypt in the 18th or 19th centuries. By the time we as tourists arrive today, guidebooks and television documentaries have shown us in minute detail what temples and tombs look like and the ways in which they functioned in Ancient Egypt. Yet for all our information, early travellers were often better equipped to appreciate what they saw. After French scholar Jean-François Champollion (1790–1832) began to decipher hieroglyphics from 1820, many visitors arrived having learned how to read ancient inscriptions. They would have also read their Greek and Roman histories and the impressions of early travellers, as well as the latest accounts.

Most 19th-century visitors spoke no Arabic, though in Egypt few people spoke anything other than Arabic. Until the mid-1800s, foreigners travelled under constant threat in a country with no strong central authority, but there was romance as well as danger: new tombs and temples were being dug out of the sand, and until the mid-19th century they sailed on a river whose source remained a mystery.

When Napoleon invaded Egypt in 1798, he landed with an army of soldiers and 167 savants who spread across the country recording everything from antiquities to wildlife.

After discovering the remains of ancient Troy, German archaeologist Heinrich Schliemann went to look for the tomb of Alexander the Great. After visiting Alexandria, he concluded that popular tradition was right and that the tomb lay under the Mosque of Nebi Danial, but the Muslim authorities refused him permission to excavate there.

Travelling incognito, the extraordinary Richard Burton perfected his disguise as Mirca Abdullah in Cairo before undertaking a pilgrimage to Mecca.

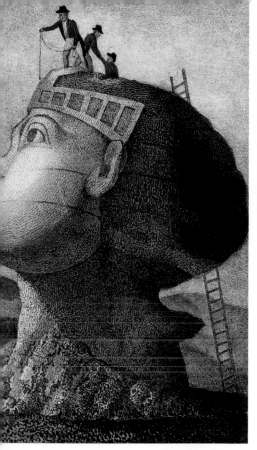

Florence Nightingale.

Ladies on the Nile

In 1849, Florence Nightingale (1820–1910) went to Egypt for the winter to recover her health and wrote, "One wonders that people come back from Egypt and live lives as they did before." She did not: by the time she got home she had written some of the finest letters from Egypt and also decided to devote her life to helping the sick.

But earlier travellers had not had it so easy. English letter-writer Elisa Fay, en route to India in 1779, was scared on the river up to Cairo, nearly suffocated under all the layers she was obliged to wear in public and was then robbed, along with the rest of her caravan, crossing the desert to Suez.

Sophia Poole, sister of Edward Lane, the Arabic scholar, lived in Egypt for seven years (1842–9) without having to compromise her Christian values, although she was a little shocked by the public baths. Miss Poole and her contemporary, English journalist Harriet Martineau, who embarked on a tour of Egypt in 1846, were among the first outsiders to write about women in Egypt. This insight was furthered by the letters of English author Lucie Duff-Gordon, who settled in Luxor in 1862 where she learnt Arabic and wrote many letters about Egyptian culture, religion and customs. In the year of her death, 1869, conditions were "soft" enough for Thomas Cook to escort his first package tour of the country. By 1886, the now Thomas Cook & Son tour company had launched a fleet of luxurious Nile steamers, aboard which the cream of Victorian society was pampered.

Egypt has long been a favourite for writers. Among those who visited in the 19th century, both Gustave Flaubert (right) and Mark Twain left classic accounts.

Napoleon's savants were led by Baron Dominique Vivant. He published his own Travels in 1802, ahead of the "Description de l'Egypte" (1809).

Between 1815 and 1819 Giovanni Belzoni, circus strongman turned antiquity-hunter, opened the Second Pyramid at Giza and Abu Simbel's Great Temple, and discovered Seti I's tomb in Luxor.

Stunning sunset over the Nile near Aswan.

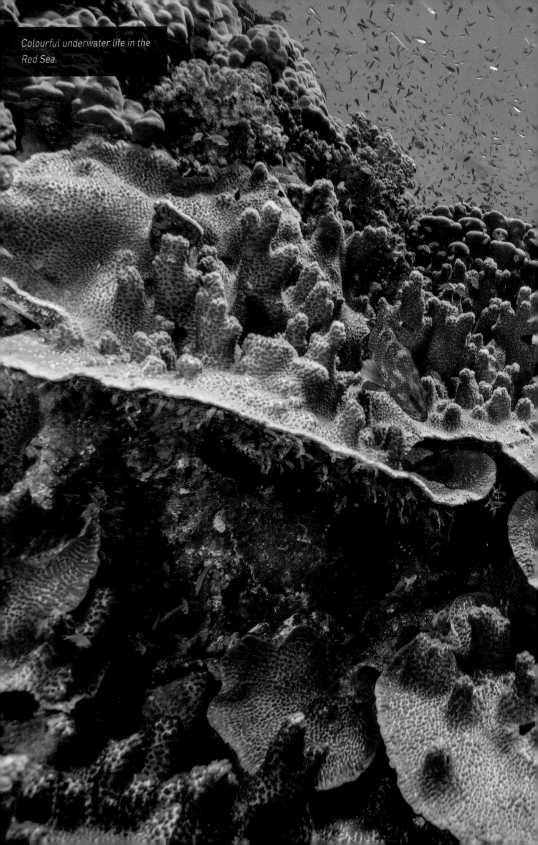

Colourful underwater life in the
Red Sea.

Touring the otherworldly White Desert.

INTRODUCTION

A detailed guide to the country, with the principal sights cross-referenced by number to the maps.

Cairo sunset and silhouetted towers.

Egypt occupies 1 million sq km (385,000 sq miles) of Africa's driest and most barren corner. It adjoins the Sinai Peninsula, which is geologically African, but geographically belongs to Asia. South and west, beyond wide barriers of desert, stretches the great body of the rest of Africa, to which Egypt is umbilically connected by the nourishing lifeline of the Nile. As it crosses the Sudanese border into Egypt, the Nile has already travelled 5,000km (3,000 miles), carving a serpentine path through swamps, rock and sand and filling the massive artificial Lake Nasser, with the Temple of Abu Simbel on one side. This lake, just south of Aswan, is among the largest man-made lakes in the world and a 20th-century achievement that changed the face of Egypt for ever.

An ancient frontier town, where Africa and Arabia mingle, Aswan is the departure point for most Nile cruises to Luxor, although some companies are now operating from Aswan south to the waters of Lake Nasser. At Luxor the vessels pause in the centre of the largest agglomeration of ancient buildings in the world, anchoring between the east bank's great temple complexes of Karnak and Luxor and the west bank's vast funerary cities.

Camel ride in the Sahara.

Further north, the river meanders on through fields dotted with water buffalo. At length it swirls beneath the many bridges of Cairo, the Egyptian capital and a buzzing, heady metropolis. To the west are the Pyramids of Giza; of the Seven Wonders of the Ancient World, only three great pyramids have withstood the ravages of time. From here the Nile moves into the Delta, spreading lushly until, much diminished, it reaches the Mediterranean. Joined to the Nile by canals is Alexandria, Egypt's most important coastal city, founded by Alexander the Great. From here, a flat coastline of fine white sand stretches east and west.

Beyond the lifeline of the river, lonely desert sands stretch for thousands of kilometres, where traditional Bedu camps, dusty mirages, lush oases and vast star-studded night skies provide endless magic. Wherever you travel in Egypt, life exists mainly in the Nile Basin, reliant on the river that has provided for its people since ancient times.

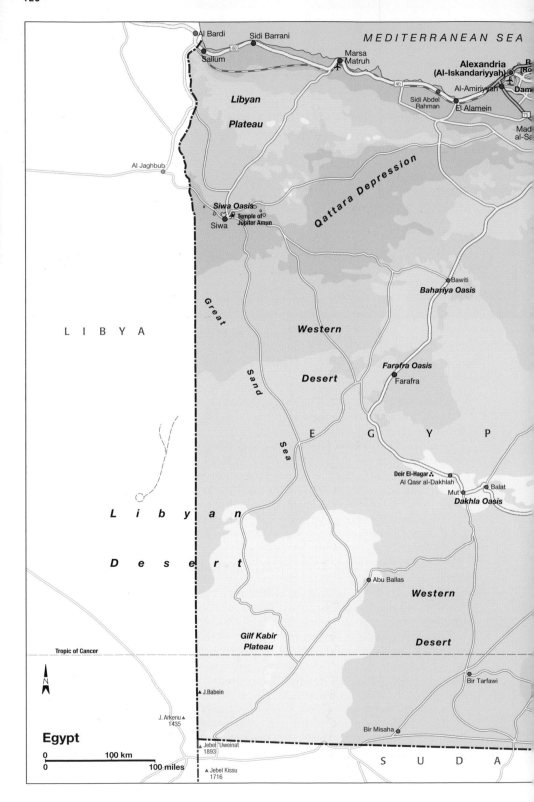

MEDITERRANEAN SEA

Al Bardi
Sidi Barrani
Sallum
Marsa Matruh
Alexandria (Al-Iskandariyyah)
B (Ro
Al-Amiriyyah
Dam
Sidi Abdel Rahman
El Alamein
Mad al-Sa

Libyan
Plateau

Al Jaghbub

Qattara Depression

Siwa Oasis
Temple of Jupiter Amun
Siwa

L I B Y A

Great

Sand

Sea

Bawiti
Bahariya Oasis

Western

Desert

Farafra Oasis
Farafra

E   G   Y   P

Deir El-Hagar
Al Qasr al-Dakhlah
Mut
Balat
Dakhla Oasis

L i b y a n

D e s e r t

Abu Ballas

Western

Gilf Kabir
Plateau

Desert

Tropic of Cancer

Bir Tarfawi

N

▲ J.Babein

J. Arkenu ▲
1435

Egypt

0   100 km
0   100 miles

Bir Misaha

S U D A

▲ Jebel 'Uweinat
1893

▲ Jebel Kissu
1716

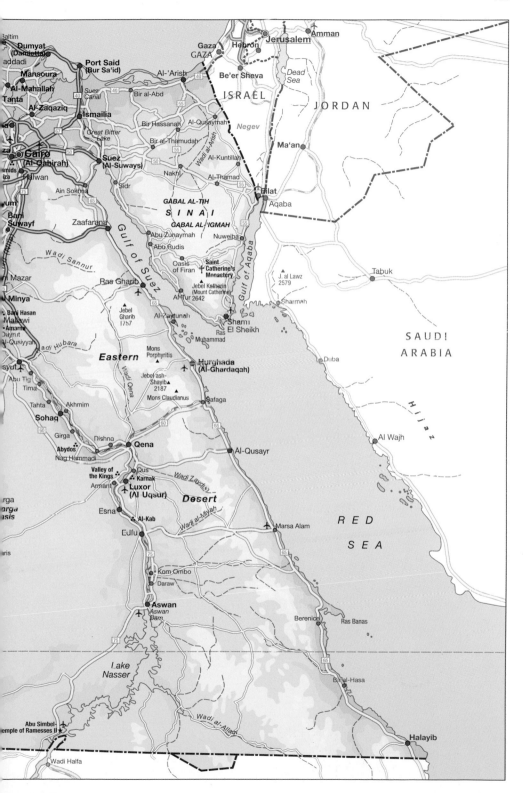

Lanterns for sale in Khan El Khalili bazaar.

CAIRO

A roaring metropolis of nearly 20 million people, Cairo is the cultural capital of the Arab world. Most visitors to Egypt spend at least a few days here, exploring its medieval mosques, sampling its fine museums and shopping in the labyrinthine Khan El Khalili bazaar.

When Ibn Khaldun, the great 14th-century Arab historian and social theorist, visited Cairo, he described it as "the metropolis of the universe, the garden of the world, the ant hill of the human species, the throne of royalty, a city embellished with castles and palaces, its horizon decorated with monasteries and with schools, and lighted by the moons and stars of erudition." What he was looking at was a city that had been devastated by the Black Death three decades earlier and had entered a long twilight of decline.

It remained nevertheless the greatest metropolis on earth, still larger in both population and extent than any city west of China. Enriched by the spice trade and the traffic in luxury goods, its sultans and emirs continued to adorn the city with extravagant architecture.

CITY OF 1,001 NIGHTS

It was during this period, sometime between 1382 and 1517, that *The Arabian Nights* were given their final form in the Cairo of the Circassian Mamluks. "He who hath not seen Cairo," says a character in one of these tales, "hath not seen the world. Her soil is gold; her Nile is a marvel; her women are like the black-eyed virgins of Paradise; her houses are palaces; and her air is

soft, as sweet-smelling as aloe-wood, rejoicing the heart. And how can Cairo be otherwise, when she is Mother of the World?"

The Mother of the World is an old lady now, somewhat long in the tooth: the gold in her soil has ceased to glitter, her Nile has been thoroughly tamed and her palatial houses are being rapidly demolished to make way for concrete high-rises, while her sweet-smelling air has achieved one of the highest pollution indexes in the world.

Main attractions

Egyptian Museum
Rawdah Island
Mosque of Ibn Tulun
Gayer-Anderson Museum
Mosque-Madrasa of
  Sultan Hassan
The Citadel
Museum of Islamic Art
The Al-Azhar Mosque and
  University
Shari Al-Muizz li-Din Allah
  al-Fatimi
Khan El Khalili

Map on page 132

Midan Talaat Harb intersection.

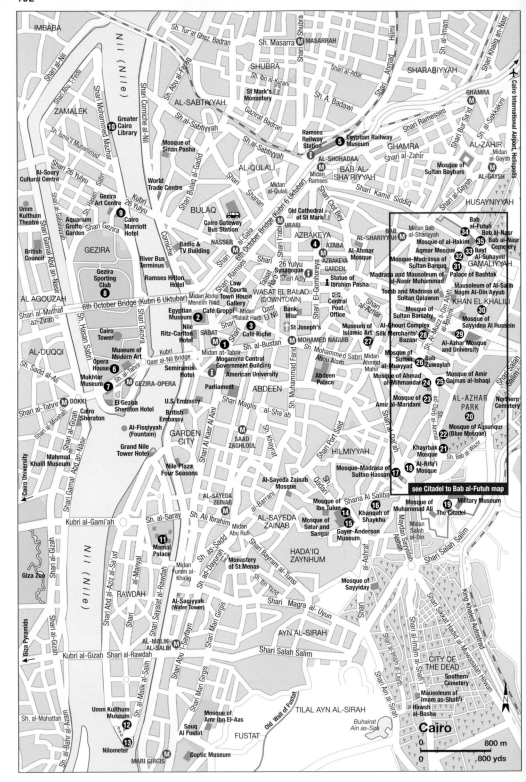

Cairo

0   800 m

0   800 yds

CENTRAL CAIRO

Modern Cairo spins on **Midan at-Tahrir ❶** (Tahrir Square), a huge square on the east bank from which all distances in Egypt are measured. It was originally named Midan al-Isma'iliyyah, after 19th-century ruler Khedive Ismail, and was a focal point for the Egyptian Revolution of 2011 (see page 96).

Despite its strategic position near the Nile, Midan al-Isma'iliyyah did not achieve its present importance until after the July Revolution of 1952. Its name was changed and the mid 19th-century barracks on its western (Nile) side, occupied throughout most of their history by British Guards regiments, were demolished and replaced by the **Corniche**, new administrative buildings and a 331-room, 13-floor hotel – formerly the Nile Hilton Hotel (built in 1958) until it was taken over to become the **Nile Ritz-Carlton Hotel** in 2015.

At the centre of the midan is a large and traffic choked roundabout (it's actually safer to cross the roads by using the Cairo Metro Sadat Station's underground subways), and on the northeast side a **statue of Umar Makram**, celebrated for his resistance against Napoleon's invasion of Egypt. Beyond is the **Umar Makram Mosque**. On the south side, the remains of a palace were knocked down and replaced in 1949 by a huge concrete block known as the **Mogamma**. Roughly translated as "the complex", the Mogamma accommodates various ministries issuing permits licences, visas, expulsion orders and other bureaucratic forms. A Kafkaesque castle of red tape, it is notorious not merely for entrapment, frustration and delay, but also for the number of suicides that have occurred in its 14-storey-high stairwell.

Situated across the street from this monster, on the southeastern corner of the midan, is the only building left from Ismail's era, a small palace dating from 1878 that houses part of the American University, though the main campus has relocated to a new site on the eastern outskirts of the city.

⊘ Fact

The Western name "Cairo" derives from "Al-Qahirah", the name of a single quarter of Misr as understood by medieval Italian merchants, who mistook it for a complete city, like their walled towns.

Umar Makram statue on Midan at-Tahrir.

⊘ CAIRO PASS

If you intend to do a lot of sightseeing while in Cairo, it may well be cost effective to purchase a "Cairo Pass". This covers admission fees for five consecutive days to more than 30 attractions in Cairo and Giza including the Egyptian Museum, Giza and Saqqara pyramids, the Museum of Islamic Art, the Citadel and Coptic Museum. It costs US$100 (US$50 for students with ID); US$ or Euro cash is accepted – no other currencies – and you cannot pay with debit/credit cards. Passes are available from the Egyptian Museum, and the ticket offices at the Giza pyramids and citadel. You will need a passport photo and a photocopy of your main passport page. The similar "Luxor Pass" (see page 215) covers admission charges to a number of archaeological sites on the west bank.

Tip

To help you get to grips with street maps of Cairo, bear in mind the following:

bab = gate
bayt = house
kubri = bridge
madrasa = school/college for Islamic instruction
midan = square
qasr = palace
shari = street

EGYPTIAN MUSEUM

On the north side of Midan at-Tahrir stands the **Egyptian Museum** ❷ (www.antiquities.gov.eg; Sat–Thu 9am–7pm, Fri 9–11am, 1.30–7pm; no photography allowed; a good guidebook to the museum is available from the museum shop and there is a useful audio guide in English, French and Arabic).

The museum was first commissioned in 1835 by the government, who were desperate to stop widespread plundering and looting of the country's many archaeological sites. It moved between several locations until this present building was built in 1902 under Pasha Abbas Hilmi. It now holds more than 100,000 of the world's greatest collection of Egyptian artefacts, from statues to mummies, jewellery and mosaics. Unfortunately, it is now far too small to house this massive collection; some of the exhibits are cramped and dusty, not to mention badly lit and labelled, and many objects within the storerooms have never been on public display. But this is all set to change with the opening of the new Grand Egyptian–Museum (GEM), which is presently under construction at Giza near the pyramids and is due to open in 2020 (see page 170). Some artefacts from the Egyptian Museum, along with objects relocated from other museums, will move to GEM. In fact, the amazing items from the tomb of King Tutankhamun (including many that have never been on display before) have already moved to there in preparation for the opening; as such, at the time of writing they are not on public display.

In the meantime, there's still much to see at the Egyptian Museum, including wonderful objects from the lesser-known Royal Tombs, discovered un-plundered at Tanis in the northern Delta in 1939. The golden objects are simply stunning, dating to the 21st and 22nd dynasties (around 1000 BC) when Tanis was the capital of kings who originated in Libya to the west. Coinciding with the outbreak of World War II, this discovery went almost unnoticed, and even today few people know about these gorgeous objects. Had they been

Giant sphinx at the entrance to the Egyptian Museum.

discovered at any other time, these finds would likely have been as famous as Tutankhamun's relics. Tanis has since gained notoriety as the fictional setting of the original Indiana Jones film, where the Ark of the Covenant was "rediscovered".

On the ground floor, large objects are arranged chronologically, running clockwise, so that a left turn from the foyer leads to the famous **Menkaure Triads** from Giza, showing King Menkaure (4th Dynasty) flanked by the goddess Hathor and another female figure representing Upper Egypt, while a right turn leads to Hellenistic painting and statuary.

No-one should miss anything if time is not a consideration, but visitors in a hurry should turn left through the entrance to see the treasures of the **Old Kingdom**. Look out for the **Narmer Palette** in the first room, recording the first unification of Upper and Lower Egypt by the legendary (and possibly mythical) King Narmer (also known as Menes), and generally considered to mark the beginning of Egyptian history and art (c.3,000 BC). Among other Old Kingdom highlights is a large black statue of Chephren, the builder of the second pyramid at Giza, seated on a lion throne. In Room 42, look out for the unusual wooden statue of Ka-Aper, known as **Shaykh al-Balad**, with rock crystal and alabaster eyes, as well as a painted limestone **seated scribe**, with vivid inlaid eyes. In the next room is the magnificent double sculpture of **Prince Rahotep and his wife Nofret**, a symbol of marital bliss, as well as the venerated dwarf **Seneb** with his family.

Reflecting a total revolution in Egyptian art under Akhenaten (see pages 44 and 196) is the **Amarnah art** in Room 3. More naturalistic than art previous to the Amarnah period, the pharaoh is depicted with lips, emaciated cheeks and a large belly. Akhenaten is usually seen with his family adoring the sun-god Aten.

Room 4 has a marvellous display of ancient **Egyptian jewellery**, while a few of the famous **Fayyum portraits**, faces painted on wooden panels placed over the mummy, are on display in Room 14.

Rooms 53 and 54 on the upper floor contain a fascinating collection of **mummified animals and birds**, illustrating the animal cults of ancient Egypt, while in Room 43 there are objects from the tomb of **Yuya and Thuya**, including a magnificent gilded mask inlaid with gems.

The **Mummies Room** houses the mummies of many notable pharaohs, found in a cache in Deir al-Bahri, Luxor, in 1875. Above all, they show the pharaohs' humanity, including their individual characteristics and defects. Note that the mummies may also move to the Grand Egyptian Museum in the future.

QASR EL NIL STREET

Running northeast from in front of the museum is **Shari Qasr El Nil**, once the city's main shopping street and still displaying a few vestiges of

> **Tip**
>
> Taxis are the best way of getting around Cairo. Though vehicles are often very battered and traffic jams can be horrendous, fares are extremely cheap. Although most taxi drivers speak only Arabic, you will usually manage to convey where you want to go successfully. Sharing a taxi is not unusual, particularly during rush hours.

Inside the Egyptian Museum.

the architecture and vintage glamour from when this part of downtown Cairo was planned in the late 19th and early 20th centuries. After adequate civic infrastructure was completed in 1874, Ismail decided that buildings here had to be large, grand and constructed using expensive materials – therefore excluding small shops and houses. Throughout its early years, the street attracted many of the Egyptian elites, socialites, celebrities and businesspeople.

Today the headquarters of the main banks, travel agencies, airline offices and restaurants now line most of Shari Qasr El Nil, but notable historic buildings that still exist include the **Automobile and Touring Club of Egypt** at No. 10, founded in 1924 and a haunt of King Farouk, who loved playing poker here for outrageous stakes. About 100 metres/yds further on, at Midan Talaat Harb, is the famous Art Deco **Café Groppi**. This once-luxurious establishment was founded in 1924 by an Alexandrian-Swiss family catering to Cairo's elite and British army officers. In the years before World War II, it served afternoon teas, aperitifs, confectionery, patisserie and delicatessen items. King Farouk was said to be very impressed with the chocolate made at the café and sent chocolates to King George and his two daughters, Elizabeth and Margaret. The establishment fell into decline from the 1980s when it became dilapidated and a bit seedy, but closed in 2016 for extensive renovations, supported by the National Committee for the Development and Protection of Cairo's Heritage. At the time of writing, it had not yet reopened, but check the website (www.groppi-eg.com) for developments.

On the southern side of Midan Talaat Harb, on the corner of Shari Talaat Harb, is **Café Riche** ❸ (daily noon–midnight), which opened in 1908 and was at various times a meeting place for intellectuals and revolutionaries. Leaders of the 1919 revolution against the British had secret meetings in the basement and used the café's printing machine to create political pamphlets. Just over 30 years later, Nasser frequented the café while planning his 1952 overthrow of King Farouk, while during the Egyptian Revolution of 2011 it again served as a refuge to many protesters in the city. Today the narrow restaurant is good for a coffee and a look at the historic photographs on the walls.

AZBAKEYA

East of Shari Qasr El Nil and Midan Talaat Harb, Shari Mohammed Sabri Abou Alam indicates the overlapping of Ismail's new quarter with old Misr as it was before the French marched in, and leads to **Azbakeya** ❹, which was founded as a pleasure zone in the 15th century but had evolved into an upper-class residential area by the time Napoleon established his headquarters here in 1798.

On Shari El-Gomhoreya, the **Abdeen Palace** was built between 1863 and

Shari Qasr El Nil.

1874 by Ismail, serving as the royal residence until the monarchy was abolished in 1952. Today it's one of the presidency's residences open to visitors, and part of the ground floor has been turned into a museum (entrance on the east side; Sat–Thu 10am–3pm), displaying a vast collection of weaponry, medals, historical documents, silverware and state gifts to the former royal family, among other items.

The focus of Azbakeya was once a picturesque seasonal lake that filled during the Nile flood, and luxurious dwellings were built along its southern and eastern shores. Local resistance to the French reduced most of these to ruins, but under Muhammad Ali, Azbakeya was soon rebuilt and dotted with new administrative offices. After 1837, when the lake was drained and its site converted into a park, several hotels began to move their premises into Azbakeya from the old European quarter along Shari al-Muski to the east. One of them, the New British Hotel (1841), known under the name of its first owner – Shepheard's

– was renowned for its opulence, with stained-glass windows, gardens and terraces, and great granite pillars resembling those of the ancient Egyptian temples. Sadly it was destroyed by fire in 1952, but a new one was built on the Corniche in 1957, which still operates today.

In 1868 Ismail reduced the park to the octagonal **Azbakeya Garden** (now closed to the public) and the remainder of the old lake site was opened for development. New squares were created and public buildings were erected, the most striking of which was a theatre for opera. Built entirely of wood and completed within five months during 1869, the old Cairo Opera House saw the premier of *Aida* in 1871 and later became renowned for its collections of manuscripts, scores, costumes and sets, all of which were consumed by fire when the building burnt down in 1971. The site is now occupied by a high-rise car-park, but the heroic equestrian statue of Ibrahim Pasha, commissioned by Ismail, still stands in what would have been the square

Neat landscaping at Abdeen Palace.

in front of the old Opera House. To the east of this are remains of the department stores that were the great retail centres of their time. The Sednaoui Building (1913) is still in business, but the earlier Tiring Building (1910), with its rooftop giant globe, is now mainly residential.

Two of Ismail's new streets, both still fashionable – Shari Abd El-Khalik Tharwat and Shari Adly, where the largest of Cairo's synagogues stands – lead westward from Ibrahim's statue, while Shari El-Gomhoreya continues north along the western edge of the Azbakeya Garden to Midan Ramses and the main railway station, where you'll come to the **Egyptian Railway Museum ❺** (Sat–Thu 9am–2pm). On display are models, historic drawings and photographs, as well as locomotives and carriages used by the royal family dating back to the first railway in 1853 between Cairo and Alexandria.

GEZIRA AND ZAMALEK

The newer districts of Cairo are not without appeal. On **Gezira Island**, joined to the mainland by three bridges, two of them near Midan at-Tahrir, you'll find **Gezira** in the south and **Zamalek** in the north. These adjoining suburbs are both popular with wealthy Cairenes and European residents and have several cultural attractions.

Crossing the Qasr al-Nil Bridge from Midan at-Tahrir, the first of these is the Japanese-built **Opera House ❻** (Dar el-Opera el-Masreyya), which has been the main performing-arts venue in Cairo since it opened in 1988 and offers some of the finest productions of ballet, opera and symphonies in Egypt. The cultural complex consists of seven theatres, a music library and the **Museum of Egyptian Modern Art** (Sat–Sun, Tues–Thu 10am–2pm, 5–8pm), which houses contemporary paintings and sculptures by 20th and 21st-century Egyptian artists.

Across the road from the Opera House, in the park at the southern end of the island, is the **Mahmoud Mukhtar Museum ❼** (Tues–Sun 10am–2pm, 3–5pm; no photography), housing bronze, stone, basalt, marble,

Long views from the Cairo Tower.

granite and plaster works by Mahmoud Mukhtar (1891–1934), Egypt's greatest modern sculptor and one of a handful of 20th-century Egyptian artists to achieve international recognition. Just up the road, the Saad Zaghloul statue is one of his, as is his giant sphinx and goddess entitled *Egypt's Awakening* on Midan Al Gamaa at the entrance of the university and zoo.

North of here is the 187-metre (614ft) high **Cairo Tower** (daily 8am–midnight), erected in 1961 and providing remarkable views of the city. A windy day, when some of the pollution is blown away, offers the best views, but queues can be long to access the tiny lift. The tower's open lattice design was intended to mimic the lotus plant, an iconic symbol of Ancient Egypt. There's a café one floor down – and a revolving restaurant two floors down – from the outdoor observation deck at the top.

Further north are the grounds of the **Gezira Sporting Club 8**, which was founded in 1882, originally called Khedivial Sporting Club. Today it offers golf, tennis, squash, croquet, horse riding, cricket, swimming and other sports.

Zamalek covers all of the island north of the sporting club. The quiet, leafy streets and 19th-century apartment blocks and villas make this one of the most attractive parts of the city and a favoured residential area for many fashionable Cairenes and expatriates. The district has many fine restaurants, bars and cafés, and nearly a quarter of the 140-odd foreign embassies in the city are in Zamalek (see page 138).

Opposite the northern entrance to the club is a charming house built in the 1920s for *Nabil* (Lord) Amru Ibrahim, a great-great-grandson of Ibrahim Pasha, as a *salamlik* (reception suite) in the khedival style, with rooms dedicated to Fatimid, Turkish and Persian periods. It is now home to the **Gezira Art Centre** (1 Shari El Masrafyt; Sat–Thu 9am–7pm; no photography), which has several galleries rotating contemporary exhibitions. Standing just across the street immediately to the east is the **Cairo**

The Cairo Tower.

Fountain in the extensive gardens of the Marriott Hotel.

Manial Bridge, leading to Rawdah Island.

Marriott Hotel , one of the tallest buildings in the city with just over 1,000 rooms in two 20-floor towers – Gezira and Zamalek. It opened in 1983, but the central block incorporates Khedive Ismail's palace, which was built to host Napoleon's wife Empress Eugénie during the celebration of the opening of the Suez Canal in 1869. The original vast grounds of the palace survive today in the enclosed garden attached to the Marriott – the Garden Promenade Café is a popular meeting place in Zamalek.

FOREIGN EMBASSIES

Along the island's eastern bank, north of Shari 26 Yulyu bridge, are splendid Art Deco mansions built in the 1930s; they are mostly occupied by foreign embassies, but there is one that can be visited. On Shari Mohammed Mazhar, the **Greater Cairo Library** ⑩ (Thu–Sat 10am–3pm; free; no photography) is housed in the impressive former palace of Princess Samiha Kamel, a daughter of Sultan Hussein Kamel (ruled Egypt 1914–17). It has a distinguished architectural style that combines the Mamluk, Ottoman and European motifs. Access for casual visitors is around the back of the building, and to the right, where a passport or ID must be left at the gatehouse. It is very much a working environment, with rooms for study, but refurbishments have been handled well and it offers fine views across the river.

GARDEN CITY AND RAWDAH ISLAND

Just south of Midan at-Tahrir is the well-planned and leafy district of **Garden City**, laid out on the site of an old estate of Ibrahim Pasha. It is the location of several more embassies, including the British and American ones, as well as some large hotels along the Corniche, including the prestigious Nile Plaza Four Seasons Hotel. While there are few sights or much to do here, it's relatively quiet and you can arrange felucca trips on the Nile from the Four Seasons, or simply take an evening stroll along the Corniche – popular with young Egyptian couples as an inexpensive date spot. Vendors rent out plastic chairs and sell glasses of tea.

To the southwest and across a narrow channel of the Nile, is **Rawdah (or Roda) Island**, which is dominated by the huge Grand Nile Tower Hotel (formerly the Grand Hyatt Cairo) on the northern tip. There are still some gems to be found on the island. Once belonging to the Muhammad Ali family is **Manial Palace** ⑪ (daily 9am–4pm) built between 1901 and 1929. It was left to the Egyptian nation in 1955 by Prince Muhammad Ali, the younger brother of Khedive Abbas Hilmi Pasha and a first cousin of King Farouk. It includes a museum exhibiting Farouk's game-shooting trophies; the prince's own beautiful residence with its furnishings; and a 14-room museum housing family memorabilia. The gardens

have been returned to their former splendour.

On the southern tip of Rawdah Island, but in fact much more easily accessed via the footbridge from the Corniche near Old Cairo (see page 140), is the smaller Monastirli Palace. This contains the **Umm Kulthum Museum** ⑫ (daily 9am–4pm), dedicated to the life and work of Egypt's best-loved singer, songwriter and actress (see page 141). On show are her iconic sunglasses, good-luck handkerchiefs, photos and video clips of her performances, as well as her correspondence with previous leaders and politicians.

In the same compound, at the southern tip of Rawdah Island, is the **Nilometer** ⑬ (daily 9am–4pm), clearly visible from across the river (it is distinguished by a conical cap). This is a reconstruction made in 1893 of a 17th-century Ottoman dome destroyed by the French in 1800; its interior is covered with fine Turkish tiles. The substructure, however, which is the Nilometer itself, dates from 861, which makes it the oldest intact Islamic monument in Cairo and the only survivor from the Abbasid period. Comprising a calibrated stone column standing upright in a stone-lined pit with a staircase, it is particularly notable for the use of pointed arches at the highest intake level – 300 years before the appearances of such arches in Europe. Before the dams at Aswan were constructed, the Nile rose every summer and the strength of the inundation was shown by the level of water covering the notches cut into the central vertical column. The greater the depth of water, the more tax the farmers had to pay.

BABYLON – "OLD CAIRO"

The remains of Roman and Christian Babylon are found in the area known as **Misr al-Qadimah**, which confusingly translates into "Old Cairo" (though it

should not be mistaken for representing more than a foretaste of Cairo's medieval glory). Here too are interesting remains from Egypt's Christian era, as well as one monument from the years immediately following the Arab conquest.

Cairo developed at a point halfway between Memphis and Heliopolis where a road crossed the river, using the present Rawdah Island as a stepping stone. Since there were no other roads across the Delta, this one not only connected the Old Kingdom's administrative and religious capitals, but also was the main passage into Egypt from the east, giving access to the rest of the country. During the Late Dynasty period a small fortress was built here and, after a canal linking the Nile with the Red Sea was completed by the Persian occupiers under Darius I (521–486 BC), the site became even more important.

The Greeks called it **Babylon**, a name that should not be confused with Mesopotamian Babylon, which probably derives from an Egyptian name

The Nilometer.

such as *Pi-Hapi-n-On* or *Per-Hapi-n-On*, meaning "The Nile House of On". Under the emperor Trajan (AD 98–117), after more than a century of Roman occupation, during which Heliopolis had long been moribund, the old canal was reopened and a new fortress was built, one of three to control the whole of Egypt.

Egyptians themselves knew their country by many names, of which the most common during the Roman period was probably Kemet, "The Black Land". Throughout the rest of the Semitic-speaking Middle East, Egypt was called **Misr**, the name it still bears in Arabic today. When the Arabs conquered Misr in AD 641 and founded a new capital next to the walls of Babylon, this capital acquired the name of the country as a whole. This became more and more appropriate as new quarters with new names were added and it expanded to become the metropolis not only of Egypt, but also of the Arab world, a huge city containing many distinct areas with their own names.

Appreciative tourists outside el Mu'allaqah.

VISITING OLD CAIRO

The remains of the Roman fortress of Babylon, which was largely intact until the British occupation, can be visited in conjunction with the churches and museum of the Coptic quarter. They can be easily reached by metro; the metro stop is **Mari Girgis** (on Line 1 towards Helwan) and stands opposite the modern Greek Orthodox church of the same name. A visit to the churches and the fortress is pleasant as the area is peaceful and picturesque. The grounds of the **Coptic Museum** Ⓐ (daily 8am–4pm) begin south of the tower and are entirely within the fortress walls. Founded by private benefactors on land belonging to the Coptic Church, the museum was taken over by the government in 1931. Though there are many ancient Christian sites in Egypt, there are none in which the churches themselves have not been abandoned, destroyed or rebuilt inside and out. It is therefore only the Coptic Museum that gives an idea of what the interior of a 5th-, 6th- or 7th-century church

Old Cairo

0   50 m
0   50 yds

N

Shari Mari Girgis

Mosque of Amr Ibn al-As, Souq Al Fustat

El-Imam Malik

Fustat

Cemetery

Convent of St George

Church of the Holy Virgin (Qasriyyat al-Rihan)

Church of St George

Monastery of St George

Church of St George (Greek Orthodox)

Ticket Office for Museum

Church of St Sergius

Remains of Roman Tower

Coptic Museum (New Wing)

Church of St Barbara

Roman Walls

Cemetery

MARI GIRGIS Ⓜ

Coptic Museum (Old Wing)

Ⓐ

Ⓒ Ben Ezra Synagogue

Ⓑ

St Virgin Mary's Church (el Mu'allaqah)

Roman Walls

Greek Orthodox Cemetery

Rabbinical Cemetery

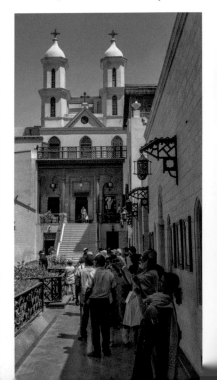

was like. Objects that were excavated in Upper Egypt and in the monastery of St Jeremiah at Saqqara are of particular interest.

The museum's most prized relics are the Coptic textiles and the "Nag Hammadi Codices" (see page 59), a collection of nearly 1,200 papyrus pages bound together as books – the earliest so far known with leather covers – sometime soon after the middle of the 4th century. Written in Coptic, the codices draw syncretically upon Jewish, Christian, Hermetic, Zoroastrian and Platonic sources and have thrown extraordinary light on the background of the New Testament, particularly the Epistles, by revealing that Gnosticism, hitherto supposed to be only a Christian heresy, was in fact a separate religion.

THE CHURCHES

Babylon is mentioned in St Peter's first epistle, most scholars now concede, in connection with St Mark's Egyptian mission, and local legend claims it as one of the many places in Egypt where the Holy Family rested. The monks and martyrs who elsewhere created the heroic age of the Coptic Church seem to have passed it by, and there are no specific documentary references to any church structure earlier than the Arab conquest. Babylon could not have had much importance as a Christian centre until four centuries later, when it had long since been absorbed into Misr. The Patriarchate of St Mark, robbed of the saint's relics by Venetians in 828, was transferred there from a declining Alexandria sometime after 1048.

Churches and monastic settlements were scattered not only at Babylon but also all over the future site of Misr. Many were later destroyed, but some were undoubtedly incorporated into later structures. Built above the southern gate of the Roman fortress, with its nave suspended over a passageway and reached by 29 steps, for example, is the **St Virgin Mary's Church Ⓡ** (daily 9am–5pm), referred to locally as **el Mu'allaqah** (meaning "The Suspended" – or the "Hanging

Ruins of Babylon, Misr al-Qadimah.

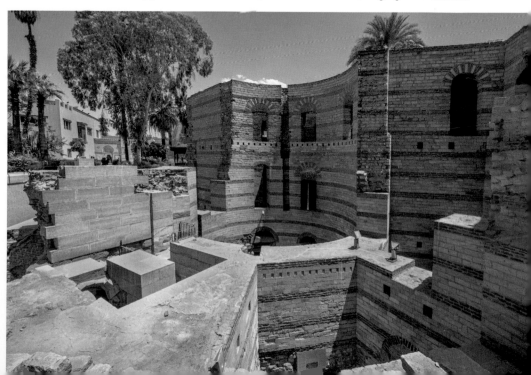

Church" in English). Once through the carved wooden doors in the beautiful twin-towered facade, the church is divided into three main aisles, with three sanctuaries dedicated to saints Virgin Mary, George and John the Baptist. Notable features include the timber ceiling, intended to resemble the interior of Noah's Ark, and the marble pulpit supported by 13 columns meant to represent Jesus and his 12 disciples. It has been a seat of the patriarchate for centuries, and one portion is claimed to date back to the 4th century. Within the walls of the fortress are several other churches with an almost equal claim to antiquity – the **churches of St Sergius and St Bacchus, St Barbara, St Cyril and St John**; a second Church of the Virgin, known as **Qasriyyat al-Rihan** ("Pot of Basil"); and a **convent of St George**. Outside the fortress walls, but still within Old Cairo, are no fewer than a dozen more churches that were well documented in medieval times.

The oldest, finest and most portable objects have all been removed either to the Coptic Museum (see page 142) or to other collections around the world, but one of the sanctuaries of the Hanging Church has the remains of fine frescoes attributed to the 7th or 8th century, and the buildings of the convent of St George include an intact reception hall belonging to a Fatimid-period house, with magnificent wooden doors 7 metres (22ft) high.

These churches are all Coptic Orthodox, but during Lent they become pilgrimage sites for Catholics as well. In the 17th and 18th centuries the Franciscan friars had the right to celebrate mass in the sanctuary of the Holy Family at the church of St Sergius and St Bacchus, which marks a traditional resting place of the Holy Family and is thus venerated by both Catholic and Orthodox believers.

Also within the walls of Old Cairo is the **Ben Ezra Synagogue** Ⓒ (daily 8am–4pm), which is a reminder of Egypt's role not only in fostering the Sephardic Rabbinical tradition but also in providing a home for Karaite Jews (before the 10th century) and

Service at St Barbara's.

Ashkenazi Jews (from the 16th century onwards). Originally a church dedicated to St Michael the Archangel, the building was closed under the Fatimid caliph Al-Hakim (996–1021), then sold to the Sephardic community. Among other functions it served as a genizah, a repository for documents made sacrosanct by being sworn under oath, which could not be casually discarded without sacrilege. It was discovered a few years ago during the restoration of the synagogue. Since these documents cover several centuries and include such mundane items as contracts, bills of sale and letters of credit, they constitute an extensive record of medieval Mediterranean trade.

After exploring the churches, the modern domed building of **Souq Al Fustat** (daily 10am–7pm) is well worth a visit, just a two-minute walk north of the Mar Girgis metro station. It is an artisanal craft market with vendors selling high-end handicrafts like Bedouin embroidery, mosaics, jewellery and leather products, and opened in 2002 with a grant from Unesco when

the Coptic area went under a restoration. A few metres beyond it on the north side is the **Mosque of Amr Ibn al-As ●** (daily 9am–4pm, closed Fri during prayers noon–1pm). Built in AD 642 with palm trunks and fronds, it was the first mosque erected in Egypt and all of Africa, although it has been enlarged several times since then.

EASTERN (ISLAMIC CAIRO)

In 872 the Abbasid caliph's name was removed from the Nilometer by order of the city's 38-year-old Turkish governor (AD 868–84), Ahmad Ibn Tulun, who would not only declare himself independent, but also within 10 years make Misr the centre of an empire stretching from southern Turkey to Sudan. Cramped by the growth of Fustat, the Abbasid caliphs had already built themselves a new military quarter, **al Askar**, to the north; but Ibn Tulun felt the need for something grander. The result was **Al-Qata'i** ("The Quarters"), a new town large enough to include a walled hippodrome, a hospital, a menagerie, mews, gardens, markets,

Ben Ezra Synagogue.

Afternoon sun at the Mosque of Ibn Tulun.

◉ FUSTAT

Immediately to the east of Old Cairo, in an enormous untidy area now covered with newer ramshackle buildings, is the site of **Fustat**, the first Muslim capital at Misr, founded by Amr ibn al-As in the course of the Arab conquest. Previous excavations here uncovered the remains of elaborate water storage and drainage systems, and the foundations of private houses and apartment blocks. There is little to see today to suggest the historical importance of Fustat, but many of the thousands of objects found here made of wood, paper, ivory, glass, metal or ceramics, ranging in date from the 8th to 14th centuries, and in provenance from Spain to China, can be seen in the Museum of Islamic Art (see page 153).

baths, residential quarters (classified by nationality), reception and *harim* ("harem") palaces for Ibn Tulun himself, and a large governmental complex, which was attached to a great congressional mosque.

When the Abbasids repossessed Misr for the caliphate in 905, the **Mosque of Ibn Tulun** ⓮ (Shari Al Saliba; daily 8am–4pm), rightly considered one of the architectural glories of the Muslim world, was the only building left standing in Al-Qata'i. It is the oldest mosque in the city surviving in its original form, and is the largest in Cairo in terms of land area. It has undergone several restorations, the first in 1297 and the latest within the decade.

Built in the imperial style of the Abbasid court at Samarra in Iraq, where Ubn Tulun had lived as a young man, the mosque is built of red brick and stucco – original materials, rather than granite, limestone and marble borrowed from other sites, as is often the case in later mosques. The mosque is impressive both for its simplicity and its grand scale – its courtyard alone covers 2.5 hectares (6.5 acres) and the sycamore-wood frieze of Qur'anic verses around the court is more than 2km (1.25 miles) long.

The unusual spiral minaret was probably inspired by the minaret in Samarra, Iraq, although legend has it that a distracted Ibn Tulun rolled up a piece of paper and told the architect to use that as the design.

GAYER-ANDERSON MUSEUM

Adjoining the mosque's northeast corner is the **Gayer-Anderson Museum** ⓯ (Midan Ahmad ibn Zulein; daily 9am–4pm, closed for Friday prayers). Two restored houses, Beit el-Kiridiliya (1632) and Beit Amna Bent Salim (1540), have been joined together to create a delightful larger dwelling with a *salamlik* (reception suite) and *haramlik* (harem suite). Both are filled with objets d'art, antique furniture, carpets, silks and embroidered Arabian costumes from all over the Middle East, the collection of Gayer-Anderson, a British major and army doctor, who restored the houses and lived here in the 1930s and 40s. The entrance to the museum leads from the Mosque of Ibn Tulun.

About 500 metres/yds northwest is the **Al-Sayeda Zainab Mosque** (daily 8am–4pm), another revered site of pilgrimage, particularly for women. Amid a forest of columns, the tomb of the grand-daughter of the Prophet Muhammad is inside a shrine behind a solid-silver grille, dazzlingly illuminated.

Outside the Gayer–Anderson Museum, Shari Tulun leads eastward (left). After less than 100 metres/yds it reaches **Shari Al Saliba**, the start of the **Qasabah** (see page 146), medieval Cairo's main street. The Qasabah linked all the city's parts on a north–south axis; at the height of Cairo's medieval prosperity this street was more than 13km (8 miles) long.

⊘ SABIL-KUTTUBS – FOUNTAIN SCHOOLS

To the early Arabs who brought Islam to Cairo from the harsh deserts of Arabia, water was one of the most precious commodities, to be harnessed and dispensed to all. The Prophet Muhammad is quoted as saying that the two greatest mercies were "water for the thirsty and knowledge for the ignorant", so that a continuous water supply and flow of knowledge were seen as essential for the wellbeing of these expanding Islamic communities. Within the crowded alleyways of Ottoman Cairo, small decorated buildings called *sabil-kuttubs* (literally meaning fountains of books) were provided by wealthy benefactors (often the Mamluk sultan himself) to quench the public's thirst for water and knowledge.

The *sabil* on the ground floor supplied free water to anybody who required it, while upstairs in the *kuttub* was a Koranic school and library for the education of children. Built from stone or marble and decorated with elaborately carved wood or finely wrought metal, each example of these delightful buildings is different from the next.

With the provision of a modern water supply system throughout the old city, most of these buildings have fallen into disrepair, but a number have been lovingly restored and there are now many fine examples scattered around the city.

SHARI AL SALIBA

There is so much of the rest of medieval Cairo still to see that it is best to take the Qasabah piecemeal. The first major part is rich in fine architecture. On the northeast side of Shari Al Saliba is a delightful Ottoman-style *sabil-kuttub* (fountain school; see box, opposite), built in 1867 by the mother of Abbas I, the successor of Muhammad Ali, and beautifully restored in 1984 by the Ministry of Antiquities.

Unmistakeable just beyond the northeast and southeast corners of the intersection are the massive facades of two madrasas (theological schools) built by the Amir Shaykhu, commander of the Mamluk armies under Sultan Hasan ibn Al-Nasir Muhammad ibn Qalawun (1334–61), who ordered his murder in 1357.

Shaykhu's **madrasa** (built in 1349, on the left) and his **khanqah** ⑯ (built in 1355, on the right) represent two classic Cairene architectural types, both introduced two centuries earlier by Saladin. Persian in inspiration, the madrasa provided a courtyard mosque made cruciform by four vaulted halls *(iwans)*, where instruction could take place in the four systems of legal thought regarded as orthodox by Sunni Muslims (Hanafi, Malaki, Shafi'i and Hanbali).

A *khanqah* is a Muslim "monastery", a mosque with dwelling areas that serve as a hostel for Sufis (Muslim mystics). Shaykhu's restored *khanqah* accommodated some 700 Sufis in 150 cells of varying comfort, surrounding a mosque with a courtyard. These two buildings frame Shari Al Saliba as one looks in the direction of the Citadel, creating a gorgeous Oriental-style vista.

Further up Shari Al Saliba, towards the Citadel, is the first free-standing *sabil-kuttub* in Cairo (built by Qaytbay in 1479), beyond which the street emerges into the **Midan Salah ad-Din**. This enormous square was the site of

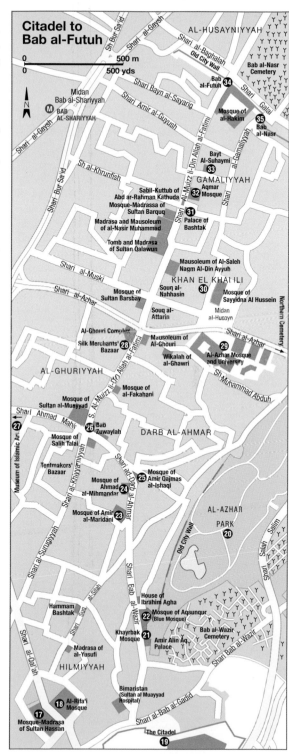

Citadel to Bab al-Futuh

0 ———— 500 m
0 ———— 500 yds

AL-HUSAYNIYYAH
Old City Wall
Bab al-Futuh ㉞
Bab al-Nasr Cemetery
Mosque of al-Hakim ㉟
Bab al-Nasr
Midan Bab al-Shariyyah
BAB AL-SHARIYYAH
Shari al-Gaysh
Sh Bur Sa'id
Shari al-Gaysh
Shari al-Baghalah
Shari Amir al-Guyush
Shari Bayn al-Sayarig
Shari Galal
Bayt Al-Suhaymi ㉝
Sh al-Khrunfish
Shari Bur Sa'id
GAMALIYYAH
Aqmar Mosque ㉜
Sabil-Kuttub of Abd ar-Rahman Kathuda
Mosque-Madrassa of Sultan Barquq ㉛
Palace of Bashtak
Madrasa and Mausoleum of al-Nasir Muhammad
Tomb and Madrasa of Sultan Qalawun
Mausoleum of Al-Saleh Naqm Al-Din Ayyub
KHAN EL KHALILI
Souq al-Nahhasin ㉚
Mosque of Sayyidna Al Hussein
Shari al-Muski
Shari al-Azhar
Mosque of Sultan Barsbay
Souq al-Attarin
Midan al-Husayn
Northern Cemetery
Al-Ghouri Complex
Silk Merchants' Bazaar ㉘
Mausoleum of Al-Ghouri
Wikalah of al-Ghawri
Al-Azhar Mosque and University ㉙
Shari al-Azhar
AL-GHURIYYAH
Mosque of al-Fakahani
Sh. Muhammad Abduh
Mosque of Sultan al-Muayyad
Shari Ahmad Mahir ㉗
Bab Zuwaylah ㉖
Mosque of Salih Talai
DARB AL-AHMAR
Museum of Islamic Art
Tentmakers' Bazaar
Mosque of Ahmad al-Mihmandar ㉔
Mosque of Amir Qajmas al-Ishaqi ㉕
Shari ad-Darb al-Ahmar
Mosque of Amir al-Maridani ㉓
AL-AZHAR PARK ⑳
Old City Wall
Salah Salim
Shari al-Suruqiyyah
Shari Bab al-Wazir
Hammam Bashtak
Shari Suq al-Silan
House of Ibrahim Agha
Mosque of Aqsunqur (Blue Mosque) ㉒
Khayrbak Mosque ㉑
Amir Alin Aq Palace
Bab al-Wazir Cemetery
AL-AZHAR
Madrasa of al-Yusufi
HILMIYYAH
Bimaristan (Sultan al Muayyad Hospital)
Al-Rifa'i Mosque ⑱
⑰ Mosque-Madrasa of Sultan Hassan
Shari al-Bab al-Gadid
The Citadel ⑲
Shari al-Qal'ah

Stunning view across Cairo, with the Mosque-Madrasa of Sultan Hassan and Al-Rifa'i Mosque in the foreground.

first Ibn Tulun's hippodrome and then the Mamluks' polo-ground, where their pageants, races, matches, musters and military displays took place under the gaze – and the guns – of the Citadel.

MOSQUE-MADRASA OF SULTAN HASSAN AND THE AL-RIFA'I MOSQUE

At the northwestern corner of this square loom two colossal religious buildings: the **Mosque-Madrasa of Sultan Hassan** ⑰ (Midan Salah ad-Din; daily 8am–4.30pm), built between 1356 and 1363; and the **Al-Rifa'i Mosque** ⑱ (same hours and ticket as the Mosque-Madrasa of Sultan Hassan), which was built to complement it architecturally between 1869 and 1912. Visitors sometimes fail to understand that these two buildings were constructed more than five centuries apart, since the modern mosque shows perfect respect for its older neighbour across the street in fabric, scale and style.

Inside the Al-Rifa'i Mosque, Mamluk motifs have been reproduced with luxurious fidelity, demonstrating recognition of the Mamluk style as Cairo's trademark, an almost "official" style and thus particularly suitable in a mosque identified with the ruling dynasty. Originally endowed by the mother of Khedive Ismail, it houses her tomb as well as those of the khedive himself and four of his sons, including Husayn Kamil (1853–1917) and King Fuad (1868–1936). The former royal family is buried here, including King Farouk.

A great parade of Sufi orders, with chanting, banners and drums, takes place annually in Cairo on the eve of the Prophet's birthday. It traditionally begins at the Al-Rifa'i Mosque, marches down Shari Muhammad Ali, up Shari Bur Sa'id, then down Shari Al-Azhar – wide new European-style streets constructed by the dynasty between 1873 and 1930 – to end at the popular Mosque of Sayyidna Al Hussein (closed to non-Muslims), which was built by Khedive Ismail.

The Mosque-Madrasa of Sultan Hassan Madrasa, situated just across the street from the Al-Rifa'i Mosque,

provided a daunting model, since it is probably the greatest of the Bahri architectural monuments, and second only to the Mosque of Ibn Tulun in grandeur of conception among all the historic buildings in Cairo. The walls are 36 metres (117ft) high and so solidly built that the mosque was twice used as a fortress – first in 1381 during a Mamluk revolt and then again in 1517 during the Ottoman invasion.

Originally four minarets were planned, including two over the entrance portal, but in February 1360, while the building was still under construction, one of these two fell, killing 300 people, and the second was never built. One of the two remaining minarets collapsed in 1659 and was replaced by the present smaller version, an Ottoman construction in the Mamluk style, in 1672, when the dome was also replaced. The architectural daring that caused the difficulties is made clear by the original minaret at the western corner; it is over 80 metres (262ft), taller and larger than any other in Cairo.

The complex originally included a market, apartments and a well at its northern end. The original wooden doors at the entrance, covered with bronze and filigree silver in geometric patterns, were removed by Sultan al-Muayyad in 1416 to be used in his mosque near Bab Zuwaylah, where they are still visible, and most of the original marble floor was stripped by Selim the Grim for shipment to Istanbul after the Ottoman conquest. What is left, however, is stunning.

THE CITADEL

The Citadel ⑲ (Mon–Fri 8am–5pm, Sat–Sun 8am–4pm), entered from **Bab al-Gabal Ⓐ** (also known as Bab al-Muqattam) reached from the Salah Salim highway, was begun by Saladin in 1176 as part of a grand scheme to enclose all of Misr within walls. In 1182, by which time he had gone north to fight his last campaigns against the crusaders, it was complete, and though it was later modified it was never without a military garrison.

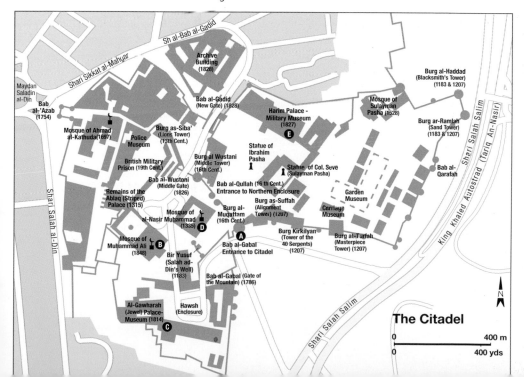

The Citadel

0 ——— 400 m
0 ——— 400 yds

In 1218 Sultan al-Kamil, Saladin's nephew, took up residence in the Citadel, and from that time until the construction of Abdeen Palace in the mid-19th century it was also the home and seat of government of all but one of Egypt's rulers, including Ottoman viceroys. The Lower Enclosure contains the famous gate-passage where Muhammad Ali conducted a massacre of Mamluks in 1811 (see page 79). It can be approached by an 18th-century gateway, restored in 1988, but it is best seen from the terrace of the Police Museum on the upper level, which contains the Southern and Northern enclosures, nearly two-thirds of the Citadel's entire area.

Visible from nearly anywhere in the city below, on the pinnacle of the Southern Enclosure, is the **Muhammad Ali Mosque** Ⓑ. Also called the Alabaster Mosque because of the shining marble that covers its inner and outer walls, it was built between 1830 and 1857. Designed by a Greek architect in accord with Ottoman models, it owes nothing to Egypt but the materials from which it is made and a few intermingled Pharaonic and Mamluk decorative motifs, but it adds a wonderful picture-postcard element to the city's skyline. The clock in the courtyard was a gift made by Louis-Philippe of France in 1846, a belated exchange for the obelisk of Ramesses II from Luxor Temple, now standing in the Place de la Concorde in Paris, which Muhammad Ali had given the French in 1831. The pasha himself is buried here under a marble cenotaph.

The view from the belvedere near the mosque is remarkable on a clear day, when it is possible to see the Giza Pyramids. Across a little court is the **Al-Gawhara Palace** Ⓒ (daily 9am–5pm), built by Muhammad Ali in 1814 but gutted by fire during a theft in 1972. The ruins have been intelligently refurbished and converted into a museum of the mid-19th century, when it served as a vice-regal *salamlik* (reception) palace.

Below the Muhammad Ali Mosque, to the northwest, between the mosque and the gateway to the Northern Enclosure, is the great 14th-century **Al-Nasir Muhammad Mosque** Ⓓ, dedicated to the father of Sultan Hasan. Built in 1318, enlarged in 1335, but stripped of its gorgeous marble by the Ottomans after 1517, it shows Persian-Mongol influence in its unique minarets, and an incredible variety of Egyptian sources in its columns: levied from Pharaonic, Greek, Roman and Coptic sites, they constitute a survey of Egyptian architectural styles.

North of the mosque of Al-Nasir Muhammad are two gates: one downhill to the left leads into the Lower Enclosure; the other, around a corner to the right, leads into the Northern Enclosure. Within the Northern Enclosure is the **Military Museum** Ⓔ, which is housed in Muhammad Ali's Harim Palace, built in 1827. The inside is packed with military memorabilia and historical weapons covering Egyptian Army history from Pharaonic times to

Muhammad Ali Mosque interior.

the present, including one of Tutankhamun's war chariots.

In the far corner of the Northern Enclosure is the **Sulayman Pasha Mosque**, the first Ottoman mosque to be built in Cairo (1528). Nestled next to an old Fatimid tomb, it is set in a small garden, which must have afforded a cool and leafy touch of the Bosphorus to the homesick Janissaries who lived here after 1517.

AL-AZHAR PARK

From 2005, the Aga Khan Trust for Culture undertook a formidable US$30-million project in a city with one of the lowest ratios of green space in the world to create the 30-hectare (74-acre) **Al-Azhar Park** ⑳ (daily 9am–10pm) near the Citadel. The scheme included the excavation and restoration of the 12th-century Ayyubid Wall (which had been entirely covered in the accumulated rubbish of several centuries), the installation of three large freshwater tanks, which provide water for fountains and a lake with fantastic views over the medieval city, and a formal garden with trimmed

hedges and lawns. It's a popular recreational space, especially for family picnics at the weekends, and there are also several good cafés and restaurants open until late in the evening.

A WALK THROUGH MEDIEVAL CAIRO

Medieval Cairo can be known only on foot, and one of its greatest walks begins at **Bab al-Jadid**, the northern gate of the Citadel, and runs to Bab Zuwaylah. The street has other names – at-Tabbana, Bab al-Wazir – but is best known as **Darb al-Ahmar**. From outside the Citadel, Bab al-Jadid can be reached by walking up towards the Citadel from Midan Saladin, then turning left to climb a road running parallel to its walls, bearing on to a shady street running downhill at the first intersection.

From here, the route to Bab Zuwaylah first runs through an area that was cleared for pleasure gardens by Saladin, then became fashionable during the reign of Al-Nasir Muhammad, when many of his sons-in-law began building there

⊙ Tip

While the ruins can be seen at any time, most of the still-functioning mosques in medieval Cairo are open daily 9am–4pm (except prayer times) and donations are welcome.

Camouflage tank at the Military Museum.

⊙ Tip

While most mosques are open to non-Muslim visitors, and general opening times are listed, note that during the five prayer times you will not be able to enter; each prayer lasts 5–15 minutes. Avoid Friday's Salaat-ul-Jumu'ah, the "congregational" prayer, just after noon, as this is one of the most exalted Islamic rituals and the mosques are at their busiest. Visitors need to be respectfully dressed – no shorts, miniskirts or bare shoulders – and shoes should be removed. Women must cover their heads.

First, on the left down a very short side street, are the ruins of what was Cairo's main infirmary in medieval times (1418), the **Bimaristan** or **Sultan al-Muayyad Hospital**; on the right appear the **madrasa and tomb of Amir Aytmish al-Bagasi** (1348), the remains of the **tomb and *sabil-kuttub* of Amir Tarabay as-Sharifi** (1503) and the **tomb of Azdumur** (early 16th century). A hundred metres/yds further down the street on the right (east) is the **Amir Alin Aq Palace** (1293), in ruins with the exception of the portal, occupied and remodelled by the treacherous Amir Khayrbak; appointed viceroy of Aleppo by Sultan al-Ghuri, Khayrbak betrayed him by defecting to the Ottoman side in the Battle of Marj Dabiq near Aleppo in 1516. He built his tomb (1502), mosque and *sabil-kuttub* (1520) next the palace, creating a northward view that is one of the most frequently photographed in Cairo.

On the left (west) across the street from the **Khayrbak Mosque ㉑** is the start of a 14-unit apartment house dating from 1522. Just beyond Khayrbak's mosque on the right (east), meanwhile, is a 17th-century house, with the 1347 **Mosque of Aqsunqur ㉒**, one of Al-Nasir Muhammad's sons-in-law, next to it. Adorned with Damascene tiles installed in 1652 by Ibrahim Agha, the first owner of the house, the mosque is also known as the "Blue Mosque". The 1992 Cairo earthquake damaged the arches of the mosque's porticoes, but they were reinforced in the mid-1990s to prevent additional deterioration.

Across the street from the mosque, next to the 16th-century apartment house, is a 17th-century *sabil* (fountain) and tomb, and on the east side another of Ibrahim Agha's houses (1652) with his adjoining *sabil* (1639). Beyond the *sabil* is a small Ottoman religious structure, with an Ayyubid minaret (1260). A little further down the street, another 17th-century *sabil-kuttub* appears on the left, and a 14th-century tomb on the right.

Jutting into the street from the left is the **Mosque of Amir al-Maridani ㉓**

Inside the Museum of Islamic Art.

(1340), notable for its carved minbar and marble and mother-of-pearl mihrab, which gives an idea of what Al-Nasir Muhammad's mosque at the Citadel must have been like before the Ottoman conquest. Further along on the same side of the street is the **Mosque of Ahmad al-Mihmandar** ❷ (1325), which has a 17th-century *sabil-kuttub* next to it. Finally, on the right as the street turns a corner and Bab Zuwaylah comes into view, stands the exquisite funerary **Mosque of Amir Qajmas al-Ishaqi** ❷ (1481); it is connected with his *sabil-kuttub* by a bridge over a side street.

Darb al-Ahmar has undergone serious restoration over the last decade. It runs east and west and leads – after a change of name – past **Bab Zuwaylah** ❷ (see below) and the Tentmakers' Bazaar to the **Museum of Islamic Art** ❷ (Midan Ahmed Maher, Shari Port Said; www.miaegypt.org; Sat–Thu 9am–5pm, Fri 9am–noon, 2–5pm). Relocated here in 1903 from its original home at the Fatimid Mosque of Al-Hakim, and recently reopened after three years of extensive renovation and reorganisation in 2017, this museum has more than 1,700 items on display (and thousands more in storage) and is considered one of the world's finest collections of Islamic applied arts. The ceramics, woodwork, carpets, textiles, manuscripts, calligraphy, metalwork, stonework and arms date from the 7th to 19th centuries, exhibited chronologically beginning with the Umayyad era, before continuing with the Abbasid/Tulunid, Fatimid, Ayyubid, Mamluk and Ottoman periods. The entrance on Shari Port Said features a facade with decorations and recesses inspired by Egyptian Islamic architecture from these various periods.

BAB ZUWAYLAH

Built in 1092 as the southern gateway of al-Qahirah, the beautifully restored **Bab Zuwaylah** (daily 8.30am–5pm), or Bab Zuweila, is the most distinguished of the old Fatimid gates. Originally a palace enclosure, it was opened to commercial development by Saladin, and through it runs the Qasabah, once the main artery of the medieval city and a single enormous bazaar. It is also known as Bab al-Mitwalli after the Islamic saint, Mitwalli al-Butb, who supposedly lived by the gate and worked miracles. As such, even until the early part of the 20th century, the gate was hung with rotting teeth, filthy rags and all sorts of monstrous tokens of sickness and disease in the hope that the saint could cure people's ailments. Directly on top of the gate are two minarets that were added to its turrets some four hundred years after it was built. Belonging to the **Mosque of Sultan al-Muayyad** (1415), which stands just inside the gate to the left, they also demonstrate that by the end of the 14th century, Bab Zuwaylah had ceased to be regarded as primarily military. Across the street, with an attached *sabil-kuttub*, is the facade of a caravanserai-emporium

The soaring towers of Bab Zuwaylah.

⊙ Tip

Bab Zuwaylah is considered to be the most majestic of Fatimid Cairo's old gates, and after careful restoration, the western gate tower, the turrets and the two minarets are open to the public, and there are far-reaching views over the medieval and Islamic districts of the city from the top.

Looking out over Shari Al-Muizz li-Din Allah al-Fatimi and beyond.

called **as-Sukkariyyah** (from the Arabic *sukkar*, the source of the word for "sugar" in several European languages), which has given this district just within the southern Fatimid walls its name.

SHARI AL-MUIZZ LI-DIN ALLAH AL-FATIMI

On the other side of Bab Zuwaylah, the Qasabah is called **Shari Al-Muizz li-Din Allah al-Fatimi**, or simply Muizz – named after Al-Mu'izz li-Din Allah, the fourth caliph of the Fatimid dynasty. It is a delightful place to walk and admire what is the greatest concentration of medieval architecture in Cairo, and the 1km (0.6-mile) stretch up to Bab al-Futuh in the north was restored between 1997 and 2008 and is now a pedestrian-only zone. One of the main aims of the renovations was to replicate the original appearance of the street as much as possible; for example, newer buildings higher than the level of the old monuments were brought down in height and painted in like colours, while cobblestones were

added to the street itself. Unless otherwise stated, mosques and other sites are open daily 9am–5pm.

About 450 metres/yds up the street is the commercial district of the **Fahhamin Quarter**, the site of the **Silk Merchants' Bazaar ㉘**, a street market that was once the most famous in Cairo. At one time covered but now open-air, it is still bursting with textile trade. Here the **Al-Ghouri Complex** (daily 9am–5pm) is beautifully restored and stands on both sides of Shari Al-Muizz li-Din Allah; the mosque and madrasa on the western side, and the khanqah, mausoleum and *sabil-kuttub* on the eastern side. Sultan Qansuh Al-Ghouri (1501–16) died in a battle against the Ottomans in Aleppo, which resulted in a complete defeat for the Mamluks, after which they lost their prominence in Egypt.

At this point Shari Muizz's north–south axis is dissected by the modern east–west traffic of **Shari al-Azhar**, cut through old Misr in 1930 to provide a tram service for the greatest and most long-lived of the Fatimids' foundations

– the **Al-Azhar Mosque and University**  (daily 9am–5pm). Lying a short distance down Shari Al-Azhar to the east, Al-Azhar was built in AD 970 as the first mosque of Fatimid Cairo; a madrasa was added in 988. Finally, in 1961, Al-Azhar was re-established as a university under Nasser's government when a wide range of secular faculties were added. As such it is considered the world's second-oldest continuous educational institution (after the University of Al Kairaouine in Fez, Morocco), and is still Egypt's supreme religious authority attracting Islamic scholars from around the world. It is believed that university black graduation gowns originated from here, inspired by the flowing robes of Al-Azhar's students. The entrance to the mosque is the splendid 15th-century **Bab al-Muzainin** ("barbers' gates").

On the other side of Shari Al-Azhar, the Qasabah, or Muizz, continues north until, just beyond a 15th-century madrasa, it is interrupted by another modern street, **Shari al-Muski**. Traditionally associated with old Christian and European quarters, by the end of the 19th century it was lined with European-owned shops. Al-Muski is now a chaotic and busy pedestrian street, where wholesale traders offer their wares to small merchants from all over Egypt.

Back on Muizz, the first major street to the right (east) leads to the warren of alleyways at **Khan El Khalili** ⑳, famous formerly for Turkish goods and now the tourists' bazaar, although many traditional workshops continue to operate in the surrounding area, and the adjoining goldsmiths' souq, for example, is still popular with locals. There is a variety of goods for sale designed for the tourist trade including silverware, stained-glass lamps, incense, carpets, spices, gold jewellery, perfume, papyrus, gallabiyahs and belly dancing costumes. Naturally, haggling is expected, and some might find it annoying to be badgered by the vendors, but it's a colourful place where visitors can get any kind of Egyptian souvenir all under one roof.

Further north on the Muizz is where you'll find the finest selection

⦿ Tip

The great north–south thoroughfare called the Qasabah is medieval Cairo's main street and can still be followed on foot from Ibn Tulun northward for more than 5km (3 miles). However, the best place to take a stroll is the 1km (0.6-mile) stretch along Al-Muizz li-Din Allah al-Fatimi between the two gates – Bab Zuwaylah and Bab al-Futuh – which is a pedestrian-only zone.

Khan El Khalili, one of Cairo's most important souqs.

The yellow stone walls of the Mosque-Madrassa of Sultan Barquq.

of restored buildings. This section of the Qasabah was known as Bayn al-Qasrayn, "Between the Two Palaces", in recognition of the two huge 10th-century Fatimid palaces that once stood facing each other on this site and which were progressively replaced by religious buildings and mausoleums of Ayyubid and Mamluk sultans. Cairo's principal slave market was also held here in Bayn al-Qasrayn, where Mamluks and girls, mainly Circassian and Greek, continued to be bought and sold until the time of Muhammad Ali.

First on your right is the **Mausoleum of Al-Salih Nagm Al-Din Ayyub**, constructed by the Ayyub sultan As-Salih Ayyub in 1243, which commands great views over this historic quarter from its minarets. Next, to the left, the magnificent **Qalawun Complex** (daily 9am–5pm) was built by three of the most important Mamluk sultans. First, you'll come to the great **Tomb and Madrasa of Sultan Qalawun**, built in 1285; next door are the **Madrasa and Mausoleum of al-Nasir Muhammad**, built 40 years

later by his son; and the next entrance through bronze-plated doors leads to the **Mosque-Madrassa of Sultan Barquq**, constructed between 1384 and 1386.

Facing the huge Qalawun Complex are the remains of the **Palace of Bashtak ③** or Qasr Bashtak (daily 9am–5pm), built by the Mamluk Amir Bashtak in the 14th century with beautiful *mashrabiyyah* windows in a high plain facade and a fountain of inlaid marble in the centre.

On the crossroads is the elegant Ottoman *sabil-kuttub* of Abd ar-Rahman Kathuda, showing a mixture of Mamluk and Ottoman influences.

Further north, on a stretch of the Qasabah where items such as copper bean-pots and finials for mosques are made, stands the 12th-century **Aqmar Mosque ③**, originally sited at the northeast corner of the great eastern Fatimid palace and one of Cairo's oldest mosques, built in 1125–6. It is unusual in that it has lavish decoration – friezes, niches and recesses – across the entire facade.

Around the corner at the second turning afterwards, on a restored side street called the Darb el-Asfar, stands one of the best examples of a 17th-century Ottoman-era Cairene house, the **Bayt Al-Suhaymi** ㉝ (daily 9am–5pm). Built in 1648, it is more typical but less furnished than the Gayer-Anderson Museum house (see page 146), but illustrates not only the standard division of rooms into a *salamlik* (reception room) and a *haramlik* (harem suite), but also the ingenuity with which architects used courtyards, fountains set in sunken floors, high ceilings and north-facing wind catchers on the roof to counter the stifling heat of a long Cairene summer.

Just before Shari Al-Muizz li-Din Allah al-Fatimi exits through Bab al-Futuh, you'll come to the **Mosque of Al-Hakim**, the Fatimid caliph. Finished in 1013, it was restored in 1980 by the Bohora, an Isma'ili Shi'ite sect who are based in Dombay but trace their ancestry back directly to the Fatimids, who have imported features that give the building a touch of India.

Bab al-Futuh ㉞ (daily 9am–5pm) stands at the end of Shari Al-Muizz li-Din Allah al-Fatimi and faces north, and was built by the Fatimids' Armenian general Badr al Gamali in 1087. It is the final of the remaining three gates of al-Qahirah; **Bab al-Nasr** ㉟ lies to the southeast and is attached to Bab al-Futuh by a 330-metre (1,080ft) stretch of wall. It is said that armies heading north of al-Qahirah would depart through Bab al-Nasr, the "Gate of Victory", and return through Bab al-Futuh, the "Gate of Conquest". Badr's Armenian architects were skilled military specialists and their work originally made use of blocks quarried and carved under the pharaohs, some of which were scratched with Napoleonic graffiti more than seven centuries later.

WEST OF THE NILE

The suburbs on the west bank of Cairo are reached by five bridges; three across Gezira Island and two across Rawdah Island. As Zamalek on Gezira Island gets more crowded, many

⊙ **Tip**

In addition to the shops and stalls at Khan El Khalili, there are tiny hole-in-the-wall traditional cafés serving Arabic coffee, mint, hibiscus or aniseed tea and usually fruit-flavoured shisha. One of the oldest and most famous is Fishawi's Ahwa, which was established in 1773 – ask for directions, as everyone knows it.

Ablutions fountain in the courtyard of the Mosque-Madrasa of Sultan Barquq.

fashionable Cairenes and foreigners are opting to live in modern apartment blocks in the suburbs of **Mohandessin** and **Dokki** immediately across from these islands. The area has less character but has good shops, bars and restaurants.

In **Dokki** is one of Cairo's quirkiest museums, the **Agricultural Museum** (Ministry of Agriculture, next to the 6th of October Bridge; daily 9am–2pm). Founded in 1938, it was one of the first agricultural museums in the world (second only to the Royal Agricultural Museum in Budapest) and covers 11 hectares (27 acres) of gardens and several pavilions, including the Museum of Ancient Egyptian Agriculture, the Cotton Museum and Museum of the Social Life of the Arab Nations.

Giza, in ancient times merely a stopover between Memphis and Heliopolis, is now a rapidly expanding governorate in its own right that begins on the west bank below Dokki and covers a large area all the way to the pyramids in the southwest (see page 166). Just

opposite the Cairo University on Shari Charles De Gaulle is the **Giza Zoo** (8.30am–4pm, until 5pm in summer). Established in 1891, the zoo is one of the oldest in the world, with a comprehensive collection of animals – but is unfortunately now in a rather poor state and not recommended.

Close to the river, next door to the Cairo Sheraton, a grand villa contains the rarely visited but fascinating **Mohamed Khalil Museum** (1 Shari Kafour; Sat–Thu 8am–5pm). Mahmoud Khalil Pasha was the Egyptian Prime Minister twice (1928 and1937) and a keen collector; this is his fine private collection of furniture and valuable 19th- and 20th-century paintings. On display are great works by Van Gogh, Gauguin, Monet and Renoir, as well as several Rodin sculptures.

NORTHERN CAIRO

To the north of the city towards the modern airport was ancient Heliopolis. It was the centre of the royal cult of Ra, the universal sun-god. Originally called On, the city the Greeks later

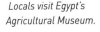

Locals visit Egypt's Agricultural Museum.

called **Heliopolis** (City of the Sun) stood 25km (15 miles) northeast of Giza and thus 32km (20 miles) from Memphis, but on the opposite side of the Nile, in the modern district of El Matareya. The primary theological centre of Old Kingdom Egypt, it was finally displaced in importance by Thebes, but not before its priests had developed elaborate rituals, liturgies and mythologies that revolved around the sun-god Ra and a host of lesser deities known as the Great Company.

It is recorded that Ramesses III (1182–1151 BC) endowed Heliopolis with some 12,000 serfs and more than 100 towns, not to mention statues, gold, silver, linens, precious stones, birds, incense, cattle and fruit.

Even in ancient times, Heliopolis had begun to suffer a decline that led to systematic pillaging. Strabo, visiting in 24 BC, recorded its desolation and 14 years later a pair of obelisks erected by Tuthmosis III (1504–1450 BC) were removed by the Romans to adorn their new Caesarium, the Temple of Julius Caesar in Alexandria. Some 19 centuries later, during the reign of Khedive Ismail, these two monuments found their way out of Egypt and became the "Cleopatra's Needles" of London and New York (though they have nothing to do with any of the real Cleopatras). Only one obelisk, from a pair erected in the reign of Senusert I (1971–1928 BC) survives in situ.

The Holy Family are said to have come here to escape King Herod and rested under what is known as the **Virgin's Tree** (daily 10am–4pm). The original sycamore tree is long dead, but a third-generation tree is surviving quite well on the site. Paintings and biblical references of this journey are also to be seen inside the nearby **Church of Virgin Mary**. Both sites are about 800 metres/yds northwest of El Matareya metro station (Line 1 towards El-Marg).

From the church, continue up the busy road away from the Virgin's Tree for about 1km (0.6 miles), to the only remains of ancient Heliopolis, the 1940 BC **Obelisk of Senusert I** (daily 10am–4pm) in a small park but, as so often is the case in the suburbs, surrounded by rubbish.

OUTLYING ATTRACTIONS

The regeneration of the northern area for the influx of Europeans got underway at the beginning of the 20th century, when Edouard Louis Joseph, or Baron Empain, a Belgian millionaire and industrialist, developed modern "Heliopolis" (nothing to do with the ancient city of the same name). Some of the grand buildings of this time survive. The main road from the airport, for example, offers a brief glimpse of the **Baron Empain Palace** set back on the left-hand side. Built in 1906 to be the baron's own palatial residence, it is not unlike a Hindu temple – the French architect was said to be inspired by Angkor Wat in Cambodia. For many years it was a crumbling ruin, but

Mohamed Khalil Museum.

Baron Empain Palace.

extensive restorations began in 2017 and it is likely to open to the public by 2020.

On the same side of the road, closer into the city, is the October War Panorama (Wed–Mon), in a circular building surrounded by fighter jets, missiles and tanks. Inside are sculptures showing famous battles throughout Egyptian history, ending with a 20-minute narration in Arabic (English on headphones) of the 1973 October War against Israel. Actual film footage is shown downstairs. The tomb of the man behind that surprise attack on Israel is located about 2km (1.25 miles) east of here along the busy al-Nasr highway, the main road to Suez. The **tomb of President Anwar Sadat** is below an open pyramid-style memorial, across the road from the scene of his assassination.

The **Muhammad Ali Pasha Shubra Palace** is in northern Shubra, the district directly north of Ramses Railway Station. This luxurious property was once connected to the Abdeen Palace by a grand boulevard, and it was built as a pleasure palace for the Muhammad Ali family by Turkish and Armenian architects. Construction started in 1808 during the early years of his reign and was completed in 1922; however the complex kept undergoing alterations well into the 1870s. It features a large central pool where the pasha would entertain his wife and 125 concubines, where water from four lion fountains poured over carvings of fish, creating an illusion of them swimming. Surrounded by open colonnades and marble terraces, the rooms were built in various opulent European, Arabic and Turkish styles and had highly decorated ceilings.

The palace was restored as part of the project to renovate historic medieval Cairo from the mid-1990s. However, it was closed again in 2012 because of further deterioration of the buildings, and when a car bomb exploded adjacent to the palace in 2015, targeting the nearby National Security Agency's headquarters, the palace was damaged once more. The Ministry of Antiquities has agreed to restore it again, so keep an eye out for developments.

The striking tomb of President Anwar Sadat.

THE NORTHERN AND SOUTHERN CEMETERIES

The Northern and Southern cemeteries are known locally as Qarafa, but Westerners delight in also calling them "The City of the Dead".

The Northern and Southern cemeteries are vast Islamic-era necropolises in a strip around 6.5km (4 miles) long on the edges of historical Cairo in the southeast of the city. The cemeteries actually grew up at different times and are separated by the limestone spur on which the Citadel was built: it's believed that the Southern Cemetery dates back to when the early city of Fustat was founded in AD 642, while the Northern Cemetery was developed by Mamluk sultans in the 14th and 15th centuries as they sought space to build their own grand funerary monuments outside the overcrowded city. The early graves were unadorned, but from AD 969 and the Fatimid era, monumental mausoleums were built and people visited ancestors' graves, customs elaborated by the Mamluk sultans.

As far as anyone knows, throughout their history the necropolises have been home to living inhabitants too. The very first residents were thought to have been burial staff, custodians tending the graves, Sufi mystics and people simply wanting to be close to their deceased relatives. Migration to the necropolises began in earnest in the 19th century.

Muhammad Ali Pasha himself had a lavish mausoleum built in the Southern Cemetery for his family, relatives and devoted servants in 1816, known as the Hoch el Pasha ("Courtyard of the Sir"). When he died in 1849, he was initially entombed here; his body was later moved to a marble tomb at the Citadel's Muhammad Ali Mosque (see page 150) in 1857. Hoch el Pasha has six domes, and inner courtyards and chambers heavily decorated by Islamic motifs. At the time of writing it was about to undergo restoration works.

Following his example, many royal officials and members of the elite also constructed ornate mausoleums and funeral complexes, which in turn required custodians and workers, whose housing was provided. Additionally, in the late 19th century and increasing into the 20th century, modernisation led to the demolition of many buildings in Cairo's historic districts, displacing much of the poor and working class to the outskirts, leading to a large increase in the number of people living in the cemeteries.

In some areas, permanent habitation for the living was tolerated and even received some government assistance. Several of the tombs have been pilgrimage sites for centuries, particularly the 13th-century mausoleum of Imam al-Shafi'i. The area east of the mausoleum became a densely populated neighbourhood named after him, and in 1907, it was connected to the rest of Cairo by a streetcar line, and later, during Nasser's presidency in the 1960s, proper public housing and schools were provided.

From the 1960s there was a surge of rural poor migrating into the city. Housing shortages forced the newcomers to erect unofficial houses wherever they could find space to build; where possible, they incorporated older structures – such as the large mausoleums in the cemeteries. In 1992, when the Cairo earthquake made 50,000 people homeless, some moved into their family tombs.

Today, the population in the cemeteries is almost impossible to determine but could be as much as half a million. The relatively large and solidly built tombs often make a better alternative to squatting or low-quality housing in the inner city. Some even have electricity and running water, while there are medical centres and schools in the districts.

It is advisable to enter these areas on a supervised tour or with a reputable guide.

Local youth in the Northern Cemetery.

ISLAMIC CAIRO

Centuries of Muslim rule have left Cairo with an astonishing legacy of Islamic architecture.

The army of Muslim general Amr ibn al-As crossed into Egypt from Palestine in 639, and after the success of his siege of Babylon two years later the rest of the country surrendered to Muslim rule. 'Amr founded the garrison city of Fustat, but when the Abbasids seized control of the empire in 750 they built a military suburb, al-Askar, near the city, establishing the trend of developing a new suburb whenever the regime changed. This protected older buildings rather than demolishing them, and left us a great legacy of Islamic architecture.

In the late 9th century, Ahmad Ibn Tulun established a new city, al-Qatai, to the north of Fustat, but all that remains of this centre is his mosque, considered to be one of the greatest Islamic monuments in Egypt.

During the 10th century, under the Fatimids, a new walled city, known as al-Qahirah (Cairo), was built, but this time purely for Shi'a officials, soldiers, servants and slaves. Some of the important landmarks of this new city are still to be seen today – Al-Azhar, Bab Zuwaylah, the main gateway in the south and Bab al-Futuh in the northern wall. It was under the young Ayyubid leader Salah ad-Din (better known as Saladin) who came to power in 1171, that Sunni control was re-established as he began a system of madrasahs or religious schools, in order to prevent the return of Shi'a influence. Ayyubid control ended in 1250 when the Mamluks rose up under a series of strong rulers like Sultan Qalawun. Cairo became a modern capital with hospitals, monumental mosques and mausoleums that stand today as the zenith of Mamluk architecture. Their greatest leader, Muhammad al-Nasir, urbanised the area between the walled city at Bab Zuwaylah and the isolated Citadel, where Sultan Hasan later built his madrasah.

The greatest building from the later Mamluk period is the mosque of Sultan Mu'ayyid, built on the site of a prison where he himself was once held prisoner, just inside the Bab Zuwaylah.

Many mosques built around tombs of important religious figures have become sites of local pilgrimage. The tomb o Sayyida Zeinab is inside a large mosque and is one of the most popular. Up to a million people gather here in the first two weeks of October, when Sayyida is venerated.

This beautifully decorated niche, known as a mihrab, indicates the direction for prayer. Inside his madrasah, Sultan Hasan wanted worshippers to pray not only towards Mecca, but also towards him. His tomb lies just behind the mihrab, but sadly his body is not inside, as it disappeared immediately after his assassination in 1361.

Al-Azhar Mosque.

The Al-Azhar Mosque

The Al-Azhar was the first mosque to be built by the Fatimids in AD 972. The Fatimids were a Shi'a sect that originally came from Tunisia, claiming descent from Fatima, daughter of the prophet Muhammad, from whom they took their name. The bright courtyard of the mosque is surrounded by ziggurat-topped arches, supported by single, double and triple columns and dominated by three minarets and a dome. A forest of columns inside the prayer hall leads to the delicate geometrical designs inside the mihrab.

The main gateway is known as the Barber's Gate, because it is where students had their heads shaved before entering the attached al-Azhar University. This is acknowledged as the world's oldest university, dating from AD 988, and most of the infrastructure came from an earlier centre of learning at Zebid in Yemen, at a time when the Fatimids controlled the entire Red Sea region. Interestingly, the Al-Azhar is now considered to be the highest seat of learning of Sunni religious thinking.

The continuity of Islamic architecture in Cairo is shown by the Rifa'i Mosque, built just a century ago. Across the road is the Sultan Hasan madrasah, the grandest of Cairo's Mamluk buildings, dating from the 14th century, which it complements perfectly.

Muhammad Ali Mosque at Cairo's Citadel is also known as the Alabaster Mosque for the shining marble casing on its walls. Built between 1830 and 1857, it was actually designed by a Greek architect.

Finely clad camel at the pyramids.

GIZA, MEMPHIS AND SAQQARA

The Pyramids of Giza are the most famous symbol of
Egypt. And among the country's other highlights are the
Step Pyramid and the decorated tombs of Saqqara, all
accessible on an easy day trip from central Cairo.

The modern city of Cairo occupies a position at the head of the Nile Delta that has been of strategic importance for some 5,000 years and that has consequently seen many urban foundations, of which Cairo itself is merely the largest and the latest.

Many visitors are told by guides to consider the west bank of the Nile as the land of the dead and Giza as the necropolis of Cairo, in the way the Valley of the Kings was to Karnak and Luxor. But it is important to remember that the first capital of Egypt, Memphis, was itself on the west bank. Sadly, there is precious little to see of Memphis, but its necropolis at Saqqara and a string of later pyramids and burial constructions offer plenty to interest visitors. With Cairo so crowded and polluted, it is a joy to drive through the stretches of verdant countryside and open desert that run south and west of the capital. And horse riding, readily available at the pyramids, can be a pleasant distraction to walking around the ancient sites, if only for an hour or two.

A DAY'S TOUR

If you are travelling independently, it is worth hiring a taxi for a day to take you on a tour of Giza, Memphis and Saqqara. This can be arranged at the reception of your hotel. It is

Close-up of the Great Pyramid of Khufu.

also worth spending some time trying to understand the importance of the locations on the west bank before seeing the sites themselves, even if you are on an organised tour, for the speed of these tours can make it hard to grasp the history and chronology of the sites.

It is also important to plan your visit. If you want to enter the Great Pyramid of Khufu, for example, you need to get there early, as numbers are restricted (tickets are sold from 8am each day).

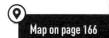

○ **Main attractions**

The Pyramids of Giza
Memphis
Saqqara
Dahshur
Maydum

Map on page 166

GIZA

The only survivors among the Seven Wonders of the Ancient World, the Pyramids of Giza (called *al-Ahram* in Arabic) are not hard to find. Standing at the end of a boulevard (Shari' al-Ahram) on the desert plateau above the western edge of Giza, across the river from Cairo, they can frequently be glimpsed from the city centre, shimmering in the distance through the haze of heat and dust.

THE PYRAMIDS

The most striking aspect of the **Pyramids of Giza ❶** (plateau daily Oct–Mar 8am–5pm, Apr–Sept 7am–7pm) is their size. But even with all the facts and figures, it is still hard to believe that these ancient structures remain in such a good state of preservation. The vision and workmanship of people 4,500 years ago in creating structures that would be the world's tallest until the 14th century is staggering.

The **Great Pyramid of Khufu Ⓐ** (Cheops in Greek, ruling approximately 2589–2576 BC) was originally 150 metres (480ft) high and incorporates some 2.3 million stone blocks averaging more than 2.5 tonnes in weight. The second ruler of the 4th Dynasty, Khufu took pyramid building to a completely new level. Building on the experience of his father King Snefru, who constructed the first "true" pyramid at Dahshur (see page 175), Khufu envisaged a tomb on such a gigantic scale that it would serve to preserve him for eternity.

Contrary to popular belief, however, the Great Pyramid is neither the biggest pyramid in the world – that distinction belongs to the Quetzalcoatl pyramid at Cholula, south of Mexico City, which covers an area more than three times as extensive – nor was it built by slaves. Teams of skilled labourers on three-month hire were supplemented by a permanent workforce of local quarrymen. Other crews cut limestone and granite construction blocks at Tura, (near modern-day Cairo) and Aswan and transported them across or down the Nile to the building site.

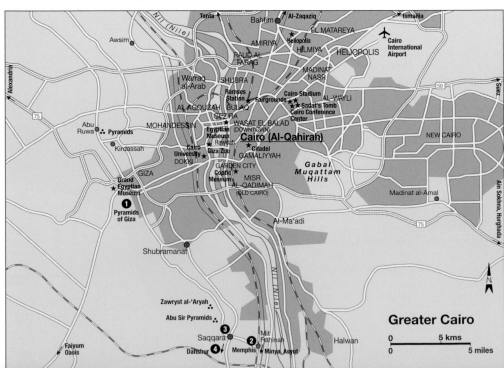

Greater Cairo

Other stones – as recent excavations at the so-called "Lost City of the Pyramids" show – were quarried from just below the pyramids, about 400 metres/yds south of the Sphinx. This quarry was then filled with the debris from the demolished mud construction ramps. Excavations of the workmen's camp have revealed the houses, bakeries and tombs of the pyramid builders, with inscriptions. Analysis indicates that the workforce comprised around 20,000 skilled builders over a 20-year period, contradicting Herodotus' 5th-century BC account of an estimated 100,000 slaves labouring for over 30 years.

Stripped of their smooth white Tura limestone upper casing and extensively quarried lower down for granite from the 11th century onwards, the sides of the Great Pyramid slope at an angle of 52 degrees, the approximate gradient for all the pyramids built after Snefru's Bent and Red pyramids at Dahshur. The four sides of the pyramid are only slightly off the cardinal points, at a time when the magnetic compass was unknown.

Except for their size, the isolated silhouettes of all the later large pyramids in Egypt would have looked exactly like the Great Pyramid. Each would have also stood within an enclosed complex, like Zoser's at Saqqara (see page 172), and would have been particularised by inscriptions, and by a painted or gilded cap.

ENTERING THE GREAT PYRAMID

The interior of the Great Pyramid can be visited and includes a grand gallery with a corbelled roof that is itself regarded as one of the most remarkable architectural works of the Old Kingdom. Entry is restricted to a few hundred people each day. Tickets can only be bought on the day, from 8am from the ticket office.

The tunnel, which was forcibly hacked out by treasure seekers, leads initially to the "Ascending Corridor" and then the remarkable "Grand Gallery". The main burial chamber is a small room built of red Aswan granite, as is the large open sarcophagus that still remains in the centre. Shafts

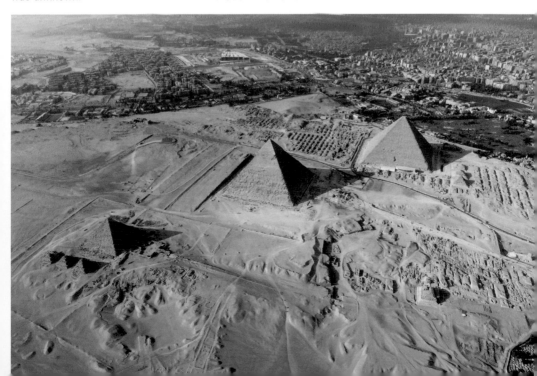

The Pyramids seen from the air.

⊙ Tip

Each evening the Pyramids host two one-hour sound and light shows, held in front of the Sphinx, in which an actorly voice relates their history. An English-language performance is held every evening at 7.30pm (6.30pm in winter) and headphones are provided to translate into other languages. You can easily arrange for a taxi to take you there, wait and return; www.soundandlight.show.

The reconstructed Solar Boat.

leading upwards from here point towards heavenly bodies.

East of the Great Pyramid is the site of Khufu's mortuary temple, identified by the remains of a basalt pavement, north and south of which are two boat pits (see below). Near its base are two more pits, one of which was excavated in 1954, when a complete dismantled river barge was found, probably secreted there in connection with the sun cult.

Beautifully reassembled, for now the cedar-wood vessel can still be admired in the **Solar Boat Museum** Ⓑ (daily 9am–4pm) next to the Great Pyramid over the hole where the boat was first found. Photographs and explanations documenting the 13 years of excavation and reconstruction can be examined on the ground floor, together with original grass ropes and reed matting from the double-roofed cabin of the boat. Note, however, that there are plans underway to move the solar boat to the new Grand Egyptian Museum (see page 170), in time for its long-awaited opening in 2020.

The causeway leading from the Great Pyramid's mortuary temple to its valley temple is largely ruinous and cannot be excavated at its lower end, thanks to the encroachment of modern buildings. But just south of it, close to three subsidiary pyramids, the only undisturbed tomb thus far found of the Old Kingdom was uncovered in 1925. The sarcophagus was empty, but it was identified as the **tomb of Queen Hetepheres**, wife of Snefru and mother of Khufu, and yielded extraordinary objects, including a carrying chair and a portable boudoir, with linen curtains as well as a gilt bed and chair.

PYRAMID OF KHAFRE

The next pyramid belongs to Khufu's son, **Khafre** Ⓒ (Chefren, 2576– 2551 BC), which looks taller than his father's but is actually smaller (it lies at a higher elevation, on a platform cut out of the sloping hillside, and is built at a steeper angle than the Great Pyramid). Look towards the top, where a lot of the outer limestone casing is still to be seen. The internal structure of

⊙ SOLAR BOATS

Between the two largest Giza pyramids is a glass building containing one of the solar boats that was buried alongside Khufu's pyramid – although plans are afoot to move it to the Grand Egyptian Museum (see page 170) for its 2020 opening. The boat was discovered in 1954, in a dismantled state comprising 1,224 pieces of polished cedar, buried in a narrow pit. The rebuilt solar boat is suspended above, with several walkways and platforms allowing views of the remarkable workmanship. A slightly smaller boat, also dismantled in antiquity, was discovered in another nearby pit, but this has been kept in-situ and resealed for preservation.

The real use of these boats is unknown, but they might have been used on the Nile to transport the king's body (there is a faint watermark), or for symbolic use in the afterlife.

passages is much simpler than that of the Great Pyramid, leading to a single chamber.

The Pyramid of Khafre is the most complete in relation to its surrounding complex, which includes the **Sphinx ⓓ**. Intended originally to represent a guardian deity in the shape of a lion, the Sphinx had Khafre's face (it is said to be disfigured and beardless thanks to Mamluk artillery practice). Later associated with the sun-god and with Horus of the Horizon, as a Greek drinking song scratched on one of its toes during the Ptolemaic period attests, the Sphinx was the object of pilgrimages, especially during the 18th Dynasty.

In front of the Sphinx stands a granite stele set up by order of Tuthmosis IV (1423–1417 BC), who records a dream he had when still a prince: while he was resting under its shade during a hunting expedition, the Sphinx spoke, promising Tuthmosis the kingdom if he would clear away accumulated sand from around its feet. For many centuries the story has circulated as a folk tale or joke involving later rulers: in one 20th-century version the hero was Gamal Abdel Nasser and the Sphinx asked for an exit visa.

PYRAMID OF MENKAURE

The third of the royal pyramids at Giza was begun by **Menkaure ⓔ** (Mycerinus, 2532–2504 BC), the successor of Khafre. By far the smallest, it was apparently left unfinished at Menkaure's death and hurriedly completed by his son, Shepseskaf, whose own tomb is at Saqqara. There are signs of haste throughout the complex, even in the pyramid itself. Brick was used to finish off the mortuary temple, causeway and valley temple, though they were begun in limestone and some of the blocks weigh 200 tonnes, showing that the failure to complete it in limestone was by no means due to a decline in technical mastery.

The great period of pyramid building, with its huge use of man-power and commitment, blossomed during this early period of Egyptian history and was never achieved again. There are

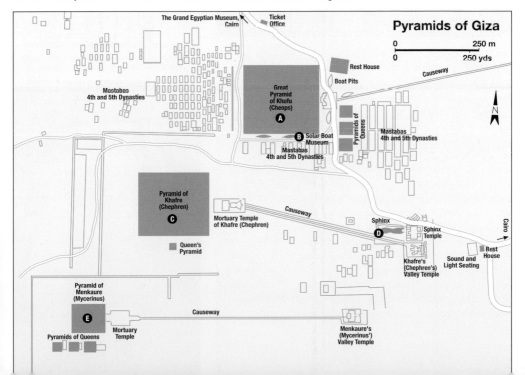

smaller pyramids from later periods, but these are poor imitations.

About 1km (0.6) miles beyond the Menkaure Pyramid is a **viewpoint** on the edge of the desert. Organised groups are driven there to take photographs, and to get hassled by souvenir sellers and camel-ride touts. Take a look around this viewpoint as there are some fossils in the sandy depressions, showing that this area was once underwater.

Security for visitors is tight at the Pyramids, and it is impossible to wander too far off the beaten track, making it difficult to fully appreciate the scale of the Giza Pyramids area. Tourist police with machine guns perched on camels provide a photo that many tourists take back with them.

MEMPHIS AND SAQQARA

The most important of Cairo's predecessors was the city of **Memphis** ❷ (daily 8am–5pm), founded by Narmer (also known as Menes), traditionally regarded as the first king of the 1st Dynasty, and said to have been the first to unite both Upper and Lower Egypt.

The colossus of Ramesses II is on display at Mit Rahinah's museum.

The city was built on land reclaimed from the Nile in about 3100 BC and lies 24km (15 miles) by road south of Cairo on the western side of the Nile.

Memphis can be reached by driving down the eastern side of the Nile and crossing the river south of Halwan. Another way is to cross the river directly into Giza and then drive south, either along the main highway to Upper Egypt, or along the attractive agricultural road that runs south from the Giza Pyramids.

The ruins of Memphis surround the village of **Mit Rahinah**, which derives its name from a temple of Mithras built here under the Romans, long after the days of the city's greatest glory when the cult of Ptah was worshipped here at a temple adorned by huge statues. But even when power transferred to Thebes, Memphis remained an important city.

There is little to see at Memphis except the **Alabaster Sphinx** and one of Ramesses' two colossi. The legs of this statue have been eroded, but the upper body, head and arms are beautifully carved and adorned with the

⊘ GRAND EGYPTIAN MUSEUM

The Grand Egyptian Museum (GEM) is presently under construction near Al Remaya Square in Giza, 2km (1.25 miles) north of the pyramids. Due to open in 2020, the site covers 50 hectares (120 acres) and the museum 24,000 sq metres (258,000 sq ft). With more than 100,000 exhibits, it will be the largest archaeological museum in the world dedicated to a single civilisation. Already, the full Tutankhamun collection of 5,000 items has been moved here from the Egyptian Museum in Cairo, and many of these will be displayed for the first time. Previously, only about a third of the treasures have ever been on public display, as the Egyptian Museum does not have the right light, temperature and other conditions to expose them, and isn't equipped with the proper technology to maintain and protect the artefacts. Other objects will be relocated from storages and museums in Luxor, Minya, Sohag, Asyut, Beni Suef and Alexandria, among other places. The building itself is triangular in shape and has glass walls, from which there are full views of the pyramids. At the front, a large plaza dotted with date palms will host a 3,200-year-old, 11-metre (36ft) tall statue of Ramesses II, moved from Ramses Square in Cairo in 2018. For progress on the museum's opening, check www.gem.gov.eg.

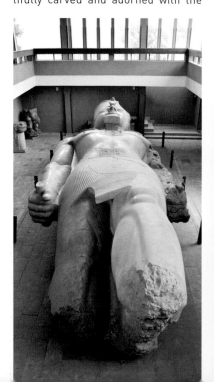

king's cartouche; the workmanship can be appreciated at close quarters.

Most of the constructions at Memphis were of mud brick, which after centuries of neglect have simply dissolved back into the earth. Any heavy stone buildings either sunk slowly into the soft Nile silt or their blocks were reused elsewhere.

More finds have been brought to light in recent excavations, and are scattered around, but visitors will probably want to enjoy the serenity of the surrounding groves of date palms, meditate briefly on the perishability of power, then push on up the road to Saqqara, the great necropolis of the ancient capital of Memphis. The famous Step Pyramid of Zoser can be seen appearing over the tops of the many palm-tree groves as you approach from the Nile Valley.

SAQQARA

The site of **Saqqara ❸** (daily 8am–4pm) lies on the desert plateau about 3km (1.75 miles) west of Memphis. This vast cemetery, which spans a period from the 27th century BC to the 10th century AD, is possibly named after Sokar, god of the burial sites.

A welcome addition to the site is the modern **Imhotep Museum ❹** (admission is included in that of the Saqqara site; no flash photography), opened in 2006 in an attempt to redistribute many of the treasures in the Egyptian Museum to more relevant locations. Of the many highlights are objects found inside Saqqara's pyramids and tombs, including a delightful wooden model of a rowing boat with human figures from the tomb of Khennu, a royal scribe of the Middle Kingdom. The mummy of King Merenre I, who ruled for five years from 2297 BC, is the oldest complete mummy yet found. Don't miss the haunting limestone bas-relief of the "Starving Men of Unas" from the causeway ramp of 5th Dynasty King Unas, it shows the ribcages of the starving Bedouin before they are given food by the king.

The ticket office at the entrance to the necropolis stands above the valley temple attached to the **Pyramid of Unas ❻**. Built in the 24th century BC

⊘ Tip

If you have plenty of time to spare, it is worth spending a whole day in Memphis and Saqqara. You could follow local tradition and take a picnic to enjoy in the ruins of the monastery of St Jeremiah.

Step Pyramid of Zoser.

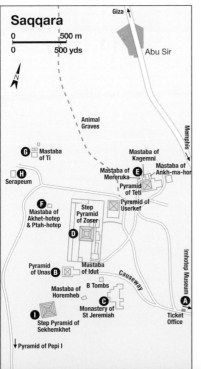

⏱ Tip

Allow plenty of time to visit the Imhotep Museum, as it really helps to explain the importance of the Saqqara site.

by the last king of the 5th Dynasty, this houses the earliest pyramid text. The ceremonial causeway linking the two has been excavated and the pyramid at the end is one of the least difficult for visitors to enter. Quite close to the parking space below the enclosure on the opposite side of the causeway to the Pyramid of Unas are the ruins of the **Monastery of St Jeremiah** ⓒ. Founded in the second half of the 5th century and destroyed by the Arabs in about AD 960, the monastery buildings include two churches, a refectory, a bakery, an oil press and cells for the monks. The monastery was the source of most of the objects in rooms 6 and 7 of the Coptic Museum in Cairo.

Dominating the whole area, however, is the **Step Pyramid of Zoser** ⓓ (3rd Dynasty, built 2668–2649 BC), the earliest of all the pyramids and the first great monument in the world to be built of hewn stone. The entire complex within the enclosure, including shrines, courtyards and the Step Pyramid itself, was the conception of a single man, Imhotep, Zoser's chief of works, who some consider to be the first recorded genius in history. An inscription left behind by a New Kingdom tourist venerates him as "he who opened the stone". He was later identified with magic, astronomy and medicine, finally becoming deified in the 6th century BC. Translating motifs from more perishable materials, such as wood or papyrus reeds, into stone, the Zoser complex displays many features that became a permanent part of the Egyptian architectural vocabulary and a few that have apparently remained unique.

The Step Pyramid can be entered only with special permission (a tour takes several hours), but a cross-section would reveal its complexity, arising from the fact that it began as a *mastaba* (from an Arabic word, meaning "bench" that refers to the usual oblong shape), a one-storey tomb of common type. Even here Imhotep showed his originality, for his *mastaba* was square rather than oblong and built of stone rather than the usual mud brick.

Looking at the pyramid, you can clearly see the separate interior

The Bedouin offer camel rides to tourists.

⏱ IMHOTEP

The exact role of Imhotep is unknown but he is seen as the first engineer, architect and physician in history as well as being a high priest and official of King Zoser. For the tomb of his king, Imhotep initially built a *mastaba* in stone blocks, which needed precise cutting and handling. Having completed it, there was enough strength to build another on top, and so on. His achievements were recognised by later dynasties, and he was elevated to a god; later on, Greeks identified him with Asklepios, their god of medicine. Imhotep's undiscovered tomb is probably somewhere near Saqqara and may contain many of his secrets. To cinema fans, Imhotep is better known as the inspiration for the series of films entitled *The Mummy*, showing him coming back to life and wreaking havoc.

structures where the outer casing has collapsed. It is possible that the surrounding life-after-death structures are copies of real buildings used by the king in Memphis. One curious small stone annexe at the rear of the Step Pyramid, known as the *serdab*, contains a statue of the king (not original), able to look out at the world through two eyeholes cut in the wall. The strange slope of this front wall is at the same angle as the pyramid, which serves as the *serdab*'s back wall.

VIZIERS' TOMBS

Not to be missed, no matter how short your visit, are two 6th-Dynasty *mastabas*, the **tombs of Mereruka and Kagemni** ❸, who were both viziers of King Teti (2345– 2333 BC). Nestled next to the Pyramid of Teti, northeast of the Zoser complex, these two structures promise nothing on the outside, but contain the most outstanding tomb reliefs of the Old Kingdom. Carved with lively scenes of domestic life, they show the interests and pursuits of the Old Kingdom nobility. hunting, horticulture,

husbandry, music and dancing, preparations to ensure that the next world would be as bountiful as this one. The artist's carved workmen exchange hieroglyphic one-liners; and such is the acuteness of his observations that more than 50 different species of fish have been identified by modern experts.

Almost as satisfying are the scenes in the *mastaba* of **Ankh-ma-hor** (known as the "Doctor's Tomb"), a few steps away, which show similar pursuits but are best known for their depictions of craftsmen (jewellers, metal-workers, sculptors) and also physicians conducting surgical operations.

Directly west of the Pyramid of Teti, a kilometre away and connected with it by a dirt road parallel to what was once an avenue of sphinxes, is a rest house serving cold beer and soft drinks. Close to here, to the left of the dirt road, is the 5th-Dynasty double **mastaba of Akhet-hotep and Ptah-hotep** (his son) ❻, high officials under the kings preceding Unas.

On the right-hand side of the road is the **mastaba of Ti** ❻, their slightly

Colourful reliefs on the walls of the Mereruka and Kagemni tombs.

older contemporary. Here, too, more remarkable scenes from daily life are depicted, including children's games (Ptah-hotep) and boat building (Ti).

THE SERAPEUM

Below the rest house is the **Serapeum** , the catacomb of the sacred Apis bull, whose rites were witnessed by Herodotus during his 5th-century BC sojourn in Egypt. Inside the labyrinthine tunnels, the mummified bulls were buried in huge stone sarcophagi set in subterranean galleries.

Situated immediately to the north are graveyards containing the mummies of other animals: baboons, now extinct in Egypt, though they can still be found in the Sudan, and ibis (three species were known to the ancients, identified by modern experts as sacred, bald and glossy: see pages 240–1). They are now very rare, though the name is frequently given locally to the cattle egret, which are seen everywhere in rural Egypt, often perched on the backs of water buffalo and cattle.

FURTHER TOMBS

Just south of the Zoser complex, across the causeway of Unas, are the **B Tombs** (separate admission charge). Not as impressive as the tombs north of the Step Pyramid, but much quieter and still beautiful, are the joint **tomb of Niankhkhnum and Khnum-hotep**, overseers of the royal manicurists to Pharaoh Niuserre (5th Dynasty); the **Tomb of Neferherenptah**, the overseer of the royal hairdressers, with a fine bird-hunting scene; and **tomb of Irukaptah**, overseer of the royal butchers.

Further along are the **Persian Tombs** (525–404 BC), some of the deepest tombs in Egypt.

Beyond here is the unfinished **Step Pyramid of Sekhemkhet** ❶, Zoser's successor (2649–2643 BC), overlooking an area where there has been a great deal of archaeological activity. Here in 1975, while looking for the tomb of Maya, an official of the Egypt Exploration Society discovered a tomb prepared for Horem-heb, Tutankhamun's general, who would become a pharaoh himself (1343–1315 BC). Eleven years

Entrance to the Zoser funerary complex.

later, Maya's tomb was finally found, but not before an enormous amount from other burials had been revealed.

Further south, accessible on foot, by donkey, horse or camel (which can be rented at the resthouse) or by 4x4 vehicle, are the **pyramid complex of Pepi I** (2332–2283 BC); the **pyramid complex of Djedkare Isesi** (2414–2375 BC) with the pyramid of a queen nearby; the **tomb of Shepseskaf** (2504–2500 BC); the **pyramid complex of Pepi II** (2278–2184 BC); and three other pyramids, one belonging to Userkare Khendjer.

In the Saqqara area alone, in fact, no fewer than 15 royal pyramids have been excavated, creating a zone more than 5km (3 miles) long. And what has been discovered thus far is only a tiny fraction of what lies still buried under the sands, including – somewhere – the tomb of Imhotep, the great architect.

The relationship of all these monuments to Memphis is made clear by the fact that "Memphis" is derived from one of them: the Pyramid of Pepi I, which was called Men-Nefer,

"established and beautiful". But the Saqqara monuments are only part of the Memphite necropolis, which actually extends north along the desert plateau beyond Giza to Abu Ruwash and southward to Dahshur and Mazghunah, a total distance of about 33km (20 miles). The two pyramids to be seen from Saqqara south across the desert in the distance are the Bent and Red pyramids at Dahshur.

DAHSHUR

The peace and quiet beauty of the palm groves around **Dahshur ❹** have attracted many of Cairo's professional class, who have built rural retreats here. The most pleasant time of year to visit the site (open daily winter 8am–4pm, summer until 5pm) is mid-winter, when a lake forms within an artificial embankment below the Black Pyramid.

The **Black Pyramid** was built of brick but unused by Amenemhet III (1842–1797 BC), one of Egypt's most colourful kings. The dark colour that gives it its name arises from the fact that it has been systematically

Tourist in the tunnel of the Red Pyramid at Dahshur.

stripped of its original white lime-stone covering. The view of the pyramid across the lake is one of the most charming in Egypt, worth the 5km (3-mile) drive from Saqqara. Its inscribed capstone is in the Egyptian Museum in Cairo.

There are two other 12th-Dynasty pyramids here, another from the 13th Dynasty, and a third not yet identified. Most striking, however, are two 4th-Dynasty pyramids, built by Snefru (2613–2589 BC). The southernmost of the two is the third-largest pyramid in Egypt and is easily distinguished, standing about 300 metres/yds further into the desert, beyond the Pyramid of Amenem-het III, not only by its bulk, but by its shape, which has led to it being called the **Bent Pyramid**: the 54-degree slope of its sides changes halfway up to an angle of 43 degrees, for reasons that may be rooted in religious symbolism, or may simply be because it had to be finished in a hurry. In 2019, the Bent Pyramid was opened to the public for the first time since 1965 (daily 9am–4pm). Visitors can now climb down a 79-metre (260ft) -long tunnel to reach two inner chambers.

The Bent Pyramid made internal use of cedar trunks imported from Lebanon, still intact, as beams, and is externally the best-preserved of all the pyramids, thanks to an ingenious construction method that made stripping its surface particularly difficult.

About 600 metres/yds northwest of the Bent Pyramid, between it and the Red Pyramid, are the remains of Snefru's mortuary temple, rededicated to Snefru during the Middle Kingdom and under the Ptolemies. Snefru was the father of Khufu, better known as Cheops, the Greek form of his name, builder of the Great Pyramid at Giza.

Visible about 2km (1.25 miles) away almost directly north is the pyramid's companion, sometimes called the **Red Pyramid**, which uses a 43-degree angle throughout its height. This is the earliest known pyramid to have been completed as a "true" pyramid, built less than 60 years after Imhotep's great discovery.

Khufu's own immediate successor, Djedefre, constructed a pyramid at **Abu Ruwash**, 10km (6 miles) northwest of Giza, which marks the northernmost limit of the Memphite necropolis; and 5km (3 miles) south of Dahshur, at **Mazghunah**, are two ruined pyramids possibly marking the southernmost limit of the necropolis.

MAYDUM

Out on a limb, 55km (34 miles) south of Saqqara is the **Pyramid of Maydum** (daily 8am–5pm), which probably dates from the end of the 3rd Dynasty or early 4th Dynasty and represents the transition from the Saqqara-type step pyramid to the "true" pyramidal forms found at Giza. This structure, with its burial chamber above ground, could have been built by an earlier king and finished by King Snefru. Also referred to as the **Collapsed Pyramid** due to the removed outer casing, it looks like a ruined tower surrounded by rubble.

Climbing the Red Pyramid.

Dahshur palm grove.

📷 THE PYRAMIDS

The magnificent Pyramids of Giza, tombs of the ancient pharaohs, are the only survivors of the Seven Wonders of the Ancient World.

The builders of the pyramids were kings of the 3rd–6th dynasties of the Old Kingdom (2686–2181 BC). About 80 structures have been identified, but most are in a poor state of preservation. Their use is still debated, but most experts agree that they were the tombs of pharaohs. The evolution of burial sites from early *mastaba* ("bench" in Arabic) to step pyramid, on to the "true" pyramids, is a fascinating journey of spiritual ideals and hit-and-miss engineering. One theory for the pyramid shape is that it represents the benben, a triangular-shaped stone found in early temples, associated with the sun-god Ra and the creation of life. In hieroglyphics, the benben is represented as a pyramid shape.

Throughout this pyramid-building period, there were five major developments. The first was Zoser's step pyramid at Saqqara, which had six steps and a burial chamber below ground. Half a century later this was copied by King Snofru, first king of the 4th Dynasty, who planned an eight-stepped pyramid covered in limestone blocks, known as the Maydum or "Collapsed" Pyramid. He also built the "Bent" Pyramid at Dahshur further north, then embarked on a third and final one, known as the Red Pyramid – the first "true" pyramid. Built with much shallower angles, this is a graceful construction, containing a single burial chamber above ground. Snofru's son Khufu learned from his father's experiments and embarked on the fifth version, which became the Great Pyramid at Giza.

In his marvellous 1947 book *The Pyramids of Egypt*, I.E.S. Edwards says that "the temptation to regard the true pyramid as a material representation of the sun's rays and consequently as a means whereby the dead king could ascend to heaven seems irresistible".

The Pyramids of Giza comprise one of the most famous sites in the world. Contrary to popular opinion, they were built not by slaves but by teams of skilled labourers and local quarrymen.

The tiny entrance into the Red Pyramid leads to steep internal passageways with almost no air circulation inside (not for the claustrophobic!).

Coloured lithograph of the pyramids, 1848.

Building materials

The pyramids that we see today would have looked very different when they were built. All the major pyramids had coverings of highly polished stone at one time, but over the millennia these have been stripped away, leaving the rough surfaces of the limestone construction blocks, which each weigh around 2 tonnes. The best remaining examples of this covering are the "Bent" Pyramid at Dahshur and towards the top of the Khafre Pyramid at Giza. The most popular covering material was polished white limestone from the Tura quarry in the Muqattam Hills, on the opposite side of the Nile overlooking Cairo.

Occasionally darker granite from Aswan was used, but because it was very hard and difficult to smooth – and because of the additional costs of transporting it along the Nile – the granite was laid in smaller bands. The best example of this is along the lower level of the Menkaure Pyramid at Giza. There is evidence that some pyramids also had small granite caps (pyramidia), often covered in electrum (gold, silver and copper mixture) to reflect the rays of the sun.

The Step Pyramid of King Zoser was the vital link between mastaba tomb and the first "true" pyramid. The idea of his massive tomb being a "stairway to heaven" for the king's "ka" or "spirit", can be clearly understood.

This tomb near the Great Pyramid of Khufu is typical of the smaller constructions built around the tomb of the pharaoh. These are the burial chambers of important ministers and viziers or other members of the royal family.

The sphinx, with a lion's body and a man's head, was carved out of a natural outcrop of rock, left behind when the causeway to Khafre's pyramid was being built.

The peculiar White Desert.

THE OASES OF EGYPT'S WESTERN DESERT

Since at least 5000 BC, man has been exploiting nature's gifts in this curve of oases in Egypt's Western Desert, the most remote of which retains its distinct culture and language.

The very word "oasis" conjures a string of romantic images – swirling sands, covered-up Bedu, mirages, the thirsty caravan stumbling into a pool of sweet water set amid swaying palms. Little of this vision has any foundation in modern reality: the caravans have all but vanished, banditry has (mostly) been suppressed, and the Bedu have traded in their camels for Toyotas. Not even the vestiges of modern man, however, in the form of asphalt, high-tension wires and water pumps, are capable of concealing the truths of a harsh climate, where shifting sands can block roads for days and where the foolhardy can still meet death by thirst, exposure or the sting of a scorpion. Nor have 21st-century wonders obscured the essential miracle of water, gushing hot or cold from barren rock to irrigate acres of garden in the midst of a wasteland.

THE SAHARA

From the Nile, the Sahara stretches 5,000km (3,000 miles) westward to the Atlantic. The world's greatest expanse of desert is broken only by dots of green, where human habitation has survived the spread of sands. Contrary to popular imagination, oases generally lie in rocky lands where wind and time have scratched out vast depressions whose depths allow natural underground aquifers to reach the surface.

Lakeside tea shop, Siwa.

In Egypt's Western Desert, a single aquifer flows north from Sudan, running in an arc of five oases roughly parallel to the Nile. Prehistoric remains show that man has been exploiting nature's gift since at least 5000 BC. Under the pharaohs the four Nileward oases – Kharga, Dakhla, Farafra and Bahariya – formed a useful line of defence against Libyan tribes.

These days the desert and the oases are popular with wealthy Cairenes and expats who happily exchange the city's noise and pollution for a weekend of

Main attractions

Faiyum oasis
Siwa oasis
Bahariya oasis
Farafra oasis
Dakhla oasis
Kharga oasis

Map on page 182

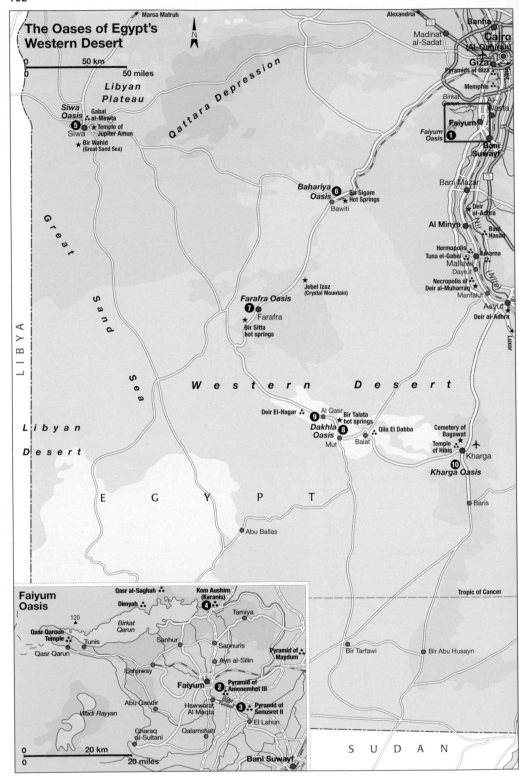

The Oases of Egypt's Western Desert

0 | 50 km
0 | 50 miles

Marsa Matruh

N

Libyan Plateau

Qattara Depression

Alexandria

Madinat al-Sadat

Banha

Cairo (Al-Qahira)

75

Giza
Pyramids of Giza

Memphis

Siwa Oasis
Gabal al-Mawta
⑤
Siwa
★ Temple of Jupiter Amun
★ Bir Wahid (Great Sand Sea)

Birkat Qarun

Al-Wasta

Faiyum ①

Faiyum Oasis

Bani Suwayf

Bani Mazar

75

G r e a t

Bahariya Oasis ⑥
Bir Sigam ★ Hot Springs
Bawiti

Deir al-Adhra

Al Minya

Bani Hasan

Hermopolis
Tuna el-Gabel
Mallawi
Dayrut
Amarna

L I B Y A

S a n d

★ Jebel Izaz (Crystal Mountain)

Farafra Oasis
⑦
Farafra
★ Bir Sitta hot springs

Necropolis of Deir al-Muharraq

Manfalut

Asyut
Deir al-Adhra

Luxor

S e a

W e s t e r n   D e s e r t

L i b y a n

D e s e r t

E   G   Y   P   T

Deir El-Hagar ◦◦ ⑨
Al Qasr
Bir Talata ★ hot springs
Dakhla Oasis ⑧
Mut
◦ Qila El Dabba
Balat

Cemetery of Bagawat ★
Temple of Hibis ★
Kharga ✈ ⑩
Kharga Oasis

Abu Ballas

• Baris

Tropic of Cancer

Bir Tarfawi •
• Bir Abu Husayn

S   U   D   A   N

Faiyum Oasis

Qasr al-Saghah ◦◦
Kom Aushim (Karanis) ④
Dimyah ◦◦

120 ▲

Birkat Qarun

Tamiya

Qasr Qaroun Temple ◦◦
Tunis
Qasr Qarun

Sanhur

Sanhuris

Ayn al-Silin

Pyramid of Maydum ◦

Ibshaway

Abu Gandir

Faiyum
② Pyramid of Amenemhet III

③ Pyramid of Senusret II

Wadi Rayyan

Hawwarat Al Maqta

Gharaq al-Sultani

Qalamshah

El Lahun

Bani Suwayf

0 | 20 km
0 | 20 miles

peace and quiet in the desert. The government is slowly becoming aware of the area's potential for adventure tourism. In coming years, the oases are likely to feel a lot less remote.

HISTORY OF THE REGION

The camel, the only beast capable of five days march without water, was introduced by invading Persians in the 6th century BC and provided the oases with their first great leap forward, matched in importance only in the 20th century with the introduction of electricity and the car. The camel helped to revive the desert economy. The new beast was no help to the Persian emperor Cambyses, however, when he dispatched his army from Kharga across the desert to Siwa in 525 BC. According to Herodotus, all 50,000 men were buried in a sandstorm.

The Ptolemies, who administered Egypt like a vast agricultural estate, set about improving the productivity of the region. Archaeological remains show that cultivation grew to its furthest extent under their rule; new wells were dug with Alexandrian technology and the complex systems of water distribution that still persist were brought into use. The Roman conquest led to a reversal of fortunes. The internal unrest of the late Roman period saw banditry increase at the expense of sedentary agriculture, while persecutions forced Christians to take refuge in the desert. Wells that had been regularly repaired and cleaned were allowed to dry up, as a general decline in population, lasting up to the 20th century, set in.

FAIYUM OASIS

Sprouting from the west bank of the Nile like a tender leaf, **Faiyum ❶** (also spelt Fayoum), some 100km (62 miles) southwest of Cairo, is referred to by some as Egypt's largest oasis. Others deny that it is an oasis at all, as it is fed not by springs but by the Bahr Yussef, an ancient Nile canal. Until recently, Faiyum was called Al-Fayyum, roughly meaning "the Sea Lake"; it was renamed when it was made capital of the modern Faiyum Governorate. An excellent road across the desert

Pigeon house, Siwa Oasis.

connects Faiyum to Cairo, two hours away (leaving Cairo from behind the Giza Pyramids). Alternatively, it can be reached from the more scenic Nile road to Upper Egypt. Some 48km (30 miles) south of Cairo's edge, the road draws parallel to the Pyramid of Maydum (see page 176).

ANCIENT HISTORY

In prehistoric times, Al-Fayyum was a marshy depression that collected the Nile's overflow during the flood season. Its wetlands were a favourite hunting ground of the Old and Middle Kingdom pharaohs until the 12th Dynasty's Amenemhet I (1991–1962 BC) drained the swamps, building a regulator at al-Lahun, the point where the river periodically breached its banks, and allowing the formation of a permanent reservoir, Lake Moeris to the Greeks, now called Lake Qarun (Birkat Qarun).

With this lake at the depression's northern end stabilised, agriculture could be introduced, and Al-Fayyum began to flourish. It received a further boost under the Ptolemies, who reclaimed more than 1,200 sq km (450 sq miles) of fertile land, reducing the lake to about twice its present size. Improved agricultural methods were introduced, and new-fangled Greek hydraulics – water wheels of a unique type still seen today) – permitted extensive terracing.

Al-Fayyum experienced an influx of Greek settlers during the Ptolemaic period. The so-called Fayyum Portraits – portraits painted on wood and attached to the faces of mummies – in the Egyptian Museum in Cairo and frequently seen in other museums around the world, show typical Graeco-Roman influences.

Al-Fayyum was an early and highly successful effort at land reclamation. Further improvements in the 19th century turned it into the "Garden of Egypt", but the 20th century unfortunately brought with it overpopulation and intensified agriculture that resulted in water overuse, the shrinking of the lake and salinisation – today the water is now more saline than seawater, and the freshwater fish and invertebrates that once thrived here have largely disappeared.

Nonetheless, agriculture is still the mainstay of the economy in the region, although now most freshwater is steered out of Bahr Yussef from the Nile by a network of irrigation canals. Cotton, rice, tomatoes and other vegetables are grown and much of the cultivated land is dotted by groves of palm trees.

FAIYUM CITY AND AROUND

With a population of more than 350,000, the city of Faiyum is itself strung out along Bahr Yussef, but has lost much of its former charm and has little to offer visitors other than the heavily eroded 12th-Dynasty obelisk of Senusert I (1971–1928 BC) on a roundabout, and four rather rickety waterwheels near the central square feeding water off the canal.

Fishermen launch a boat on Lake Qarun.

Nine kilometres (5.6 miles) southeast of Faiyum at Hawwarat Al Maqta, the **Pyramid of Amenemhet III ❷** (1842–1797 BC; daily 7am–5pm) was the site of what Herodotus in the 5th century BC called the Great Labyrinth. Amenemhet III built his first pyramid at Dahshur (the so-called "Black Pyramid"), but even after 15 years of work there were construction problems and it was abandoned. Instead, he built a new one here – which is where he is entombed. Amenemhet III is also attributed with building the Bahr Yussef canal.

Further along the same road, 21km (13 miles) southeast of Faiyum at El Lahun, stands the 12th-Dynasty **Pyramid of Senusret II ❸** (daily 7am–4pm), often called the Pyramid of Lahun. It was the tomb of Senusert II (1897–1878 BC). Perched on top of a rock, it is believed that the builders utilised the outcrop to anchor the pyramid to reduce construction time and cost. All that remains today are the mud brick internal walls; although the completed pyramid was originally encased in white limestone, an inscription found indicates that the casing was removed in the 19th Dynasty for reuse in a different structure built by Ramesses II.

AROUND LAKE QARUN

Lake Qarun is the Faiyum's greatest attraction. The western end, approached through the villages of **Sanhur** and **Ibshaway**, is the more peaceful stretch. The village of **Tunis**, where artists from Cairo have built some beautiful houses, has a potters' school and workshop started by the Swiss potter Evelyne Porret (see margin box). Several of her students ended up opening their own pottery studios nearby, and there are now several in the village. A handicrafts festival is held here every autumn.

Further on, the Ptolemaic **Qasr Qaroun Temple** (daily 8am–4pm) is thought to have been built in around 323–30 BC but has not been dated more precisely due to the absence of inscriptions. Constructed of blocks of yellow limestone, it has been restored and by climbing one of the two square spiral staircases, from the roof you can enjoy a good view of the desert to the south and west and the cultivated land to the north and east. South of here is a series of further lakes, with swimming at **Wadi Rayan**. Beaches at the lake's eastern end, where most of the hotels and fish restaurant are, fill up with Cairenes on holidays and weekends.

Past the eastern tip of the lake is **Kom Aushim**, or ancient **Karanis ❹**. Dating from the Ptolemaic period are extensive ruins of a temple dedicated to the crocodile-headed god Sobek, a Serapis temple and a later Roman temple to Zeus Amun. Karanis was located on a desert caravan route running from Memphis to Al-Fayyum, and the ruins today are found on a huge mound which rises 12 metres (40ft) from the plain surrounding Kom Aushim. At the time of building it would have been on the shores of Lake Qarun. The town was founded by Ptolemy II in the 3rd century BC, primarily as a garrison for

⊙ **Shop**

Two Swiss potters, Evelyne Porret and Michel Pastore, have a pottery school in Tunis where you can buy the school's striking ceramics. Alternatively, you can buy them from Nagada, a textile- and interior-design shop in Cairo (13 Refaah Street in Dokki; tel: 02-3748 6663; www.nagada.net).

Cooling off at Wadi Rayan's water fall.

⊙ Tip

Siwa is famous for its lush gardens and fruit orchards and is the major producer of both olive oil and dates in Egypt. More than one million date palms fill the cultivated area, and shops specialising in dates are located around Siwa's Market Square; as well as regular ones, you'll also find dates stuffed with almonds and chocolate.

his troops. The **Kom Aushim Museum** (daily 8am–4pm) displays artefacts found in the Faiyum region, including a huge head of a Roman god, pottery and coins. The museum also exhibits two of the famous "Faiyum Portraits" (others can be seen in the Cairo Museum). These were personal portraits painted on wood or linen which covered the face of the mummy towards the end of the Graeco-Roman times. Portrait subjects were usually portrayed in the prime of life, always wearing their finest clothes and jewellery, and they greatly influenced Coptic art in Egypt.

SIWA OASIS

Lying 780km (485 miles) west of Cairo, the most remote and perhaps the most engaging of Egypt's oases, **Siwa** ❺ is unusual in Egypt in that it has a distinct culture and its own language, related to the Berber languages of North Africa. It evolved as a well-watered stopping point in the desert, on the Haj pilgrimage route from the coast of northeastern Libya through to the Red Sea, and thus developed many Berber connections.

Until the 1980s when a highway was completed connecting it to the coastal town of Mersa Mahruh, it was completely isolated from the rest of the country. Today the modern Libyan border lies only 50km (31 miles) to the east.

It is not your stereotypical palm grove with a watering hole, but Siwa covers a large area of date palms and olive trees fed by underground springs – and there's a central salt lake. The oasis' population is currently about 33,000, mostly Berber, and the main centre is **Siwa town**. It is dominated by the remains of the ancient hill-top settlement known as **Shali Ghadi**, a fort-like tight collection of ruined and slowly collapsing mud-brick houses. The Siwis moved from here after it was severely damaged by unprecedented heavy rains in 1926 and instead built their houses on the surrounding plains, which now make up the town. You can climb to the top of Shali Ghadi for great views across the oasis' sea of date palms.

The **Siwa House Museum** (Sat–Thu 9am–2pm) was built thanks to a grant from the Canadian government to safeguard the architectural heritage and the uniqueness of the oasis. The house is constructed of *karshif*, a salt-impregnated dried mud, the same as the crumbling houses in Shali Ghadi, and the roof and door are made of palm fronds. Inside is a collection of everyday objects, including silver jewellery, musical instruments, traditional clothes, ceramics and handmade baskets.

On the rock of Aghurmi, 4km (2.5 miles) from the centre, sit the remains of the **Temple of Jupiter-Amun** (Sat–Thu 9am–5pm, Fri 7am–noon), or the Temple of the Oracle, which dates from the 6th century BC and is the home of the famous oracle that confirmed Alexander the Great in his status as a god – he came here to ask the god Amun (also referred to as Zeus or Jupiter-Amun) if he was really his son.

Another major historical site is **Gabal al-Mawta** (Mon–Thu 8am–2pm, Fri

Bedouin driving a tuk-tuk at Siwa Oasis.

7am–noon), less than 1km (half a mile) north of Siwa town, where tombs have been cut out of the rock of a conical ridge. Paintings cover some of the walls, especially in the tomb of Si-Amun, but much was destroyed when the tombs were used as shelters during the Italian air raids of World War II. The oasis was a strategic location for the Allied Long Range Desert Group as they penetrated deep behind German/Italian lines.

Among the orchards, palm and olive groves, lie numerous bubbling springs, and indeed, the water is so plentiful at Siwa that large salty lakes have formed and drainage is a major problem. Follow the track to the Temple of Jupiter-Amun and you will reach **Ain Juba**, the ancient Cleopatra's Spring or Fountain of the Sun, whose crystal-clear waters are said to have purifying properties. The queen herself was said to have once taken a swim, and this circular pool is now enclosed by stone. You can bathe in its balmy waters that remain a constant 29°C (84°F). The couple of cafés here have shaded areas with lounge seating, but remember the spring is used by local people so proper dress attire is required – in fact when bathing, women should also wear a t-shirt.

About 12km (7.5 miles) southwest of Siwa is the beginning of **Bir Wahid** or the "Great Sand Sea", which is the section of the Saharan sand dunes that stretches westward more than 300km (187 miles) into eastern Libya. This area around Siwa features spectacular dunes and hot- and cold-water pools and lakes. To get here you need to use local transport; plenty of tuk-tuk and 4x4 drivers wait around for tourists to offer them tours, and sandboarding is also on offer.

To the northeast of Siwa, meanwhile, is the Qattara Depression, covering about 19,605 sq km (7,570 sq miles). At an altitude of 133 metres (436ft) below sea level, this is one of the lowest points in the world, and its bottom is covered with salt pans and sand dunes.

There are an increasing number of hotels – ranging from budget hostels to a 5-star ecolodge – in the oasis, and the tourist trade is now firmly rooted as part of the local economy. But this has not managed to affect to core of the Siwi way of life yet, and it is a very conservative community. The town itself is pretty compact and the central area is easily walkable, while bicycles can be rented to get to the outlying sites.

BAHARIYA OASIS

Bahariya ⓺ is reached from Cairo by an excellent road that leads westward off the Faiyum desert road behind the Giza Pyramids. About 330 rather dull kilometres (205 miles) later is a new settlement around Egypt's only iron-ore mines. Not far beyond the mines the road descends to the **Bahariya Oasis**, which lies in a depression of the Western Desert covering around 2,000 sq km (770 sq miles). Bahariya consists of many villages, of which **Bawiti** is the largest and the administrative

Washing in a hot spring in the Sahara, Bahariya.

⊘ Tip

The desert route between Bahariya and Siwa is inaccessible because it runs through a closed military zone. As such, buses and all other traffic from Cairo goes first the 448km (278 miles) to Marsa Matruh on the Mediterranean coast (see page 270) and then heads southwest 300km (190 miles) to Siwa. Many Cairo tour operators offer 3–4-day tours out to Siwa.

centre. Agriculture is the mainstay of the economy and guavas, mangos, dates and olives are grown in jungle-like proliferation, but many local people also work in the regional iron-ore industry. Bawiti sits atop a rock out-crop. To the north, cliffs drop abruptly into a sea of palms. Bawiti's gardens spread for several kilometres along the base of this cliff. Within the gardens, land is so precious that there are few walkways and it is often necessary to paddle through the irrigation channels. The people here are known as the Waḥātī, meaning "of the oasis" in Arabic, and are generally descendants of Bedouins from Libya and various other people who settled here over time from the Nile Valley.

Archaeologists have revealed an ancient Egyptian cemetery at Bawiti, thought to be the largest ever uncovered. Excavation is still ongoing, but it is estimated that there are as many as 10,000 mummies in a 6.5km (4-mile) strip of desert dating from the Greco-Roman period. The tomb complex, dubbed the Valley of the Golden

Mummies (see box), is not open to the public, but the **Golden Mummies Museum** (daily 8am–4pm) houses 10 of the gilded mummies. The lighting is subdued to protect the delicate materials and no photography is allowed.

Around Bawiti and its sister village of **Al Qaser** are numerous ancient sites, not all accessible and not all interesting. More to the taste of tourists are the **Bir Sigam Hot Springs**, 7km (4.5 miles) east of Bawiti on the Cairo road. Here the water emerges from a gorge to flow into the surrounding orchards, some of which reach a scalding 47°C (115°F) – they reputedly have medicinal and restorative properties. Few things are as memorable as a moonlit bath under palm trees in the crisp air of the desert.

FARAFRA OASIS

From Bahariya, a well-travelled road goes southeast, through 185km (115 miles) of some of Egypt's most spectacular scenery, including the **White Desert** (see page 190) to the **Farafra Oasis ❼**. The village of some 15,000 inhabitants has some fine old mud-brick houses built up against the side of a hill, and the oasis has more than 100 natural springs. By drilling new wells, the agricultural area has expanded in recent times and nowadays it produces more than it needs, exporting the excess output to Cairo and the Nile Valley. The palm gardens on the edge of town are lush, green and full of date palms, olive trees and orange groves. Farafra is also well known for cultivating watermelons.

In spite of good road connections, Farafra feels a long way from anywhere (it is 200km/120 miles from Dakhla Oasis, the next town on the desert loop). There are no Pharaonic sites to visit, the main attraction being the village itself. Wander around and visit **Bir Sitta**, sulphurous hot springs 6km (3.75 miles) west of the village, which are now harnessed in a concrete pool. The steaming

⊘ VALLEY OF THE GOLDEN MUMMIES

Like many good discoveries, this one happened by accident in 1996 when the hoof of a donkey being ridden by the guardian of the Temple of Alexander at Bahariya disappeared into a hole. The result was the uncovering of four tombs containing over 100 mummies, many with beautifully gilded faces, dating from the Roman period of the 26th Dynasty some 2,500 years ago. More of these important tombs have been excavated, and while work at this exciting site is continuing, it is anticipated that as many as 10,000 mummies may lie in a necropolis that could perhaps cover a surface area of about 36 sq km (14 sq miles).

During the Roman period this region became wealthy from the production of wine, and this affluence is reflected in the high quality of workmanship and the gilding and painting on the sarcophagi. Most of these mummies were mummified using the old method, cartonnage, which consisted of covering the face with a mask made out of linen and plaster, onto which the mouth and eyes were painted to give a clearer image of the face, before it was decorated with colourful reliefs. Some of the best examples of the mummies, including that of a woman with gold-plated breasts, are now on view at the small Golden Mummies Museum at Bahariya.

hot 38°C (100°F) waters are said to aid muscle and joint recovery.

DAKHLA OASIS

Dakhla Oasis ❽ ("the inner oasis") measures approximately 80km (50 miles) from east to west and 25km (15 miles) from north to south. It has a population of around 80,000 spread across 16 villages. Well supplied with water from more than 500 springs and pools, the area is a major producer of wheat, mangoes, olives, dates, figs, mulberries and citrus fruits, all of which are exported throughout Egypt; indeed, no trip to Dakhla would be complete without a walk through its fragrant fields and gardens. The New Valley Project, an ambitious scheme to bring water from Lake Nasser to irrigate the Western Desert, has more than doubled Dakhla's size in recent years, but it retains more of its original laid-back charm than Kharga, to which it is connected by a 190km (120-mile) road and daily buses.

Like the rest of the Egyptian oases located in the Western Desert, Dakhla Oasis is situated inside a depression. The first important village in the depression is **Balat**. In the 13th-century it was the terminus of a direct caravan route from Asyut in the Nile Valley, and a hive of mud-brick dwellings testifies to medieval prosperity. Tombs were unearthed here in the 1980s when archaeologists found treasures including terracotta pottery and copper jewellery – now on display in the Kharga Archaeological Museum (see page 191). **Qila El Dabba** (daily 8.30am–4pm) is located about 1.6km (1 mile) to the west of the village, where mud-brick mounds conceal oval pits with descending staircases to the various antechambers and burial chambers. They belonged to the rulers of the oasis and their families in the 6th Dynasty. The most impressive are that of Pepi II, the ruler of the oasis from 2246 until 2152 BC, and Khentika, the

ruler from 2289 to 2255 BC, with the mortuary chambers being decorated with wonderful bright colours.

Dakhla's capital is **Mut**, some 35km (22 miles) further west. The town contains most of Dakhla's hotels; provisions may be bought here, and there are a number of decent restaurants, but there is little to see – the old town's mud-brick Roman settlement, which was inhabited until the beginning of the 20th century, has been allowed to fall into ruin. Located about 2km (1.25 miles) to the northwest is the most popular tourist attraction: the **Bir Talata** hot springs, with pool and rest house. The water is rich in iron and sulphur, which reputedly helps cure many illnesses. In fact, many of the other warm sulphurous springs of the oasis are equally pleasant. Thirty kilometres (18 miles) to the north of Mut on the Farafra road, the town of **Al Qasr ❾** perches on a mound between the desert and the fields and dates to the 12th century, probably built on the remains of a Roman-era settlement. Like Balat, it

⊙ **Tip**

From Bahariya, about 90km (56 miles) before Farafra, the drive passes by Jebel Izaz, otherwise known as the Crystal Mountain. This small hill of flower-like glittering calcite crystal (quartz) around a small arch in the centre is an obligatory photo stop on the route.

Dakhla Oasis greenery.

*White Desert rock
formation.*

is a honeycomb of little lanes running between mud-brick houses. Although cement is gaining ground, mud bricks are often preferred since they retain heat at night and coolness during the day. Al Qasr has wonderful gardens, a fortress and a mosque dating from the Ayyabid era and a restored madrasah (Qur'anic school).

About 10km (6 miles) further along the main road towards Farafra is the 1st-century AD sandstone temple of **Deir El-Hagar** (daily 8.30am–5pm). After being buried for many centuries by the huge sand dune that can still be seen to the south, it was uncovered, restored and partially reconstructed during the 1990s. Dedicated to the Theban deities Amun, Mut and Khonsu, construction began during the reign of Roman Emperor Nero (AD 54–68). A processional way leading from the main gateway up to the entrance has the remains of a series of round columns, which would have been part of pillared halls. The sanctuary itself was decorated with a magnificent astronomical ceiling,

*Deir El-Hagar
sandstone temple.*

dating to the rule of Hadrian (AD 117–38), with painted reliefs including an arching figure of the goddess Nut representing the sky and the god Geb who symbolises the earth. This fallen zodiac ceiling has been reassembled for viewing outside the temple building. A few small sphinxes found in this area can now be seen in the Kharga Archaeological Museum (see opposite).

KHARGA OASIS

Kharga  ("the outer oasis") is the largest and most developed of Egypt's oases, by virtue of its proximity to the Nile and because it is the seat of the New Valley Governorate. Five kilometres (3 miles) north of Asyut, a paved road leads past industrial complexes up into the desert. About 230km (143 miles) of barren gravel later, the road suddenly descends a magnificent cliff into the **Kharga Depression**, which extends southward, narrowing at its extremity, for 100km (60 miles). Descending from the plateau on the left-hand side are the remains of the

⊘ THE WHITE DESERT

West of the string of oases that make up the Bahariya settlements is a large expanse of exposed limestone known as the White Desert. Erosion by wind and rain over many thousands of years has sculpted these massive blocks into strange shapes that loom out of the desert landscape like monstrous white ghosts.

For visitors with 4x4 vehicles the area makes a popular weekend excursion from Cairo, spending a couple of nights camping in the desert. If you don't have your own vehicle, the best way to see this remarkable area is to join an organised tour from Cairo. It is also sometimes included in itineraries travelling overland from Siwa to Cairo via Bahariya, again spending the night camping under the stars.

old railway track that once linked the area to the Nile Valley.

As one crosses the flat bottom of the depression, a few straggly trees appear on the road side, inauspiciously announcing the beginning of cultivation. Then modern concrete and glass buildings and Nasserite housing blocks begin to sprout, marking the entrance to Kharga town. Visitors to the oasis should realise it is merely an administrative centre and has little of the appeal normally associated with oases such as Siwa or Bahariya, although much of the population consists of resettled Upper Egyptians, and the hotels, duck farms and packaging industries point to some degree of prosperity.

The desert town used to be an important stop on the famous Forty Days Road, a trade route connecting Sudan and the south with the oases and the north. Used to transport ivory, gold and slaves, as well as camels, it was a lucrative route, as the number of protective forts along its length testify. Camel traders still used the route until relatively recently, but these days most of the journey is completed by truck.

The **Kharga Archaeological Museum** (daily 9am–4pm) is located in the centre of town and houses two floors of archaeological finds from the Kharga and Dakhla regions. Items on display date from prehistoric times through to the Roman and Ottoman eras and include tools, jewellery and textiles, as well as sphinxes from Deir El-Hagar (see opposite), a statue of Horus, some Pharaonic reliefs and a collection of Coptic pottery.

About 2km (1.25 miles) northeast of the town, not far from the main road, lies a cluster of monuments. Chief among them is the **Temple of Hibis** (daily 8am–4pm), important as one of the few remnants of Persian rule. Built of local sandstone, it was mainly built under Darius I, but the colonnade was not completed until the reign of Nectanebo II in the 4th century BC and other additions date from the Ptolemaic period. It is well preserved, having been buried in sand until its discovery in the early 20th century, and lies in a palm grove beyond the remains of a ceremonial pool and an avenue of sphinxes. The carving style within shows local influence, while the content of the reliefs – deities, the burial of Osiris and a winged Seth struggling with a serpent – follows a standard pattern.

At the edge of cultivation to the north of the temple lies the Christian **Cemetery of Bagawat** (daily 8am–4pm), a huge area of mud-brick domes and vaults, some of which date back to the 3rd–7th centuries and therefore representing one of the earliest Christian cemeteries in the world. Some of the tombs have very vivid illustrations from the Old Testament, depicting the stories of Adam and Eve, Noah's Ark, the Exodus and even Jonah being ejected out of the whale's stomach. It is worth engaging the services of one of the guardians (tip expected) to show you the highlights of the site.

Enjoying a desert sunset near Bahariya.

Workers in a field, Asyut.

MIDDLE EGYPT

A visit to Middle Egypt, a region little changed for thousands of years until the building of the Aswan Dam, helps to explain the Middle Kingdom shift of power from Memphis to Thebes.

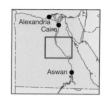

For 19th-century visitors sailing along in their *dahabeyyahs* (sailing boats), their only means of reaching Upper Egypt, the lush countryside south of Cairo offered a first taste of adventure on their great journey up the Nile.

Even today Middle Egypt offers a rich and varied experience, and those with time to spare and patience will discover a place in Egypt far removed from the mass tourism evident in parts of Upper Egypt. Many spectacular ancient tombs and temples lie in a rural landscape that has barely changed in centuries, and where the majority of farmers still work the land by hand.

In addition, Middle Egypt provides many clues to understanding Egypt's ancient history. The Middle Kingdom tombs at Bani Hasan help to explain the shift of power from Memphis to Thebes, and the change in burial patterns from the Old Kingdom pyramids at Giza and Saqqara to the tucked-away royal tombs in the Valley of the Kings at Thebes in Luxor.

Middle Egypt was also the chosen base for the most radical of all pharaohs, Akhenaten, who during the New Kingdom period, moved his capital Akhetaten from Luxor to Amarna, located 50km (31 miles) south of Al Minya. And just 50 years later Seti I built his magnificent temple complex at Abydos to confirm the restoration

Columns of Temple of Seti I.

of the old regime that Akhenaten had tried to overthrow.

SECURITY ISSUES

This region has long been associated with religious conservatism and Islamic fundamentalism, and during the 1990s, there were outbreaks of violence in the region's sprawling towns, including a series of attacks on tourists and government officials. For many years, travel in the region was unpredictable and it was a virtual no-go area for tourists; foreigners

⊙ **Main attractions**

Al Minya
Deir al-Adhra
Tombs at Bani Hasan
Amarnah
Temple of Seti I, Abydos
Temple of Dendarah

Map on page 194

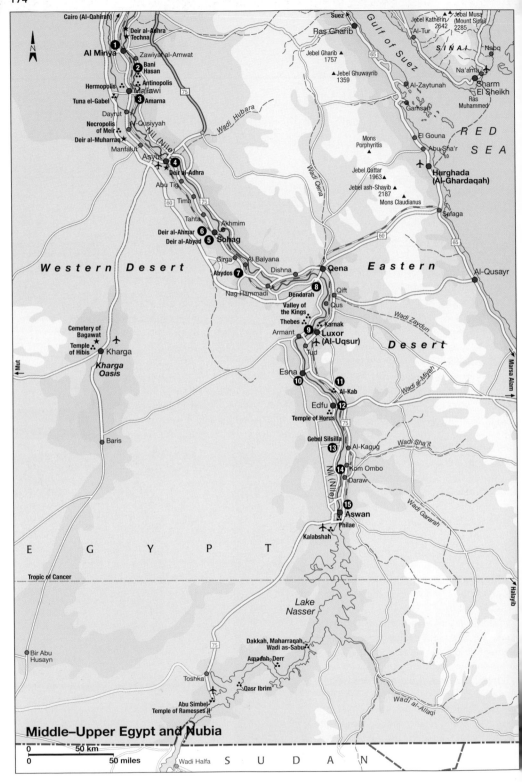

N

Cairo (Al-Qahirah)
Deir al-Adhra
Techna
Al Minya ①
Zawiyat al-Amwat
② Bani
Hasan
Hermopolis
Antinopolis
Tuna el-Gabel
Mallawi
③ Amarna
Dayrut
Necropolis
of Meir
Al-Qusiyyah
Deir al-Muharraq ★
Manfalut
Asyut ④
Deir al-Adhra
Abu Tig
Tima
60   75
Tahta
Akhmim
Deir al-Ahmar ⑥
Deir al-Abyad ⑤ **Sohag**
Girga   Al Balyana
Abydos ⑦   Dishna
Nag Hammadi
Dendarah ⑧
Valley of
the Kings
Thebes   Karnak
Armant   ⑨ **Luxor**
(Al-Uqsur)
Tud
Esna
⑩   ⑪
Al-Kab
Edfu ⑫
Temple of Horus
Gebel Silsilla
⑬   Al-Kagug
⑭ Kom Ombo
Daraw
⑮
Aswan
Philae
Kalabshah

Suez
Ras Gharib
Jebel Katherin
2642
Jebal Musa
(Mount Sinai)
2285
Al-Tur
SINAI
Nabq
Jebel Gharib
1757   65
Jebel Ghuwayrib
1359
Al-Zaytunah
Garnsah
Na'ama
Sharm
El Sheikh
Ras
Muhammed
El Gouna   RED
Abu Sha'r
Mons
Porphyritis   SEA
Jebel Dattar
1963
Hurghada
(Al-Ghardaqah)
Jebel ash-Shayib
2187
Mons Claudianus
Safaga
60   65
Al-Qusayr

Wadi Hubara
Wadi Qena
Eastern
Desert
Wadi Zaydun
Wadi al-Miyah
Marsa Alam

Western   Desert
Cemetery of
Bagawat
Temple
of Hibis   Kharga
**Kharga
Oasis**
Mut
Baris

Qena
Qift
Qus

E   G   Y   P   T
Tropic of Cancer
Wadi Sha'it
Wadi Gararah

**Lake
Nasser**
Bir Abu
Husayn
75
Dakkah, Maharraqah,
Wadi as-Sabu
Amadah, Derr
Toshka
Qasr Ibrim
Abu Simbel
Temple of Ramesses II
Wadi al-Allaqi
Halayib

Middle–Upper Egypt and Nubia

0   50 km
0   50 miles
Wadi Halfa   S   U   D   A   N

were only allowed to travel by rail or road in police convoy, and cruise ships were prevented from undertaking the 10-day journey from Cairo to Luxor, making it difficult to visit the sights independently or spontaneously.

However, no foreigners have been attacked since the 1990s and the Interior Ministry has recently eased restrictions, including cancelling the police convoys (as they have done further south, too) – replacing them instead with frequent police check points on the roads. The towns in Middle Egypt are well connected by buses from Cairo and tourists will have no problem using these. Additionally, since 2017 the classic cruise journey between Cairo and Luxor/Aswan has been revived, and cruise boats now leave regularly from Cairo heading south to Aswan and from Aswan to Cairo. Trips range in length from 10 to 15 days depending on the direction of the trip and chosen point of departure (Cairo, Aswan or Luxor). Still, bear in mind that the situation can change from place to place and from day to day, so get on-the-ground advice before visiting the region. Foreigners will certainly be turned away at road blocks at the slightest sign of trouble.

CHANGING LIFESTYLES

Until the building of the Aswan Dam, which regulates the flow of the Nile and produces hydroelectricity, the lives of the *fellaheen* (peasants) had barely changed in thousands of years. Their routines were regulated by the annual rise and fall of the river and the sowing and harvesting of crops, occasionally interrupted by a *mouled* (local saint's festival). Over the past few decades many things have changed. The towns and cities have massively expanded, often over precious agricultural land; educational opportunities have improved, offering children life chances other than farming, and almost every household now has electricity and satellite TV. Whereas it used to be the sun that dictated the pattern of the day, it is now more often than not foreign or Egyptian soaps on TV that draw the *fellaheen* home in the evening.

Farmers in Sohag.

AL MINYA

The first place of much significance on the journey south of Cairo is **Bani Suwayf**, but this is an administrative hub and of little interest to visitors. Worthier of attention is the provincial capital of **Al Minya ①**, on the west bank of the Nile, 245km (153 miles) south of Cairo. It has a good choice of hotels and a more relaxed atmosphere than the other cities in Middle Egypt, and makes a good base for exploring the surrounding sights of Deir al-Adhra (just north of the town: see below), Tuna al-Gabal, Bani Hasan and Hermopolis. Known as "the Bride of Upper Egypt" on account of it lying on the cusp of Lower and Upper Egypt, Al Minya is considered a city of the south by northerners, but if you talk to any southerner, they will deny that Al Minya is part of their heritage. It has some interesting colonial-era buildings in the old section of town near the central midan, Tahrir Square, from a time when Greek and Egyptian cotton barons did business in the area. There are also pleasant walks along the Nile,

Akhenaten Museum.

and you can see it carving its way up north, flanked by rows of green fields and palm trees. The new **Akhenaten Museum** (daily 9am–5.30pm), a striking and surprisingly large concrete pyramid-shaped building on the east bank (just over the bridge from town), showcases a collection of statues of Akhenaten and his wife, Queen Nefertiti, along with busts of their daughters, a replica of his tomb and other artefacts. A 3-metre (10ft) -tall statue of Akhenaten is located in the museum's entrance gate. Akhenaton, born Amenhotep IV, ruled Egypt from 1352 to 1336 BC. Shortly after taking power he changed his name and outlawed the age-old religion in favour of monotheistic worship of Aten, the sun-god.

DEIR AL-ADHRA

Twenty-one kilometres (13 miles) north of Al Minya on the east bank of the Nile brings the curious traveller to an extraordinary monastery, the **Deir al-Adhra** (Monastery of the Virgin), perched on top of a cliff, 130 metres (426ft) above the river, and approached by 166 steps hewn into the rock. It is said to have been founded in AD 328 by St Helena, mother of Byzantine Emperor Constantine, a dubious attribution, but one that corresponds in date at least to the archaeological evidence and the plan of the church. Coptic tradition says that the Holy Family rested here on their flight from the Holy Land, and many miracles are ascribed to its picture of the Virgin, said to weep holy oil. Hundreds of Coptic pilgrims flock here on the week-long feast of the Assumption in August and make the precipitous ascent. Visitors are welcome (although a donation is expected) and a priest will likely show you around; there's even a little café. You can get to the monastery by minibus from Minya to Samalut and then a boat across the river.

THE TOMBS OF BANI HASAN

On the east bank of the Nile 18km (11 miles) south of Al Minya, and approached by a battered old ferry, is the village of **Bani Hasan ❷**, above which 39 Middle Kingdom tombs have been cut into the cliffs (open daily 8am–5pm).

The powerful feudal lords who are buried here ruled almost independently of the Middle Empire during the 11th and 12th dynasties (2040–1782 BC). Twelve of the tombs are decorated with scenes similar to those at Saqqara, but are painted in fresco rather than carved in relief. Biographical accounts describing the military and administrative pursuits of the aristocratic owners are depicted, as well as pastimes, occupations and trades such as hunting, fishing and dyeing cloth.

Four tombs are open to the public, including the tomb of **Baqet**, an 11th Dynasty monarch, which in addition to scenes of hunting and harvesting depicts a catalogue of 200 wrestling positions; the tomb of Baquet's son, the governor **Kheti I**, presenting interesting depictions of daily life in the Middle Kingdom; the particularly grand tomb of **Amenemhat**, which has a portico and a courtyard as well as fine paintings; and the beautiful tomb of **Khnumhotep**, which includes vividly coloured scenes of his family life, trading and hunting.

MALLAWI AND HERMOPOLIS

Sixteen kilometres (10 miles) south of Bani Hasan, and back on the west bank, are the scant remains of the ancient town of **Antinopolis**, founded by Hadrian in memory of his friend and favourite, the beautiful boy Antinous, who was drowned here, perhaps willingly, as a human sacrifice.

At **Mallawi**, a few kilometres further on, a road leads to the right, bending northward through fields of sugar cane, where a little railway runs in and out to transport the crop to a nearby molasses factory. The road passes through the village of Al Ashmunin,

which partially covers the ruins of ancient **Hermopolis**, city of Thoth, the god of wisdom and writing and the reckoner of time, and therefore equated by the Greeks with Hermes. Ancient Egyptians believed that this site was the primeval hill from where the sun-god Ra emerged to create the world out of chaos.

It is worth taking the time to wander around the rather confusing overgrown hummocks, which are all that remain of this once-flourishing provincial capital. The ruins of a huge **Temple of Thoth**, two giant quartzite baboons and a church of the Virgin are about all that can be identified.

Across the fields on the edge of the desert, 7km (4.5 miles) west of Hermopolis, is the necropolis called **Tuna el-Gabel** (daily 8am–5pm) containing several interesting graves, in particular that of Petosiris, which illustrates the link between Egyptian and Greek art. Petosiris belonged to a family of high priests of Thoth during the time that Alexander liberated the Egyptians from the hated Persians at the end of

The ruins of ancient Hermopolis.

⊘ **Fact**

After Akhenaten's death, his successor, Tutankhaten (later to change his name to Tutankhamun) abandoned Akhetaten for Memphis and Thebes and reinstated Amun-Ra as the chief god of Egypt. Akhetaten quickly went into decline.

the 4th century BC. In the decoration of his fine tomb he chose to have the conventional offering scenes depicted in the fashionable new Greek style. Here the stiff virgins characteristic of the New Kingdom are replaced by a parade of buxom young women in fluttering see-through draperies, and the men are wearing hitched-up *gallibiyas* and straw hats, not unlike the people visible on the roads of Middle and Upper Egypt today.

There has been serious ongoing archaeology work in the Tuna el-Gabel area recently, with a series of impressive finds. In 2018, eight tombs were discovered containing 40 coffins of Pharaonic priests, one of which is believed to have been a high priest to the god Thoth; the priest's mummy was decorated with blue and red beads and bronze gilded sheets. More than 1,000 ushabti statues, jewellery, potteries and jars, a gold mask and 40 sarcophagi, some bearing the names of their owners in hieroglyphics, were also found in the tombs. Furthermore, in 2019 it was announced that the well-preserved mummies of

more than 50 men, women, children and their pets had been discovered in a family grave dating back to the beginning of the Roman era.

AMARNA

Returning to Mallawi, the next site of importance is **Amarna** ❸ (daily 8am–4pm Oct–May, until 5pm in summer), the open plain on the east bank of the Nile where the rebel pharaoh Akhenaten and his wife Nefertiti made their brief bid to escape from the stuffy and over-bearing establishment of Thebes in the 14th century BC. Their new capital Akhetaten, the Horizon of Aten, was the capital of Egypt for only 30 years, until Akhenaten's death in 1336 BC. His successor moved back to Thebes, and this city was abandoned for ever.

Though the story is appealing and romantic, the site of Akhetaten in the hot dusty bowl of the Amarna plain can be disappointing, as the ruins are hard to understand, even though the original outlines of the buildings are still discernible. Archaeologically, however, it has yielded a vast amount

The Northern Palace at Amarna.

of information and some beautiful objects, including the famous head of Nefertiti (now in Berlin).

The site is extensive, as the city of Akhetaten spread out over 14km (9 miles). The easiest way to visit is to hire a taxi from Mallawi and take the irregular car ferry at Et-Till, 5km (3 miles) south of Mallawi, which lands close to the most visited parts of Amarna. Make sure you tell the taxi exactly which tombs you want to see and how long you are staying. There are 25 tombs but not all are open to the public, and only five have light, so bring a torch.

From what remains of buildings and frescoes, Akhetaten seems to have been a bright and cheerful place reflecting the king's delight in his family and the everyday world. "Because Thou has risen," he says in his wonderful *Hymn to the Sun*, found in the tomb of Ay, "all the beasts and cattle repose in their pastures; and the trees and green herbs put forth their leaves and flowers. The birds fly out of their nests; and their wings praise Thy Ka as they fly forth. The sheep and goats of every kind skip about on their legs; and feathered fowl and birds also live, because Thou hast risen for them."

From the landing stage at Et-Till, a dirt track follows the original Royal Road, which cuts straight to the centre of Akhetaten. Remains of the Great Temple of Aten (now covered in Muslim tombs), the Archives where the famous Amarna letters were found, and the Royal Palace, are discernible just south of Et-Till.

A pedestrian bridge, from where the royal couple waved at their subordinates, connected the Royal Palace with the State Palace across the Royal Road. The famous unfinished head of Nefertiti (now resident in Berlin) was found in a sculptor's workshop in the residential quarters, now mostly covered by sand.

Of the 19 southern tombs, located about 8km (5 miles) from the landing,

that of Ay (prepared during Ay's lifetime but never used, as he was actually buried in Thebes) is undoubtedly the finest, with wall paintings depicting street and palace scenes, and Akhenaten and his wife presenting Ay with a golden collar. The tomb of Mahu, Akhenaten's chief of police, is the best-preserved on the site.

To the north, outlines of Nefertiti's Northern Palace and courtiers' villas can be traced. Incorporating reception rooms, bedrooms, bathrooms with basins and toilets, kitchens, and storerooms, the houses were surrounded by gardens with trees and pools. Air condition was affected by wind catchers, which faced the northerly breezes. These architectural details can be seen in paintings in the Egyptian Museum in Cairo (see page 134). The seven northern tombs often show depictions of daily life in Akhetaten, as well as the royal couple and their family.

ASYUT

A few kilometres further south on the west bank, **Asyut ❹** (Assiut) has

Central Asyut.

a population of almost half a million and stands on a bend in the river 378km (236 miles) south of Cairo. In the 19th century it marked the end of the Forty Days Road from Darfur in Sudan, and slaves from Sudan and the Libyan desert were sold in its important market. Then, thanks to the cotton boom during the late 19th and early 20th centuries, its wealthy merchants built palatial villas here and lived on a grand scale, with black-tie dinners and weekly races. Most of these families eventually moved north, however, and Asyut is rather provincial today. But it is the regional capital and the largest town between Cairo and Aswan. There's a decent crop of hotels, a pleasant corniche with cafés and juice bars, and the airport is served by daily EgyptAir flights from Cairo.

The large Coptic community here takes care of several early monasteries north and further south of the town including the **Deir al-Muharraq** (Burnt Monastery), 12km (7.5 miles) north of Asyut. It is claimed that Mary and Jesus spent six months and 10 days here on their flight into Egypt from King Herod, their longest stay in Egypt. Copts believe that the **Church of al-Adhra** (Church of the Virgin), built over an ancient cave and consecrated in AD 60, is the oldest church in Egypt. There are still about 120 Coptic monks in residence; you can visit by taxi from Asyut and a priest will show you around (donations expected).

SOHAG

South of the town of **Sohag**, 115km (71 miles) south of Asyut, are two of Egypt's most visited monasteries. The **Deir al-Abyad** ❺ (White Monastery; daily 7am–dusk), founded in the 5th century by St Shenuda, one of the fathers of Coptic Christianity, has many striking similarities with Pharaonic temple design and is built of white limestone (hence its name). The monastery was once home to over 2,000 monks, but these days only about 25 remain.

Nearby **Deir al-Ahmar** ❻ (Red Monastery; daily 7am–midnight) was founded by Besa, one of Shenuda's disciples, and is dedicated to St Bishoi. Monasticism started in Egypt around AD 320, after Pachom from Esna founded the first community. He first served in the Roman Army, which convinced him that his monks should be strictly disciplined and of service to the community. Shenuda, at the end of the 4th century, went even further and introduced strict rules for every aspect of a monk's life. The monastery today is occupied by a growing number of monks, and several new churches at the site serve the Coptic communities of the surrounding villages. In this case the name is derived from the red (burnt) brick on the outer walls.

ABYDOS

Abydos ❼ (daily 7am–6pm; bring a torch), 165km (103 miles) north of Luxor and 10km (6 miles) southwest of Al Balyana, is one of Egypt's most

Deir al-Abyad near Sohag.

spellbinding spots. The area was used as a burial place from *c.*4000 BC until well into Christian times, around AD 600. The site has been systematically excavated since 1977, and many important finds have come to light, including the tombs of kings from before the 1st Dynasty, causing Egyptian chronology to be extended by a zero dynasty. In 1991 two large ships carrying the dead were found, thought to be 5,000 years old. The earliest known tomb of a pharaoh, dating back to around 3150 BC, was discovered in 1993, containing some of the oldest known examples of hieroglyphic writing.

In the dawn of history, Wepwawet, the jackal deity and the original god of Abydos, roamed the desert's edge guarding the ancestral burial grounds below the dip in the western hills. At sunset the ancients imagined the golden glow to be the staircase to the afterworld and they wished to be buried at its foot.

PLACE OF PILGRIMAGE

Most of all, however, Abydos is associated with the legend of Osiris. From the Middle Kingdom onwards, every pharaoh as well as hundreds of thousands of pilgrims left some token of their presence or a false stele at Abydos, hoping to gain favour with Osiris in his capacity as Judge of the Court of the Hereafter. The area is thus a mass of funeral stele, burial grounds, former temples and memorials. But it was the New Kingdom pharaoh Seti I (1291–1278 BC) who was responsible for the most beautiful tribute to Osiris, his seven-sanctuaried temple, the Great Temple of Seti I.

Seti came to power around 1291 BC, some 40 years after the monotheistic regime of Akhenaten at Al-Amarnah had collapsed. The nation was still recovering from the shock of this apostasy, and Seti wished to reaffirm his faith in the traditional gods and restore them to their former pre-eminence. To this end he rallied all the resources of the land to build and adorn a new temple at Abydos, in which he recorded his devotion to the six main gods: Osiris, his wife Isis, their son Horus, Amun-Ra, Ra Hor Akhty and Ptah. He also

⊘ Tip

Tour operators in Luxor organise full-day tours combining Abydos and Dendarah. Alternatively, hire a private taxi from Luxor and go at your own pace. However, it's a long day; expect about 10 hours to explore both sites and the driving.

Exquisite reliefs inside the Second Hypostyle Hall, Temple of Seti I.

⊘ THE OSIRIS LEGEND

Legend relates (with multiple variations) how the just ruler Osiris was killed by his evil and jealous brother Seth. Isis, Osiris' weeping sister/wife, faithfully searched the banks of the Nile for his dismembered body. The pieces of Osiris were buried at different places in both Upper and Lower Egypt, but importantly his head was believed to be buried at Abydos. She eventually found all the pieces, except for the penis, and bound them carefully together with strips of cloth. Isis used her magical powers to revive her husband just long enough to conceive their son Horus. She fashioned a phallus from Nile mud, turned herself into a bird and, hovering over the body of her husband, became pregnant.

It was at Abydos that Osiris was resurrected and assumed his powers as the lord and judge of the afterlife.

honoured his forebears by recording their names in a list of kings. This assemblage of 76 cartouches has been of immense importance to researchers and historians.

TEMPLE OF SETI I

The temple is entered through a mostly ruined pylon leading into the **First Hypostyle Hall**, which was completed by Seti's son Ramesses II. Beyond this is the **Second Hypostyle Hall** with 24 papyrus columns, decorated with some of the finest reliefs in the whole country. These exquisite reliefs on fine white limestone show Seti engaged in performing a multitude of rites in honour of Osiris and the company of gods. The reliefs on the walls on the right are particularly noteworthy.

Further on are the seven sanctuaries of the six mentioned gods and of Seti himself; these would have contained their barques behind closed wooden doors. Seti himself died before the temple was completed, leaving his son Ramesses II to finish the decoration of the courtyards and colonnades, in a clearly less sophisticated way.

In the south wing of the temple, entered from the Second Hypostyle Hall is a long passage known as the **Gallery of the Kings**, where Seti I and his son Ramesses are shown honouring all the kings that came before them, from King Menes to Seti I. North of Seti's temple is the much less well preserved **Temple of Ramesses II**, his son, dedicated to the same gods.

The cult of Osiris and Isis later moved south to the Cataract Region, but the annual festival of Abydos lingered for almost 400 years. Every January the great drama was re-enacted, with a cast of thousands – crowds of pilgrims came from all over Egypt to participate. A gold-plated image represented Osiris; the pharaoh himself took the part of Horus; and the priests and priestesses masqueraded as Wepwawet, Seth, Isis, Nephthys and supporting cast.

The Christians finally sacked the temple in AD 395.

Vestiges of powerful magic still cling to the sacred precincts. It is not

The Osireion, behind Temple of Seti I.

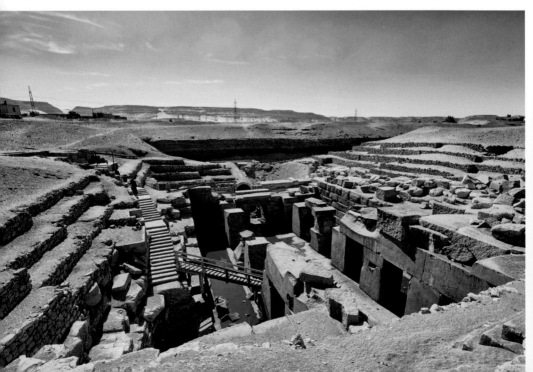

unusual to see local women circling the pool of the mysterious building, often said to be the burial place of Osiris but in fact a cenotaph of Seti I, called the **Osireion**. In more recent times the temple attracted the Englishwoman Dorothy Eady, who believed she was the reincarnation of a temple priestess and Seti's lover. She spent the last 25 years of her life living at Abydos, where she provided archaeologists with details of how temples worked in ancient times. Known as Umm Seti, the Mother of Seti, she died in 1981.

DENDARAH

Excursions from Luxor and the longer Nile cruises include the **Temple of Dendarah** ❽ (daily 7am–6pm), located on a bend in the river 60km (37 miles) north of Luxor on the west bank, opposite the provincial modern town of **Qena** (about halfway between Abydos and Luxor). Like those of Esna, Edfu, Kom Ombo and Philae, and others lost under Lake Nasser, the temple dates from the Ptolemaic period, and is around 1,000 years more recent than the New Kingdom temples.

The temple is dedicated to Hathor, the cow goddess, known as "The Golden One", goddess of women, who was also a sky and tree goddess, sometimes equated with Aphrodite by the Greeks. As in Kom Ombo and Philae, the sick travelled here to be cured by Hathor's healing powers.

Despite being damaged by the Christians, who chipped out the faces and limbs of many figures, Dendarah is one of the best-preserved Egyptian temples and its adjunct structures can all be easily identified. It has retained its girdle wall, its Roman gate, two birth houses and a sacred lake, as well as its crypts, stairways, roof and chapels.

Its most distinctive feature is its great hypostyle hall, with its 24 Hathor-headed columns and a ceiling showing the outstretched Nut, the sky-goddess, swallowing the sun at evening and giving birth at morning. The zodiac on the ceiling is the best-preserved in the whole of Egypt. The hall was decorated during the reign of Tiberius and is dated AD 34.

The dark courts and crypts in the interior give evidence of various festivals in which Hathor was involved. The most important of these feasts was the annual New Year Festival, during which the goddess was carried up the western staircase to the roof for the ritual known as the "Union with the Disc", returning down another staircase to the east. On the walls of the stairways the order of procession of the gods in full regalia is clearly shown. There are interesting graffiti on the roof, including names of Napoleon's soldiers. On the back wall of the temple is one of the very few contemporary representations of Cleopatra with Caesarion, her son by Julius Caesar.

Beside the birth house stand the ruins of one of the earliest structures of the Christian era, a basilica built in sandstone, the interior of which features a beautifully carved niche.

Beautiful detail inside the Temple of Dendarah.

Elephantine Island.

Columns in the Great Hypostyle
Hall at Karnak.

UPPER EGYPT

The monuments of Upper Egypt are breathtaking. The great temples of Luxor and Karnak and the funerary complexes of the west bank form the largest agglomeration of ancient buildings in the world.

During the 19th century, as more and more archaeological discoveries were being made and the mystery of hieroglyphics unravelled, wintering in Egypt became fashionable for the well-to-do. They would hire a private houseboat, complete with crew and cook, at the port of Cairo, and sail upstream, stopping here and there to explore the ruins and visit local dignitaries. Their impressions were conscientiously set down day by day in letters home or in Morocco-bound diaries, as they sat under the awning on deck, glancing up to watch the palm-fringed shore slipping peacefully by.

Luxor (ancient Thebes) was the high point on their journey, a concentration of magnificent temples and tombs, with comfortable hotels that offered the chance to get off the boat and relax in the superb winter climate.

It is still possible to spend a fulfilling week or two in Luxor, relaxing by the Nile, visiting the temples on the east bank and making forays over to the west bank to see the ancient necropolis of Thebes. But for a truly memorable visit, make time to travel south of Luxor to Aswan, along a 215km (135-mile) stretch of river that is both picturesque and rich in ancient sites; Esna, Edfu and Kom Ombo all offer spectacular Ptolemaic

Daraw Camel Market.

temples, and Aswan, the regional capital and an important university town, has one of the most beautiful settings in Egypt. With fewer monuments, it is the ideal place to end your trip, shopping in the hassle-free souq or circling its many islands by felucca.

The best time to make the journey down south is in the cooler months between October and April. Most of the luxury cruise boats run three-, five-, or eight-day trips starting from Luxor or Aswan (see page 228).

⊙ Main attractions
Karnak
Luxor Temple
Luxor Museum
Mortuary temples
Valley of the Kings
Tombs of the Nobles
Esna
Edfu
Kom Ombo
Aswan

Map on page 194

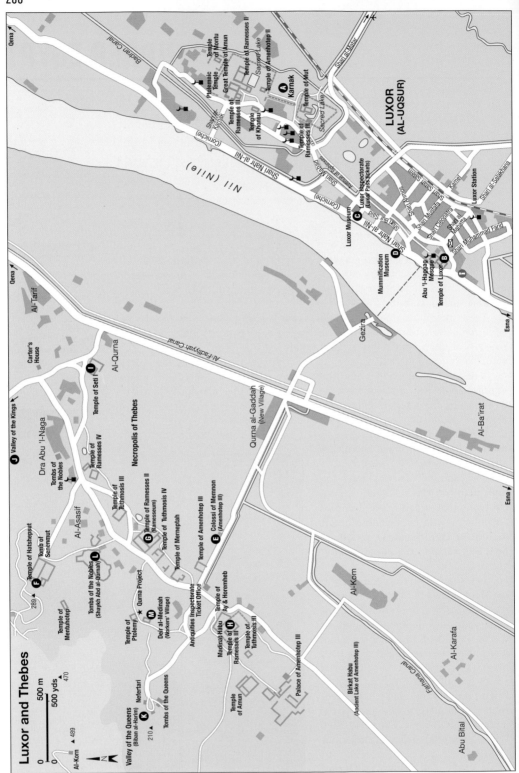

208

Luxor and Thebes

0 ──────── 500 m
0 ──────── 500 yds

N

LUXOR (AL-UQSUR)

Qena

Qena

Badran Canal

Sharī al-Matar

Sharī al-Karnak (Corniche)

Temple of Montu

Temple of Amun

Temple of Ramesses II

Sacred Lake

Temple of Amenhotep II

Ptolemaic Temple

Great Temple of Amun

Ⓐ Karnak

Temple of Mut

Temple of Ramesses III

Temple of Khonsu

Temple of Ramesses III

Sacred Lake

Shari Nahr al-Nīl (Corniche)

Nīl (Nile)

Al-Fadliyyah Canal

Luxor Museum

Shari al-Matar

Sharī Mustafa

Amūn of Sphinxes

Ⓒ Luxor Inspectorate (Luxor Pass tickets)

Mummification Museum

Shari Nahr al-Nīl

Ⓓ

Gezira

Abu 'l-Haggag Mosque

Ⓑ Temple of Luxor

Shari al-Mahatta

Shari Cleopatra

Shari Salim Salim

Sharī al-Mustafa

Kamel

Luxor Station

Shari al-Salakhana

Shari Mohammad Farid

❶

Esna

Esna

Necropolis of Thebes

Al-Tarif

Carter's House

Al-Qurna

Temple of Setī I **❶**

Ⓙ Valley of the Kings

Dra Abu 'l-Naga

Tombs of the Nobles

Temple of Ramesses IV

Al-Asasif

Temple of Tuthmosis III

Temple of Senenmut

Ⓕ Temple of Hatshepsut

289 ▲

Temple of Mentuhotep

Tombs of the Nobles (Shaykh Abd al-Qurnah) **Ⓛ**

Qurna Project ★

Temple of Ramesses II (Ramesseum) **Ⓖ**

Temple of Tuthmosis IV

Temple of Merneptah

Temple of Amenhotep III

Ⓔ Colossi of Memnon (Amenhotep III)

Temple of Ptolemy

Deir al-Medinah (Workers' Village) **Ⓜ**

Antiquities Inspectorate Ticket Office

Temple of Ay & Horemheb

Madīnat Hābu **Ⓗ**

Temple of Ramesses III

Temple of Tuthmosis III

Palace of Amenhotep III

Al-Kom

Birkat Habu (Ancient Lake of Amenhotep III)

Al-Ba'irat

Quna al-Gaddah (New Village)

Valley of the Queens (Biban al-Harim)

210 ▲

Nefertari **Ⓚ**

Tombs of the Queens

Temple of Amun

Al-Karafa

Farfana Canal

Abu Bital

Al-Kom

▲ 489

470 ▲

LUXOR

Luxor ❾, 675km (420 miles) south of Cairo, is the most important and the most spectacular site in all Egypt. Al-Uqsur (the Palaces) is the Arabic name for ancient Thebes, the splendid capital city of the New Kingdom (1570–1070 BC) rulers, whose glory still glowed in the memories of classical writers a thousand years after its decline. Here the booty of foreign wars, tribute and taxes poured into the coffers of the pharaohs of the 18th and 19th dynasties, each of whom surpassed his predecessor in the construction of gorgeous temples and tombs, creating a concentration of monuments that rivals that of any imperial city before or since.

ORIENTATION

The east bank, where the sun rises, was the side of the living, and the location of the two great temple complexes of Luxor and Karnak; the first in the modern city centre and the latter a 30-minute walk north. Today, most of the hotels and restaurants are on the east bank, as well as the souqs, banks and offices. The west bank is the place of the dead, a vast necropolis containing the tombs and mortuary temples of the New Kingdom pharaohs. There are fewer hotels and restaurants on the west side, but it is favoured by independent travellers who want closer contact with the locals or peace and quiet away from the many tour groups.

A ferry (from the landing on the Corniche near Luxor Temple) runs between the east and west banks, and there is also a road bridge, 6km (3.75 miles) south of town.

LUXOR'S TEMPLES

Under the New Kingdom pharaohs, when Thebes became the seat of power, Amun, once just a local god, took on the qualities of Ra, the sun-god of Heliopolis, becoming Amun-Ra and rising to a position of ascendancy over all the multifarious gods of Egypt. With his consort Mut and his son Khonsu he formed the Theban Triad.

Two tremendous temple complexes were established in honour of these gods, the Temple of Karnak and the Luxor Temple. Both were built over extensive periods of time and were constructed from the inside outwards; the original founders built sanctuaries on spots that had probably been venerated for centuries, and successive pharaohs added progressively more grandiose courtyards, gateways and other elaborations.

The temple complex of Amun-Ra at **Karnak** Ⓐ (daily 6am–5.30pm in winter, 6am–6.30pm in summer; to get there, walk north along the Corniche or take a taxi or calèche) and its neighbouring buildings, 3km (1.75 miles) north of the centre of Luxor, constitute the most awe-inspiring of all the Egyptian monuments. Apart from the immense conglomeration of elements that makes up the temple itself, it also has a particularly complicated plan. Unlike most other temples

⊙ Tip

The wealth of sites in and around Luxor make sightseeing both exhilarating and exhausting. To get the most out of your time wear light and loose cotton clothes, comfortable shoes, sunglasses, sunhat and sun lotion, take plenty of water with you, and try to read up on the sights beforehand. A torch for dark corners is also useful.

Carved columns with a guide for scale, Karnak.

in Egypt, it was developed over many centuries on both an east–west axis, with six pylons, and on a north–south axis with four pylons. These 10 pylons, together with intervening courts, halls and enclosures, surround the nucleus of the sanctuary.

Karnak, known as Ipet-Sut, "The Most Esteemed of Places", was one of the most important religious and intellectual centres in antiquity, and for more than 13 centuries successive pharaohs were proud to enhance its magnificence.

Put aside two half days to see the most important monuments, one starting early in the morning to be seduced by the temple's mystery, and one in the afternoon when the stones and carvings glow in the sun.

The local god Amun-Ra became more important during the early Middle Kingdom, and during the 12th Dynasty several temples were erected in his honour. Their foundations were found underneath the later temples. The origins of the Karnak Temple as we now see it are attributable to the royal

family of the 18th Dynasty (1550–1292 BC), who made Amun-Ra the state god, and whose rise to power brought the city of Thebes to the heights of glory. Three Tuthmoses and Queen Hatshepsut were responsible for most of the inner parts of the temple.

An avenue of ram-headed sphinxes leads to the unfinished **First Pylon**, built by Nectanebo I during the 30th Dynasty. The **First Court**, enclosed by colonnades on both sides, includes several shrines: the **Temple of Seti II**, the **Colonnade of Taharga** and the **Temple of Ramesses III**. The **Second Pylon**, built using blocks from earlier structures, leads into one of the architectural marvels of the world, the **Great Hypostyle Hall**. Seti I (1291–1278 BC) completed the mighty work started by Amenhotep III, and built the largest hall of any temple in the world, with 134 huge columns, covering an area of 6,000 sq metres (19,700 sq ft). It was completed under Seti's son, Ramesses II (1279–1212 BC), who placed the colossi of himself at the entrance. The northern walls are decorated with

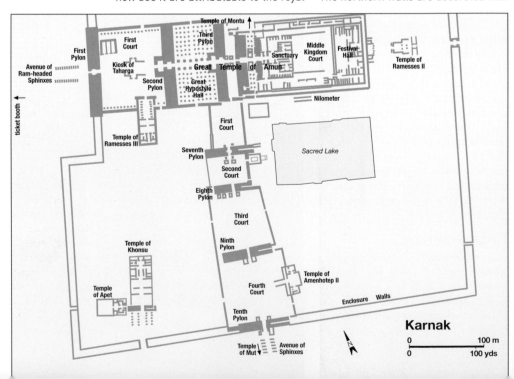

Karnak

remarkable bas-reliefs of Seti I's battles in Syria and Lebanon, while the southern walls show similar themes, in a much cruder style, of Ramesses II's Battle of Kadesh.

Behind the Fourth Pylon lies the inner core and oldest part of the temple, starting with the Hypostyle Hall of Tuthmosis III. In this court stands one of the obelisks erected by his step-mother Hatshepsut (the second toppled over centuries ago and has been placed near the **Sacred Lake** (see page 216). Hatshepsut dominated the family after her husband and brother Tuthmosis II's death in 1518 BC. Tuthmosis III despised his coregent/stepmother, and as soon as she was out of the way, proceeded to hack her name away from cartouches, substituting his own. He walled up most of the 320-tonne obelisks that she had erected, thus unwittingly preserving her work in pristine condition.

Tuthmosis III (1504–1450 BC) proceeded to reign long and brilliantly, waging 17 successful campaigns and extending the Egyptian Empire from Syria to the Sudan. He brought back thousands of prisoners and immense quantities of booty, as well as new varieties of trees and plants, new ideas and new fashions. The annals of his career are inscribed on the walls surrounding the **sanctuary** and extend to his great **Festival Hall** and to the southern courts.

Succeeding generations added new pylons, courts and subsidiary temples, all lavishly and colourfully illustrating their conquests, like a great stone history book. Amenhotep III contributed a pylon and the **Temple of Mut**. Though the capital moved away to the Delta and the importance of Thebes declined thereafter, Karnak continued to be expanded and embellished, such was the awe in which Amun-Ra was held. At the end of the Ramesside line the **Temple of Khonsu** was built, in which reliefs clearly show the rise to kingly status of the priests.

In the 6th century BC the Persians did a certain amount of damage when they sacked Thebes, but the incoming Greeks set things to rights. Alexander,

The Sacred Lake, Karnak.

⊘ TEMPLE STRUCTURE

Temples in general all followed the same principles. For the ancient Egyptians, the precinct represented a little replica of the cosmos at the time of the creation. It was set apart from the everyday world and demarcated by a mud-brick girdle wall. Usually, but not always, the temple had an east–west axis, so that the rising or setting sun could strike right into its innermost recesses. Giant wedge-shaped pylons or gateways flanked tall gold-plated doors and were decorated on the outside with enormous reliefs of the pharaoh symbolically subduing his enemies.

Within the gates were courtyards, with small kiosks or barque stations (storage places for the boats of Egyptian gods) for visiting gods. Other shrines appeared in later times, including the birth rooms in which the divine progeniture of the pharaoh was established. Before the entrance of the covered part of the temple stood enormous statues of the pharaoh in human or animal form and/or obelisks. Inside was a hypostyle hall with a forest of columns. All was lavishly decorated.

Proceeding through a vestibule into the offering court and then the inner parts of the temple, the ground rises by degrees, the roof gets lower until the sanctuary, which represents the mound of creation, is quite dark. Only the pharaoh and the priests were allowed into this holy of holies, where a gold-plated image of the presiding god was kept.

⊘ Fact

From time to time the temple god would be brought out from his seclusion, suitably dressed and perfumed, to receive offerings of bread and beer, or to pay visits to other gods. Probably the image could be made to move its hand or bow its head.

his brother Philip Arrhidaeus (who replaced the original sanctuary with one of rose granite) and, subsequently, the Ptolemies restored and continued to make additions to the temple.

LUXOR TEMPLE

Luxor Temple ⓑ (daily 6am–9pm, until 10pm in summer) is relatively long (230 metres/780ft) and narrow, and lies in the centre of Luxor. Like Karnak Temple, to which it was connected by the 3km (1.75-mile) -long processional Avenue of Sphinxes, it was dedicated to the Theban Triad, but Amun of Luxor had a slightly different form and function, as a divinely fertile figure. Of the 1,350 human-headed, lion-bodied sphinxes that once lined the Avenue of Sphinxes, 650 have recently been excavated and restored in a project that began in 2005 and was completed in 2017. They are now open to the public, and today visitors can walk the entire 3km (1.75-mile) stretch of the avenue on a broad stone path between them to reach each of the two temples. There

are some sphinxes lost to the ravages of time, but almost every pedestal remains.

Known as the "Harem of the South", Luxor Temple was the residence of Amun-Ra's consort Mut and her son Khonsu, while the statue of Amun was kept in Karnak. During the annual Opet Festival his statue was brought in a procession of holy barques to be reunited with his wife. Nowadays, during the annual *mouled* (festival) of Abu 'l-Haggag (Luxor's patron saint), feluccas are carried up to the mosque of Abu 'l-Haggag (see opposite) in a ceremony that is a survival of the ancient festival.

Nineteenth-century visitors to Luxor observed that the glorious city of Thebes had shrunk to a miserable village piled on top of metres of dirt and debris. Only the heads of the colossi of Ramesses, half the granite obelisk and the capitals of the columns were still visible; and even these were battered and blackened with smoke. Excavations of the site started in 1885 when the houses

The mosque of Abu 'l-Haggag at Luxor.

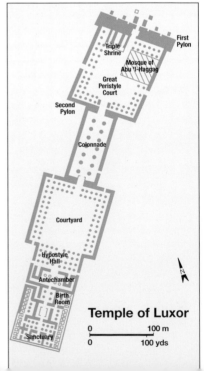

Temple of Luxor

First Pylon
Triple Shrine
Mosque of Abu 'l-Haggag
Great Peristyle Court
Second Pylon
Colonnade
Courtyard
Hypostyle Hall
Antechamber
Birth Room
Sanctuary

0   100 m
0   100 yds

were removed piece by piece, but the people of Luxor took a stand when it came to removing the mosque of Abu 'l-Haggag, built in 1077, so it was left in situ, hanging above a corner of the courtyard built by Ramesses II. It has since been restored.

The Luxor Temple is easier to grasp than Karnak, as it is much smaller and the major part was built by one pharaoh, Amenhotep III (1386–1349 BC), with substantial later additions by his successors. The gigantic **First Pylon**, on which his triumphs were displayed, was built by Ramesses II. It was originally fronted with six colossi of the pharaoh, but only one standing and two seated statues remain. One of the obelisks still stands in place, but its twin, presented to the French in 1829, adorns the place de la Concorde in Paris. **The Great Peristyle Court**, which today incorporates the medieval mosque, was also added by Ramesses II, and in the southern half stand more of his colossal granite statues.

Amenhotep III, who built the **colonnade** with papyrus-bud columns,

was succeeded by his son, Akhenaten (1350–1334 BC), the revolutionary pharaoh who moved the capital away from Thebes to Al-Amarnah (see page 45). His reforms collapsed immediately after his death, however, and the capital returned to Thebes, the old hierarchy of priests was re-established, and his successors Tutankhamun and Horem-heb dutifully took up the embellishment of the Luxor Temple again. On the walls of the processional colonnade, the skilful sculptors of Tutankhamun depicted the annual Opet Festival (see opposite) showing the gods of Karnak, accompanied by a procession of priests, musicians, singers, dancers and sacred cows, parading down to Luxor on the west, and going back to their own temple on the east.

During the restoration of the **Second Court**, also built by Amenhotep, a large cache of statues was found, now in the Luxor Museum (see page 214). Beyond this, the **Hypostyle Hall**, with 32 columns representing papyrus bundles, leads into a smaller hall. In Roman

Great Peristyle Court columns and colossi.

⊘ TEMPLE COLUMNS

You will see two main types of column in Egypt's ancient temples. The first imitate natural vegetation, with bases and capitals shaped like bundles of papyrus or lotus flowers (depicted either closed or open) or palms (very common in the Ptolemaic temples). Sometimes, in hypostyle halls, they are clustered thickly together to represent the marsh of creation, a conception that was often completed by a ceiling adorned with pictures of heavenly bodies to recreate the sky. Some of the best examples of vegetal columns are found in the hypostyle halls in the Karnak and Luxor temples.

The second type of column is the more functional polygonal column, an early form of the Doric column, often with fluted sides.

Ceremonial axe in the Luxor Museum.

Main entrance to the temple complex of Amun-Ra, Karnak.

times this was converted into a church, and some of the Christian frescoes are still visible.

The **sanctuary** area dates from the reign of Amenhotep III. In the **Birth Room**, his mother Mutemwia is shown being impregnated by Amun and giving birth to the infant pharaoh, whose body and spirit are formed on the potter's wheel by the ram-headed creator-god Khnum. The facts of life are indicated with delicate symbolism.

A return to the floodlit temple at night allows one to take a better look at its magnificent reliefs.

LUXOR MUSEUM

Luxor Museum Ⓒ (daily 9am–4pm, 5–10pm in summer, 9am–9pm in winter), north along the Corniche, houses a small but impressive collection found in the Luxor area. The objects have been carefully placed and lit, and are well labelled, so that every single item looks like a masterpiece. Most of the museum's ground floor is dedicated to the period of the New Kingdom, and works include a beautiful bust of

the young pharaoh Tuthmosis III and a fine wall painting of Amenophis III. A further wing is devoted to the glory of Thebes during the New Kingdom and two royal mummies. Another gallery on the ground floor (near the exit) displays an important cache of statues that were discovered in 1989 excavations in Luxor Temple, under one of the courtyards near the Birth Room of Amenophis III.

A ramp leads up to the upper floor of the museum, where there are interesting reliefs from Akhenaten's temple in Karnak as well as spectacular heads of the same pharaoh in the typical Amarnah style (see page 44) and a variety of smaller objects found in Tutankhamun's tomb, including *shabti*, models of servants that were intended to serve the pharaoh in the afterlife).

MUMMIFICATION MUSEUM

The **Mummification Museum** Ⓓ (daily 9am–9pm) houses a 21st-Dynasty mummy and a well-documented array of tools and materials used in the ancient art of mummification,

including the tools to extract the vital organs and the Canopic jars in which the removed lungs, stomach, intestines and liver were placed. Only the heart – considered to be the essence of a human being – was left inside the body, ready to be weighed by Anubis against the feather of truth in the afterlife. There were four jars in all, each presided over by a son of Horus: Amset, human-headed; Hapi, baboon-headed; Duamutef, dog-headed; and Qebehnsenuf, hawk-headed.

Also on display are some of the more essential goods the deceased would want on the final journey to the other world; familiar from other museums in Egypt, their function is finally made clear.

THE WEST BANK

The Nile valley is wide at Luxor and the mysterious pink limestone mountains about 4km (2.5 miles) across the lush green plain west of the Nile are so honeycombed with treasures and secrets that the average day or two spent among them is unlikely to be enough.

The west bank of the Nile was the necropolis of Thebes for more than 3,000 years. The New Kingdom pharaohs chose to be buried in the hidden Valley of the Kings, and they built their mortuary temples on the edge of the cultivation so that they would be remembered for eternity. The queens and royal children were buried in the nearby Valley of the Queens, the nobles and courtiers in the Tombs of the Nobles, and even the workers who laboured on the royal tombs had their own cemetery, the Workers' Village, known as Deir al-Medinah. Most of the tombs were cut deep in the rock, hidden in the valleys of the Western Desert hills.

GETTING TO THE WEST BANK

The west bank can be reached by the local ferry, which departs roughly every 15 minutes and takes five minutes to cross from the landing opposite Luxor Temple (last ferry back 9.30pm in winter, 11pm in summer), or by taking one of the launches for private hire moored along the bank. From the ferry landing

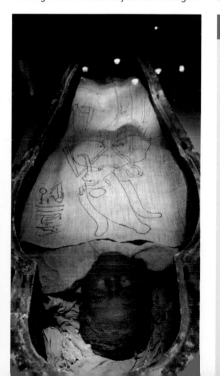

Mummy of a high priest of Amun-Ra at the Mummification Museum – not for the faint of heart.

⊘ WEST BANK TICKETS

Admission charges are payable for each site on the west bank and are generally EGP20–40 each. Three tombs require extra fees; Seti I (EGP1,000), Queen Nefertari (EGP1,000) and Tutankhamun (EGP200). Tickets for many of the sites are obtained from the ticket booth beside the Antiquities Inspectorate's office at the crossroads beyond the Colossi of Memnon and just to the north of Medinat Habu (taxi drivers will bring you here). However, the Temple of Hatshepsut, the Assasif tombs (available at the Hatshepsut ticket office), the Valley of the Kings and the Valley of the Queens have their own ticket offices.

Alternatively, you can purchase a "Luxor Pass", which is valid for five days. The standard pass costs US$100 (US$50 for students with ID), and the premium pass – which includes access to Seti I and Queen Nefertari – US$200/US$100. Only US$ or Euro cash is accepted and you cannot pay with debit/credit cards. Passes are available from the Public Relations Office in the Luxor Inspectorate, which is found behind the Luxor Museum on the east bank; Mon–Sat 9am–3pm. You will need a passport photo and a photocopy of your main passport page.

you can either take a taxi for the day to transport you from site to site or rent a bicycle. (Note that it does get very hot in summer and cycling is only advisable between October and May).

Alternatively, a bridge, 6km (3.75 miles) south of Luxor town, connects the east and west banks and makes it possible to visit the west bank by taxi from Luxor; the journey takes between half an hour and an hour.

Tour groups based in Luxor hit the west bank at around 8am, and from 10am, bus tours from the Red Sea resorts arrive. Your best bet for the least crowds is to come here in the afternoon, or if you're an early riser, at 6am when the tombs open. All sites are open daily 6am–5pm, unless otherwise stated. Note that photography is not permitted in any tombs.

MORTUARY TEMPLES

The pharaohs of the 18th Dynasty broke with the pyramid tradition and began to hide their tombs deep in the mountainside, hoping to elude tomb robbers. On the edge of the valley,

at some distance from their resting places, each pharaoh constructed his own mortuary temple.

The mortuary temples of Hatshepsut, Seti I, Ramesses II and Ramesses III still stand (those of other pharaohs have mostly collapsed). The two **Colossi of Memnon E**, standing in the fields by the side of the road, are the most visible reminder of the Temple of Amenhotep III, the famous Memnon. After the one on the right was hit by an earthquake in 27 BC, it made a gentle singing noise at dawn which the Greeks believed to be Memnon singing for his mother Eos. The Roman emperor Septimus Severus had it restored in AD 199, after which the singing stopped.

TEMPLE OF HATSHEPSUT

The **Temple of Hatshepsut F** (1498–1483 BC) is somewhat different from the other temples, being set back in a spectacular natural amphitheatre. Three gracefully proportioned and colonnaded terraces are connected by sloping ramps. The sanctuary areas are backed up against the mountain and partially hollowed out of the rocks. On first approach the temple looks strangely modern, but it is easy to imagine how grand the complex must have been when the courts were filled with perfumed plants, fountains and myrrh trees.

Hatshepsut's divine birth and exploits are recorded on the walls behind the colonnades of her temple. They include an expedition to Punt in Somalia, from where frankincense trees, giraffes and other exotica were brought back to Egypt. The cutting and transportation of the two great obelisks set up by Hatshepsut at Karnak are also recorded. The temple was designed by Senenmut, evidently a great favourite of the queen. His portrait is hidden behind a door; and his own tomb is nearby.

The upper ramp has benefited from many years of restoration. The

On the approach to the Temple of Hatshepsut.

sanctuaries of Hatshepsut and of the sun show some fine reliefs, while the central sanctuary of Amun, dug into the rock, points towards her tomb in the Valley of the Kings. It was at this temple, in 1997, that 58 foreigners and four Egyptians were gunned down by Islamic terrorists.

THE RAMESSEUM

Some of Ramesses II's (1279–1212 BC) mortuary temple, the **Ramesseum G**, is in ruins, but like other monuments of this pharaoh (who reigned for over 60 years and had 80 children) what remains is majestic. In front of the Hypostyle Hall lie parts of the largest granite colossus on record, the statue of Ozymandias (Ramesses' coronation name), which inspired the poet Shelley in his poem, *Ozymandias*:

I met a traveller from an antique land
Who said:
"Two vast and trunkless legs of stone
Stand in the desert[...]
And on the pedestal these words
appear:
'My name is Ozymandias, king of kings:
Look on my works, ye mighty, and
despair!'
Nothing beside remains. Round the
decay
Of that colossal wreck, boundless and
bare
The lone and level sands stretch far
away."

One foot alone measures 3.3 metres (11ft). The famous Battle of Kadesh (1274 BC) is depicted on the pylons. More interestingly is a representation of Thoth, the ibis-headed secretary god (see pages 48–9) writing Ramesses' name on the leaves of the sacred tree. Vestiges of the adjoining palace where the king came to spend a few days supervising work on his "Mansion of Eternity" can be seen.

MADINAT HABU

Ramesses III (1182–1151 BC), however, is not eclipsed by his famous forebear. Although he modelled his mortuary temple, **Madinat Habu H**, 1km (0.6 miles) southwest of the Ramesseum, on that of his father, the scale is even more extravagant. The surrounding mud-brick walls may have partly collapsed but the temple is one of the best-preserved in Egypt, and the easiest to understand as it reflects all the principles of the classical temple. In ancient times it was known as the "Mansion of Millions of Years".

The temple is not on the tour-group circuit, and in fact, not much visited at all. In the late afternoon, in the last glow of the sun, one can still feel something of the awe and spirituality the place must have inspired in ancient times.

The enclosure is entered through the Syrian-style gatehouse from which stairs lead to the pharaoh's private apartments. The grand **First Pylon** is decorated with reliefs glorifying the king's military victories. Religious ceremonies took place in the First Court, flanked by colonnades on

Ramesses III relief from the Medinat Habu.

Vast head of Ramesses II at the Ramesseum.

Valley of the Kings.

either side. On the south side, the colonnade with papyrus columns formed the facade of the adjoining Royal Palace. Coptic Christians later used the Second Court as a church and carved their symbols on the pillars, but a few Osiris figures survived as well as coloured reliefs under the western colonnade. Only the lower parts of later buildings remain; the upper part, including three small hypostyle halls and 52 side chambers, was used as a quarry by builders.

To the right of the entrance portal is a small **18th-Dynasty temple**, the oldest part of this complex, which is built over even earlier structures. The site of Madinat Habu enclosed the sacred site known as the Mound of Djeme, where it was believed the eight gods of creation were buried. Further east is a **Sacred Lake**.

MORTUARY TEMPLE OF SETI I

The well-restored small mortuary **Temple of Seti I ❶** is where 19th-century visitors began their west-bank tour. Once a favourite subject for painters, these days it is well off the beaten track and rarely visited. The setting is wonderful, overlooking a palm grove, and the visitor finds a tranquillity that may have reigned in these sacred places in ancient times. Built by Seti I (1294–1279 BC), who also built the great Hypostyle Hall at Karnak and the superbly decorated temple at Abydos, it was dedicated to the worship of Amun and of Ramesses I. The first and second pylons and court are ruined, but the remaining walls have some exquisitely executed reliefs. Off the Hypostyle Hall are six shrines and a small chapel dedicated to Ramesses I, Seti's father, who died before having built his own mortuary temple. Archaeologists have found the earliest example of a palace within a memorial temple, as in the temple at Madinet Habu.

VALLEY OF THE KINGS

After being embalmed and mummified, the New Kingdom pharaohs were transported in solemn cortège to the **Valley of the Kings ❶**, hidden

in a secluded wadi in the Theban hills. They were buried in rock-cut tombs, bedecked with gold and jewels, and surrounded by treasures and replicas of all they would need in the afterlife.

As soon as a pharaoh ascended to the throne, he would begin to build his tomb, which was intended to preserve the royal mummy for eternity. However, many died before the lavish decoration of their tomb was finished, which now gives an interesting insight into the different stages of the whole process. Although serious precautions were made to dissuade intruders, the treasures hidden inside were too much of an attraction to be left alone. As the power of the rulers of the 20th Dynasty decreased, breaking into tombs became commonplace, mainly by the craftsmen who had worked in them, or by the supervisors themselves. By the end of the New Kingdom the priests reburied the mummies in secret caches in the surrounding mountains, which were not discovered until the end of the 19th century.

THE VISITORS CENTRE

The entrance to the valley is from the **visitors centre** (6am–4pm in winter, until 5pm in summer; the standard ticket is valid for three tombs, and extra tickets are required for Tutankhamun). In the air-conditioned hall, guides explain the history behind the Valley of the Kings, while visitors can see a model of the site, use the computers to find out more information or watch a short film about Howard Carter's discovery of Tutankhamun's tomb. The adjoining tourist bazaar sells cold drinks and snacks. A noddy train (another ticket) then takes visitors about 500 metres/yds to the entrance of the valley, but it is easy enough to walk.

There are 63 principal tombs, and undoubtedly more to be discovered. In most of the tombs, long, elaborately decorated corridors lead down through a series of chambers and false doors to the burial vault. The entrance passage is painted with texts and illustrations from mortuary literature and the *Book of the Dead*. In

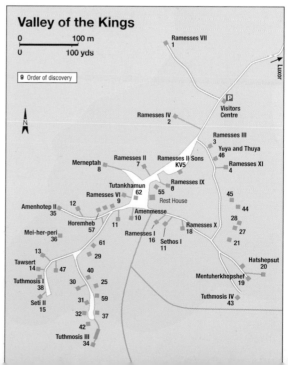

Valley of the Kings

0   100 m
0   100 yds

🚩 Order of discovery

Ramesses VII 1

Luxor

Ramesses IV 2

🅿 Visitors Centre

Ramesses III 3

Yuya and Thuya 46

Ramesses II Sons KV5

Ramesses XI 4

Merneptah 8

Ramesses II 7

Ramesses IX 6

Tutankhamun 62

55

Rest House

45

Ramesses VI 9

Amenhotep II 35

12

Amenmesse 10

44

28

Horemheb 57

11

Ramesses X 18

27

Mei-her-peri 36

Ramesses I 16

Sethos I 11

21

13

61

29

Tawsert 14

47

40

Hatshepsut 20

Tuthmosis I 38

30

25

Mentuherkhopshef 19

Seti II 15

31

59

Tuthmosis IV 43

32

37

42

Tuthmosis III 34

⊘ Tip

A gasp of wonderment escaped our lips, so gorgeous was the sight that met our eyes: a golden effigy of the young boy-king, of most magnificent workmanship.

Howard Carter

this, the pharaoh takes his last journey, passing through the 12 gates of the 12 hours of the night, beset by serpents, crocodiles and other malevolent beings. He arrives at the Court of Osiris where he is met by a delegation of gods; he makes his confession and his heart is weighed for its truthfulness and purity. A hideous monster waits to devour him should he fail the test but, evading the torments of hell, he is eventually received into the company of heaven.

Only a few of the tombs are open to the public at one time, as a rotation system has been introduced to protect the tomb walls from further deterioration caused by flashlights and respiration.

THE TOMB OF SETI I

The finest and largest tomb in the valley, now seemingly permanently closed to the public, is the **tomb of Seti I**. Like the carvings in his temple at Abydos (see page 218), the tomb's walls are decorated with magnificent, subtly coloured reliefs, and the anteroom to the burial chamber has an important astronomical ceiling. The sarcophagus is now in the Sir John Soane Museum in London, and the mummy in the Egyptian Museum in Cairo.

THE TOMB OF TUTANKHAMUN

Only one of all these tombs miraculously escaped the attention of tomb robbers, who were already ransacking them within just a few years of their construction. The famous small **tomb of Tutankhamun** (1334–1325 BC), the boy-king, was not discovered until 1922, when Howard Carter, under the patronage of Lord Carnarvon, chanced upon it after a search of seven long years. The tomb (additional admission charge) contained more than 5,000 precious objects buried with the young pharaoh, whose embalmed remains were still in situ in a complex system of gold and bejewelled mummy cases and coffins within coffins. A gilded chariot, beds, chairs, stools and headrests covered in gold leaf, alabaster lamps and vases, weapons, sandals, statues of servants, amulets and all kinds of other objects in perfect condition were crammed into the small space of the tomb. The majority of the treasure was until recently displayed in the Egyptian Museum in Cairo, but has since been moved to the new Grand Egyptian Museum (GEM), which is presently under construction in Giza and is due to open in 2020 (see page 170). This tomb, more than others because it is one of the smallest, has suffered from its popularity, and the colours have suffered from humidity caused by respiration. Since its discovery, there have been rumours of a "curse" put upon those who dared to enter the tomb, which perhaps began when the man who financed Carter's excavations, Lord Carnarvon, died soon afterwards at his Cairo hotel.

The world-famous tomb of Tutankhamun.

THE TOMBS OF THE RAMESSES

Ramesses I ruled for only one year so his tomb is a simple affair, but the decoration in the burial chamber is superb with scenes of the pharaoh hanging out with the gods and extracts from the *Book of Gates*. The **tomb of Ramesses II** is the largest in the valley (his 67-year reign gave him plenty of time to work on it). Unfortunately, he chose the wrong location as the tomb has been flash-flooded several times, and the decoration is in bad condition.

The longest tomb was built by **Ramesses III** and has beautiful painted sunken reliefs representing the various ritual texts. Closest to the entrance is the **tomb of Ramesses IV**, who died before finishing it. The tomb was robbed in antiquity and the paintings are not in good condition, but it has the valley's only image of the goddess Nut swallowing and spitting out the sun every day. The **tomb of Ramesses VI** has some fine astronomical scenes. The most visited tomb is that of **Ramesses IX**, which has colourful paintings from the *Book of the Dead*.

OTHER OUTSTANDING TOMBS

One of the earliest tombs open to the public belonged to **Thutmosis III**, but it takes quite a climb to reach it. It is unusual in that the decoration resembles the early papyri, and it looks almost like a cartoon. The **tomb of Tuthmosis IV** was also discovered by Howard Carter and it was the first tomb to use the technique of applying paint onto a yellow background.

The second-largest tomb in the valley, which belonged to Ramesses II's son **Merneptah**, has well-preserved reliefs in the upper part of the tomb.

The **tomb of Horemheb** was filled with furniture (now in the Egyptian Museum in Cairo). A steep flight of steps leads to a shaft decorated with images of Horemheb facing the gods.

The **tomb of Ay** lies 2km (1.25 miles) up a dirt track, but it is worth seeing if it is open: the burial chamber has some spectacular scenes of hunting and fishing in the marshes.

Stunning detail inside the tomb of Ramesses VI.

VALLEY OF THE QUEENS

The royal wives were buried in the **Valley of the Queens** Ⓚ (Biban al-Harim) in the hills behind Madinat Habu. Very few are open to the public, but in 1995 the restored **tomb of Nefertari**, one of the most impressive monuments on the west bank, was opened for the first time since its discovery in 1904, albeit to a maximum of 150 people a day. Also buried in the valley are a number of princes thought to have been killed in a smallpox epidemic, including the nine-year-old son of Ramesses III. The young boy is shown being led by his father to meet the gods.

TOMBS OF THE NOBLES

Divided into five groups, the Tombs of the Nobles are far less visited than the queens or kings, but are still well worth seeing. Unlike royalty, who were buried with great solemnity, the priests, scribes and dignitaries of the court, whose tombs are scattered in the sandy foothills, departed this world surrounded with scenes of the joyous good living to which they had apparently been accustomed during their lifetime. Thousands of private **Tombs of the Nobles** Ⓛ (Shaykh Abd al-Qurnah), dating from the 6th Dynasty to the Graeco-Roman period, with the majority from the New Kingdom period, were found, but only about 19 are open to the public at present. Most consist of three rooms with a forecourt, a covered columned hall and a smaller room with niches in which were placed statues of the deceased. Many of the nobles' tombs are vividly painted with naturalistic scenes of agriculture, fishing, fowling, feasting and celebrating, thereby constituting a fascinating record of everyday life in ancient Egypt. Offerings were presented to the deceased in the court outside the tomb.

TOMBS OF MENNA AND NAKHT

The **tomb of Menna** is tiny, but the decoration is extremely colourful and innovative, with the agricultural scenes particularly detailed and lively, as befits Menna's role as a scribe and overseer of the

Tomb of Nefertari interior.

agricultural activities on the royal lands during the 18th Dynasty. The **tomb of Nakht** was possibly decorated by the same artist. Though cramped, it is beautifully painted with scenes of a funerary banquet and agricultural tasks such as ploughing and sowing. Nakht was a scribe and astronomer in the Temple of Amun in Karnak.

TOMBS OF RAMOSE, USERHET AND KHAEMWET

The decorations in the **tomb of Ramose**, although unfinished, reflect the fact that he was a governor of Thebes under both Amenhotep III and his son Akhenaten. While the walls show exquisite carvings in the style of the former, some low reliefs on the back wall reveal a clear influence from the Amarnah style.

Userhet was a scribe responsible for inventorying the wheat in the royal bakeries. The walls in this tomb are somewhat damaged but there are some unusual scenes of cattle branding and hunting. The decorations in **Khaemwet's tomb** are similar to those in the tomb of Ramose, but he added scenes particular to his function as overseer of granaries and the royal scribe.

TOMBS OF SENNUFER AND REKHMIRE

Rekhmire was a vizier of Upper Egypt and mayor of Thebes during the reign of Tuthmosis III and Amenhotep II, a period of incredible prosperity for Egypt. He oversaw many great projects. Reflecting his status, his tomb is decorated with the finest paintings of arts and crafts, daily life and burial rituals. The **tomb of Sennufer**, mayor of Thebes and overseer of the Garden of Amon, has similar scenes and a ceiling painted with a vine laden with black grapes. It is an intimate tomb, giving a clear impression of the love between the deceased and his wife.

TOMBS OF KHONSU, USERHET AND BENJA

The decorations in these small tombs is fairly conventional with standard scenes of agriculture, hunting and offerings.

TOMBS OF NEFERRONPET AND NEFERSEKHERU

Also known as the **Khoka tombs**, these tombs, set apart from the others, belong to the New Kingdom scribes. They are brightly painted with strong yellow, blue and red tones. Their wives feature more prominently here than in other tombs. The adjacent tomb of Dhutmosi is closed to the public.

DEIR AL-MEDINAH, THE WORKERS' VILLAGE

For some 500 years the village of Pa Demi (the Village) or Ta Set Ma'at (the Place of Truth) housed a community of architects, masons, painters and decorators who were kept segregated from the rest of the population for generations, in an effort to keep the whereabouts of the treasure-filled royal tombs a secret.

A hot-air balloon takes off at Luxor.

Tombs of the Nobles dug into the mountainside.

Hawking souvenir gifts at Esna.

Scene from Pashedu Tomb in Deir el-Medinah.

In Christian times, the small Ptolemaic **Temple of Hathor**, still there today, was occupied by early Christian monks, which is why the village became known as **Deir al-Medinah** , "Monastery of the City". There are very detailed records of the relatively humble lives of the 50 families of the workmen in the village, their salary and their work schedule.

Archaeologists have uncovered more than 70 houses here and many tombs, which the workmen decorated in their spare time. The most interesting is the **tomb of Sennedjem**, an artist who lived under the reign of Seti I; the paintings of everyday life in his tomb are exquisite. Other tombs worth visiting belong to **Peshedu and Ipy**.

SOUTH OF LUXOR

The 215km (135 miles) between Luxor and Aswan is one of the loveliest stretches of the Nile, and the best and most popular way of seeing it is from the deck of a cruise boat, with stops at the various sights along the way. The strip of fertile agricultural land on either side of the river becomes ever narrower, until it more or less gives way to the desert closer to Aswan.

The towns are still relatively small and picturesque: fishermen beating the water to scare the fish into a net, water buffaloes wallowing in the mud, palm groves, farmers tilling the land with the same tools you see depicted in the tomb carvings. Most of the splendid monuments, temples and tombs date from the Graeco-Roman period, but there are a few much older sites, including the remains of one of the oldest temples in Egypt, at al-Kab and the quarry at Gebel Silsilla from which came the stone used in the temples in Luxor.

ESNA

The small rural town of **Esna** ⑩ lies 50km (31 miles) south of Luxor and is built over the ruins of the **Temple of Khnum** (daily 8am–4pm Oct–May, until 5.15pm in summer). A tourist souq leads from the Nile to the entrance of the temple. Only the Hypostyle Hall has been excavated and its foundation

level is 8 metres (27ft) below that of the street, an indication of the sand and debris that have piled up over the centuries since the temple was abandoned in the Roman period. Originally the temple would have been the same size as the temple in Edfu (see page 226) or Dendarah (see page 203).

The temple is dedicated to the creator god Khnum, the main god of Esna, and it was built over an older structure by Ptolemy VI. The Romans added the **Hypostyle Hall**, which has 24 columns with richly decorated floral capitals. It contains interesting reliefs and inscriptions, including the names and activities of Ptolemies and Roman emperors up until the time of Decius, murdered in AD 249. On the walls the emperors, dressed as pharaohs, are seen before the various gods of Esna, carrying out rituals related to the construction of the temple. French archaeologists have deciphered many details of the rituals of the worship of Khnum, as well as a calendar specifying when and how to celebrate. Just next to the temple

is an old caravanserai, and south is a sesame oil press and the local souq.

AL-KAB

Surrounded by an impressive mud-brick wall, and including several temples, the site of **Al-Kab ⑪**, ancient Nekheb, is 26km (16 miles) south of Esna. It's usually visited from the river on felucca or *dahabeeyah* trips. At the time of writing, however, the site was inaccessible because of ongoing excavations. In pre- and early dynastic times this was the capital of ancient Egypt, and the city's main goddess was the vulture goddess Nekhbet. Across the road and railway line, 500 metres/yds north of the ruins, you can still visit four interesting rock tombs (tip the guards), mainly of local notables from the early 18th Dynasty. Each has wonderful decorations and reliefs of daily life in vivid colours. The **tomb of Paheri**, who was a priest of Nekhbet, has some colourful agricultural scenes; the **tomb of Setau**, another priest, is similar, though it is 400 years younger than the other tombs here; the **tomb of**

Temple of Khnum at Esna.

Ahmose, a military leader, contains a lengthy biography explaining his part in the wars against the Hyksos at the start of the New Kingdom; while the **tomb of Renni**, a mayor, has detailed scenes of a banquet and funeral procession. In the desert east of Nekheb are several other temples and sanctuaries dating from the same period.

EDFU

A further 20km (12.5 miles) south, on the west bank of the Nile, is the pleasant market town of **Edfu** ⓬. The Greeks called it Apollonopolis as the sun-god Horus-Apollo was worshipped here, for it was believed to be the spot where Horus won a major battle with the evil Seth to avenge his father Osiris (see page 42). The Ptolemaic **Temple of Horus** (daily 7am–7pm in winter, until 8pm in summer) is the most complete in Egypt and is in near-perfect condition, with its great pylon, exterior walls, courts, halls and sanctuary all in place. On the outer walls, building is recorded as having begun in 237 BC by Ptolemy III Euergetes (246–221 BC), and continued until decoration of the outer walls was finished in 57 BC. Built over a much older sanctuary, it was one of the last attempts to build on a grand scale.

The massive First Pylon has carvings of King Neos Dionysos holding his enemies by the hair, in front of Horus and his wife Hathor. Regal carved-granite sparrowhawks, representing Horus, stand sentinel at the doors. The Court of Offerings has 32 columns with beautiful palm and flower capitals, and the walls are decorated with scenes of various festivals: the mock battle commemorating the victory of Horus over Seth; the joyful annual wedding visit of Hathor, who journeyed upriver from Dendarah to be reunited with her spouse, and the annual coronation of the reigning monarch who identified with Horus. A vestibule leads to a smaller and darker inner hypostyle hall, which has several antechambers with fine wall carvings, including one room, often thought to be a laboratory, with recipes for perfumes and ointments used in the rituals carved into the walls. The sanctuary of Horus has

The stunning, illuminated Temple of Kom Ombo.

the granite shrine that once contained the gold statue of Horus. In the eastern enclosure wall is a Nilometer which showed the level of the Nile flood, and thus helped predict the agricultural yield and taxes for the year ahead.

GEBEL SILSILLA

The Nile tapers to one of its narrowest points in Egypt at **Gebel Silsilla** , 42km (25 miles) south of Edfu, known as Khenu, "Place of Rowing" in ancient times. It was an important centre for the cult of the Nile, as the current was very strong here during the inundation season. Stone from its sandstone quarries was used for the temples in Luxor.

The landscape is riddled with shrines, inscriptions and chapels left by pharaohs from different periods. The most impressive of these is the rock-cut chapel (furthest north) of **Speos of Horemheb** (1323–1295 BC). On the southern side of the site is a massive rock pillar, known as capstan, believed to have once had a chain around it that connected the east and west bank (hence the name *silsilla*, Arabic for chain). The only way to get to Gebel Silsilla is by felucca or *dahabeeyah*.

KOM OMBO

Kom Ombo (daily 8am–5pm), is situated 40km (25 miles) north of Aswan, on a sandy bank where crocodiles once sunned themselves. The ancient city of Ombos owed its existence to its strategic position, on a promontory in a sweeping bend in the Nile, and to its role as an important stop on the caravan routes from Nubia to Egypt. Gold, copper, camels and African elephants were all traded here. It became more important during Ptolemaic times, but its main rise to prominence came with the erection of the Temple of Kom Ombo in the 2nd century BC.

The temple is unique in that it has two identical entrances, two linked hypostyle halls and twin sanctuaries dedicated to two different gods: the falcon-headed god Haroeris, or Horus the Elder, and the crocodile god Sobek. Older structures have been found on the site, but the main temple was built by Ptolemy VI Philometer, while the decoration was finished by Ptolemy XII Neos Dionysos (80–58 BC and 55–51 BC). On the east bank, this is the first riverside sight to greet Nile cruisers travelling north from Aswan to Luxor and looks glorious seen from the river, despite the fact that part of the Roman forecourt has fallen into the water and parts of the rear of the temple are roofless.

There is a black diorite offering table for both gods in the middle of the forecourt. Two portals lead into the outer Hypostyle Hall, which has 10 columns with floral capitals and especially fine carvings. On the left-hand side is a very fine relief of Neos Dionysos being presented to Haroeris by the lion-headed goddess Raettawy and Isis under the guarding eye of Thoth.

From here, two doors lead into a shared inner hypostyle hall where the roof was supported by 10 papyrus columns. The walls here have reliefs

Daraw Camel Market is one of Egypt's largest.

⊙ THE DARAW CAMEL MARKET

The dusty town of **Daraw** on the road from Kom Ombo to Aswan (40km/25 miles north of Aswan) distinguishes itself by hosting one of Egypt's largest camel markets (Souq el-Gimaal). Although there is a daily livestock market here (sheep, goats, cows and poultry), the best time to come is on Tuesday or Sunday mornings (6.30am–2pm) when traders sell hundreds of camels – sometimes there are up to 2,000 – and many buyers take them on to Cairo. The camels are brought from the Sudan by the Sudanese and Rachidia herdsmen on a trail known as the Darb al-Arba'in or the Forty Days Road, which is one of the last surviving trading routes through the desert – although these days many of them arrive in the back of Toyota pickup trucks, which the camel drivers rent at Abu Simbel for the final leg of the journey. The camels spend a couple of days in quarantine in Daraw before market day to rest and have their health checked out. The market is hot and dusty but full of colour and vibrancy, and this is a great opportunity to witness traditional Arabic bargaining and negotiation. Visitors are welcome – and many tour operators in Aswan organise excursions – but remember this is rural Egypt and you must dress appropriately (women should even wear headscarves).

showing Euergetes II and his sister Cleopatra VII in front of the gods. Three further vestibules are also decorated with beautiful reliefs, particularly on the rear wall of the third hall where there is a splendid carving of Philometer and Cleopatra standing in front of the moon god Khonsu, and Haroeris and Sobek. Only the foundations remain of the sanctuary of Sobek and Haroeris but behind them lies the inner temple gallery with seven chambers, closed to the public. On the walls of the outer temple gallery is a carving of medical instruments used in ancient times. In the grounds is a shrine dedicated to Hathor, a birthing house and a pool where sacred crocodiles were once kept.

In 2018, a project to drain groundwater from the temple uncovered a magnificent sandstone sphinx sculpture and two sandstone stelae. One depicts King Ptolemy IV alongside his wife and a triad of gods, while the other depicts the much older King Seti I standing in front of Sobek and Horus the Elder.

A new addition to the complex is the **Crocodile Museum**, which has air-conditioned rooms displaying 40 mummified crocodiles, ranging from 2 to 5 metres (6.5–16.5ft) long. The crocodiles are arranged on a sandy hill designed to represent a bank on the Nile inside a large glass showcase. Also on display are a collection of crocodile coffins and wooden sarcophagi; the gold and ivory teeth and eyes that were inserted into the dead crocodiles following mummification; crocodile foetuses and eggs; and statues depicting the crocodile-god Sobek, bearing a human body and the head of a crocodile.

ASWAN

Ivory, ebony, rose and gold are the defining colours of **Aswan** (215km/135 miles south of Luxor). Here, a wild jumble of glistening igneous rocks, strewn across the Nile, creates narrows between the highlands of the Eastern Desert and the sandy wastes of the Sahara. The barrier to navigation is known as the First Cataract; it was once where the civilised world stopped.

Aswan souq.

Aswan, for many at the end of a Nile trip, is a laid-back, warm place that is good for lingering for a few days. While the town has grown immensely in recent years – this is not just a tourist centre but the lively capital of the governorate and an important university town – the part to visit is still largely strewn along the Nile and on the islands. The souqs are more relaxed and less pushy than in other Egyptian towns, and there is definitely a hint of Africa in the souvenirs for sale. Taking a felucca around the islands, sniffing the scents of the botanical garden and listening to the Nubian children sing is the perfect way to watch the sun go down behind the desert on the other side. Further south are some beaches where it is safe to swim on a hot day.

During the Old Kingdom, a few travellers ventured further up the Nile in quest of gold, slaves and the occasional pygmy, leaving records of their missions inscribed on the rocks among the islands, but most expeditions were to Elephantine (see page 232), the island in the middle of the river at the foot of the cataract. Yebu, the main town on the island, was the Old Kingdom border town, and as the Nile was believed to spring up from under the First Cataract, it was also an important religious centre.

The excellent winter climate and beautiful setting of Aswan were well-known in the classical world and were described by several writers. They mentioned the temples, the garden and the vineyards of Elephantine, which were supposed to produce grapes all the year round. Both the Ptolemies and the Romans maintained garrisons at this distant southern outpost.

The greatest geographer in antiquity, Eratosthenes (273–192 BC), who held a post as librarian in Alexandria under the Ptolemies, established the approximate circumference of the earth from astronomical observations made at Elephantine and Alexandria. He noted that at the summer solstice the sun's rays fell vertically to the bottom of a well at Elephantine, whereas on the same day in Alexandria an upright stake cast a shadow, indicating that the

Karkadeh, a refreshing local drink made using hisbiscus flowers.

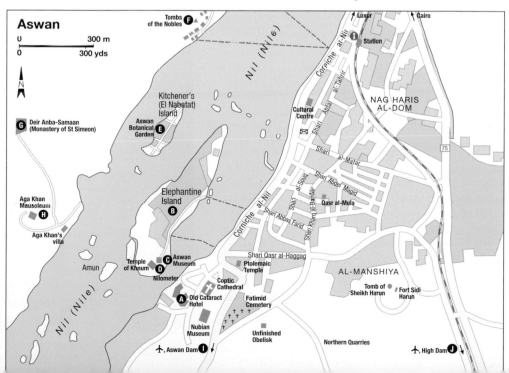

sun was seven degrees from its zenith. Since he knew the distance between the two cities, he could then proceed to work out the total circumference of the earth; and he came to within a few kilometres of the truth.

Juvenal, the Roman satirist, died here in exile at the age of 80, towards the end of the 1st century AD. But it was the merchants, more than the scholars, scientists, poets and soldiers, who left the most abundant evidence, in the form of *ostraka*, or potsherds, inscribed with records of their transactions. Nineteenth-century travellers were able to pick up pocketsful.

In the second half of the 19th century, tourists began to arrive by way of Thomas Cook steamers and *dahabeeyas*; and their many observations were noted in Morocco-bound diaries.

Elegant hotels were built to accommodate the fashionable travellers who came to spend the winter at Aswan or to plan the future development of Egypt and the Sudan. The terraces of the **Old Cataract Hotel ⓐ**, which was built in

1899 by Thomas Cook, must have been the scene of many a portentous discussion by these Victorian empire-builders.

The construction of the first **Aswan Dam** was successfully financed and the project completed in 1902. King Edward VII's younger brother came out from England for the opening with a host of onlookers, including the young Winston Churchill.

ASWAN'S SOUQ

Parallel to the Nile is the long stretch of Aswan's souq (Sharia el Souk), which still retains a hint of Africa. The little shops sell cotton, *karkadeh* (hibiscus flowers for infusion, the local drink here), Nubian baskets, dates, ebony cane and crocheted skull caps. The best time to visit is when the heat of the day has died down, late afternoon, or in the morning. Softly spoken Nubians while away their time in front of coffee shops, and women carry home the day's shopping on their heads, wearing their traditional thin black dresses with flounces trailing behind. Not so long ago, when they reached their villages

Statue inside the Nubia Museum.

⊙ THE OLD CATARACT HOTEL

Modern hotels have replaced the grand old ladies of the past in Aswan, although the magnificent Old Cataract Hotel opposite Elephantine Island survives, and in fact was closed from 2008 to 2011 for a complete restoration and is now the Sofitel Legend Old Cataract Hotel. It was built in 1899 by travel entrepreneur Thomas Cook for European travellers who had also gone on the company's pioneering Nile cruises. The Old Cataract's first newspaper advertisement appeared in *The Egyptian Gazette* on 11 December 1899, stating, "Every modern comfort. Large and small apartment rooms, library, billiard room... Electrical lights running all night. Perfect sanitary arrangements approved by the authorities". The hotel proved so popular that overflow guests were housed in tents until a 1900 enlargement doubled the number of rooms. Illustrious early guests included the Duke of Connaught, Tsar Nicholas II, the Aga Khan, Winston Churchill, Howard Carter, and of course, Agatha Christie, who set portions of her novel *Death on the Nile* at the hotel (the 1978 film was shot there). A drink on the terrace at sunset, or afternoon tea, is still a must as the views over the islands on the Nile, white-sailed feluccas, the desert on the west bank and the picturesque ruins of Elephantine are unsurpassed.

by walking across the Nubian sand dunes, these flounces brushed away their footprints in the sand.

NUBIA MUSEUM

Just south of the Old Cataract Hotel is the **Nubia Museum** (daily 9am–9pm), housed in a stunning modern building, built in Nubian style and surrounded by well-kept gardens. The importance of Nubian culture in Egypt has tended to be played down, even though the pharaohs of the 25th Dynasty came from south of Aswan. Since the flooding of Egyptian Nubia by the creation of Lake Nasser (see page 243), and the Nubian diaspora that followed, there is a serious threat that Nubian culture could disappear altogether – hence the importance of this museum. Well designed and laid out, it throws light on Nubia's history and heritage, from 4500 BC to the present day. Highlights of the museum include the fine quartzite statue of a 25th-Dynasty Kushite priest, the splendid horse armour from the so-called Ballana Period (7th–5th century BC), centring on the region

south of the First Cataract, and Nubian ceramics. A distinctive Nubian house and some prehistoric rock paintings can be found in the garden.

FATIMID CEMETERY

As in so many places in Egypt, Aswan has a multitude of burial grounds from different eras of Egyptian history. Hemmed in between the Nubian Museum and Unfinished Obelisk, for example, is a vast cemetery, known as the **Fatimid Cemetery**, with beautiful domed tombs dating from the 7th to the 12th century AD. In 2014 it was reopened to the public after an eight-year renovation that included setting up a visitor's path with signboards explaining the history of some of the 30 tombs – the caretaker will show visitors the most interesting ones for a tip. The earliest bears the name of a deceased person who was buried in AD 686, shortly after the Arab Conquest to Egypt, while the last bears a name of someone buried towards the end of the 12th century, a few years before the fall of the Fatimid Caliphate.

> ## ◯ Quote
>
> For those who wish to be wise, to be healthful, to borrow one month of real pleasure from a serious life, I would say, come and see the Nile.
>
> H.M. Stanley
>
> My Early Travels and Adventure (1895)

Ancient brick tombs in the Fatimid Cemetery.

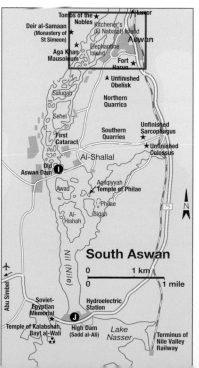

Tombs of the Nobles ★
Deir al-Samaan (Monastery of St Simeon) ★
Kitchener's (El Nabatati) Island ★
Luxor
Aga Khan Mausoleum ★
Elephantine Island
Aswan
Fort Harun ★
★ Unfinished Obelisk
Salugah
Northern Quarries
Sehel
Southern Quarries
Unfinished Sarcophagus ★
First Cataract
★ Unfinished Colossus
Al-Shallal
Old Aswan Dam
Agilqiyyah
Awad
★ Temple of Philae
Philae
Al-Hishah
Bigah
N
75
South Aswan
0   1 km
0   1 mile
Nile (Nil)
Abu Simbel
Soviet-Egyptian Memorial ★
Hydroelectric Station
Temple of Kalabshah, Bayt al-Wali ★
High Dam (Sadd al-Ali)
Lake Nasser
Terminus of Nile Valley Railway

The Unfinished Obelisk, Aswan.

Arriving at Elephantine Island by boat.

UNFINISHED OBELISK

On the other side of the road, across from the cemetery, is one of Aswan's many quarries where the **Unfinished Obelisk** (daily 8am–6pm in summer, 7am–4pm in winter) can still be seen, found exactly where it was semi-carved from the solid bedrock. The 42-metre (137ft) -long obelisk would have been the single heaviest piece of stone in ancient Egypt had the workers not discovered a crack while hewing it out of the rock. The stone had no reusable value to the stonemasons of the day, and it was totally abandoned, possibly during the reign of Queen Hapshepsut and the 18th Dynasty.

ELEPHANTINE ISLAND

Opposite Aswan, in the middle of the Nile, is **Elephantine Island Ⓑ**, the original defensive "border town" between Egypt and the Nubian lands to the south. It is much more built up than it used to be, but it remains pleasant, with several Nubian villages and their gardens, and on the southern tip, the remains of ancient Yebu – which means elephant and was probably derived from the shape of the smooth grey boulders that surround the island, looking like elephants in the water. The island is home to the **Aswan Museum Ⓒ** (daily 9am–6pm in summer, 8am–5pm in winter), set in a lovely subtropical garden and housed in the villa of Sir William Willcocks, who designed the first Aswan Dam. A gold-plated ram, ram mummies, precious stones, jewellery and amulets are on display.

The modern **annexe** next door has a wonderful collection of objects found on Elephantine, including weapons, pottery and household objects, with interesting labels in Arabic and English.

The entrance ticket to the museum includes the scant but rarely visited – and therefore atmospheric – remains of ancient Yebu, including the Temples of Khnum (see page 224), on the tip of the island, and the **Nilometer Ⓓ**. From the Old Kingdom onwards, a strict watch was kept on the rise and fall of the Nile, and its measurement

was one of the important functions of the resident governor of Elephantine and later Aswan. Up until the 19th century, when western technology started to revolutionise the management of water, frequent and regular readings were taken from the Nilometer at the southern end of Elephantine Island, and the information was communicated to the surrounding region. Those responsible for the cultivation of crops and the maintenance of embankments and canals would thus know in advance what to expect, while other administrators could calculate tax assessments.

According to an interesting text at Edfu, if the Nile rose 24 cubits at Elephantine, it would provide sufficient water to irrigate the land satisfactorily. If it did not, disaster would surely ensue. Just such a failure, which lasted for seven years – though it is not the drought mentioned in the Bible – is recorded on a block of granite a short way upstream: "By a very great misfortune the Nile has not come forth for a period of seven years. Grain has been scarce and there have been no vegetables or anything else for the people to eat."

Archaeological remains of the **Temples of Khnum** on the southern end of Elephantine are sketchy, but there is evidence that Tuthmosis III, Amenhotep II, Ramesses III, Alexander IV (the son of Alexander the Great), Augustus Caesar and Trajan all had a hand either in their construction or maintenance. Parts of the temples were still standing when the French expedition arrived in 1798 (see page 77), but were demolished about 20 years later by Muhammad Ali's son Ibrahim (at this time viceroy of Upper Egypt,) who subsequently used the temple's fine white stone to build himself a palace.

The nearby **Temple of Satet** was built by Queen Hatshepsut for the goddess of fertility and inundation. Beneath the ruins is a shaft leading to a natural whirl hole, the noise of which was revered as the "Voice of the Nile". Aramaic papyri found in the settlement record the presence of a large Jewish colony on the island.

Atmospheric ruins on Elephantine Island.

◎ Tip

An afternoon walk through the sweet-scented lanes of Aswan Botanical Garden is the perfect antidote to a hot day. If you come by felucca, your captain will drop you off at one end of Kitchener's Island and then sail round to the other to pick you up.

Swaying palms on Kitchener's Island.

KITCHENER'S ISLAND AND THE WEST BANK

The nicest way to see the sights on the west bank is to take a felucca, although faster motorboats are available, too. The feluccas usually stop at the **Aswan Botanical Garden ⒠** (daily 8am–4pm in winter, 8am–5pm in summer) on **Kitchener's Island**, also known as El Nabatat Island. In return for his military achievements in the Sudan, Consul-General Kitchener was presented with this island in 1898, for which he collected exotic plants and seeds from across the world and laid out the gardens. It has 25 different varieties of palm trees, and the main central pathway paved with pink granite is shadowed by two long rows of particularly impressive royal palms. Many visitors to Aswan are not aware that Kitchener's Island even exists, simply because it is hidden from view from the east bank by the much larger Elephantine Island.

In ancient times, the hereditary governors of Elephantine and other high-ranking officials had their tombs cut out of the cliffs on the west bank of the Nile at a spot called Qubbat al-Hawa in Arabic, or "Dome of the Winds", which can clearly be seen from the Corniche on the east bank. The **Tombs of the Nobles ⒡** (daily 8am–5pm in summer, until 4pm in winter) of the Old and Middle Kingdoms depict interesting scenes of daily life, and the views over Aswan and the Nile alone are worth the steep climb.

The ruins of **Deir Anba-Samaan ⒢** (Monastery of St Simeon; daily 8am–5pm in summer, until 4pm in winter) are nestled in sand dunes high on the hill opposite Elephantine Island. Once built on two levels of mud brick, this 7th-century monastery was first dedicated to the local saint, Anba Hedra; it was rebuilt in the 10th century and rededicated to St Simeon. The monastery once provided for about 300 monks, who used it as a base for forays into Nubia in the hope of converting the Nubians to Christianity. From where the feluccas and motorboats stop on the west bank, the road up to the monastery is a fairly steep

30-minute walk. Alternatively, camel handlers wait on the river bank and offer a (hard-negotiated) 20-minute camel ride up, which can be very enjoyable while taking in the tremendous views towards the desert and back down on to the river.

Aga Khan III, Sir Sultan Muhammed Shah, the grandfather of Kerim Aga Khan and distinguished leader of the Isma'ili sect of Islam for many years, loved Aswan for its pleasant therapeutic, timeless tranquillity and had his domed mausoleum built high up on the bluffs overlooking the river. He was buried in the **Aga Khan Mausoleum**  in 1957. The pink limestone building is a close relative of those of his ancestors, the Fatimids, whose followers' mausoleums are on the east bank. In 2000, his wife Begum Om Habibeh Aga Khan was also buried here. She is remembered for her daily ritual of placing a red rose upon her husband's tomb while she was in Egypt; when she was away, she arranged for the ritual to be carried out by the gardener. The tomb itself is closed to the public but

the site commands wonderful views over Aswan. The couple's white villa can be seen just below the tomb.

SEHEL ISLAND

Further south, just north of the Aswan Dam, is **Sehel Island** (daily 7am–4pm in winter, until 5pm in summer), home to a Nubian village. On the island's southern tip, on top of a cliff, are more than 200 inscriptions from 18th and 19th Dynasty nobles and traders who passed here on their way to Nubia and wanted to make their mark. One inscription is much older, however, dating from the 3rd Dynasty. It is called Famine Stela, and is an inscription of 42 columns of hieroglyphs that tells of a seven-year period of drought and famine, thought to be engraved during the Ptolemaic Kingdom (332–30 BC). It's located right at the top of the pile of granite boulders where the other inscriptions are, so expect a bit of a scramble up. The way to get here is by motorboat or felucca. On the way there is a great **beach** on the west bank opposite Salugah Island.

Looking out to the Aga Khan Mausoleum.

☉ DAHABEEYAHS

Medieval historians described *dahabeeyahs* or "Golden Ones" as luxurious vessels that went up and down the Nile, sumptuously decorated with two masts, lots of staff and a few comfortable private cabins and bathrooms. The same wooden boats were favoured by 19th-century travellers, too, who chose a boat and dragoman in Cairo, kitted it out and took about two months or more to sail up to Abu Simbel and back. The introduction of the Thomas Cook steamer and later the cruise boats put an end to *dahabeeyahs* – until recently. In the last decade or so, the *dahabeeyah* made a comeback, and it is undoubtedly once again the chicest and most pleasant way to travel up the Nile.

A few 19th-century vessels have been restored, but others are newly built in the old style with between four and 10 cabins with en-suite bathrooms. This is the slow way to travel: the cruise from Esna to Aswan takes six or seven days, a leisurely pace that includes the less visited sites of Al-Kab and Gebel Silsilla, a swim in the Nile and a beach where the bigger ships can't stop. The boats can moor where they like, and the scenery is just as spectacular as it was a century ago. It is more expensive to travel on a *dahabeeyah* than on a regular cruise boat but in this age of mass tourism it is a privilege to see Egypt in all its tranquillity.

THE ASWAN DAM

The taming of the river's unpredictable moods and the year-round conservation of its waters have been at the core of Egypt's history and civilisation since its earliest beginnings. In primeval times, the unharnessed flood roared down annually from the Ethiopian highlands, swamping the valley for three months before it receded, leaving behind thousands of tonnes of fertile silt which, accumulating over millennia, created the 10-metre (33ft) -thick blanket of soil that constitutes the Valley and the Delta.

The flood, however, was unpredictable and occasionally failed to appear. The consequences were disastrous, and the coordinated planning required to deal with the recurring problem was an important factor in the development of ancient Egyptian civilisation. By systems of dykes and channels, water could be trapped in basins. These systems were improved by waves of conquerors who tried their hand at governing Egypt.

In the 19th century, Muhammad Ali set about repairing and extending the canals and building barrages, which conserved enough water for a limited year-round supply. They made feasible the production of summer cash crops such as sugar, rice and cotton, which enormously increased the country's revenue.

Continuing this pattern of development, the British in their turn built the first **Aswan Dam ❶** in 1902 at the head of the First Cataract, creating a reservoir 225km (140 miles) long. At the time it was acclaimed as a great feat of engineering, and there was another marked increase in the prosperity of the country.

With the demise of the British occupation and the takeover of Egypt by Nasser's revolutionary government in 1952, the Nile Valley became a testing ground for international rivalries. The new regime focused its aspirations on the construction of a **High Dam ❷** that would generate enough electricity for new industry and rural electrification, as well as providing enough water to bring millions of new acres under

View from the High Dam.

cultivation – but it needed financial and technical assistance to realise the project. The United States was ready to help, but withdrew its offer abruptly when Nasser refused to compromise his nonaligned status. The Soviet Union stepped in with loans and technology.

For 10 years, 30,000 workers laboured on the dam. Hundreds of tonnes of rubble were shovelled into the Nile to make a barrier 4km wide and 92 metres high (2.5 miles x 300ft). Four huge channels were cut through the granite on the west side to divert the water while 12 turbines were installed on the east. By 1972 the dam was finished. The High Dam straddles the Nile 13km (8 miles) south of Aswan. Beyond it, Lake Nasser stretches for 800km (500 miles), deep into the Sudan, submerging many ancient temples and monuments (see page 243) as well as Nubian cultural relics.

The beneficial effects of the dam were immediately apparent, though it has fallen short of remedying all of Egypt's ills. Had it not been for the water stored up behind it, however, Egypt would have suffered as disastrously as Ethiopia and the Sudan during the droughts of 1972 and 1984.

An additional 3 million *feddans* (1.2 million hectares/3 million acres) to Egypt's cultivable lands, irrigated by the new assured water supply, was planned, but the leaders were so closely identified with the project that they turned a deaf ear to seasoned advice. The new lands were on poor soil, which took years to attain marginal productivity at exorbitant cost. Eventually Sadat had to admit that grand schemes for land reclamation were unrealistic.

The containment of the flood has produced other results. Houses can now be built in places that were formerly underwater for three months of the year; and in response to the huge explosion in Egypt's population, the private sector has built on precious agricultural land. Moreover, further land is being lost through the use of excessive water, causing waterlogging and salinity. The drainage system that would remedy this defect is proving to be costlier than the dam itself.

Gamal Nasser and Anwar Sadat, the two presidents responsible for the building of the High Dam, are commemorated in a memorial.

📷 STILL WILD AFTER ALL THESE YEARS

Despite the pressures on Egypt's wildlife over the past hundred years, many of the creatures that the ancients revered are still found today.

Before the building of the Aswan dams, the Nile flooded each year and its silt-rich water covered the valley. When the water subsided, the first creature that was seen to move was the scarabaeus, the dung beetle. This beetle also laid its eggs in dung or in the corpses of other beetles. Egyptians called it Kheper, and used it to represent the essence of existence, the god Kherpi. Scarab beetles can still be seen rolling their balls of dung, but many of the other animals that lived on land whose re-emergence the scarabaeus celebrated have long since disappeared.

SURVIVORS

Egyptians used many living creatures to represent their gods, but where now are the Nile crocodiles, the African elephants, the lions and ibises, the green monkeys and the baboons? Long since hunted out of existence or forced off the land as buildings gobbled it up.

Among the survivors that were common to the ancient Egyptians and are still found in Egypt today are the magnificent birds like the short-toed eagle, the long-legged buzzard, the hoopoe and the Egyptian vulture (all were used as hieroglyphics).

The Egyptians domesticated many animals including the cat, ox and cow, which feature on many tomb and temple decorations. In the river, grey mullet, catfish and Bulti fish would have been as familiar to the ancients as they are to Egyptians living by the Nile today.

Finally, while the scarab beetle reminds us of the eternal cycle that ancient Egyptians believed in, the pesky fly, also seen in hieroglyphics, reminds us that then, as now, there were trials and tribulations.

One of the great pleasures of wealthy Egyptians in antiquity was to go hunting in the papyrus marshes, particularly in the Delta. Egyptians hunted birds and other animals for sport, not to provide food, and scenes of hunting and fowling are frequently depicted in tomb paintings. The Tombs of the Nobles in Thebes have some of the best examples. This fine painting can be seen in the British Museum in London.

The Egyptian cobra was sacred to the goddess Wadjet. Egyptian cobras are still very common, and highly venomous. They often enter homes in search of food.

Cyperus papyrus.

Papyrus – the first paper

The papyrus plant (*Cyperus papyrus*), a relative of sedge grasses, used to grow abundantly in Egypt, particularly in the marshy Delta. In antiquity, Egyptians put papyrus to a number of uses. They wove it into mats, plaited it for ropes, bundled it together to form light rafts – perfect for fishing in the marshes – and pressed and wove it into a suitable medium on which to write. The creation of this technique was largely responsible for the explosion of literacy in ancient Egypt. Until then stone had been the main means of conveying the written word.

Making papyrus sheets was time-consuming and labour-intensive, so even in antiquity they were reserved for writing that was intended to last, for religious texts and important legal works. More ephemeral information was put down on slates or on pottery shards.

Because of its proliferation and importance, the papyrus was one of the symbols of Upper Egypt and its form was recreated in the shapes of pillars in several hypostyle halls.

Papyrus continued to be used for important texts into the 10th century, but the manufacturing technique was lost soon after paper was imported from the East and wasn't rediscovered until the 20th century, by which time papyrus had vanished from most of the country. Recently, there has been some replanting.

To see papyrus being made today, you can visit the Egypt Papyrus Museum in Giza in Cairo (see page 165), which also sells a wide range of high-quality copies of famous papyrus scenes.

The sacred ibis is now extinct in Egypt, but can still be found in parts of sub-Saharan Africa and in Iraq.

The jackal, another sacred beast, lives on the edge of the desert in Egypt, where the Egyptians still bury their dead.

Temple carving of an ancient Egyptian scarab beetle. Scarabs were used to symbolise the sun, immortality and protection, and adorned amulets, seals and ornaments.

Vibrant colours and decorations adorn a traditional Nubian house.

ABU SIMBEL AND NUBIA

The temples and tombs of Nubia, lying south of the First Cataract, were threatened with extinction by the Aswan Dam, but thanks to worldwide cooperation, many of Nubia's treasures can once again be viewed from the water.

For thousands of years the First Cataract south of Aswan marked the border between Egypt and Nubia, the land south of Aswan up to Khartoum in Sudan. This arid sun-seared Nubian land, about 22,000 sq km (8,500 sq miles), is now dominated by Lake Nasser, among the world's largest artificial lakes.

After the building of the High Dam in 1971, Nubia disappeared under the lake's water, and its entire population of some 100,000 people were uprooted from their ancestral homes, with half relocated in Egypt (in Kom Ombo, about 14km/9 miles north of Aswan, see page 228), and the rest in Kashem al-Girba in northeastern Sudan. Most of Nubia's major monuments were also transported to new locations, one as far afield as the Metropolitan Museum of Art in New York.

To the ancient Egyptians, Nubia was known as Ta-Sety, the Land of Bowmen, as the Nubians were famous for their bows. The word Nubia is thought to have come from the ancient Egyptian word *nbw* (gold), for Nubia was also an important source of ivory, copper and gold for the Egyptians. The area between the First and the Second cataracts is known as Lower Nubia (Wawat in ancient Egypt) and further south between the Second and Sixth cataracts is Upper Nubia (Kush).

EXPLORING NUBIA

Many tourists include a day excursion to Abu Simbel in their programme, but increasingly, as the sites along the Nile get more and more inundated by tourists, the attraction of a few days of peace and quiet on the very unspoilt and unvisited Lake Nasser has grown immensely. A few cruise boats tour the monuments around the lake – and in many cases this is the only way of accessing the temples that were salvaged from the water and located on higher grounds – and increasingly companies organise

⊙ Main attractions
Philae
Temple of Kalabshah
Amadah Temple
Qasr Ibrim
Abu Simbel

◉ Map on page 243

Temple of Kertassi.

HISTORICAL NUBIA

Mineral-rich but desolate, ancient Nubia traded iron ore, copper and gold for grain and other produce. As Egypt declined, so Nubia prospered.

For many centuries Nubia was the link between Egypt and Africa, but it was not a regular trade corridor because of its inhospitable environment, and the natural barriers presented by the cataracts. But it was a largely barren land, while Egypt, on the other hand, had an abundant agricultural surplus, and so even in ancient times Nubians turned to their rich northern neighbour for vital food supplies, especially grain. And Egypt, though ever fearful of attack from the south, was ready to fulfil the Nubians' requirements in return for the right to exploit their rich mineral resources. During the New Kingdom when Egypt gained ascendancy over Nubia, much of the era's great wealth was derived from Nubian gold and copper.

Nubian homes are often colourfully decorated.

ANCIENT NUBIA

When the civilisation of ancient Egypt was in decline, the kingdom of Upper Nubia prospered, and in around 600 BC, the Nubians moved their capital from Napata southward to Meroe (Shendi) in a fertile bend in the river, where, free from invasion, well-placed for trade, and rich in iron ore and wood for iron smelting, they developed a culture that was at once a continuation of the Egyptian-influenced Napatan culture and a totally individual African entity.

The Meroitic kingdom spread northward until, by the reign of Ptolemy IV (181 BC), the king of Meroe, Argamanic, controlled the Nile to within sight of Elephantine at Aswan. There the Nubians remained until the Roman conquest of Egypt in 30 BC, when the Romans signed a treaty with them, turning all northern Nubia into a buffer zone.

Nubia embraced Christianity between the 5th and 6th centuries, when numerous churches were built, and some ancient temples were converted into churches.

FROM CHRISTIANITY TO ISLAM

When Egypt was conquered by the Arabs in the 7th century, they concluded a treaty with the Christian Nubian king and Nubia officially remained Christian until the 12th century, when many Nubians embraced the Muslim faith. Mass conversion to Islam was triggered when tribes from Arabia settled in Lower Nubia and began to impose their religion and political organisation on the people. They intermarried with Arabs and their children came to be called *Bani Kanz*, or the Kenuz tribe. Most of the resettled Nubian population in Kom Ombo belong to this tribe. By the end of the 15th century, Nubians, with the exception of only a few settlements, were Muslim.

Surviving documents in a host of languages, including "Old Nubian" (which has yet to be deciphered), Arabic, Coptic and Greek, provide a wealth of information about the Nubian people in the form of private and official letters, legal documents and petitions, which date from between the end of the 8th and the 15th century. Most of these documents come from Qasr Ibrim (see page 247).

fishing safaris (see page 246), looking for the giant Nile perch and other fish.

THE FLOODING OF NUBIA

When the creation of Lake Nasser threatened to swallow up many Nubian monuments, the governments of Egypt and Sudan launched an appeal to save and record as many of them as possible. The international response was impressive. Between 1960 and 1970, in the most concentrated archaeological operation ever undertaken, scholars, engineers, architects and photographers from more than 30 countries fought against time to preserve what they could, and 23 temples were saved. Many of these were left in Nubia but lifted out of harm's way: the Temple of Amadah, for example, was raised as a unit weighing 800 tonnes, put on rails and dragged up a hill to safety, while the Temple of Derr was rebuilt nearby; another temple, built by Queen Hatshepsut, was dismantled, crated, loaded onto 28 lorries and taken to the Sudan, where it was reassembled in the National Museum at Khartoum.

PHILAE

During the Ptolemaic period, the cult of Isis moved 8km (5 miles) south of Aswan to the island of **Philae** ❶ (daily Oct–May 7am–4pm, June–Sept 7am–5pm), near Bigah Island, identified with the burial place of Osiris (see page 201). On Philae, a particularly beautiful **temple** was dedicated to Isis and became the most important shrine in Egypt over the next 700 years. Pilgrims came from both north and south to invoke the healing powers of the goddess, and continued to do so long after Christianity had been adopted as the national and imperial religion. As well as the Temple of Isis, many subsidiary temples, shrines and gateways were added to enhance the cult centre.

The construction of the first Aswan Dam in 1902 resulted in the partial submersion of Philae during eight months of the year. There were strong objections from conservationist quarters but, as Winston Churchill caustically observed, to abandon plans for the dam would have been "the most senseless sacrifice ever offered on

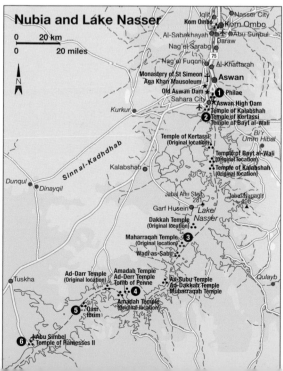

Isis carving on the temple at Philae.

Nubia and Lake Nasser

0   20 km
0   20 miles

⊙ Tip

To get to Philae: Most cruises that ply the river between Luxor and Aswan stop at Philae. Many operators offer day tours from Aswan that also include visits to the Unfinished Obelisk and the Aswan High Dam. To visit independently, take a taxi from Aswan to the Marina Philae Temple on the south side of the old Aswan Dam where official motorboats wait to transport visitors to Agilkia Island. Expect to pay around EGP10 per person for the return boat ride and tip the boatman if you want to stay longer than the usual hour.

Trajan's Kiosk, Philae.

the altar of a false religion". The dam was built, Philae was indeed inundated – and still more so in 1932 when the dam was heightened for the third time. But visitors were able to row and even swim about among the foliated capitals of the long colonnades and glimpse the ghostly reliefs on the walls in the water below.

When the High Dam was built between 1960 and 1971, Philae was threatened with total and permanent immersion. This time it was rescued by a huge international mission. A 1.6km (1-mile) -long coffer dam was constructed round the island, and all the water within was pumped out. Stone by stone the temples were dismantled, and transported to nearby **Agilkia Island**, which had been levelled and remodelled to receive the masterpiece of reconstruction that visitors see today. The total cost was in the region of US$30 million, a fortune at the time.

VISITING PHILAE

Small boats take tourists from the boat landing at Shellal, in Aswan, to Agilkia Island, where stairs lead from the landing to the oldest part of the Philae complex: the **Kiosk of Nectanebo I** (30th Dynasty) and the **Outer Temple Court**, flanked on both sides by colonnades. The entrance to the **Temple of Isis** is marked by the 18-metre (60ft) -high towers of the **First Pylon**, where reliefs show the Ptolemies in traditional Pharaonic poses. To the left of the Central Court is the **Birth House of Ptolemy IV** (221–205 BC) with fine reliefs depicting the god Horus rising from the marshes. A stairway inside the **Inner Sanctuary of Isis** leads to the **Osiris Chambers**, decorated with exquisite reliefs illustrating the Osiris myth (see page 201). Inside the sanctuary, reliefs show Isis suckling her son Horus as well as the young pharaoh.

To the right of the **Second Pylon** is the small **Temple of Hathor**, the patroness of music, with a good relief of musicians. On **Hadrian's Gate** an interesting relief depicts the source of the Nile as the Nile god Hapi, who pours water from two jars, a scene alluding to the ancient Egyptian belief that the

source of the Nile was to be found at the First Cataract, from where it flowed both north towards the Mediterranean and south towards the Sudan).

The most photographed part of the temple is probably **Trajan's Kiosk**, (AD c.100), displaying floral columns and reliefs of the Roman Emperor Trajan making offerings to Isis and Osiris.

THE TEMPLE OF KALABSHAH

For most of the year, the only way to get to the **Temple of Kalabshah** ❷ (daily 9am–5pm) is by boat, but sometimes when the water is low, it can be reached via a 10-minute walk from Aswan's boatyard. However, seeing the temple in all its grandeur from the water is worth the extra expense and hassle.

The original site of Kalabshah, ancient Talmis, was 50km (31 miles) further up the Nile, and today the temple lies somewhat forlorn in the shadow of the High Dam, where it was relocated in 1970. The temple, dedicated to the Nubian fertility god Marul (Mandulis to the Greeks), was

built around 30 BC during the reign of Emperor Augustus, over an older Ptolemaic temple. During the Christian era it was used as a church. An impressive stoneway leads up to the First Pylon. The colonnaded court and hypostyle hall beyond the pylon have varied floral capitals, clearly suggesting a garden. Inside the sanctuary, the emperor is seen in the company of the entire Egyptian pantheon. A stairway leads to the roof, with magnificent views over Lake Nasser.

The smaller temple of **Bayt al-Wali** (House of the Governor), was also relocated here, having stood on a site near the original Kalabshah Temple. Carved into a sandstone hill, it was built by the viceroy of Kush to commemorate Ramesses II's successful military expeditions in Nubia. The well-preserved and brightly coloured reliefs show the victorious pharaoh receiving heaps of exotic goods as tribute. Just north of the Kalabshah Temple are the picturesque remains of the **Temple of Kertassi**, with a few Hathor and papyrus columns

◉ Tip

A spectacular sound and light show at Philae, with three shows every evening in English, French and Spanish, relates the history of the Temple of Isis. For a schedule, ask at the tourist office in Aswan or consult the website at www.soundandlight.show. Tour operators offer package deals that include entrance fees, river transport, a guide and hotel pick-up and drop-off.

Arriving at Philae by boat.

◉ THE CATARACTS

The First Cataract at Aswan is one of six original cataracts in the Nile, all found in the river's so-called "Great Bend" between Aswan and Khartoum, where due to tectonic shift the river veers away from its normal north–south course.

Although the word cataract derives from the Greek word *kataraktes* (meaning downfall of water), the cataracts are actually broad stretches of shallow water strewn with large boulders and islands rather than waterfalls, although they can incorporate rapids. They often create a very picturesque scene, as at Aswan, one of the loveliest stretches of the Nile. Presenting natural obstacles for boats, the cataracts hampered the Nile's navigability during antiquity except during times of flood. Today, the Second Cataract lies under Lake Nasser.

⊙ Tip

To get to Kalabshah:
Boats to Kalabshah dock on the western side of the High Dam (reached by taxi). The return trip costs about EGP60 per person; tip the boatman if you want to stay longer than the usual hour.

DAKKAH, MAHARRAQAH AND WADI AS-SABU

The rest of the temples from here to Abu Simbel can only be visited by boat, as part of a cruise. Leaving from the Saad al Ali maritime station beside the Aswan High Dam, the cruise boats pass the temples of Kalabshah and Kertassi and the Bayt al-Wali, on the western shore, before heading into open water. The lake is broad here and the hills gently sloped, but further south the landscape closes in where the Nile used to run through a narrow passage between steep hills. It is a unique sight. Antiquities used to be spread along the Nile between the First and Second cataracts but, as with Kalabshah, many were grouped together during the salvage operation, which makes seeing them easier, even if it has taken some of the drama away.

The next group of **temples ❸** – Dakkah, Maharraqah and Wadi as-Sabu – lies some 140km (87 miles) south of Aswan, also on the western shore.

Camel ride to Dakka.

Dakkah was begun, 40km (25 miles) north of its present site, by the 3rd-century local king Argamani, reusing stones from earlier buildings. Despite extensive additions under the Ptolemies and the Roman Emperor Augustus, the temple was never finished, as is apparent from the lack of decoration on parts of the pylon.

The nearby temple of **Maharraqah** originally stood 30km (18 miles) north of its present site at the frontier marker of Ptolemaic Egypt. It is a later building than Dakkah, constructed in the Roman period and dedicated to Isis and Serapis.

Wadi as-Sabu (the Valley of Lions) is the most complete of this group. The temple, originally located 2km (1.25 miles) further southwest, takes its name from an avenue of sphinxes that lead to a temple built by the viceroy of Kush for Ramesses II. Colossal figures of the pharaoh stand at the entrance and line pillars in the court. The outer areas of the temple were built of sandstone, but the vestibule, antechamber and sanctuary

⊙ LAKE NASSER FISHING

A few companies offer big-game freshwater fishing safaris on the lake on "live-aboard boats", guaranteeing most people their biggest freshwater catch ever. The lake is home to 32 different fish species in total including two species of tilapia, tiger fish, and the giant vundu catfish. But it is the Nile perch that is the greatest draw – one of the largest freshwater fish in the world. The largest recorded Nile perch caught on Lake Nasser weighed in at a whopping 176kg (392lb). Fishing-safari operators include African Angler (www.african-angler.net) and Nubie Adventure (www.nubieaventure.com).

were carved out of the rock. The figures of Ramesses, Amun-Ra and Ra-Harakhte, which once occupied the sanctuary, gave way to an image of St Peter when the temple was converted into a church.

AMADAH TRIO

Forty kilometres (25 miles) south of Wadi as-Sabu, three monuments now stand near the original west-bank site of the Temple of Amadah. The small 18th-Dynasty **Amadah Temple** ❹ was built a couple of kilometres away from its present site by Tuthmosis III and Amenhotep II. The illustrations of planning and building the temple (in the innermost left-hand chapel) are worth finding. The nearby rock-cut **Temple of Derr** was moved 11km (7 miles) north to its present site. Like the Wadi as-Sabu temple, it was dedicated to Amun-Ra and Ra-Harakhte; its figures were badly damaged by Christians using it as a church. Also here is the **tomb of Penne**, a local governor (1141–1133 BC), moved from Anibaah, 40km (25 miles) south.

QASR IBRIM

About 15km (9 miles) north of Abu Simbel is **Qasr Ibrim** ❺. Now an island, before the flooding it was situated on the eastern bank where three massive peaks of rock rose from the river. Crowning the middle peak was a ruined town, whose fortress commanded the valley for miles around in all directions.

This *qasr* (castle) is all that emerges above the level of the lake today, but it must have been a striking landmark in Pharaonic times when the first temple-fortress was built. Excavations have revealed inscriptions dating from the 16th century BC and there are remains of a significant Byzantine cathedral. It is known that the Romans, Saladin, the Ottoman emperor Selim and Muhammad Ali all stationed garrisons here.

ABU SIMBEL

The mostly Nubian village of **Abu Simbel** ❻, 280km (174 miles) south of Aswan, has some restaurants and cafés, as well as a few comfortable hotels. It is a relaxed kind of place,

The shores of Lake Nasser, the world's largest artificial lake.

○ Tip

To get to Abu Simbel: Do not rent your own car and drive there, as you need to be a licensed tour operator to pass the security checkpoints. The drive takes about three hours and will probably start very early — some tour buses start heading to the site as early as 4am. Allow a visit of three hours and then three hours back to Aswan again. It can be worth staying overnight, but book accommodation in advance (see the companion app for listings). Alternatively, there are up to three flights a day each way (only one on Sunday): www.egyptair.com.

The four seated colossi at the Temple of Ramesses II.

where people play backgammon in cafés or listen to Nubian music at night. The lake looks beautiful at different times of the day, but it's especially wonderful to visit the temple at the crack of dawn before the crowds arrive, or late afternoon.

The largest and most magnificent monument in Nubia, the famous **Temple of Ramesses II** (Oct–Apr 6am–5pm, May–Sept 6am–6pm, later if arriving planes are delayed) was carved out of the mountain face between 1274 and 1244 BC, to confirm Ramesses II's might to all those who sailed down the Nile from the south, particularly the prosperous Nubians. The rock temple was dedicated to the main gods of Upper and Lower Egypt, Amun-Ra and Ra-Harakhte, but also to the deified pharaoh himself.

Over the centuries the desert sands covered up most of the temple's facade, and it was lost to the world until 1813, when the Swiss explorer Jean-Louis Burkhardt discovered it by chance as he travelled up the Nile. Only one head stuck out of the sand,

and it took the Italian explorer Giovanni Belzoni several years to clear enough sand to enter the temple.

Salvaging the temple from Lake Nasser presented a formidable challenge to the rescuers. Unlike other temples, Abu Simbel was not free-standing; the facade was the cliff face itself hewn in imitation of a pylon and dominated by four colossi of a youthful Ramesses II. The salvage operation entailed sawing the temple into more than 1,000 transportable pieces, some weighing as much as 15 tonnes, and reassembling them at a new site 60 metres (200ft) higher than the original site. The ground was levelled, and a great reinforced concrete dome was made to cover the temple.

The moving of the temple, which took more than five years from 1966 to 1972, was regarded at the time as one of the wonders of modern engineering. The reconstruction is nearly perfect and every year on 22 February and 22 October, only one day later than when the temple was in its original position, the dawn rays of the sun reach to the

heart of the sanctuary to revive the cult statues.

The four seated 20 metre (66ft) -high colossi of Ramesses II dominate the facade. The pharaoh considered himself a reincarnation of the sun-god Ra. At his feet are some of his children, and the supporting balustrade has kneeling and bound African captives on the south side and Asian captives on the north side. Look out for the graffiti left by earlier travellers, particularly on the two southern colossi; on the left leg of the second statue is a Greek inscription from mercenaries who passed by in the 6th century BC.

The **portal**, topped by a statue of the falcon-headed sun-god, leads into the **Great Hypostyle Hall**. This central hall is flanked by eight 10-metre (33ft) -high Osiride statues of the king in a double row facing each other, against a corresponding number of square pillars.

The **northern wall** of the Hypostyle Hall is decorated with the Battle of Kadesh, in which the young Ramesses II confronted the Hittites in Syria. It is one of the most extraordinary and detailed reliefs to be found in the Nile Valley. There are more than 1,100 figures and the entire wall, from ceiling to bedrock, is filled with activity: the march of the Egyptian Army with its infantry and charioteers, its engagement in hand-to-hand combat and the flight of the vanquished prisoners, leaving overturned chariots behind them. There are also scenes of camp life.

The reliefs on the **southern wall** are decorated with scenes of the king kneeling in front of several gods. The side chambers off the hall were used for storage and for keeping treasure. The much smaller **Second Hypostyle Hall** has just four large pillars and is decorated with scenes of offerings. Next is the **vestibule** that leads to the **sanctuary** carved out of the mountain to a depth of 55 metres (180ft). Inside this is an altar and the seated statues of Ptah of Memphis, Amun-Ra of Thebes,

the deified Ramesses II and Ra-Harakhte, the sun-god of Heliopolis; they are all the same size, indicating equality between the king and the gods.

Outside and south of the temple is a small **chapel** dedicated to Thoth, the god of learning, and five stele dedicated to high officials of Ramesses II. Unfortunately, at the time of writing it is no longer possible to enter the steel-enforced concrete dome that supports the temple (which gives a fascinating insight into the salvage process).

The small **Temple of Queen Nefertari**, which lay to the north of the great temple of her husband Ramesses II, was also saved. Nefertari was the most beloved of the wives of Ramesses II; and the pharaoh took the unprecedented step of having the facade of this temple decorated with statues of himself, his wife and their children. The goddess Hathor, to whom the temple is also dedicated, lovingly attends to the sun-god during his day's passage, so Nefertari is depicted watching admiringly as her husband kills his enemies.

⊙ Tip

A sound and light show is staged daily at Abu Simbel, with projections on the great and minor temple facades showing how they once looked. Earpieces are provided, allowing visitors to listen to the commentary in English, Arabic, French, Italian, Spanish, German, Russian, Chinese and Japanese (www. soundandlight.show; daily 7.15pm and 8.15pm).

Inside the Temple of Queen Nefertari.

Wooden fishing boats on the shores of Alexandria's Eastern Harbour.

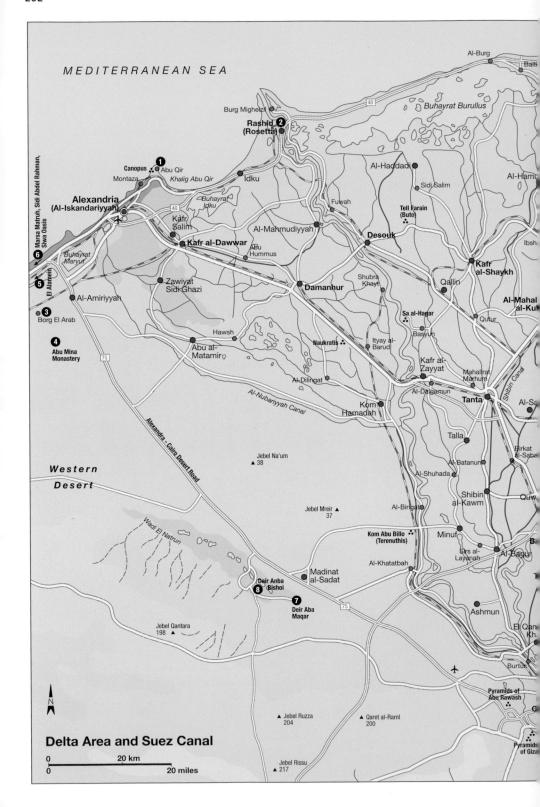

MEDITERRANEAN SEA

Al-Burg

Balti

40

Buhayrat Burullus

Burg Mighelzil

Rashid
(Rosetta) ②

Al-Haddadi

Al-Ham

Canopus ① Abu Qir

Montaza

Khalig Abu Qir

Idku

Sidi Salim

Al-Ham

Marsa Matruh, Sidi Abdel Rahman, Siwa Oasis

Buhayrat Idku

Fuwah

Tell Farain
(Buto)

Alexandria
(Al-Iskandariyyah)

Kafr
Salim

Al-Mahmudiyyah

Desouk

Ibsh

Kafr al-Dawwar

Abu Hummus

Kafr
al-Shaykh

⑥

Buhayrat Maryut

Damanhur

Shubra Khayt

Qallin

Al-Mahal
al-Ku

⑤ El Alamein

Zawiyat Sidi Ghazi

Sa al-Hagar

Qutur

Al-Amiriyyah

Hawsh

Naukratis

Ityay al-Barud

Basyun

Kafr al-
Zayyat

③

Borg El Arab

Abu al-
Matamir

Mahallat Marhum

Tanta

Al-Sa

④

Abu Mina
Monastery

75

Al-Dilingat

Al-Nubariyyah Canal

Al-Daigamun

Shibin Canal

Kom
Hamadah

Talla

Birkat
al-Saba

Western

Jebel Na'um
▲ 38

Al-Batanun

Desert

Al-Shuhada

Shibin
al-Kawm

Quw

Alexandra - Cairo Desert Road

Jebel Mreir ▲
37

Al-Birigat

Wadi El Natrun

Kom Abu Billo
(Terenuthis)

Minuf

B

Sirs al-
Layanah

Al-Baqu

Deir Anba
Bishoi

⑧

Madinat
al-Sadat

Al-Khatatbah

⑦

Deir Aba
Maqar

75

Ashmun

El Qan
Kh

Jebel Qantara
198 ▲

Burtus

N

Pyramids of
Abu Rawash

Delta Area and Suez Canal

▲ Jebel Ruzza
204

Qaret al-Raml
200

G

0   20 km

Pyramids
of Giza

0   20 miles

Jebel Rissu
▲ 217

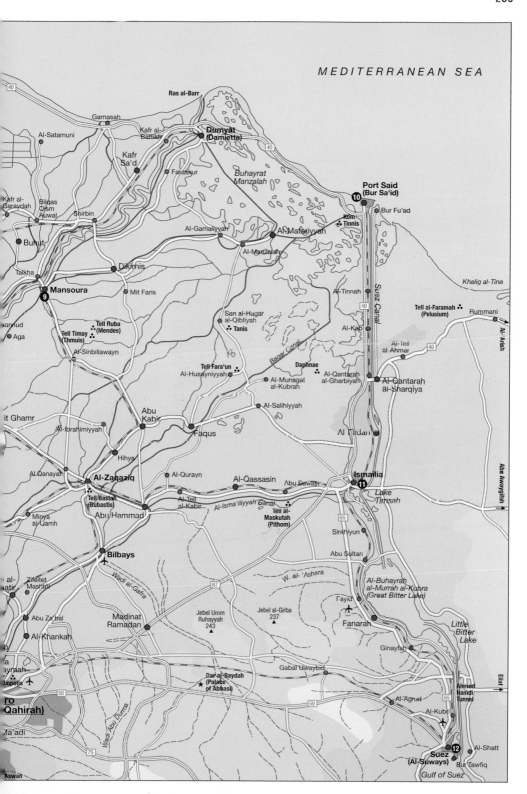

MEDITERRANEAN SEA

Ras-al-Barr

Gamasah

Al-Satamuni

Kafr al-Battikh

**Dumyat
(Damietta)**

Kafr
Sa'd

Faraskur

*Buhayrat
Manzalah*

**Port Said
(Bur Sa'id)**

⑩

Bur Fu'ad

Kafr al-
Garaydah

Bilqas
Qism
Auwal

Shirbin

Al-Gamaliyyah

Al-Matariyyah

Kom
Tinnis

Buhut

Al-Manzalah

Talkha

Dikirnis

Mit Faris

Mansoura

⑨

San al-Hagar
al-Qibliyah

Tanis

Al-Tinnah

Khalig al-Tina

Al-Kab

Suez Canal

Tell al-Faramah
(Pelusium)

Rummani

ammud

Aga

**Tell Timay
(Thmuis)**

**Tell Ruba
(Mendes)**

Al-Sinbillawayn

Bahr Canal

Al-Tell
al-Ahmar

Tell Fara'un

Al-Husayniyyah

Daphnae

Al-Munagat
al-Kubrah

Al-Qantarah
al-Gharbiyah

**Al-Qantarah
al-Sharqiya**

Al-Arish

it Ghamr

Al-Ibrahimiyyah

Abu
Kabir

Al-Salihiyyah

Faqus

Al Firdan

Hihya

Aba Awaygilah

Al-Qanayat

Al-Zaqaziq

Al-Qurayn

Al-Qassasin

Abu Suwayr

Ismailia

⑪

*Lake
Timsah*

**Tell Bastah
(Bubastis)**

Al-Tell
al-Kabir

Al-Isma'iliyyah Canal

**Tell al-
Maskutah
(Pithom)**

Minya
al-Qamh

Abu Hammad

Sirahiyun

⑥⑤

Abu Sultan

Bilbays

Wadi al-Gafra

W. al- 'Achara

**Al-Buhayrah
al-Murrah al-Kubra
(Great Bitter Lake)**

Zifeitet
Mashtul

⑥⑦

Fayid

al-
atir

Abu Za'bal

Madinat
Ramadan

*Jebel Umm
Ruhayyah
243*

*Jebel al-Girba
237*

Fanarah

*Little
Bitter
Lake*

Al-Khankah

Ginayfah

aymah

ⓘopolis

ro
Qahirah)

⑤⓪

*Dar al-Baydah
(Palace
of Abbasi)*

Gabal Uwaybid

Al-Agrud

Ahmed
Hamdi
Tunnel

Eilat

Ma'adi

⑤⓪

Al-Kubri

⑥⑤

Wadi Abu Duma

⑦⑤

⑫

**Suez
(Al-Suways)**

Al-Shatt

Aswan

Bur Tawfiq

Gulf of Suez

ALEXANDRIA AND THE NORTHERN COAST

Modern Alexandria is the second-largest city in Egypt. Set on the shores of the Mediterranean, it has long been a popular holiday spot for Cairenes, a refuge from landlocked Cairo's searing summer heat.

A visit to Alexandria, even if only for a couple of days, is the perfect counter-balance to the intensity of Cairo. With its string of beaches and Mediterranean outlook, Alexandria is much more laid-back and a good place to relax. Here, the Nile is no longer the lifeblood of the community; instead the Mediterranean Sea and its maritime influences hold sway.

Even though it was an important centre of the Hellenistic civilisation and the capital of Ptolemaic, Roman and Byzantine Egypt for almost 1,000 years – making it the most renowned city of the ancient world after Athens and Rome – sadly there is very little left of the buildings and monuments that graced the city during these periods. An odd column or two on the skyline, dank catacombs deep under modern pavements, a Roman pillar propping up the gateway to a pre-Revolutionary patrician villa and a growing inventory of masonry, columns and statues beneath the Mediterranean, are all that is left of this glorious past. Today's Alexandria covers a stretch of coast extending about 32km (20 miles) and is filled with concrete apartment buildings, office blocks and traffic-filled streets. But it does feature an interesting crop of museums, and over the past few years the city, which has more than 5.2 million inhabitants and

is the Mediterranean's largest urban centre, has seen considerable cosmetic rejuvenation and has recovered a little of its former prestige. While bustling Cairo is steeped in tradition, Alexandria is shaped by Mediterranean values. It is a city less about sights and more about ambiance.

ALEXANDER'S LEGACY

When the 25-year-old Macedonian conqueror Alexander the Great arrived in Egypt in 332 BC, he realised that he needed a capital for his newly

Main attractions
Bibliotheca Alexandrina
Alexandria National
  Museum
Kom al Dikka
Citadel of Qaitbay
Anfushi Tombs
Catacombs of Kom El
  Shoqafa
Montaza Palace
Rosetta
El Alamein
Wadi El Natrun

Map on page 252

Tuk tuks in Karmouz district.

conquered Egyptian kingdom and that, to link it with Macedonia, it would have to be located on the coast. Early in 331 he sailed northward from Memphis down the Nile, then westward along the coast. At a small fishing village called Rhakotis, on a spit of land between the sea and a freshwater lake, with limestone quarries and easy access to the Nile, he founded his city, gave orders to build it and promptly departed. He never saw his new metropolis completed, as he was never to return, except in death.

When he died in 323 BC in Babylon, Alexander's remains were taken to Memphis for burial, but the priests sent the funeral cortège away. "Do not settle him here," they said, "but at the city he built at Rhakotis. For wherever his body must lie, that city will be uneasy, disturbed by wars and battles." So the conqueror of Asia was returned to the city he had established eight years earlier, where he was buried in a grave now lost somewhere below the foundations of modern Alexandria. And the priests were wrong: Memphis today is a sand heap littered with ancient fragments, while Alexandria, although buffeted by many wars and battles, has somehow stood the test of time.

THE PTOLEMIES

After Alexander's death, Egypt fell to a Macedonian general, Ptolemy, who had been present at the founding of

Alexandria. He made it his new capital and established a dynasty that lasted until 30 BC. The first Ptolemies busily set about adorning their city. They also encouraged scholarship, and under their rule Alexandria became a haven and refuge for intellectuals. The first Ptolemies meanwhile decided that they needed a great monument in their new city, which could be seen by ships at sea and provide a guide for sailors through the limestone reefs that line the shore. Thus the lighthouse on the island of Pharos, one of the Seven Wonders of the Ancient World, came into being (see page 272), built during the reign of Ptolemy II Philadelphus (280–247 BC). A fortress as well as a beacon, this huge lighthouse stood at the eastern end of Pharos, where it dominated both the Eastern Harbour, which sheltered the royal fleet, and the Western Harbour. Lillle remains of the lighthouse today beyond a few Aswan granite blocks, although some of its statues and masonry have been found beneath the harbour in recent years (see page 272).

The Ptolemies' intellectual achievement was epitomised by the Great Library attached to the Mouseion in Alexandria. In many ways, the Mouseion, a shrine to the Muses, resembled a modern university, but the scholars, scientists and literary men it supported were under no obligation to teach. They could devote their entire time to their studies. The Great Library was, alas, burnt down during Caesar's wars and the Mouseion's buildings have disappeared under subsequent rubble.

External threats, nationalist rebellion, intrigue at court and family strife made the Ptolemaic dynasty increasingly dependent on Rome. By 89 BC, thanks to the debts it owed to this new power, the Ptolemaic dynasty was under Roman control. In 51 BC, while rivals squabbled in the Roman Senate, a 17-year-old girl was crowned Queen Cleopatra VII in Alexandria. Three years later she was ready to play the temptress, first at Caesar's feet, then at Mark Antony's. And as long as she lived, Alexandria preserved its

The Corniche is a pleasant place for a stroll.

autonomy. At her death, it became a Roman city.

DECLINE AND RENAISSANCE

As Rome acquired increasing sway over its new colonies in the east, Christianity, a brand-new religious movement, drew disciples. More than any other city in the Roman Empire, Alexandria was the intellectual capital of the new religion.

The conflict between the Church and State came to its height in the first years of the 4th century under the emperor Diocletian, who demolished churches, demoted all Christian officials and enslaved or killed the rest, as many as 60 a day for a period of five years, according to the traditions of the Coptic Church. This persecution prompted the Christian flight to the desert, which led to the founding of the first monasteries, and made such a strong impression on the Egyptian Church that the Coptic calendar (also sometimes called the Alexandrian calendar) begins at AD 284, marking the start of "the Era of Martyrs".

Stanley Bridge at sunset.

In 641, Alexandria fell to the Arab General Amr ibn al-As, who stormed into Egypt with an army of some 3,500 Bedu horsemen. They brought with them a new, rapidly growing religion, Islam.

This new religion would certainly have been hostile to a pagan Alexandria and was uneasy with a Christian one, but the Arab conquest was on the whole a humane affair and little damage was done to property. The city's two venerable libraries, which the Arabs are sometimes accused of destroying, had long been burnt by pagans and Christians. But it was Cairo that would blossom under Egypt's Arab masters, while the once great, glittering city of Alexandria gradually dwindled, especially after a Frankish raid in 1365, when all the public buildings were destroyed and 5,000 citizens were carried off into slavery.

The turning point in Alexandria's renaissance came with Napoleon's invasion of 1798, when he recognised the town's strategic maritime importance and initiated its revival. Subsequently, from the early 19th century and during the reign of Muhammad Ali, a new city was built on top of the old one. Ali also introduced its famous cotton industry and built the Mahmoudiyah Canal in 1820. This once more linked Alexandria to the hinterland, encouraging Egypt to look not only towards the Mediterranean again, but beyond it, to Europe. The cotton trade created great wealth, and a steady influx of Greeks, Italians, French and English turned Alexandria into a pseudo-European city, complete with wide, grid-planned streets, foreign schools, clubs, restaurants, casinos, businesses and banks.

The 1952 Revolution changed all that. The new government eventually expelled most foreigners and confiscated their lands or nationalised their businesses, while Egyptian capital and enterprise fled abroad.

A lot of the ancient city only came to light during a construction boom in the early 1990s. As old buildings were being demolished to make way for new ones, archaeological teams were allowed to excavate. One of the most important developments in understanding ancient Alexandria was the declassification of the harbour (ancient *portus magnus*) as a military zone in the 1990s. Underwater excavations have so far uncovered 2.2 hectares (5.5 acres) of buildings in the eastern section. Of special interest is the site of Mark Antony's uncompleted palace, the Timonium.

BIBLIOTHECA ALEXANDRINA

One of the most exciting developments in the city in recent decades – and one that has given the city a renewed cultural focus – is the **Bibliotheca Alexandrina** Ⓐ (www.bibalex.org; Sun–Thu 10am–7pm, Fri 2–7pm, Sat noon–4pm; separate admission charges for each museum), which is located on the Corniche to the east of the historic Steigenberger Cecil Hotel.

This vast modern library was inspired by the original Mouseion Library, which was the pride of the ancient city and the world's first-ever centre for scientific research. The impressive glass and steel building, an architectural evocation of the sun rising on the eastern Mediterranean, is intended to be an international centre of knowledge and culture, with the capacity to hold 8 million books in many languages, and 50,000 rare manuscripts. The manuscripts include Spanish donations documenting the period of Moorish rule, and French documents dealing with the building of the Suez Canal. In 2010, the library received a donation of half a million books from the National Library of France (Bibliothèque Nationale de France), which now makes it one of the largest Francophone libraries in the world.

There are reading rooms on 11 cascading levels and six specialised libraries, including rare books and special collections; arts and multimedia; children's; and one for the visually

Ⓞ Tip

Alexandria is served by flights from Cairo to Borg El Arab International Airport, 50km (31 miles) along the coast to the west, and hourly buses from Cairo, which take no more than three hours. Trains too take about three hours from Ramses Station; be sure to get off at the Misr train station, the central station in Alexandria, rather than the suburban Sidi Gaber station, which serves the eastern suburbs and is where most locals get off.

Trams began operating in Alexandria in 1863.

⊙ Tip

Central Alexandria is easily explored on foot. Alternatively, you might want to try the trams, which began operating in 1863. There are now 20 lines serving 140 stops. Useful routes are blue trams Nos 1 and 2 east to Montaza, and yellow trams Nos 15 and 25 along the Corniche west to Ras El-Tin and Anfushi. Taxis are also plentiful and cheap and can be hired by the day.

impaired. Other facilities include a concert hall, a planetarium, an antiquities museum and a further museum dedicated to former Egyptian president Anwar Al Sadat.

ALEXANDRIA NATIONAL MUSEUM

A good place to begin unravelling Alexandria's past is the **Alexandria National Museum** Ⓑ (daily 9am–4.30pm), which is set in a fine Italian-style villa, once the residence of a prominent timber trading business-man, and the United States Consulate, on Shari El-Horeya. The museum illustrates the city's history with beautifully displayed and labelled artefacts from various eras. The layout is chronological, with the basement devoted to the Pharaonic period, displaying numerous statues of different ancient Egyptian rulers and gods and very interesting portraits of Menkaure, Ikhnaton and Hatshepsut; the ground floor to the Graeco-Roman period, with statues including a sphinx; while the top floor is devoted to Coptic, Islamic and modern Alexandria, showing coins, candle holders, icons and various other items. Panels in every room explain various facets of religion and history, and the most interesting section is the exhibit of sculptures that were found in the Eastern Harbour (see page 272). The museum also shows a film of how these items were pulled out of the sea.

THE ROMAN ODEON AND NABI DANIEL

On Shari Al Naby Danyal, not far from the Misr train station, are the extensive excavations of **Kom Al Dikka** Ⓒ (daily 9am–4.30pm). Below Muslim tombs dating from the 9th to the 11th century, archaeologists have found baths, houses, assembly halls and the site where Christian mobs burnt objects from the Serapeum. The main attraction is the small 2nd-century amphitheatre with marble terrace seating and well-preserved mosaic flooring. Some fine mosaic floors of a Roman villa, known as the Villa of the Birds, are also on show.

Follow Shari Al Naby Danyal back towards Shari El-Horeya. The point

Tourists visit the ruins of the 2nd-century amphitheatre.

where the two streets meet has been the chief crossroads of the city for more than 2,300 years. Here, from east and west, the Canopic Way (Shari' Tariq al-Hurriyyah) once ran from the Gate of the Sun to the Gate of the Moon, and in ancient times was lined from end to end with colonnades.

A short walk south along Shari Al Naby Danyal will bring you to the **El Nabi Daniel Mosque** ❷, on the left side of the street with an entrance set back. It was built at the end of the 18th century and restored in 1823 by Muhammad Ali. Mistakenly believed to lie over the tomb of the prophet Daniel, it is actually the burial place of Shaykh Danyal al-Maridi, who died in 1407. It is also falsely believed to be the site of the Soma, where Alexander is buried. Inside the mosque, the caretaker will beckon you over to peer down a great square hole into the crypt where Danyal lies along with one Lukeman the Wise, a religious story-teller, keeping company (it is alleged) with Alexander and some of his successors.

THE LITERARY SCENE

Near the ancient crossroads on Shari El-Horeya is the Italian-style **Alexandria Opera House**, or Sayyid Darwish Theatre, which opened in 1921 and was restored to its former splendour in the early 2000s. It regularly holds performances including from the Cairo Symphony Orchestra.

During the early 20th century a literary revival took place in Alexandria, led by Constantine Cavafy (1863–1933), called "the poet of the city" by Lawrence Durrell. E.M. Forster, who lived in Alexandria and wrote its history, first met Cavafy in 1917 and was responsible for introducing him to the English-speaking world. Just north of the Opera House at 6 Cavafy Street, also known as Sharm El Sheikh Street, the Greek poet's apartment where he lived most of his life is today the **Cavafy Museum** ❸ (Tue–Sun 10am–4pm), thanks to the efforts of the Greek Consulate. It displays furniture, letters and poems, as well as portraits and photographs of Cavafy and his close friends.

❖ CLEOPATRA'S NEEDLES

The Roman occupation of Egypt was followed by the looting of ancient artefacts to adorn the major piazzas of Rome, and today there are almost twice as many obelisks in Rome as there are in Egypt. However, not all of them made it to Rome. After defeating Cleopatra, Augustus Caesar ordered the removal of two granite obelisks at the Temple of the Sun at Heliopolis, originally made during the reign of the 18th Dynasty Pharaoh Thutmose III, but they only travelled as far as Alexandria. There they rested for almost 2,000 years until the late 19th century when Egypt presented one to London and another to New York. The ship carrying the obelisk to London almost sank. It was raised on the Embankment in London in 1879. The other arrived a year later and now stands in New York's Central Park.

Alexandria's courthouse building.

Tip

The best time to photograph the Citadel of Qaitbay is just before dusk, when the warm reds and oranges of an Alexandrian sunset turn the sandstone building the colour of rich honey.

Lawrence Durrell's celebrated novels, published between 1957 and 1960, *The Alexandria Quartet*, were to a large extent inspired by Constantine Cavafy's poetry, and all the characters in the *Quartet* meet at least once at the Pastroudis Café to drink *araq*. Sadly, not only did the Pastroudis Café close down in 2004, but Durrell's ornate villa where he wrote was demolished in 2017 as it was beyond repair. The city he describes, however, is still palpable. The **Cecil Hotel** 🄵, built in 1929, is still there, and you can imagine Justine swinging in through the doors, however much the hotel has changed over the years.

At the heart of the former European zone, the Cecil Hotel sits on the corner of the large square of Midan Saad Zaghlol and the **Corniche**. In the centre of the Midan is a statue of Saad Zaghlol, the nationalist hero who tried to negotiate Egypt's independence after World War I, while the Corniche, which was built in 1870 by Italian-Egyptian architect Pietro Avoscani, is a pleasant promenade that runs for

16km (10 miles) along the seafront. This is where Alexandrians come to stroll and enjoy the cool of the evening. The two obelisks that once stood near the Cecil Hotel, the famous Cleopatra's needles, are now in London and New York (see page 261).

CITADEL AND THE PHAROS

At the end of the breakwater of the Eastern Harbour west of the Cecil Hotel, sitting on the site of the ancient Pharos of Alexandria lighthouse, is the handsome **Citadel of Qaitbay** 🄶 (daily 8am–5pm). One of the Seven Wonders of the Ancient World, the lighthouse, constructed in 279 BC, was a marvel of its day. It rose to an estimated 100 metres (330ft) and hydraulic machinery may have been used for carrying fuel to the top. Within its square base were as many as 300 rooms, to house mechanics and operators; above were an octagonal storey and a circular storey, topped by a lantern with a beacon.

The lantern collapsed as early as the 8th century, followed by the circular

⊘ THE PHAROS OF ALEXANDRIA

Besides the pyramids, the other Wonder of the Ancient World in Egypt was the lighthouse of Alexandria, the Pharos. Initially built by the Ptolemaic Kingdom, during the reign of Ptolemy II Philadelphus (280–247 BC) to indicate the entrance of the harbour, it was turned into a lighthouse by the Romans. A floor mosaic of the Pharos found at a Byzantine church at Qasr Libya 900km (560 miles) west (now in northern Libya) shows that it was a hemispherical dome on top of a square building. At an estimated 100 metres (330ft) in height, for many centuries it would have been one of the tallest man-made structures in the world.

Contemporary descriptions talk of a mirror of polished steel to reflect the sun by day and a fire by night, or describe a device made of glass, so fashioned as to enable a man sitting under it to see ships at sea that were invisible to the naked eye. If true, the latter suggests a kind of prism, the secret of which Alexandrian mathematicians may have discovered only for it to be lost when the Pharos fell. It was severely damaged by three earthquakes between AD 956 and 1323 and became an abandoned ruin.

storey. In 881, Ibn Tulun made some restorations, but the 1100 earthquake toppled the octagonal storey and foiled his efforts. The Pharos still served as a lighthouse, however, until the square base was finally destroyed in another earthquake in the 14th century.

In 1477, Sultan Al-Ashraf Sayf al-Din Qa'it Bay built the citadel that still stands on the site, incorporating some of the debris from the Pharos – you can make out granite and marble columns, for example, in the northwest section of the enclosure walls. The Sultan built the fortress to defend Alexandria from the advances of the Ottoman Empire, although his efforts were in vain as the Ottomans took control of Egypt in 1512. The current citadel, however, is not all original, having been heavily damaged in the British bombardment of Alexandria in 1882, the preliminary to the British invasion and occupation. It was rebuilt at the turn of the 20th century, and it was again restored in 1984. It is an impressive piece of defensive architecture and has a labyrinth of passageways, large chambers, towers and walls to explore. The inner walls contain the soldiers' barracks and weapons stores, on the first floor is a mosque, and there are sweeping views of the city, including the Bibliotheca Alexandrina, from the battlements. It's also home to the small **Qaitbay Maritime Museum**, which exhibits relics from sea battles from the Roman, Napoleonic and British eras, and another three pillars likely to date from the lighthouse. The part of the Corniche leading to the citadel has a small fishing port, where nets are hung along the jetty to dry, and the Yacht Club of Egypt – there are plenty of boats bobbing around. The area is usually crowded with families enjoying the sea views, restaurants and ice-cream shops.

RAS EL-TIN AND ANFUSHI

Westward along the seafront, 3km (1.75 miles) from the citadel, is the 19th-century **Ras El-Tin Palace**  ("Cape Fig Palace"). Built by Muhammad Ali, but altered by later rulers of

The striking Citadel of Qaitbay.

Egypt, this enormous Italian renaissance palace is one of the official residences of the President of Egypt.

East of the palace on Shari Ras al-Tin, near the end of the tramline, are the Ptolemaic **Anfushi Tombs** ❶ (daily 9am–4pm), with decorations that marry Greek and Egyptian styles. Their stucco walls are painted to imitate alabaster and marble blocks and tiles.

At this point, you can turn into the old Turkish quarter of **Anfushi** at the heart of what was once the island of Pharos.

Continuing southeast along Shari Ras el-Tin you will reach **Shari Faransa** (Rue de France). You are now in one of the most "native" parts of the city, where you may like to stop to look at the **Terbanh Mosque**. Built in 1684, it has a distinctive pale-yellow exterior, with plaster over a red and black Delta-style facade of bricks and wooden beams. On its left side note the ancient columns at the entrance to the cellars. Two huge Corinthian columns mark the entrance to the mosque itself and support its minaret.

In ancient times Pharos was joined to the mainland by a causeway called the **Heptastadion**, which gradually became a permanent broad neck of land. Along it to the south, Shari Faransa runs into **Midan at-Tahrir**, formerly Place Muhammad Ali. A statue of the pasha on horseback (by the 19th-century French sculptor Henri Alfred Jacquemart) still graces the midan. The southern end of the square marks approximately the former mainland coastline and what was the seafront of the village of Rhakotis, an older name for Alexandria before the arrival of Alexander the Great.

THE SOUTHERN QUARTER

The densely populated and fairly poor district of Karmouz, just over 2km (1.25 miles) south of the Corniche, features narrow market streets with numerous fruit and vegetable stalls and teahouses, and two of the city's best-known historical sites; to get here take a taxi or the tram.

Located at the bottom of a hill – which was once home to the citadel

The catacombs of Kom El Shoqafa combine Egyptian and Roman elements.

of Rhakotis – you'll find **Pompey's Pillar** ❶ (al-Amud as-Sawari, the Horseman's Pillar; daily 9am–4.30pm) surrounded by a wall; it's all that's left of the acropolis of the Ptolemies.

The citadel of Rhakotis, dedicated to the worship of Osiris, was erected long before Alexander arrived on the scene. The Ptolemies in their turn constructed a temple of Serapis on its summit. Here, with a collection of around 700,000 manuscripts given to her by Mark Antony, Cleopatra endowed the second great Alexandrian library, which remained attached to the **Serapeum** until the temple itself was destroyed by a Christian mob. Not much remains: some tunnels in the rocks with crypts and niches and a few marble pillars.

Pompey's Pillar is the principal attraction: a solitary 30-metre (98ft) -high pillar of pink Aswan granite, which was the largest of its type outside Rome and Constantinople. When European travellers arrived in the 15th century it caught their attention and they named it after Pompey, saying that his head was enclosed in a ball at the top. It actually has nothing to do with Pompey: according to an inscription on its base, it was dedicated to the Emperor Diocletian in 291; it may once have had an equestrian statue on top, which would explain its Arabic name.

In 1803, a British ship commander, John Shortland, flew a kite over Pompey's Pillar and dropped a rope ladder at the top. He then climbed it, waved the Union Jack, and drank a toast to King George III. A short walk south of Pompey's Pillar are the Catacombs of **Kom El Shoqafa** ❷ (daily 8am–4pm). Come out of the enclosure of Pompey's Pillar, turn right up a crowded street and at the top you will come to a small crossroads. Just beyond it is the entrance to the catacombs. Immediately inside the entrance are four very fine sarcophagi of purplish granite. You are now on the

Kom El Shoqafa ("mound of shards") and the tombs here constitute the largest Roman-period funerary complex in Egypt. They date from about the 2nd century AD, a time when the old religions began to fade and merge with one another, as demonstrated in the curious blend of classical and Egyptian designs.

The catacombs are set out on three different levels, the lowest being flooded and inaccessible. The first level is reached by a wide circular staircase lit by a central well, down which the bodies were lowered by ropes. From the vestibule you enter the rotunda, with a well in its centre, upon which eight pillars support a domed roof. To the left is the banquet hall.

From the rotunda, a small staircase descends to the second level and the amazing central tomb is revealed. Here the decorations are fantastic and in a hotchpotch of styles. Bearded serpents on the vestibule wall at the entrance of the inner chamber hold the pinecone of Dionysus and the serpent-wand of Hermes, but also wear the double

The hulk of a sphinx and Pompey's Pillar behind.

Royal brooch collection in the Royal Jewellery Museum.

Illuminated Montaza Palace.

crown of Upper and Lower Egypt, while above them are Medusas in round shields. Inside the tomb chamber are three large sarcophagi cut out from the rock. Roman in style, decorated with fruits, flowers, Medusas and filleted ox heads, none of them has ever been occupied and their lids are sealed. Over each of the sarcophagi is a niche decorated with Egyptian-style reliefs. Now turn and face the entrance. On your right stands the extraordinary figure of Anubis – with a dog's head, but dressed as a Roman soldier, with sword, lance and shield. On the left is the god Sobek, the crocodile god, with a cloak and spear.

ART AND PARKS

Slightly out of the centre, at 27 Sharia Ahmed Yehia Basha in Zizinia, is the beautiful 19th-century palace of Princess Fatma Al Zahraa, now housing the **Royal Jewellery Museum** (Sat–Thu 9am–4pm, Fri 10–11.30am, 1.30–4pm). Very little is known about Princess Fatma, the great-great-great grandchild of Muhammad Ali, with the exception of her evident taste in interior decoration. The palace features deep carpets, marble staircases, stained-glass windows and carved, gilded ceilings. The superb collection covers a period from Muhammad Ali to the excessive and extravagant monarchy of King Farouk. After the Egyptian Revolution in 1952, all the royal jewellery was expropriated and remained in government stores for a long period before it made its way to this museum, which now exhibits more than 11,000 pieces. As well as jewellery and royal crowns and tiaras, these include bronze and gold cups, gold clocks and watches, and Roman, Persian, Byzantine and Coptic coins. Among the most impressive exhibits are Muhammad Ali's monumental sword, in the shape of a snake and decorated with 600 diamonds; Farouk's grooming set comprising huge crystal bottles capped with heavy gold lids and embossed with the royal coat of arms; and the crown of his wife, Queen Farida, ornamented by more than 1,500 diamonds. In fact, even diamond-encrusted garden tools from the Farouks are on display. Understandably, there's a serious security system in place.

One stop further on tram No. 2 is **San Stefano**, home to the **Mahmoud Said Museum** (daily except Mon 10am–6pm) at 6 Sharia Mohammed Pasha Said, behind a huge shopping mall. It is housed in the stately villa of Mahmoud Said (1897–1964), the son of a prime minister, the uncle of Queen Farida and one of Egypt's best-known modern artists. The museum contains his wonderful paintings dating to the 1930–50s and works by his contemporaries and today's artists. One room is dedicated to Said's female nudes – one in 10 of his paintings were nudes, which he regarded as embodying pure and intrinsic Egyptian beauty. Mahmoud Said is the only Arab artist to date to have paintings selling for more than US$1 million at auction.

At the end of the bay is **Montaza Palace** , built as a summer residence in 1892 by Khedive Abbas II, the ruler of the Khedivate of Egypt and Sudan from 1892 to 1914. In 1932, the larger **Al Haramlik Palace** was added by King Fuad, the last successor of the Muhammed Ali dynasty before the 1952 Revolution, also as a summer palace. The palaces were renovated during the 1970s to serve as an official presidential residence during the summer months, but today Montaza now functions as the characterful El Salamlek Palace Hotel. It has suitably palatial rooms and suites, splendid public areas, a small casino and various restaurants. If nothing else, come for afternoon tea on the terrace and a walk through the lovely 140-hectare (350-acre) gardens – a popular spot for a picnic. The complex also has five beaches for swimming.

Near the zoo and just north of the Mahmoudiyah Canal are the elegant **Antoniadis Gardens**  (daily 8am–5pm) in Smouha. These peaceful formal gardens covering 48 hectares (120 acres) surround the 19th-century villa of the Greek philanthropist Sir John Antoniadis (1818–95), who was president of the Greek community in Alexandria and was knighted by Queen Victoria. The garden has a collection of Greek mythology statues as well as a Roman tomb and cistern.

EAST TO ROSETTA

Alexandria's **Corniche** extends some 16km (10 miles) eastward. There are a number of public beaches between the Eastern Harbour and Montaza, but they are crowded and polluted, and incessant building has turned most of the Corniche into an ugly string of high-rise buildings.

Eight kilometres (5 miles) east of Montaza, with the gardens of the Montaza Palace (see above), is **Abu Qir** , famous for battles fought here in 1798 and 1799. This seaside shanty town is home to some good seafood restaurants with open-air terraces right on the sea.

The next spot of interest is **Rashid**  (Rosetta), 65km (40 miles) from Alexandria on the western branch of the Nile near the sea. It was here that the Rosetta Stone, which enabled Champollion to decipher the hieroglyphics of the pharaohs, was discovered by Pierre Bouchard, a Frenchman working for Napoleon, in 1799. About the size of a gravestone, it was of very hard granite with three parallel bands of inscriptions. The defeat of the French by the British led to the stone passing into British hands and into London's British Museum. A replica of the original can be seen in the Egyptian Museum in Cairo.

Rosetta became the principal port of the northern coast in the 17th- and 18th-centuries and many *wikalahs* (warehouses with lodging rooms attached) and merchant houses were constructed, built in typical Delta style. Unfortunately, most of these are neglected and modern buildings

Ferry in Rashid.

surround them. Still, look for the finest house, **Bayt Ramadan**, just west of the main square, which has a harem for the women in the household on the first floor, and a private hammam (bathhouse) on the top floor. Other traditional houses in the area include **Bayt al-Toqatli**, the impressive **Bayt Amasyali**, which has a splendid facade, and next door to it **Bayt Abu Shaheen**. The Arab Killy house, named after an 18th-century Ottoman governor of the city, is today the **Rachid Museum** (Sat–Thu 9am–4pm, Fri 9am–noon and 2–4pm), just off the main square, which also has a copy of the Rosetta Stone, while the upper floors are furnished to illustrate life in these houses.

WEST TO BORG EL ARAB

The coast road west of Alexandria is unprepossessing for the first 30km (18 miles) until you pass the **Agami**, which started out some decades ago as a few bathing huts and simple beach houses in a grove of trees, but has now mushroomed into an overgrown resort with swimming pools, discotheques and fast-food places.

Before the turn-off to the town of **Borg El Arab** on the hill on your left is the ancient temple of **Taposiris Magna**, whose name is preserved in the modern Abu Sir. It is contemporary with the founding of Alexandria and was dedicated to the cult of Osiris. The ruined tower to the east is a Ptolemaic lighthouse, the first of a chain that stretched all the way along the North African coast. It looks, in miniature, very much as the Pharos would have appeared.

To the south lies the lake bed of **Maryut** (ancient Mareotis), in spring vibrant with wild flowers. If you drive south across the lake bed, you can make out the remains of the ancient causeway, to your left, which connected ancient Taposiris with the desert.

Over the crest of the hill is the crumbling town of **Borg El Arab** ❸, the brainchild of W.E. Jennings-Bramley, governor of the Western Desert under the British, who decided in the early 1920s to build a Bedu capital

Ptolomaic ruins, Taposiris Magna.

using stone from the ruins of Roman villas, which dotted the area. Modelling his village as a fortified medieval Italian hill town, he invited friends to build holiday homes within its turreted walls. The Borg El Arab Airport lies just to the east.

From here, you may want to continue inland and visit the ruins of the **Abu Mina Monastery ④**. To reach it, drive south out of Borg El Arab through an industrial development and turn left at the first crossroads you come to. This road will take you to the turn-off to the monastery. Before long you will spot the twin towers of a new monastery, founded in 1959, a popular pilgrimage spot for modern Copts. Drive on by and very shortly you will see a low line of hillocks to your right, the site of the ancient monastery of Abu Mina; the hillocks are the scrapheaps left behind by several generations of enthusiastic archaeologists. The foundations of the primitive church and the basilica of Arcadius can be discerned.

The crypt where St Mina was buried lies at the foot of a marble staircase, which was incorporated into the portico of the basilica, but his relics rest in the modern monastery. A baptistry with a font lies to the west. North of the basilica are the hospice and baths that were fed by healing springs, with cisterns for hot and cold water. These remains were designated a Unesco World Heritage Site in 1979.

EL ALAMEIN

Further along the coast road, 105km (65 miles) west of Alexandria, is **El Alamein ⑤**, the site of a series of World War II battles that began in the summer of 1942 and turned the tide of war in favour of the Allies. Of the three main war cemeteries in El Alamein, the British is the first one you come to. It is on your left as you enter the town from the east. A walk around the simple tombstones, each of which carries an inscription, cannot fail to move. In the

centre of town is a **War Museum** (Sat–Thu 9am–4pm, Fri 9am–noon, 1–4pm) housing numerous artefacts of the battle such as uniforms, maps and weapons. Outside are many military vehicles and guns that were used, some of them bearing war damage. Beyond stands the stone monument to Germany's fallen soldiers, in a beautiful setting that overlooks the sea. Further down the coast is the Italian memorial, reminiscent of a railway station in a provincial Italian city.

SEASIDE RESORTS

From this point on, the coast varies between beautiful abandonment and heavy development of unfinished holiday resorts. On the left is the desert, enlivened by the occasional flash of colour from a gaily painted house or Bedu tent; to the right is the sea. If you long for a day on the beach, keep going to **Sidi Abdel Rahman**, about 25km (15 miles) past in El Alamein, some people claim it's the best beach on the coast. Out of season the hotels are rather dismal, but a new large

Spire of the new St Mina Monastery, built near the ruins of the original Abu Mina Monastery.

Tanks on display at El Alamein War Museum.

hotel, residential and entertainment complex called Marassi Resort has raised the stakes. One of the main reasons that some tour groups travel along the coast to Sidi Abdel Rahman is to take a break on the journey inland to visit the Siwa Oasis.

Alternatively, you can go to **Marsa Matruh** ❻, 72km (45 miles) further on and 280km (174 miles) from Alexandria. Its seaside is lined with hotels, but the town has little character. You can visit **Rommel's Cave** (Sat–Thu 9am–2pm, until 8pm in summer), now a museum containing the German general's personal effects and the maps he drew up here, as well as his armoury (see box). There are also British, German and Italian cemeteries in the town. The beach to the east, supposedly where Rommel went for his daily swim, is popular with families.

WADI EL NATRUN

To the west of the Delta, just off the Cairo–Alexandria desert road, the **Wadi El Natrun**, or Valley of Natron, snuggles below sea level. It was once home to over 50 monasteries; the best two are open to the public. **Deir Aba Maqar** ❼ (www.stmacariusmonastery.org; daily 9am–6pm), also known as the Monastery of St Macarius the Great, is the largest and best restored, and the monks give tours of the complex. It was founded in approximately AD 360 by St Macarius, and most of the Coptic popes have been selected from here; equally, most are buried here too. During the restoration of the big church, the crypt of St John the Baptist and that of Elisha the Prophet were discovered below the northern wall, with the site being confirmed in 11th- and 16th-century manuscripts found in the library. Dating to AD 350, the second monastery is **Deir Anba Bishoi** ❽ (daily 9am–6pm, until 7pm in summer), or the Monastery of St Pishoy – a disciple of St Macarius. It has five churches and is surrounded by a keep complete with drawbridge.

Wadi El Natrun's churches, like Pharaonic temples, have three distinct areas. The outer is reserved for laymen, the middle for initiates and the

Service at Anba Bishoi.

⦿ VICTORY AT EL ALAMEIN

For several months during early 1942, Allied troops had been forced back across North Africa under pressure from German and Italian troops intent on seizing the Suez Canal. In early July, a defiant stand by the Allies under General Auchinleck halted this advance, but it was his replacement, Lieutenant-General Montgomery (Monty), who took the fight to the Axis powers. The second Battle of El Alamein lasted almost two weeks and by 4 November 1942, Rommel, the German commander, ordered a retreat. The Allied Eighth Army pushed the Afrika Korps westward, trapping the remaining German troops in northeastern Tunisia, leading to their surrender in May 1943. Some experts say that the Allied victory at El Alamein was the turning point of World War II.

inner for clergymen. Visitors should on no account venture into the curtained inner sanctuaries.

THE DELTA

The **Nile Delta** is lush with vegetation and veined with canals. From the barrage at **El Qanater El Khayreya** just north of Cairo, where parks surround locks and sluices built under the British occupation, to the marshy waters of lakes **Idku**, **Burullus** and **Manzalah**, the Delta fans out like a palm tree reaching for the Mediterranean. To both the west and the east, deserts are receding in the face of extensive land-reclamation projects, while in the Delta, *fellaheen* (peasants) pack their bags and leave to seek their fortune in Cairo or the oil-rich Gulf.

The prehistoric Delta was a swampy tidal estuary interspersed with islands. Centuries of effluvia built up a silty land mass that eventually split the river in two. During the annual flood, river water turned the Delta into a vast lake. The ancient Egyptians therefore built their towns on hills and hummocks, which appeared like islands when the inundation was at its height.

Diligent canal building, after the union of Lower and Upper Egypt in the Old Kingdom, tamed the swamp. With the growth of trade and rivalry between Egypt, Phoenicia and the Greeks, the Delta grew in importance, encouraging later pharaohs to establish headquarters in the Delta near the sea.

Each area of the Delta has its particularity. **Mansoura** ❾, the "victorious", was founded on the site of the Mamluks' triumph over crusaders under Louis IX. With its gracious Nileside villas dating from the age when cotton was king in the Delta, the city is regarded as the queen of the Delta.

Dumyat (Damietta) rivalled Alexandria in the Middle Ages and is now the centre of Egypt's furniture industry; and **Desouk** is identified with a festival *(moulid)* in honour of its saint, Ibrahim El Desouki. The Delta's largest town, **Tanta**, is known for its October *moulid*, drawing people from all over Egypt for the festival of Al Sayyed Ahmed Al Badawi

> ⟳ **Tip**
>
> Monasteries are closed to the public during periods of fasting: Sexagesima Monday to Orthodox Easter (61 days), Advent (25 November–6 January), before the Feast of the Apostles (27 June–10 July) and before Assumption (7–21 August).

Farmer and his water buffalo in the Nile Delta.

📷 UNDERWATER ARCHAEOLOGY

The Lighthouse of Alexandria, also called the Pharos of Alexandria, was built during the reign of Ptolemy II Philadelphus (280–247 BC). It was one of the Seven Wonders of the Ancient World, but time and earthquakes brought it down and the ruins now lie beneath the Mediterranean.

Ancient Alexandria was one of the great cities of the world. Befitting its role as a major Mediterranean seaport, it had a grand waterfront, capped by the Pharos. The Eastern Harbour, at whose entrance the Pharos stood, was fronted by the royal palace, which was constantly enlarged and embellished. Cleopatra built a new temple on the waterfront in honour of Mark Antony, which Augustus Caesar finished in honour of himself. In front of it stood two older obelisks brought from the south. This temple, the palace and all but a few stones of the Pharos disappeared in the aftermath of earthquakes.

Modern Alexandrians always knew they were sailing and swimming over the ruins of their city, but it wasn't until 1968 that Unesco sponsored an expedition to send a team of marine archaeologists to the site. The first underwater maps were made around that time by Honor Frost, a Briton working with Unesco. But given this was then a military zone, exploration was put on hold until French archaeologists led by Jean-Yves Empereur rediscovered the remains of the lighthouse in 1994. Empereur's most significant findings were 36 blocks of granite, 30 sphinxes, five obelisks and columns with carvings dating back to Ramsses II (1279–1213 BC).

Meanwhile, a second team under Franck Goddio worked on what was dry land in antiquity in the early 1990s at the opposite side of the Eastern Harbour from where Empereur had worked. This team revealed additional remains of wharves, houses and temples which had all

A scuba diver examines an amphora at Alexandria's "underwater museum".

Underwater archaeologist Franck Goddio shows off a bronze cult statue. Goddio is the grandson of navigator Eric de Bischop, inventor of the modern catamaran.

Three impressive statues (the nearest is of Hapi, god of the annual flooding of the Nile) are pulled from the waters around Alexandria.

fallen into the sea as a result of earthquakes, and they also claimed to have discovered Cleopatra's marble-floored 3rd-century BC palace and Mark Antony's uncompleted palace, the Timonium. In fact, these finds are more likely to date from later than the Ptolemaic period, suggesting they were abandoned after Cleopatra's death when Egypt was absorbed into the Roman Empire.

Some statues and masonry were brought to the surface, including a colossal statue of a Ptolemy pharaoh, which was reassembled underwater after excavation and cleaning. In 2005, the area was declared an underwater museum and it is possible to go diving and see the ruins, although unfortunately pollution and cloudy water can make it difficult to view the artefacts – and accelerate their erosion. Try the Sub Marine Diving Center (www.submarindiving.com) or Alexandra Dive (www.alex-dive.com).

Excavated artefacts are shown onboard the Princess Duda research boat.

An archaeological diver plunges into the sea from the Princess Duda.

Franck Goddio (in blue) and his team raise a sphinx from the depths. Its head is believed to depict Cleopatra's father, Ptolemy XII.

Sitting on the dock of the bay in Ismailia.

THE SUEZ CANAL

The Suez Canal is arguably the most vital traffic artery in the world. When it opened to shipping in 1869, it cut distances between Europe and India in half.

Picture a huge ocean-going ship drifting through a sea of sand. Seen across flat desert, the hallucinatory effect of the Suez Canal underlines the revolutionary impact the waterway has had not only on the nation of Egypt, but also on the structure of international commerce. By the mid-19th century, with the expansion of both trade and empires, its economic potential was becoming increasingly obvious.

AN OLD IDEA

The idea of building a canal that would link the Mediterranean with the Red Sea is an ancient one. The first channel connecting the Nile and Red Sea might go as far back as the 12th Dynasty (c.1800 BC). Certainly the 26th Dynasty pharaoh Necho II aired such a proposal at the end of the 7th century BC, with a project to join the Gulf of Suez to the Nile, down which ships could continue to the Mediterranean. According to Herodotus, an oracular pronouncement that he would merely be "labouring for the barbarians" disuaded Necho from completing excavations. The job was therefore left to Egypt's Persian conquerors a century later, under Darius; their work was followed by Ptolemaic and Roman re-excavation.

During the centuries before the Arab conquest, however, this old canal silted up and the Muslims' brilliant general

Fishermen on the canal, Ismailia.

Amr ibn al-As suggested that a new and better one should be cut across the narrow isthmus of Suez. Cautioned by the caliph Omar that it would be hard to defend and that Greek pirates might use it as a route to attack the holy city of Mecca, he satisfied himself with renovating the existing canal. It flourished for another century before being blocked on orders of the Abbasid caliph al-Mansur.

It was not until the 19th century, with the growth of European power in the region and the energetic promotion

Main attractions

Port Said
Ismailia
Suez

Map on page 252

THE SUEZ CANAL

Engineered by the French, built by the Egyptians and coveted by the British, the Suez Canal has historically been a troubled but lucrative waterway, and in recent years has witnessed considerable investment and development.

Construction of the Suez Canal began in 1859. It took 10 years, with 25,000 labourers working three-month shifts, to cut the 160km (100-mile) channel. The total cost, including the building of the Sweetwater Canal for drinking water from the Nile, reached £25 million, of which Egypt put up more than two-thirds. Amid extravagant fanfare, with assorted European royalty in attendance, the canal was opened to shipping in November of 1869, transforming trade and geopolitics as dramatically

Construction of the Suez Canal near El-Qantara.

as the Portuguese and Spanish discoveries of the 15th century. At the same time Cairo acquired an extravagant new opera house and a new palace (now the Marriott Hotel) to entertain and accommodate the important guests who attended the opening.

However, Egypt's mounting debts forced the sale of its stake to the British Government for a paltry sum of £4 million sterling. As London's *Economist* dryly commented in the year of its opening, the canal was "cut by French energy and Egyptian money for British advantage". The strategic importance of the canal to the British Empire was one of the excuses for occupying Egypt in 1882.

THE FORTUNES OF FIVE WARS

Britain imposed draconian measures on Egypt while defending the canal in both world wars. For Egyptians, foreign possession of the canal came to represent the major reason for the anti-imperialist struggle. Not until 1954 did Nasser achieve the withdrawal of British troops occupying the Canal Zone.

In 1956, hard up and seeking to finance the High Dam, Nasser turned as a last resort – having been refused financing by the United States – to nationalising the canal, from which Egypt received only a tiny portion of the revenue. Unreconciled to the rapid decline of its empire, Britain responded by invading, with the collusion of Israel and France, in what became known as the Suez Crisis. Only the intervention of the USA and the Soviet Union resolved the crisis, marking a turning point in international relations. Ten years later all that remained of Britain's empire were Gibraltar, Hong Kong and a few remote islands. Meanwhile Egypt had become dependent upon Russia.

In June 1967, the Israelis again attacked Egypt in the Six Day War, and held the Sinai Peninsula up to the edge of the canal. Heavy bombardment during the War of Attrition that followed the Israeli conquest shattered the canal cities and made refugees of their 500,000 inhabitants. For six years, until the successful Egyptian counterattack of the Yom Kippur War in October 1973, the waterway was closed to traffic.

of the French engineer Ferdinand de Lesseps that Amr's idea could be brought to fruition. A Suez Canal Company was formed by public subscription in Europe and an agreement was reached with the viceroy Said and his successor Khedive Ismail, whereby Egypt provided both capital and labour for the job itself.

THE CANAL CITIES

PORT SAID

Port Said ⑩ (Bur Sa'id) and its twin city, Port Fouad, on the other side of the canal, were built in 1859 during canal construction. Port Said sits on an artificial landfill jutting into the Mediterranean and is named after the khedive of Egypt, Said Pasha. From here, southbound convoys of ships depart every morning at 3.30am, passing the green domes of the Suez Canal Authority building to begin the journey to the Red Sea.

Once the major point of entry for tourists stepping off the great Peninsular and Orient (P & O) passenger lines, Port Said is now the Hong Kong of Egypt, where Cairo consumers flock for duty-free goods. Despite the damage of three wars and the current emporium atmosphere, this resilient town retains a good deal of character, including some fine period buildings from the middle of the 18th century. To the north, it's flanked by a wide expanse of Mediterranean beach, popular with domestic tourists: there are lines of deck chairs, umbrellas and colourful windbreakers for hire and endless views of the ships queuing up on their approach to the canal.

ISMAILIA

Situated on **Lake Timsah** halfway between Port Said and Suez, **Ismailia ⑪** (al-Isma'iliyyah) was built to accommodate European workers of the Suez Canal Company during construction of the canal. With its tree-shaded avenues and colonial-style houses, it is the queen of the canal cities and retains a certain gentility from the 1950s, when British officers escaped the hardships of their desert postings to relax here

Suez Canal Authority monument on the bank of the New Suez Canal, Ismailia.

A monument to the Yom Kippur War, in the shape of an AK-47, on the eastern shore of the Suez Canal.

Mosque in Bur Tawfiq.

at the French and Greek clubs. There are several fairly good hotels and restaurants; and from uncrowded lakeside beaches ships transiting the canal – which is much wider here as the lake opens out – can be watched.

There are few places in the world where you can watch giant tankers and container ships glide past at 15km (9 miles) per hour so close and so quietly. The ships take between 11 and 16 hours to pass through, so you are almost certain to see a line of them at Ismailia around midday.

Ismailia has a few sights in addition to the canal. You can take a taxi to the small **regional museum** (daily 9am–4pm), which has a good selection of mainly Greek and Roman finds, including a large 4th-century mosaic with mythological creatures. One of the most impressive items is a Hellenised face on a marble coffin from the Ptolemaic period.

Near the centre of Ismailia is the former **house of Ferdinand de Lesseps**, the builder of the Suez Canal, and close by a mosaic of the grand opening ceremony. In the central town square is the large new mosque of Abu Bakr Saddiq.

SUEZ

The canal's southern terminus, **Suez** ⑫ (al-Suways), was Egypt's major Red Sea port for hundreds of years; thus it's an important transit point for millions of Muslims making the pilgrimage to Mecca *(hajj)* from North Africa and Turkey. The town has an important trading history as the main port at the northern end of the Red Sea. It was, for example, crucial in the coffee trade from the southern Red Sea port of Mocha in Yemen, for coffee accounted for over 60 percent of Egypt's imports at the end of the 18th century. The wreck of a 17th-century cargo ship at Sadana Island at the entrance to the Gulf of Suez has been excavated to reveal a cargo of coffee, porcelain, pepper, spices and incense bound for Suez.

The port's harbour is now at **Bur Tawfiq**, an artificial peninsula where the canal meets the **Gulf of Suez**. Israeli bombardments flattened the town in the 1967 war, after which it was evacuated and hasty rebuilding has not enhanced its beauty. It's an ugly, scruffy concrete city, patched up hurriedly after the conflicts.

Suez is best observed from the Sinai side of the canal, where scores of ships can be seen lining up in the Gulf ready to make the northward passage and then manoeuvring, with the help of pilot boats, into the canal. It is an amazing sight.

THE MODERN CANAL

The canal reopened in 1975 and since the withdrawal of the Israelis from the Sinai in 1982, the canal now fully lies within Egypt. During the eight years that it was closed, super tankers were built to make the alternative voyage around the bottom of Africa more viable; once it reopened, these were too large to go through the canal, but sinc

then it has been widened and deepened to accommodate them.

Today, after several enlargements, the canal is 193.30km (120.11 miles) long, 24 metres (79ft) deep and 205 metres (67ft) wide; it can receive vessels of up to 240,000 tons. And in 2015, the "New Suez Canal" opened – a parallel canal along the middle stretch, with a length of 35km (22 miles), allowing ships to pass and travel in both directions. Almost 50 ships per day make the transit through the canal and it's a major revenue source for Egypt, earning more than US$3 billion each year. Many of the major cruise lines go through the Suez Canal. Being out on deck throughout transit is one of the world's most fascinating maritime experiences, creating the bizarre impression that you are sailing right through the desert.

Recent investment in developing links across the canal to connect the east and west banks has started to improve communications with the Sinai and to repopulate the eastern bank of the canal, which had been abandoned

during the wars with Israel. Just north of Suez is the 1.6km (1-mile) long Ahmed Hamdi Tunnel, providing vehicle access to the Sinai. It was built by the British in 1981 but leakage problems necessitated serious repairs by the Japanese within the first decade. For many years this was the only tunnel under the canal, but in 2019, four more tunnels opened: two just north of Ismailia, and two more near Port Said.

Modern bridges have been built, too. Fifty kilometres (31 miles) south of Port Said at El-Qantara, the Mubarak Peace Bridge, also known as the Egyptian-Japanese Friendship Bridge, almost 10km (6 miles) in length, was built with Japanese assistance and opened in 2001. The clearance under the bridge is 70 metres (230ft), allowing for ships to pass below. Additionally, the Al-Nasr floating bridge, connecting Port Said and Port Fuuad on the opposite eastern bank, opened in 2016. The two components extend from each bank; with the help of tugboats that push the parts together, they form a bridge that can be traversed by cars.

Ship approaching the Mubarak Peace Bridge.

The Qulaan Islands in the Red Sea.

Camels in the Sinai Desert.

SINAI

Whether treated as holy ground or as a battleground fought over by classical empires and modern nation states, the Sinai Peninsula has always been special.

The Sinai's 25,000 sq km (10,000 sq miles) of desert ranges from the spiky granite mountains of the south to the central plateau of al-Tih, on to the rolling dunes of the northern coastal plain. Volumes have been dedicated to this small arid peninsula poised delicately but obstinately as a buffer zone between Asia and Africa. The Sinai is effectively a barrier separating the two halves of the Arab world, and there have been more than 50 recorded invasions of the area since Pharaonic times (see page 285). Indeed, the Sinai has weathered as many military crossings as it has peaceful occupations. Its few prehistoric, ancient and medieval remains have only been scratched at by archaeologists, while Biblical geographers' controversies over problematic routes and sites have created an academic kaleidoscope of fact and fantasy.

A TURBULENT REGION

The shock of Israeli occupation from 1967 – following the Six-Day War – and Israel's opportunistic development of the peninsula's tourist potential ignited Egypt's fierce determination to bind the Sinai once again to the Nile Valley. In 1982, as a result of the Israel–Egypt Peace Treaty of 1978, Israel withdrew, and this time the region was inextricably bound to Egypt. The Sinai became a

tourist destination, with visitors drawn to its natural setting, rich coral reefs and Biblical history. First it attracted backpackers, who enjoyed lounging on cushions while smoking shisha at the low-budget kibbutzniks and going snorkelling, diving and on camel treks with the Bedu. Soon airports opened and brought European package tourists to bigger hotels; Sharm El Sheikh and Dahab quickly became sprawling resorts.

However, the bubble somewhat burst from the 2000s, mainly as a result of a series of terrorist attacks

⊙ **Main attractions**

Ras Sedr
Hammam Fara'un
Feiran
St Catherine's Monastery
Ras Muhammad
Sharm El Sheikh
Nuweiba
Taba

Map on page 284

Bedouin woman making tea in Dahab.

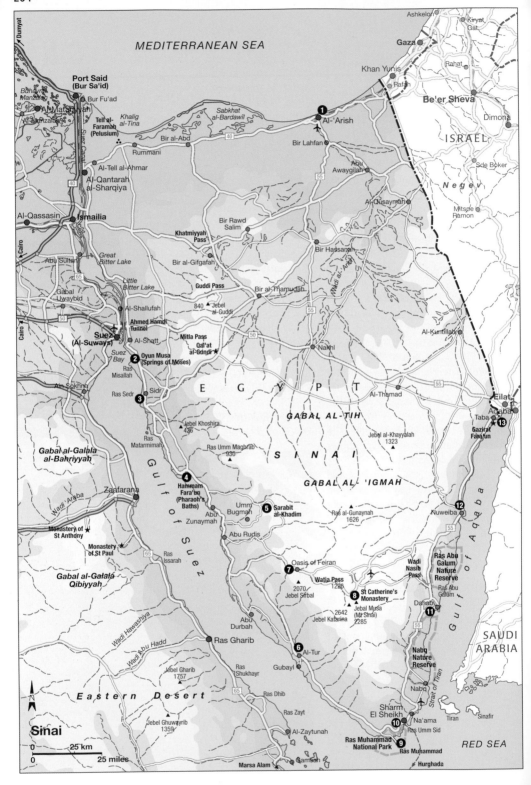

MEDITERRANEAN SEA

Ashkelon
Kiryat
Gat
Gaza
Rahat
Khan Yunis
Be'er Sheva
Rafah
Dimona
1 Al-'Arish
Port Said
(Bur Sa'id)
Bur Fu'ad
Bira al-Abd
Bir Lahfan
ISRAEL
Buhayrat
Manzalah
Al-Matariyyah
Al-Manzalah
Tell al-
Faramah
(Pelusium)
Khalig
al-Tina
Sabkhat
al-Bardawil
Rummani
Abu
Awaygilah
Negev
Sde Boker
Al-Tell al-Ahmar
40
55
Al-Qantarah
al-Sharqiya
Al-Qassasin
Ismailia
Bir Rawd
Salim
Al-Qusaymah
Mitspe
Ramon
Cairo
Abu Sultan
Great
Bitter Lake
Khatmiyyah
Pass
Bir Hassanah
Little
Bitter Lake
Bir al-Gifgafah
40
Gabal
Uwaybid
Guddi Pass
Bir al-Thamudah
Wadi al-Arish
Al-Shallufah
840
Jebel
al-Guddi
55
Ahmed Hamdi
Tunnel
Mitla Pass
50
Al-Kuntillah
Suez
(Al-Suways)
Al-Shatt
Qal'at
al-Gdndi
Nakhl
Suez
Bay
2 Oyun Musa
(Springs of Moses)
E G Y P T
Ras
Misallah
Ain Sokhna
Ras Sedr
3 Sidr
GABAL AL-TIH
Al-Thamad
55
Eilat
Taba
Aqaba
Gulf of Suez
Jebel Khoshira
436
Ras
Matarmimah
S I N A I
Jebel al-Khayyalah
1323
13 Gazirat
Fara'un
Gabal al-Galala
al-Bahriyyah
Ras Umm Maghrab
930
GABAL AL-'IGMAH
Zaafarana
4 Hammam
Fara'un
(Pharaoh's
Baths)
Umm
Bugman
5 Sarabit
al-Khadim
Ras al-Gunaynah
1626
12
Nuweiba
Monastery of
St Anthony
Abu
Zunaymah
Ras Abu
Galum
Nature
Reserve
Monastery
of St Paul
Abu Rudis
Oasis of Feiran
Wadi
Nasib
Pass
Ras Abu
Galum
65
Ras
Issarah
7
2070
Jebel Sirbal
Watia Pass
1286
Dahab
Gabal al-Galala
Qibiyyah
Wadi Araba
8 St Catherine's
Monastery
11
Wadi Hawashiya
Abu
Durbah
Jebel Musa
(Mt Sinai)
2285
2642
Jebel Katarina
SAUDI
ARABIA
Ras Gharib
6 Al-Tur
Wadi Abu Hadd
Gubayl
Nabq
Nature
Reserve
Jebel Gharib
1757
Ras
Shukhayr
Nabq
Strait of Tiran
Eastern Desert
Ras Dhib
65
Sharm
El Sheikh
10 Na'ama
Tiran
Sinafir
Jebel Ghuwayrib
1359
Ras Zayt
Ras Umm Sid
Sinai
Al-Zaytunah
9
Ras Muhammad
National Park
Ras Muhammad
RED SEA
0   25 km
Marsa Alam
Qamson
Hurghada
0   25 miles

Gulf of Aqaba

linked to Islamic extremism that targeted tourists in the area – affecting Taba and Nuweiba in 2004, Sharm El Sheikh in 2005 and Dahab in 2006. Since the Egyptian Revolution of 2011, there has been a further spate of violent incidents in the Sinai, today referred to as the Sinai Insurgency. Largely instigated by local Islamic militant Bedu, who exploited Egypt's chaotic situation and weakened central authority, these attacks have terrorised government forces and the Christian minority. Tourists have been caught up in this newer conflict too – notably the disastrous 2015 bombing of a Russian airliner taking off from Sharm El Sheikh Airport – and security fears rippling through the region have yet again created a downturn in tourism.

Today, security in the resort towns is steadily improving, though it is still advisable to get up-to-the-minute advice before visiting the Sinai. Travel to northern Sinai, where many of the local attacks are presently taking place, is not advised *at all*. Check the UK Foreign and Commonwealth Office (FCO) and other countries' travel advisories before your visit.

NORTH SINAI

Aside from seasonal Bedu encampments, North Sinai's population is concentrated on the provincial capital of **Al-'Arish ❶** (also known as El Arish). From Cairo, the main Ismailia highway leads to the Suez Canal. At El-Qantara, north of Ismailia, crossing to the Sinai is over the Mubarak Peace Bridge.

The road continues across the desert to the northeast, skirting the marshy lagoon of Lake Bardawil to reach Al-'Arish after 130km (85 miles). This city of 165,000 is the biggest in the peninsula and much recent effort has been made to turn it into a palm-fringed resort with plenty of reasonably priced hotels and restaurants popular with Egyptian holiday-makers, though the once beautiful Mediterranean beaches are hemmed in with concrete. The local Thursday souq has some good Bedu finds. Bedu crafts and jewellery are also on display at the Sinai

> **⊙ Fact**
>
> Sinai is mostly inhabited by the Bedu, or Bedouin, who claim descent from tribes of the Hejaz (Saudi Arabia) on the Arabian Peninsula, except the Jebeliya ("mountain people"), who are believed to be descendants of Caucasians.

On the road in the Sinai.

⊙ MILITARY THOROUGHFARE

The wilderness of the Sinai is one of the most strategically important locations on earth. As the land bridge between Africa and Asia it has witnessed the marching feet of countless armies. It is where the ancient Egyptians under great military pharaohs such as Tutmosis III and Ramesses II attacked their eastern Mediterranean enemies, such as the hated Hyksos. In the other direction came the armies of Assyria, Persia, Greece and Rome, all intent on conquering the powerful Nile Valley civilisations.

With the building of the Suez Canal, the region became even more important, with the Sinai essentially a "buffer zone" between east and west. During World War I there were several important battles fought by the Allies to stop Turkish forces seizing the canal as early as February 1915. From their base in Jerusalem, the Turks and Germans were attempting to stem the flow of men and supplies from the British Empire in the east.

After the establishment of the State of Israel in 1947, Egypt and its Arab neighbours fought the first Arab-Israeli war the following year. Other major conflicts followed, such as the Suez Crisis of 1956 when British, French and Israeli forces attacked Egypt, the Arab-Israeli wars of 1967 (when Israel seized the Sinai from Egypt) and 1973, ending with the signing of the Camp David Peace Accord in 1978 which saw the eventual handing back of the Sinai to Egypt.

Heritage Museum (daily except Fri 9.30am–2pm).

Just east of the town, the bare dunes begin. A few olive trees appear, marking the decline of the desert and the beginning of the fertile Palestine coastal plain. At 50km (31 miles), the town of **Rafah** marks the current border. Beyond lies Gaza. Rafah's population is a mixture of local Bedu and Palestinian refugees. Their camp – built with Canadian government aid and consequently called Canada – was brutally bisected by the border fence erected after the area's return to Egypt in 1983. The border crossing at Rafah is now closed most of the time because of the situation in Gaza.

Between Al-'Arish and Rafah a number of wadis, seasonal watercourses, lead back from the sea into the desert interior. The Bedu graze their goats and camels extensively in this region. Friendly and hospitable, they are wont to invite travellers into their ramshackle settlements – shacks slapped together with cans, boxes and the debris of four wars – for a glass of tea.

Hammam Musa (Moses' Bath), near Oyun Musa.

The desert-dwelling women of North Sinai wear gorgeous embroidered dresses and heavy silver jewellery and are extremely friendly, so the opportunity to mingle should not be missed.

To the northeast of Suez and difficult to access, lie the ruins of a medieval fortress, **Qala'at al-Gundi**. Built by Saladin to protect trade and pilgrimage routes, these fortifications attest to the importance Muslim rulers attached to Egypt's Asian gateway.

SOUTH SINAI

With its two coasts, oases, mountains and historic sites, South Sinai is a much more popular destination. North of Suez, the Ahmed Hamdi Tunnel carries traffic under the canal. Turning south, the main road follows the canal, veering eastward opposite Suez. From here it descends 320km (200 miles) along the breezy Gulf of Suez to Sharm El Sheikh.

Along this route and 20km (12.5 miles) south of the tunnel is **Oyun Musa ❷**, the "Springs of Moses", a palm grove fed by two wells of

brackish water where Moses is said to have rested with his flock. According to the *Bible*, after three days of travelling in the desert without water, Moses found the water was too bitter to drink. But after supplicating God for a solution, he was told to throw a piece of wood into the water to make it drinkable. The wells lie behind a Bedouin village settlement of the same name and the local people here believe that the water has various healing properties.

Thirty-three kilometres (20 miles) further on, the road nears the coast at the wide sandy beach of **Ras Sedr ❸**, a favourite stopping place, where there are several hotels. Many Cairenes have holiday homes here. Unlike the Gulf of Aqaba on Sinai's east coast, the Gulf of Suez is shallow and sandy-bottomed. The marine life is abundant, and there are plenty of water sports on offer. Moon Beach in Ras Sedr is one of Egypt's top wind- and kite-surfing destinations.

Beyond Ras Sedr the road bends away from the coast up into the mountains. A track to the right at this turn leads after a few hundred metres/yds to **Hammam Fara'un ❹**, the hot springs known as "Pharaoh's Baths". The seven springs produce boiling-hot mineral-rich waters that bubble from the base of the mountains right into the sea. It is a popular spot for Egyptian family bathing. The waters are said by local Bedu to cure rheumatism.

ANCIENT MINING AREA

About 16km (10 miles) into the mountains above Hammam Fara'un, a track leads left among palm trees. Negotiable only by 4x4 vehicles, it continues for 32km (20 miles) to the site of **Sarabit al-Khadim ❺** (no facilities, ask for a Bedu guide at Abu Zunaymah), a 12th-Dynasty temple that was dedicated originally to the goddess Hathor. A second shrine, for the patron god of the Eastern Desert, Sopdu, was later added. The site, which covers approximately 0.4 hectares (1 acre), has yielded more than 400 inscriptions, some of which praise Hathor,

Hatshepsut or Tuthmosis III, and others give instructions regarding the mining of turquoise in the region (turquoise, malachite and copper were all mined here).

Particularly interesting is the graffiti of the workers, some written in unknown scripts called protosinaitic. They form the link between hieroglyphics and the Phoenician alphabet from which Latin script developed. Also discovered here was the bust of Queen Tiy of the Old Kingdom, now displayed in the Egyptian Museum in Cairo (see page 134).

Inscriptions at the mines of **Wadi Maraghah**, south of Sarabit al-Khadim, date back to the 4th Dynasty and the reigns of Snefru and Khufu (Cheops), builder of the Great Pyramid. The British caused much damage to the inscriptions here when they tried to reopen the mines in 1901.

From Wadi Maraghah, a track running down the Wadi Sidri for 24km (15 miles) rejoins the main road at **Abu Zunaymah**, where it descends again from the mountains to the coast.

Beyond this ramshackle frontier settlement, where manganese from local mines of recent date is processed, the road continues to Abu Rudis. The Gulf of Suez is at this point dotted with beetle-like rigs shooting flames into the haze: this is the centre of Sinai's oil fields, most of them off-shore. Pipes, fences, tanks and prefabricated housing clutter the shore town to Balayim, 50km (31 miles) further on.

The road again leaves the coast, heading towards the mountains of the Sinai range. A checkpoint marks the turn-off to St Catherine's Monastery, while the main road continues south to Al-Tur and Sharm El Sheikh. **Al-Tur** ❻, the capital and largest town in South Sinai, is reached after 75km (45 miles) of hot driving through a wide valley. Settled in ancient times because of its good water supply and excellent harbour, it was the chief quarantine station for pilgrims returning to Egypt from Mecca. Modern Al-Tur, despite scattered palm groves and a beautiful beach, retains this way-station atmosphere. The town's population is a broad ethnic mix, many of them descended from Berber and African immigrants. From Al-Tur it is 100km (60 miles) to Sharm El Sheikh (see page 292).

GOING TO ST CATHERINE'S

Turning instead up towards St Catherine's, you enter the **Wadi Feiran**. Narrowing as it mounts, after 33km (20 miles) the dry ravine suddenly blossoms into a river of date palms. This is the **Oasis of Feiran** ❼, the largest and most fertile patch of cultivation on the peninsula. Parched for most of the year, winter rains and melting snow send down short-lived torrents to water the valley. Peppered throughout the palm groves are clusters of Bedu huts. The wadi may have been the site of the biblical battle between the Amalakites and the Israelites. Within the mountain

Trekking in the Sinai.

are the scattered remains of monasteries, chapels and hermit cells of early Christian monks who believed this to be the Elim of the *Bible*. Tranquil and serene, it is difficult to imagine that Feiran was a cathedral city in the Middle Ages. Today it is spread with the ruins of dozens of ancient churches, some dating back to the 4th century AD, and you can often visit the small operating convent here with permission.

South of the oasis, approached most easily up the Wadi 'Aleayat, rises the peak of the **Jebel Sirbal**. At 2,070 metres (7,000ft), it is not high for the Sinai range, but its isolation makes the view from its summit extensive. One school of Biblical speculators claims it as the true Mount Sinai.

From Feiran the road climbs into an open plain and after 32km (20 miles) reaches the settlement of St Catherine, where there are hotels, a campsite and the bus stop. The **St Catherine's Monastery ❶** (www.sinai-monastery.com; 9am–noon, closed on Fri and Sun and all Greek Orthodox holidays; modest attire is required) is in a wadi between Jebel Musa – most popular candidate for the site of the delivery of the Ten Commandments – and the Jebel al-Dayr just up the hill to the south.

The Roman emperor Justinian ordered the building of a fortress monastery on the site in AD 537 in order to protect the Sinai passes against invasion. Originally dedicated to the Transfiguration of Christ, the church built within the fortress was renamed after St Catherine (a 4th-century Alexandrian martyred for her derision of Roman idol-worship), after her body miraculously appeared atop Sinai's highest peak, apparently looking none the worse for wear. This miracle, coupled with the Crusaders' occupation of nearby Palestine, ensured the support of Christian rulers.

The monastery's fame spread, so that by the 14th century up to 400 monks lived there, as the grisly collection of skulls in the ossuary attests. In recent centuries Russia

A green oasis in the Sinai.

The ossuary at St Catherine's Monastery.

St Catherine's Monastery.

was the chief benefactor. The monastery now has around 20 resident monks, and remains the property of the Greek Orthodox Church. As the world's oldest Christian monastery still in use for its initial function, it became a Unesco World Heritage Site in the early 2000s.

THE MONASTERY

The path to St Catherine's leads past a walled orchard and an outer complex of buildings before reaching the monastery itself. An old basket-and-pulley system of entry has been abandoned and visitors now enter by simply walking through a portal. A small building on the left inside the wall is one of the original structures, diplomatically converted into a mosque in the 12th century. The Church of St Catherine is down the steps to the left, just behind the mosque.

The church, built by order of Justinian in AD 527, is basilical in form, with great granite columns supporting the nave. The wooden bracing beams of the reconstructed ceiling are original

and beautifully carved, one of them with a foundation inscription dating to Justinian. The doors leading to the sanctuary are flanked by two silver chests inlaid with precious stones. Both were donated by members of the Russian royal family, one in the 17th century, the other in the 19th. The sanctuary is adorned with 6th-century mosaics that are the monastery's greatest treasure. Within the arch and semi-dome of the apse is a portrayal of the Transfiguration of Christ: to his left stand Moses and St James, and on his right are Elijah and St John the Apostle.

Side aisles, lined with chapels dedicated to varied saints and decorated with ancient and modern icons, lead off from either side of the church. At the sanctuary end of the building a small alcove opens into the Chapel of the Burning Bush. Here, on a site marked by a small silver plate, God spoke to Moses while hidden in a flaming shrub. The monastery's other treasures, off-limits to visitors (unless they have a letter of introduction from

the Greek patriarchate in Cairo), include a library of rare manuscripts and a museum containing a superb collection of icons.

Just behind the monastery, a path leads ultimately to the summit of 2,285-metre (7,497ft) -high Jebel Musa, popularly known as **Mount Sinai**. There are two principal routes to the top and it takes about two-and-a-half-hours each way. The longer and less steep route, Siket El Bashait, can also be negotiated by camel (for hire in the village). The steeper, more direct route, Siket Sayidna Musa, is up the 3,750 "steps of penitence" – rough stone steps that were likely constructed in the 6th or 7th century. The climb is fairly easy, but coming down is trickier, and care should be taken. The view from the top is magnificent, particularly at dawn or sunset. In fact, many visitors book onto tours that arrive at approximately 1am at the foot of the mountain in order to climb to the top to watch sunrise. Little café stalls on the path up serve hot coffee and tea and snacks. After dark, ensure you have a torch and certainly bring a jacket because the wind really blows at the top.

All of Sinai's mountains are very ancient, and their variety, in terms of texture, colour, shape and vegetation, is eternally fascinating – especially in the very early morning or early evening when their contours and colours are seen most clearly. Another option is to climb Jebel Katherin (Mount Catherine), the highest point in Egypt at more than 2,640 metres (8,500ft), which has an even better view. It is approached up the wadi on Jebel Musa's western side, but this is a challenging one-day trek up and down and a guide is required. But the descent from Mount Catherine to the east traverses enthralling landscapes all the way to the sea.

THE GULF OF AQABA

One of the earth's most dramatic interfaces, the **Gulf of Aqaba** is only 16km (10 miles) wide, but in places as much as 1,800 metres (6,000ft) deep. Indeed, it marks a long geological

Locals and their camels on Mount Sinai.

fault, running from the Dead Sea in the north to Africa's Great Rift Valley in the south. Coral reefs line the shores of the Gulf from Ras Muhammad at the peninsula's extremity to Taba on the Israeli border. Teeming with life and colour, they provide a striking contrast to the desolation of the land.

With Sharm El Sheikh Airport serving as the major hub to this east coast of the Sinai, the region has traditionally been a popular package-holiday destination for Europeans. However, since the bombing of a Russian airliner, which killed all 224 people on board in October 2015 soon after take-off from Sharm El Sheikh Airport, most European airlines and holiday companies withdrew. At the time of writing, while Sharm El Sheikh itself is currently considered safe, there generally remains a warning over all but essential travel by air to or from the popular Red Sea resort – although European governments are currently working with the Egyptian authorities to enable regular flights to resume. Unfortunately, however, there has been a dearth of tourism on the east coast in recent years.

Ras Muhammad ❾ is a coral peninsula thrusting its head into the Red Sea at the southernmost tip of the Sinai. It is a national park and one of the outstanding snorkelling and diving areas in the world. At the Shark's Observatory a coral ridge falls over 80 metres (262ft) into the open sea and the wary diver or snorkeller can float along its edge (under 1 metre/3ft deep at high tide) and look out into an underwater paradise.

North of Ras Muhammad, on a beautiful natural harbour much damaged by the ill-planned building of successive occupants, is the town of **Sharm El Sheikh** ❿, international gateway to the region and the hub of a series of resorts that merge into one another – Ras Muhammad (see above), Na'ama Bay, Coral Bay, Shark's Bay (a good family resort) and Ras Nasrani. **Peace Road**, running a little way inland, links all the bays together (taxis and minibuses ply the route).

Gateway to Ras Muhammad National Park.

Old Sharm lies a little way inland, as authentic a piece of Egypt as you will see on this part of the Sinai coast, with small shops on backstreets and an unhurried atmosphere: it is well worth a visit.

Eight kilometres (5 miles) farther on, **Na'ama Bay** is the centre of Sinai's tourist boom, with hotels, restaurants, camping grounds and diving shops. It is over-developed but it makes a good base for visiting local beaches. Some of the best for diving and snorkelling are The Tower, Ras Umm Sid, Ras Nasrani and Nabq. Equipment can be rented at one of many diving centres, where boat trips to Gazirat Tiran, an island in the middle of the straits with superb corals, can also be arranged. Shipwrecks dot the shoreline, testifying to the difficulty of navigation between the reefs.

DAHAB

Hotel complexes spread further and further beyond the airport, but the next major coastal settlement is **Dahab ⑪**, 90km (56 miles) north. Sediments washed down from the mountains have created a broad sandy plain here. An Israeli-built town on a sandy cove, it has hotels, restaurants, camping and diving facilities and a reputation as the "Ibiza of Egypt". It is world-renowned for its wind- and kite-surfing as reliable winds provide superb flat-water conditions inside Dahab's sand spit. The scuba diving is also excellent thanks to coral reefs just offshore, and there are several dive schools.

Across the plain 2km (1.25 miles) to the west, the Bedu village of **Assalah** sits next to a palm-lined horseshoe bay. Here low-budget travellers stay in reed huts on the beach, which is lined with informal cafés.

Nuweiba ⑫ is 75km (45 miles) further north, a slightly superior resort, although cheap accommodation in beachside reed huts and relaxed alfresco cafés can be found in Tarabin to the north. There are wide sandy beaches, but the reefs here are not as good as further south. Nuweiba functions primarily as a port for the daily passenger- and car-ferry to Aqaba in Jordan, which is operated by Jordanian company AB Maritime (www.abmaritime.com.jo). The ferry allows travel between Egypt and Jordan without transiting through Israel.

Taba ⑬ is 60km (37 miles) north of Nuweiba. This small Egyptian town near the northern tip of the Gulf of Aqaba is the location of Egypt's border crossing with neighbouring Eilat in Israel. There are a number of hotels here, traditionally popular with Israelis, but Taba has been blighted with terrorism incidents in recent decades, including the 2004 bombing of the Hilton Hotel, and the bombing of a coach in 2014, which injured all passengers on board and killed two South Korean tourists. Nevertheless, if you are entering Egypt overland from Israel and the Palestinian Territories, Taba has all the facilities you could need, and there are onwards buses and long-distance taxis.

> **⊙ Tip**
>
> The resorts and dive shops in Dahab organise day and overnight 4x4 and camel trekking trips into the hinterland. These trips are well worthwhile: many of the fertile wadis (valleys) are extremely beautiful and it's a great opportunity to engage with the Bedu who will be your guides and hosts.

Idyllic beach at Nuweiba.

El Gouna beach.

THE RED SEA AND EASTERN DESERT

The beauty of the landscape and an excellent climate are obvious reasons for this region's ever-increasing popularity, especially as a winter-sun destination.

The Red Sea coast of Egypt runs for 1,600km (1,000 miles) in a south-easterly direction from Suez. Despite the many offshore drilling wells and numerous oil depots, petrol stations are few and far between and trips by car must be planned with foresight. The rewards, however, are considerable. For most of its length, beautiful but desolate limestone and granite mountains border the coast, with range rising upon range, their shades of purple harmonising with deep-blue skies and blue-green seas.

But this once pristine coast is changing fast. Most of the coastline has been sold to developers and many large-scale tourist projects, from the basic to the luxurious, have already been built or are underway.

DESERT ROADS

Apart from the area east of Cairo, where sprawling suburbs and industrial zones eventually join up with the pockmarked battlegrounds of past wars in the canal area, the transition from the green Nile Valley is abrupt. Suddenly the lush cultivated land gives way to stony wilderness, in which rocks rise up in extraordinary formations, reminiscent of the pyramids and Sphinx, the sand blows and spills, and there is hardly a sign of human life for hundreds of miles.

Jeep safari in the desert.

To get to the coast from Cairo, an obvious choice would be to take the Cairo–Suez highway, which opened in 2016 and is in great condition. But this route is heavily congested with trucks heading to the Sinai and beyond via the Ahmed Hamdi Tunnel under the Suez Canal. A better alternative is to take another good highway, route 75, from Cairo and join the coast road at **Ain Sokhna**, 134km (83 miles) southeast of Cairo and 56km (35 miles) south of Suez. Effectively the nearest seaside resort to the capital, this

Main attractions
Monastery of St Anthony
Monastery of St Paul
El Gouna
Hurghada
Eastern Desert
Safaga
Marsa Alam

Map on page 296

is a popular year-round getaway for wealthy Cairenes thanks to a strip of swaying date palms, white sand and clear green-blue sea. It has a string of high-rise holiday resorts, private villas and a smattering of cafés and shops. But perhaps the best reason to stop is to ride the Porto Sokhna Telepherique – a cable car that runs 1km (0.6 miles) from the Porto Sokhna Beach Resort up to the highest hill behind town, from where there are terrific views of the Gulf of Suez and the sea liberally strewn with tankers and other ships converging on the canal.

South of Ain Sokhna, the rocky skirts of the North Galala Plateau come right down to the edge of the sea and the drive along here is spectacular. An endless string of resorts lines the coastal highway, and at **Zaafarana**, 80km (50 miles) south of Ain Sokhna, the road is joined by a good road from the Nile Valley 290km (180 miles) through the desert to the west.

THE DESERT MONASTERIES

The monasteries of St Paul and St Anthony have lost much of their original remoteness, but remain important centres of Coptic Christianity.

About 25km (15 miles) west of Zaafarana, in the rugged hills at the foot of the South Galala Plateau and looking out over the desolate Wadi Araba, stands the **Monastery of St Anthony ❶** (daily 9am–5pm, closed Lent and Christmas), the 4th-century Christian hermit whose temptations were enthusiastically illustrated by painters of the Renaissance. The monastery was founded by Anthony's followers after his death in AD 356, and is often regarded as the first monastery in the world. The oldest building in the compound is the **church of St Anthony**, which is adorned with murals from the 13th century onwards. A path from the west side of the monastery leads to a steep staircase to **St Anthony's cave**, where the saint lived as a hermit until the age of 105. His life is considered to be the inspiration for monasticism in Egypt, although others credit his contemporary, St Paul (see page 60).

When the daily visitors have gone, the monks lead a quiet life of work and prayer, very much as they did 15 centuries ago, when the original Desert Fathers retired from the injustice of the world to seek a better way of life.

Retracing the road through Zaafarana, it is an hour's drive to the monastery of Anthony's contemporary, St Paul, tucked into a fold of the Red Sea Mountains. Smaller, more dilapidated and more remote, the **Monastery of St Paul the Hermit ❷** (daily 9am–5pm, closed Lent and Christmas) sees fewer visitors. St Paul (AD 230–342) was the earliest known hermit but, when he was visited in his cave at the age of 113 by St Anthony, St Paul recognised him as being spiritually his superior. St Paul's cave is in the **church of St Paul**, which also contains his remains.

RED SEA RESORTS

The resort of **El Gouna ❸**, 21km (13 miles) north of Hurghada, is Egypt's most luxurious purpose-built holiday village to date. A Cairene businessman, Samih Sawiris, bought the plot of land with the intention of building a few holiday homes for family and friends, but before long his business instincts got the better of him, and he seized the opportunity to create something unique in Egypt. At its conception in 1989, El Gouna was originally planned as a self-contained community, but it is now almost considered a town in its own right (albeit a privately owned one). Today, it has a hospital, an international school, a private airport, three yacht marinas, a mosque and a Coptic church; even the local football team, El Gouna FC, plays in the Egyptian Premier League. Gardens, canals and several man-made lagoons add to the impression of peacefulness, and there are numerous swimming pools and several good beaches. The myriad things to do include water sports, tennis,

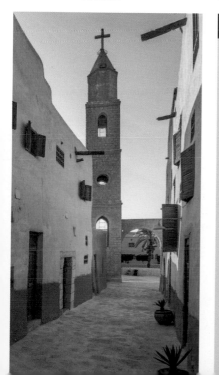

Monastery of St Anthony.

☉ THE PARTING OF THE RED SEA

The story of Moses parting the Red Sea is one of the most famous of the Biblical stories. The account of the fleeing Israelites tells how Moses led the Jewish slaves out of Egypt, pursued by Pharaoh's army (Exodus 13–15). Arriving at the Red Sea, they were trapped between the desert, mountains and sea until Moses raised his arms and parted the waves, allowing the Israelites to walk between the walls of water. Reaching the other side, Moses ordered the sea to close again, thus drowning the Egyptian Army.

With our modern understanding of natural phenomena, it is possible to find an explanation for this miracle, as well as other Biblical stories, such as the Ten Plagues of Egypt. There are three main theories for the parting of the waves: a tsunami, an earthquake (or volcanic eruption) and wind setdown. The first two are usually dismissed due to the short time in which the seabed would be exposed, but a strong wind (as also described in Exodus) might force back a body of water so that it resembled a wall of water along one side.

A combination of these natural events could easily give rise to the Biblical account, especially if they occurred in quick succession. However, experts cannot even agree about the location of the crossing, whether it is the Gulf of Aqaba or the Gulf of Suez.

Fruit market in El Dahhar, Hurghada.

go-karting and horse riding, and use of the 18-hole golf course designed to United States Professional Golfers Association (USPGA) standards by Fred Couples and Gene Bates, created determinedly out of the barren desert sands. A second golf course designed by Karl Litten opened in 2012. A small museum (daily 10am–2pm, 4–9pm) displays good replicas of many well-known examples of ancient Egyptian art.

Wealthy Egyptians, Gulf Arabs and Europeans have hurried to buy beachfront villas, while visitors can stay in one of the 18 attractive hotels ranging from three to five stars. The inspiration for most of the design has come from traditional Nubian architecture, revived by the late Egyptian architect Hassan Fathy, and from the Mediterranean – there's plenty of whitewash and some corners could be mistaken for old towns on the Cycladic Islands in Greece.

At weekends, the place is crowded with wealthy young Cairenes, and for the overseas visitor who wants everything on tap and has little interest in what lies outside, El Gouna is perfect; otherwise Hurghada gives more options for shopping and nightlife and the opportunity to experience a "real" Egyptian town.

HURGHADA

In recent years, what was a small sleepy fishing village, **Hurghada** ❹ (Al-Ghardaqah), 420km (250 miles) south of Suez, has grown into a booming resort town – the largest on the Red Sea coast. The town has a large range of accommodation, from basic hotels catering for backpackers to up-market resorts. A long strip of holiday villages continues to spread further south and has now reached a long way past the airport. Many of these villages, which rival each other for splendour, the size of their pools and the number of rooms, are operated by international four- and five-star chains.

The Hurghada area can now be regarded as comprising three separate sections – at the northern end, the old downtown (known as El

Dahhar) is the most "Egyptian" part with souqs, local restaurants, general authentic bustle and most of the budget hotels; the mid-section, or new downtown (known as Al-Sakkala), is crowded with mid-range hotels on the public beach; and south from here is the developed strip running along the coast for over 20km (12.5 miles), with more private self-contained high-end resorts and Western-style shopping malls.

El Dahhar was the original village and has some of the Red Sea's earliest hotels, built between the Gabal al-Afish hill and the sea. The hill itself is slowly being hacked away as houses and hotels push further back, and it could disappear completely within the next few years. Between El Dahhar and Al Sakkala are the naval dockyards and the port, from which the ferry to Sharm El Sheikh departs.

Al-Sakkala is very much like any modern Mediterranean package resort. Shops and fast-food restaurants run along its main street, off which are side roads down to the

beaches. Several boat and dive operators run from the marina here. The road rejoins the coast to reach the abandoned circular Sheraton Hotel, which was built in the 1970s as the resort's first hotel. The fact that this entire stretch of Corniche from El Dahhar is still referred to by everyone as Sheraton Road shows how little was here in the early days, when the old Sheraton was a lonely outpost way south of old Hurghada. Beyond here today are endless up-market resorts catering for everything the beach-loving tourist requires.

The modern town is not particularly attractive, the small public beaches are sometimes littered with rubbish, and the large souq area offers the usual souvenir shops filled with leather, brasswork, papyrus, furry camels, statuettes and so on. That said, Hurghada is the ideal antidote to an overdose of antiquities. The water is warm all the year round except for a few weeks in December and January; the sun is always shining and even in the hottest months there is a good

Hurghada mosque and port.

Bright colours at a hotel pool in Hurghada.

Windsurfing at Hurghada.

breeze, which can sometimes turn into a strong wind. The beaches are small, but the hotel pools are large and more than compensate.

Each of the major beach resorts offers activities and excursions. Things to do include diving, snorkelling, glass-bottomed boats trips, sailing, kite- and windsurfing, fishing, 4x4 and quad-bike desert safaris to meet local Bedu, and two- or three-day trips to Luxor or Aswan.

The **Hurghada Grand Aquarium** (Safaga Village Road; www.hurghada aquarium.com; daily 9am–7pm) offers insights into the Red Sea's rich marine life. A trip here affords the opportunity to observe the many types of fish close-up, including sharks, turtles, rays and stone fish. **Sindbad Submarines** (tel: 65 340 4227; daily 9am–3pm) dive to a depth of 25 metres (82ft) and allow visitors to view the underwater life through large portholes – an activity guaranteed to delight children.

There's an international airport in Hurghada with direct flights (including many charter flights) from the UK, Germany, Russia, the Ukraine and others. There are domestic flights from Cairo (one hour) and Sharm El Sheikh (35 minutes). There is also the option of coming from Cairo by luxury coach, but given that it's a seven hour drive, this can mean departing very early morning and getting back late at night. The coach ride between Hurghada and Luxor takes five hours. The modern ferry service between Hurghada and Sharm El Sheikh operates four times a week and takes two hours.

EASTERN DESERT

In Pharaonic times the **Eastern Desert**, particularly the mountains, was a source of gold and other precious metals, ornamental stone and other building materials, which contributed greatly to the wealth and prestige of the pharaohs and were later coveted by Assyrians, Persians, Greeks and Romans.

Thousands of prisoners in chains were used for the extraction of these

riches and many died in the process. The gold was arduously mined and smelted, and both granite and limestone were quarried and transported to Thebes for the construction of temples and other monuments.

The Romans established permanent quarrying camps in the mountains, the ruins of which are visible from the road between Hurghada and Safaga. They were particularly partial to the purple stone known as porphyry, which comes from **Mons Porphyrites** (Mountain of Porphyryr) below **Gabal Abu Dukhan** (Father of Smoke) and which is accessed along **Wadi Umm Sidri** (4x4 vehicles only, with local guide).

The stone was in great demand for the adornment of palaces and temples and was brought out of the Egyptian mountains until as late as the 5th century. Great blocks were quarried and then dragged 180km (112 miles) through the mountains and over the desert to Qena, where they were transported down the Nile and then across the Mediterranean to Rome.

The largest columns were used to build the great temple at Baalbek in modern Lebanon, though eight of these were later moved to Constantinople to support the roof of the city's great Hagia Sophia church.

There is not much left to see at Mons Porphyrites – just toppled columns, inscribed blocks and a ruined fort – but it is worth taking a closer look if only to enjoy the landscape and peacefulness of the spot.

Another mountain nearby, **Mons Claudianus** (Mountain of Claudius), yielded a white-specked granite, also much in demand in ancient Rome; again, all that is left are the jumbled remains of a Roman town.

ANCIENT EGYPTIAN PORTS

Further on down the coast, famous ancient ports continued to thrive even after the discovery of the Cape route in the 15th century, but have largely fallen into disuse since the building of the Suez Canal. In antiquity and even in Ottoman times, these ports – Safaga, Al-Qusayr, Marsa Alam, Berenice

Hikers in the Eastern Desert.

⊘ DESERT WILDLIFE

The geological formations of the Eastern Desert are varied and strange, yielding stones and sands of amazing shapes and colours. It can look like a barren landscape, but in fact flora and fauna are plentiful, especially in the wadis, and all the more wonderful for their tenacity. There are numerous species of small migratory birds and large resident ones, including the Egyptian vulture and the sand partridge; in spring and autumn migrating cranes may be seen high above. Once in a while a gazelle or an ibex streaks across the open plain and disappears among the rocks; often a sandy picnic place is crisscrossed with bird and animal tracks. Jerboas, jackals and foxes leave dainty pad marks, while rabbits, gazelles and hyenas leave heavier prints.

and Halayib – were connected to the Nile Valley by caravan routes, along which laden pack animals took spices, silks, pearls and precious woods from Arabia, Persia, India and the East African coast. Meanwhile, Muslim pilgrims from the hinterlands thousands of miles away, sometimes travelling for years, embarked at these ports for Mecca.

Safaga ❺, however, which is 62km (39 miles) south of Hurghada, is still very much alive. Not particularly attractive with a grid of untidy streets, it's primarily a port town, exporting phosphates that are mined in the region. During *hajj*, ferries operate from here transporting Muslims in the Nile Valley across to Saudi Arabia en route to Mecca. Cruise ships also dock here, although passengers are immediately whisked off on shore excursions to either Luxor or Hurghada. But a small tourist area has nevertheless developed at the northern end of the bay with a choice of hotels; almost permanently windy, the town is particularly popular with wind- and kite-surfers as well as divers to the nearby reefs.

Safaga lies 165km (103 miles) from the Nile town of Qena to the west, on an excellent tarred road. From Qena it's another 70km (44 miles) south to Luxor, so this is the fastest and most logical route from the Red Sea resorts to the Nile Valley – although expect many police checks along the way. It's also a convenient way to travel along the Nile Valley from Cairo to Luxor, cross to the Red Sea, and then return north up the coast towards Suez (or the other way around).

Al-Qusayr ❻ (also known as El Quseir) was, until the 10th century, the largest trading port on the Red Sea and the most popular port for Muslims making the pilgrimage to Mecca in Saudi Arabia. The Ottomans tried to revive the port – and the small town is still dominated by the 16th-century fort of Sultan Selim, now a good historical **museum** (Safaga Road; daily 9am–5pm) – but it finally lost its importance with the

Abu Dabbab Beach, Marsa Alam.

opening of the Suez Canal. Excavations of the fort have revealed private letters from the 18th century relating to the provision of wheat from Upper Egypt, as well as clay pipes, dating from the very earliest days of smoking tobacco almost 500 years ago. Al-Qusayr's former prosperity is evident in the many old Ottoman houses, although these are generally in a sadly dilapidated state.

The town also has many small mosques and shrines dedicated to the various holy men from places such as Morocco, West Africa, Somalia and India who have died here en route to or from Mecca. Immediately opposite the Ottoman fort, for example, is the shrine and mosque of Abdel Ghaffar, a Yemeni shaykh.

The sleepy town is virtually untouched by tourism but developers have discovered that the surrounding coast offers excellent snorkelling and diving, and resort hotels are quickly springing up, including the large Mövenpick Resort El Quseir, which is built in traditional Nubian style.

MARSA ALAM AND FURTHER SOUTH

About 140km (87 miles) further south, on a T-junction with the road to Edfu on the Nile, is the fishing town of **Marsa Alam ❼**. Now overtaken by tourism, it has been the focus of some frenzied construction over the last decade, with several luxury resorts and an international airport for charter flights. The main drive behind it all is the good diving and snorkelling. The development just outside the airport is **Port Ghalib**; with its hotels, villas, restaurants, shops and activities, it has grown into a southerly version of El Gouna.

A popular excursion from Marsa Alam is to **Wadi el Gemal National Park** (www.wadielgemal.org), which was designated a protected area in 2003 and is located 40km (25 miles) further south, covering both land and marine areas. Dive operators take clients to the coast and to five offshore islands for excellent diving and snorkelling, while the terrestrial section can be visited on 4x4 Jeep desert safaris that usually include a camel ride and lunch or dinner with the Bedouins.

⊘ Fact

A few kilometres north of Al-Qusayr is Al-Qusayr al-Qadim (ancient Myos Hormos), the likely departure point for Queen Hatshepsut's expedition to the Land of Punt (modern Somalia). Details of the expedition, including the frankincense trees, giraffes and other exotica – brought back to Egypt – are inscribed on the walls of the Temple of Hatshepsut at Thebes (see pages 216–7).

SCUBA DIVING

Egypt's Red Sea coast has some of the best coral reefs in the world, offering spectacular diving for novices and experts alike.

Egypt's Red Sea coasts are a diver's paradise, as their climate and geographical position make them ideal for the formation of coral, which grows on reefs called *shaab* or *erg*. Mounds of coral build up like islands, the tips of which are barely skimmed by the waves. Each coral accretion consists of numerous polyps, growing together in a colony. When one colony dies, a new one grows on top, attached to the calcium skeletons of its defunct ancestors.

The most common inhabitants are thousands of little orange cardinalfish, which move in great sparkling clouds. Butterfly and banner fish form a large, easily distinguishable family because of their oval shape, snub noses and deep lemon colour; they swim in pairs and stick to the same territory. Be ready for encounters with moray eel, whose size and snake-like appearance give them a vicious reputation. Simply remember an important rule: watch but don't touch. Just admire its graceful movements and leave it gasping for oxygen-rich water.

If you are diving the outer reefs, you also have a chance of seeing white tip sharks, a slim predator, feeding on small fish and crustaceans. In the deep south, sightings of hammerhead, grey reef and ocean white tip sharks are not uncommon, but don't expect to see all of them on one trip.

Nudibranchs, shellfish, shrimps and crabs, living in the nooks and crannies of the coral, are also fascinating. Hawksbill turtles, a species once verging on extinction, find a habitat on the coral reefs and it seems that every reef has its own resident turtle. The odds that you'll see bottlenose or spinner dolphins while diving are remote, but the chances of meeting them on the way to your dive spot are quite high. The boat crew will let you know by blowing the horn continuously, which tends to keep the curious dolphins close to the ship.

Corals are found in many shapes and colours: soft, undulating and bright red or yellow, solid and shaped like mushrooms, branching "elkhorns", and gorgonians – fan-shaped and perforated like Elizabethan lace collars. Be aware that corals take thousands of years to form and should never be touched or stood upon.

The underwater world is a peaceful environment but is not silent. You'll hear boat propellers, the sound of the waves hitting the reef and coral-crunching parrotfish.

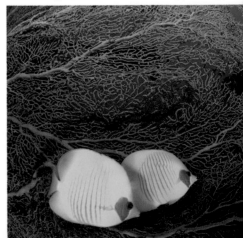

Tourist diving boats.

The best spots for diving

For land-based diving, choose Hurghada, Sharm El Sheikh or El Gouna. They serve the northern part of the Red Sea, which is also a paradise for wreck diving.

• El Gouna and Hurghada offer day trips to Shaab Abu Nuhas, where four wrecks are lined up against the reef, including the steamer *Carnatic*, which hit this infamous reef in 1869, and the more recent *Giannis D*, sunk in 1983.

• Sharm El Sheikh serves the dive sites around the Sinai Peninsula, notably the Strait of Tiran and the wrecks of the *Dunraven* and the *Thistlegorm*. The latter was a British supply ship, sunk in 1941 by Junker bombers; it sits upright in 30 metres (98ft) of water, with its load of motorcycles, trucks and even train wagons still on board.

• Safaga, some 60km (37 miles) south of Hurghada, offers dive excursions to reefs like Panorama and Abu Kefan, known for their prolific coral growth. Safaga is also a base for diving the wreck of the *Salem Express*, sunk in 1991.

• Ras Samadai, further south, is popular with those who relish the chance of snorkelling with spinner dolphins.

• Marsa Alam, in the south, the centre of live-aboard diving, is the place for die-hard divers. Live-aboards, or safari boats, allow several dives a day from a purpose-built vessel – simply jump overboard and enjoy the magnificent reefs of Elphinstone, St John's and Zabargad.

A green turtle drifts past. Also look out for the smaller hawksbill turtle.

It is possible to become a certified diver within a week. Simply enrol on a diving course: two days of pool training plus some theory will be followed by guided open-water dives, after which you will be ready to qualify. Some dive operators will also cater to snorkellers.

Trained divers love the wreck Giannis D, sunk in 1983 against the Shaab Abu Nuhas reef, as it allows entry into the engine room, crew quarters and wheelhouse.

Shopkeeper in Aswan's souq.

EGYPT

TRAVEL TIPS

TRANSPORT

By air

Egypt is served by several international airports: Aswan, Borg El Arab (Alexandria), Cairo, Hurghada, Luxor, Marsa Alam, Marsa Matruh and Sharm El Sheikh. Contacts and (patchy) information can be found on the website of Egyptian Airports Company at www.eac-airports.com.

Most major airlines have desks at Cairo International Airport and around Midan at-Tahrir in downtown Cairo.

Cairo International Airport (www.cairo-airport.info) is the busiest in the country and a first-class facility. It is located in the northeastern part of the city. Most planes from Europe approach it from the northwest, giving passengers magnificent views of the city and the River Nile. It's the hub for EgyptAir and is served by more than 60 airlines.

Borg El Arab (Alexandria) International Airport is served by Aegean Airlines, EgyptAir, some Middle East airlines such as Etihad and flydubai, and Turkish Airlines. **Luxor International Airport** has direct flights from various European cities via EgyptAir, and is also served by Turkish Airlines and several charter companies. Apart from EgyptAir, **Hurghada International Airport** is mostly served by charter airlines from Europe or low-cost carriers such as EasyJet from the UK and Condor from Germany. Most flights were suspended from **Sharm El Sheikh International Airport** after a Russian airliner was attacked in 2015, although at the time of writing some airlines from the Middle East and Eastern Europe were returning.

By land and sea

From Israel

Private or rental vehicles are not permitted to enter Egypt from Israel and the Palestinian Territories, but it is possible to enter using public transport. Taba is the only border crossing that currently accommodates tourists, and is about 10km (6 miles) south of downtown Eilat, reached by bus or taxi. It's open 24 hours, has a café on the Israeli side, duty free shops and bureau de changes. Passengers disembark from the Israeli vehicles, walk through immigration and customs on both sides, and then take an Egyptian bus or taxi. Note however, that due to the security situation in northern Sinai, tourists are presently not permitted to get direct buses from Taba to Cairo, but instead must go via Sharm El Sheikh.

There is an exit fee from Israel, and then a standard security check (metal detector and luggage scan). Remember that visas are needed for Egypt. There are no facilities for issuing visas at this border unless your visit is limited to the east coast of the Sinai, between Taba and Sharm El Sheikh, when a free two-week Sinai-only entry stamp is issued. Although regular visas may be obtained at Egyptian consulates in Tel Aviv and Eilat, Israel, this will be evidence of your visit and may prevent entry to some other Arab and Muslim countries such as Lebanon and Sudan. Far better is to get an Egyptian e-Visa prior to arrival (see page 319).

From Jordan

There is a daily passenger and car ferry between Nuweiba on Egypt's Sinai Peninsula to Aqaba in Jordan, which is operated by Jordanian company AB Maritime (www.abmaritime.com.jo). The ferry allows travel between Egypt and Jordan without transiting through Israel. It takes about two-and-a-half hours and there are comfortable seats and a shop selling snacks and drinks. During the voyage all passports are kept at a counter in the middle of the ferry. When disembarking, an escort takes the passports and accompanies passengers to the arrival terminal in Nuweiba where visas for Egypt are issued (US$25, cash only). If your visit is limited to the east coast of the Sinai, between Taba and Sharm El Sheikh, a free two-week Sinai-only entry stamp is issued. Onward buses go from Nuweiba to Dahab and Sharm El Sheikh.

From Sudan

Some Sudanese companies operate basic direct buses between Wadi Halfa and Aswan (12–13 hours). These are generally used by cross-border traders and can be chaotic and stuffed to the gills, but they are fun, and a good way to mingle with traditional Sudanese people. The border itself is about 35km (22 miles) north of Wadi Halfa, but do not rely on getting visas here; it's best to already have an e-Visa. Just north of the border, the bus, its passengers and assorted cargo crosses the Nile on a ferry – specifically built to accommodate four to five buses – at a point south of Abu Simbel just before it opens up into Lake Nasser. In theory you can only book a through ticket between Wadi Halfa and Aswan (and the other way around) but it's possible to jump off or join at Abu Simbel and forgo the minimum portion of the fare between Abu Simbel and Aswan.

A very simple ferry (traditional Nile cargo steamer) run by the Nile Valley River Transport Corporation usually travels every Monday from Wadi Halfa in Sudan at around 5pm, arriving in Aswan around lunchtime on Tuesday (roughly 18 hours). The boat crosses Lake Nasser, and goes past Abu Simbel, but it is occasionally suspended and impossible to prebook in the northbound direction. It is advisable for hardy travellers to get there a couple of days beforehand. The booking office in Wadi Halfa is located in the Nile Valley River Transport Corporation building on the same unnamed street as the Kilopatra Hotel; it is open 9am–3pm (closed Friday). Egyptian visas (cash only) can be purchased on board, and when entering Egypt from Sudan, you will need a yellow fever vaccination certificate. The ferry has some very basic two-berth cabins, otherwise sleeping is on benches or the deck, and there's a cafeteria for meals and drinks. In the other direction it departs from Aswan on Wednesday at about 3pm, and the Nile River Valley Transport Corporation office is in the shopping arcade next to the Marhaba Palace Hotel (tel: 097-230 348 or 011-2709 2709; 8am–2pm except Fri).

From Libya

The main border crossing between Egypt and Libya is Musaid-Sollum, 521km (324 miles) west of Alexandria, which is used by truck drivers and local traders. Due to insecurity along the Libyan border, however, foreigners are not permitted to cross here and it's also restricted to local people at times.

By road

The only feasible route into Egypt in your own vehicle is from Sudan (see opposite) and by crossing from Jordan on the car ferry (see opposite). All private vehicles entering Egypt must have a carnet de passage en douane, also known as a *triptyque*, from an automobile association in the country of registration. A carnet requires a deposit or guarantee of 200 percent of the value of the vehicle. It permits a car to enter Egypt for three months. Egyptian Customs charge a fee for stamping the carnet, an entry permit is issued at the border and temporary Egyptian number plates are affixed to the vehicle, which are surrendered when departing.

GETTING AROUND

From the airport

At Cairo International Airport, tourists are often targeted by taxi drivers in the arrivals hall. Note, the old black and white taxis usually do not have a meter and prices are negotiated before travelling (ask in the airport for an idea of fares), while newer white taxis have meters. Other options for transport into the city include shared shuttle minibus and limousine; Cairo Airport Travel (www.cairoshuttlebus.com) offers a number of options. Alternatively, Uber operates in Cairo, Alexandria and Hurghada and any hotel can prebook a transfer.

Although inadvisable due to overcrowding (see page 311), the best bus to take from the airport to downtown Cairo is No. 356, which runs 7am–midnight every 20 minutes from Terminal 1 via Terminal 2, Heliopolis and Abbaseya, to the Midan Abdel Moniem Riad bus station just behind the Egyptian Museum. The bus leaves from the bus stop outside the airport car park.

All the airports connected to other major Egyptian cities have taxis into their city centres. Again, hotels can organise airport transfers – book these along with your hotel reservation.

By air

For internal flights, EgyptAir and their subsidiary EgyptAir Express (www.egyptair.com) has the most regular network and flies daily from Cairo to Abu Simbel, Aswan, Borg El Arab (Alexandria), Hurghada, Luxor, Marsa Alam, Marsa Matruh and Sharm El Sheikh. Nile Air (www.nileair.com) is the largest airline after EgyptAir and flies to similar domestic destinations as well as several airports in Saudi Arabia and Iraq, among other places in the Middle East. FlyEgypt (www.flyegypt.com) is a low-cost carrier that flies from Cairo to Asyut, Borg El Arab (Alexandria), Hurghada, Luxor, Sharm El Sheikh and Sohag.

By rail

The government-owned Egyptian National Railways (www.enr.gov.eg; customer service tel: 02-2574 8279) serves the Nile Valley to Aswan, the Red Sea cities of Suez and Port Said, and the Delta and North Coast cities of Alexandria and Marsa Mutrah. Air-conditioned passenger trains usually have 1st and 2nd classes, while non-air-conditioned trains have 2nd and 3rd classes. There are at least six through trains a day, and fares are inexpensive, but unless one is travelling on an organised tour, tickets are purchased at railway stations (in Cairo inside Ramses Station at Midan Ramses); alternatively, you can book 1st and 2nd-class tickets on the website.

The most popular route for tourists is the twice-nightly air-conditioned sleeper train between Cairo and Luxor (journey time 10 hours) and Aswan (15 hours), which is operated by privately run Watania (www.wataniasleepingtrains.com). They have both comfortable reclining seats and single and two-berth sleeping compartments (depending on how much you want to pay) and a lounge/bar car. The fare includes a basic airline-style tray dinner and breakfast. This service must be paid for in foreign currency (US dollars, euros or pounds sterling) at the separate Watania sleeper office/counter at the stations. You can book a day or two before departure but as they are often booked by tour groups, it's advisable to reserve well in advance. The trains also stop in Giza en route, so you can join/depart the train there if this is where you are staying in Cairo.

By bus

Air-conditioned buses link most parts of Egypt to Cairo and Alexandria, and beyond the Nile Valley, it's often the only option. Seats may be reserved up to two days in advance. There is also a fleet of cheaper non-air-conditioned buses, but they can be crowded and stop frequently. Although bus times change without notice, departures are so frequent that this is rarely a problem.

The Cairo Gateway Bus Station (Torgoman) on Shari Al Gisr in Bulaq, close to the Orabi metro station and 1km (0.6 miles) northwest of Midan Ramses and the train station, handles most of the long-distance buses. There are numerous companies, and tickets can be bought here from different windows depending on the destination; those for air-conditioned buses should always be booked in advance. Increasingly, tickets can be booked online.

One of the better and newer companies is Go Bus (www.gobus-eg.com), which can be booked online or via the app and runs services in "classes" – economic, deluxe and elite – the latter having bigger seats,

Wi-fi and free snacks. They operate an ever-expanding network of routes from Cairo to the northern coast, down to the Red Sea coast, to Sharm El Sheikh and Dahab in the Sinai, and between Luxor and Hurghada.

Other reliable companies include Super Jet (www.superjet.com.eg), which again serves major routes around the country; West & Mid Delta Bus Company (www.westmidbus-eg.com), for Alexandria, Marsa Mutrah and Siwa Oasis; the Upper Egypt Bus Company (tel: 02-2576 0261) for the Western Oases, Luxor and Aswan (although the train is a better alternative to these); and the East Delta Bus Company (tel: 02-2419 8533) to Suez, the Canal Zone and the Sinai.

By service taxi

Collective service taxis are a faster alternative to buses, and will get you just about everywhere in Egypt. The fare is about the same as for the bus, and on the main routes there are several departures daily. These taxis, often estate Peugeots (hence their pet name of "Beejoo"), seat six or seven and leave as soon as they are full. They are nicknamed "flying coffins" as the drivers are renowned for their speed and reckless driving.

The service station where you'll find these taxis is usually next to the bus or train station in a town or city.

By car

Driving in Egypt is very demanding. Cairo and the bigger cities have congested roads, especially the highways, which can be eight lanes wide, non-working traffic lights, unruly road rules from other drivers and a chronic shortage of parking. It is not advisable for visitors to drive at night, as other drivers may not use their lights and unlit donkey carts move at a snail's pace and are very difficult to see. Always beware of other traffic, as long-distance taxis and overloaded trucks travel too fast, and are frequently driven by men who use "stimulants" to keep themselves going. When you wish to overtake, sound your horn very deliberately, as Egyptian drivers need an extra signal and most of them overuse the horn. If your car breaks down, don't abandon it, as even in remote areas another vehicle will pass by and likely offer assistance.

Road signs are similar to those used in Europe and on the main roads

are in Arabic and English. Driving is on the right; speed limits are enforced by radar. There are petrol stations, often with ATMs and mini-markets, throughout the country; fuel is inexpensive and sold by the litre.

Car-rental agencies can be found at most major hotels and airports. The best alternative is to hire a driver and car together, thus freeing yourself to enjoy the scenery. But if you do want to rent a car, foreigners must have a driver's license with a photograph, as well as an additional International Driving Permit (IDP); you must also be at least 25 years of age. Some agencies offer four-wheel-drive vehicles, with or without a driver, which are a good idea for desert travel. You will need your passport, driver's licence and a credit card. Ask your hotel to recommend a local company; alternatively, most international car-rental companies are represented in Egypt, including Avis (www.avisegypt.net); Budget (www.budget-egypt.com); Europcar (www.europcar.com.eg); Hertz (www.hertz.com); and Sixt (www.sixt.com.eg).

By Nile cruise

A cruise on the Nile is still a good way both to visit the temples and ancient sites and to sample the peaceful life along the river. You'll see local

☉ Distances from Cairo

North
Alexandria 221km/138 miles
Damietta 191km/119 miles
Marsa Matruh 448km/278 miles

South
Aswan 880km/550 miles
Asyut 359km/224 miles
Esna 719km/449 miles
Edfu 775km/484 miles
Kom Ombo 835km/521 miles
Luxor 664km/415 miles

East
Ismailia 140km/87 miles
Port Said 220km/137 miles
Sharm El Sheikh 511km/318 miles
Suez 139km/86 miles

West
Bahariyya Oasis 316km/197 miles
Dakhla Oasis 690km/413 miles
Faiyum Oasis 103km/64 miles
Farafra Oasis 420km/262 miles
Siwa Oasis 749km/465 miles

farmers, fishermen, small villages and beautiful views of the deserts and hills lining the Nile, and if you're lucky, have clear skies for spectacular sunsets. Hundreds of ships now cruise along the Nile following more or less the same itinerary but offering a wide choice of accommodation, suitable for every budget. It is advisable to book cruises before you leave for Egypt as it is usually cheaper to buy them as part of a package. Most boats travel between Luxor and Aswan in three to four days, sometimes for six days to include Abydos and Dendarah, and increasingly they sail the whole way from Cairo to Aswan.

Differences in price reflect the standard of service, the numbers and size of the cabins and the quality of the food. More expensive boats tend to have fewer and larger cabins and will make the effort to prepare good food. All boats provide guides to accompany passengers to the sites and some have small libraries on Egyptian history and culture.

But there is no doubt that cruising is no longer as romantic as it used to be. For a start most people are surprised at how little time is spent actually moving – the distances are quite short and often cruising is only about four hours each day. There are often delays at Esna due to the number of boats passing through the lock, forcing some companies to transfer their passengers to a sister boat on the other side. For the same reason not all boats dock in the centre of Aswan or Luxor; cheaper boats are often moored further along the river bank, or are wedged between other boats and therefore without any Nile views from the inside. Your travel agent should know if you will have a Nile view.

To get a real feel of what cruising used to be like before the traffic jams on the Nile, a cruise on Lake Nasser is highly recommended. A number of companies offer cruises visiting the Nubian monuments on the shores of Lake Nasser and highlights include seeing Abu Simbel at dawn before breakfast (and the crowds) or taking an aperitif at one of the rarely visited Nubian temples. Itineraries are generally three nights/four days from Aswan to Abu Simbel, or four nights/five days from Abu Simbel to Aswan.

There are numerous (sometimes overwhelmingly so) Nile and Lake Nasser cruise companies to book from. When choosing, check out specifications of a selection of boats, including size and number of cabins and where they are (you don't want to be on the bottom with no view), whether there is a pool or Jacuzzi, what nightly entertainment is on offer, and inclusions in the price such as drinks or entry fees to the sites. Finally, cruise options also vary in terms of the atmosphere, which is something you can usually gauge after reading the itinerary and reviews. Choose whatever best suits your travel style.

By dahabeeyah

For a totally authentic experience, you can sail the Nile on a historic *dahabeeyah* (literally a golden boat; see page 235). Nineteenth-century travellers, including Flaubert, Amelia Edwards, Pierre Loti, Florence Nightingale and many others, sailed the Nile on wooden boats with cabins, propelled by two Latin sails. Some of these vessels, which are a lot smaller than the cruise boats, have been restored and have started sailing the Nile again; others are being built in the same style. They make the journey from Luxor to Aswan slowly, usually taking six or seven days, and stopping at sites such as Gebel Silsilla and Al-Kab where the bigger boats can't stop. They have a chef on board who cooks fresh food bought daily from the markets and farmers along the river. There is no pool, no hot tubs and no nightly entertainment. However, the experience is truly unique. Like Nile cruises, shop around the operators and look at a selection of options.

By felucca

A traditional Egyptian wooden boat with a canvas sail, a *felucca* trip is the best way to get a feel of the Nile, although it is the most basic of the Nile options. *Feluccas* can be hired for a few hours to watch the sunset, or for two–four-day cruises with visits to temples along the way. They usually carry six to eight passengers and two to three crew and the boatmen will also cook local meals (like foul, falafel, hummous and pitta bread) and advise where it is safe to swim. They have shade from the sun, but there are no cabins or enclosed areas, and passengers sleep in the open air on a communal mattress, which also triples up as dining and relaxing space. You'll be provided with a blanket. It is advisable to sail from Aswan towards Luxor as the current will carry you downstream, and the most popular trips go to Kom Ombo (two days/one night), Edfu

(three days/two nights) or Esna (four days/three nights). To find a *felucca*, ask your hotel for a recommendation; the tourist office in Aswan can also recommend good captains and has a list of fixed prices. Some captains offer a trial tour to allow you to check out their abilities and boats. Agree on a price before starting out on the trip and do not hand out the whole amount until you get to your destination. Insect repellent, a hat, sunscreen and plenty of bottled water are essential.

LOCAL TRANSPORT

By taxi

For one of the experiences of your life, take an Egyptian taxi. Drivers seem to need to fill every empty space on the road (and sometimes the pavement). All taxis have orange licence plates and are identified by a number on the driver's door. Drivers are required to display their licence and identity numbers on the dashboard.

Official or metered prices are unrealistically low and so meters are seldom used. The fare should be agreed beforehand. At your destination, pay in exact money – it's always useful to have change. No tip is obligatory, but about 10 percent is most welcome.

Taxi drivers are usually friendly, many speak English, and most are eager to be hired by the day – ideal for seeing several scattered monuments. The fee is negotiable, but should be around EGP30–40 per hour. If you find a taxi driver you like, swap phone numbers. Uber also operates in Cairo, Alexandria and Hurghada (www.uber.com).

By bus around Cairo

The large red-and-white and blue-and-white buses in Cairo are usually extremely overcrowded. As well as being claustrophobic, they provide ample opportunity for petty theft and unwelcome sexual encounters. Given that destinations on buses are only in Arabic, they can also be confusing, and you can travel to most places much more efficiently and comfortably by metro and/or taxi.

Most buses start or pass by the Midan Abdel Moniem Riad terminal behind the Egyptian Museum on Midan at-Tahrir.

By metro around Cairo

The Cairo Metro (www.cairometro.gov.eg) is extensive and has three interchangeable lines and 61 stations across the capital. On the streets the stations are identified by blue circular signs with a big red M. It is clean and efficient and an easy way to get around, although it can get crowded at peak times (7–9am and 3–6pm). Trains run every few minutes from 5am to 1am and fares are inexpensive, usually no more than two Egyptian pounds to the furthest destination. Note that the middle two cars of every train are reserved for women. Cairo Metro Line 1 runs north–south from El Marg to Helwan through the heart of the city; Cairo Metro Line 2 runs from the northern suburb of Shoubra-El-Kheima to Giza; and Cairo Metro Line 3 connects Attaba in east-central Cairo with Abbassia and Heliopolis to the northeast. Other lines are under construction, including the extension of Line 3 to the airport.

Useful stations include:

Al-Shohadaa Station, Midan Ramses, for access to the main train station and bus stations to Upper Egypt and the Western Oases.
Gamal Abdel Nasser Station, for the downtown area around Midan Talaat Harb and Shari Qasr El Nil.
Sadat Station, Midan at-Tahrir, with 10 entrances and access to the Egyptian Museum, the American University in Cairo, Nile Ritz-Carlton Hotel, all major airline offices and the Mogamma (central administrative building).
Mar Girgis, Old Cairo, for access to the Coptic Museum, Coptic churches and Roman fortress.
Giza Station, next to the main Giza train station and handy for short bus rides to the Pyramids.

By tram around Alexandria

Trams are a slow but fun way to get around Alexandria, and there are now 20 lines serving 140 stops. The main station is Mahattet Ramleh, called Terminus, near the Cecil Hotel. Yellow-coloured trams go west, including tram No. 14 to Misr Train Station and Nos 15 and 25 along the Corniche to Ras El Tin and Anfushi. The blue trams travel east, including Nos 1 and 2 to Montaza. One carriage is reserved for women.

A

Accommodation

There's a good range of accommodation throughout Egypt, from international chain hotels offering luxury and a good range of facilities like air conditioning, room service, restaurants and swimming pools, to great value and characterful local (and often family-run) places, which may just offer a room with a fan and breakfast. Nonetheless, almost all rooms have private bathrooms (though the quality of the plumbing varies). Many hotels are set near the Nile for ease of sightseeing and you won't spend so much time in them, while on the Red Sea coast and the resort towns of the Sinai, they tend to have more of a holiday atmosphere where you are likely to spend more time next to the pool or the beach. In Cairo, the Nile Valley, the Red Sea and the Sinai, there is plenty of choice for every budget, but in less visited towns and cities there may be only basic lodgings aimed at Egyptian businesspeople. Except at the up-market end, it's not a given that hotels accept credit cards.

Admission charges

Admission charges to all monuments and historical sites are posted and paid for in Egyptian pounds – cash only. Ticket offices will not accept any other currency or credit/debit cards, and there are few places that have ATMs nearby, so ensure you have enough cash. The exception is if you opt to buy a Cairo Pass (see page 133) or Luxor Pass (see page 215); both of which cover entry fees to a number of sites over a period of five days, and can be paid for in US dollars or euro cash (no other currencies).

Two levels of charges operate at most of the major sites: one for Egyptians and a much higher one for non-Egyptians, which is fair enough considering the disparity in incomes in most cases and the high cost of maintaining the sites.

B

Budgeting for your trip

After airfares (and visas), the biggest expense in Egypt is accommodation; rates can vary from US$150–300 for a top-end hotel, to US$30–50 for a mid-range place, to as little as US$12–15 for a bed in a bare room. For transport between the destinations, flights are the most expensive choice, followed by trains and then buses. Food and drink are reasonably priced in Egypt, while major tourist site admissions vary from EGP60–200. Also allocate extra for tipping, which is more or less expected in Egypt for drivers, tour guides, and hotel and cruise-boat staff.

C

Calendars

The business and secular community in Egypt operates under the Western (Gregorian) calendar. But other calendars also have official status.

The Islamic calendar is used to fix religious observances, and is based on a lunar cycle of 12 months of 29 or 30 days. The Muslim year is thus 11 days shorter than the year in the Gregorian calendar and months move forward accordingly. In the Gregorian calendar, for example, April is in the spring, but in the Muslim calendar all months move

through all seasons in a 33-year cycle.

The Coptic calendar follows the Julian calendar, which was replaced in the West by the Gregorian calendar between 1582 and 1752, but the months carry their current Egyptian names.

The Coptic year consists of 12 months of 30 days and one month of 5 days. Every four years a sixth day is added to the shorter month. An adaption of the Coptic calendar is often used for planting and harvesting crops. It is used by the authorities of the Coptic Orthodox Church.

Muslim calendar	Coptic calendar
Muharram	Toot (begins 11 Sept)
Safar	Baaba
Rabi' il-awal	Hatour
Rabi' it-tani	Kiyaak
Gamada-l-uula	Tuuba (mid-Jan)
Gamada-l-ukhra	Amshir
Ragab	Baramhat
Sha'aban	Barmuda
Ramadan	Bashans
Shawal	Bauna
Dhu'l	Abiib
Dhu'l	Misra Nasi (5–6 days)

Children

Egyptians love children, but the very young can get bored after seeing yet another tomb, so it's best to wait until they are a little older and can appreciate the rich cultural history more clearly; prep them first – there are numerous websites and books teaching kids about Ancient Egypt. Options children might enjoy are the Egyptian Museum in Cairo, horse- or camel-riding at the pyramids, taking the sleeper train, diving and snorkelling on the coasts, camping out at the Western Desert oases, and certainly sailing on a felucca from Luxor or Aswan (even if it's just for the afternoon). Many family-friendly hotels have pools to recover from the sightseeing and heat. Hygiene in food preparation can be inconsistent, so be prepared for stomach problems and carry the appropriate medication for remedies. Additionally, hats and sunscreen are essential.

Climate

With an arid desert climate, summers are hot and dry throughout Egypt, and humidity is high in the peak months of July and August. Summer temperatures vary; in Cairo the average is around 35ºC (95ºF), while much further south in Aswan, they average 42ºC (108ºF).

Winters are mild with usually bright, sunny days and cool nights. In desert regions nighttime temperatures can drop to 0ºC (32ºF). Most regions have very little precipitation, although Cairo, the Mediterranean coast and the Nile Delta may experience a few rainy days during winter. Spring and autumn are short; during the 50 days (khamseen) between March and April, dust storms may occur.

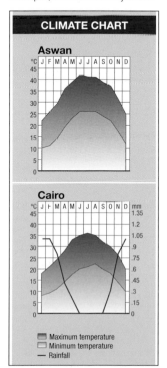

CLIMATE CHART

Aswan

Cairo

- ◾ Maximum temperature
- ◻ Minimum temperature
- — Rainfall

☉ Temperatures

Average year-round temperatures (max/min, in Celsius)			Average year-round temperatures (max/min, in Fahrenheit)		
	winter	summer		winter	summer
Alexandria	21/11	30/21	Alexandria	69/51	86/70
Cairo	21/11	36/20	Cairo	70/52	97/68
Luxor	26/6	42/22	Luxor	79/43	108/72
Aswan	26/9	42/25	Aswan	79/48	108/77

Crime and safety

Petty theft in Egypt is generally very rare, but because of variable economic reforms over the years that have created hardship, muggings and hotel and vehicle theft occasionally occur. The average Egyptian is also honest, and if you leave a bag, wallet or other personal belongings in a restaurant or other public building the chances are it will be kept safe and sound until you can retrieve it. Nevertheless, keep your passport and valuables hidden; use hotel safes; and beware of pickpockets and bag snatchers. If you are the victim of any crime and wish to report it, you should do so to the tourist police immediately, and remember that a police report is essential to claim travel insurance.

From January 2011, Egypt experienced significant domestic political turmoil during, and in the aftermath, of the Egyptian Revolution of 2011 (see page 96), which ousted President Mubarak, and then later President Morsi in 2013. This upheaval involved mass public protests, marches and civil disturbances; some of which resulted in a number of demonstrator deaths. Since then, politics has increasingly stabilised, with Abdel Fattah el-Sisi winning elections in 2014 and becoming President; for now, most people don't feel the need to protest against the government. While tourism suffered greatly during this time, 2018 was the first year that saw a significant increase in numbers and a renewed international interest in Egypt.

Meanwhile, like in several other countries, since the 1990s Egypt has been troubled by terrorism. Many attacks have been linked to Islamic extremism and targets have included government officials, the police and security services, the Christian minority and, in some cases, tourists. Attacks on the latter during the 2000s included bombings in Sinai tourist resorts – Taba and Nuweiba in 2004, Sharm El Sheikh in 2005 and Dahab in 2006 – and in each incident, tourists lost their lives.

Terrorism since the Egyptian Revolution of 2011 has mostly been focused on the Sinai Insurgency, which refers to a series of actions by Islamist militants in the Sinai Peninsula – most have occurred at churches or other places where the Christian minority reside. However, the 2015 bombing of a Russian airliner, which killed all 224 people on board soon after take-off from Sharm El Sheikh Airport, resulted in most European airlines and holiday companies withdrawing from the Sinai – although they are expected to return soon. At the time of writing however, while the resort towns are considered secure, travel to northern Sinai where many of the local attacks have taken place is generally not advised. There are presently no international travel warnings against travel for tourists in other regions. Security is tight at places visited by foreigners, and security personnel and the government are on a constant crackdown – for example at the end of 2018, 40 known terrorists were killed during raids in Giza and northern Sinai.

Customs regulations

Entry

A visitor is permitted to enter Egypt with 200 cigarettes or 25 cigars, one litre of alcohol, one litre of perfume and personal effects. Animals must have a veterinary certificate confirming their good health and a valid rabies certificate, as rabies is a problem in the country.

Duty-free purchases of liquor (three bottles per person) and other items may be made within 24 hours of arrival at ports of entry or at the special tax-free shops in Cairo, Luxor, Hurghada or Alexandria.

People travelling with expensive electronic equipment may be required to list these items in their passports so that authorities can check that they are exported upon departure and have not been sold to locals.

Departure

Although travellers are free to buy and export reasonable quantities of Egyptian goods for personal use, the export of large quantities of items will require an export licence. Egyptian-made items that are more than 20 years old are not permitted to leave the country, nor are foreign-made items deemed to have "historic value".

The export of carpets, Egyptian-made or not, is restricted. Travellers may be requested to show bank receipts as proof of payment for other valuable items. Excess Egyptian pounds may be changed back at the airport on presentation of valid bank receipts.

D

Disabled travellers

Few hotels or cruise boats and no public buildings, restaurants, theatres or historical sites provide facilities for people with disabilities. Major airlines provide services for those with disabilities upon entering and leaving the country.

Despite this, a couple of operators offer tours for wheelchair users, and the slow-walking elderly: Egypt for All, www.egyptforall.com, and Memphis Tours, www.memphistours.com, are both Cairo-based outfits offering specialised programmes

Tea time in Cairo.

that include river cruises on adapted boats, as well as hot-air ballooning, desert safaris and diving and snorkelling holidays on the Red Sea. Also bear in mind that Egyptians are very friendly and will readily lend a hand.

E

Eating out

Influenced by its many rulers – from the Ottomans to the British, the French to the Arabs – Egyptian cuisine is dominated by rich flavours. Egypt's restaurants are authentic, diverse, atmospheric and good value for money, while typical Egyptian food caters for all, with plenty of options for fish lovers, carnivores, vegans and vegetarians. Local specialities include *ta'amiyya* (falafel, and widely considered to have originated in Egypt), lamb kebabs, grilled chicken, kofta (spiced mincemeat grilled on skewers), tabbouleh (bulgur wheat, parsley and tomato), *kushari* (macaroni, lentils, chickpeas and caramelised onions in spicy tomato sauce), and dips such as baba ganoush, hummous and tahini. Breakfast usually consists of fresh bread and cheese, maybe olives or a fried egg, or *fuul* (broad or fava bean paste). There are endless places to try these types of meals and how much you pay depends on if it's a street stall, a hole-in-the wall establishment or a 5-star hotel, but generally eating out is inexpensive. Many tour groups staying in hotels, or passengers on Nile cruises, will be served buffets. In Cairo, American fast-food franchises are well represented, too.

Electricity

In Egypt the standard voltage is 220V and the frequency is 50Hz. Plug types C and F are used; C has two round pins and F has two round pins with two earth clips on the side. An international travel adaptor will cover both.

Embassies and consulates

Cairo

Australia
World Trade Centre, 1638, 11th floor, 1191 Corniche El Nile, Bulaq
Tel: 02-6261 3305
www.egypt.embassy.gov.au

Canada
Nile City Towers, 2005 Corniche El Nile, South Tower, 18th floor
Tel: 02-2461 2200
www.international.gc.ca

Ireland
18 Hassan Sabri Street, 11211, Zamalik
Tel: 02-2728 7115
www.dfa.ie

UK
7 Ahmed Ragheb Street, Garden City
Tel: 02-2791 6000
www.gov.uk

US
5 Tawfik Diab Street, Garden City
Tel: 02-2797 3300
www.eg.usembassy.gov
For complete lists and contact details of Egyptian embassies and consulates abroad, as well as foreign missions in Egypt, consult the website of the Ministry Of Foreign Affairs: www.mfa.gov.eg.

Emergencies

Fire: **180**
Ambulance: **123**
Police: **122**
Tourist Police: **126**

Etiquette

Intimate behaviour in public (kissing and cuddling) is disapproved of. Be aware, too, of the importance of dress: shirts (for both sexes) should cover shoulders, and away from hotel swimming pools or the beach, women should refrain from wearing skirts or shorts that show too

☾ Culture and customs

Whether Muslim or Copt, the Egyptians as a whole tend to be religious, and piety is important in their daily lives. So is commitment to the extended family. Each family member is responsible for the integrity of the family and for the behaviour of other members. Certainly, one result of these concerns is that the city of Cairo is generally safer than any Western metropolis.

Yet when Westerners visit Egypt, they are often apprehensive. Their views of Egyptians and Arabs, fomented by alarmist and exaggerated media stories, often bear no relation to reality at all. Travellers normally receive friendly, hospitable treatment and take home with them good feelings about the warmth and goodwill of the Egyptian people.

much. If you're visiting a mosque, men should be covered from below the shoulder to below the knee and women from wrist to ankle. Shoes must be removed at the entrance. Don't show the soles of your feet; it's considered disrespectful. Make sure you refrain from eating, drinking or smoking in public during the daytime in the holy month of Ramadan (international hotels are an exception to this rule). If eating with Egyptians, never put food into your mouth with your left hand or put it into the bowl during a communal meal.

H

Health and medical care

Evidence of yellow fever and cholera immunisation may be required from travellers who have been in an infected area up to six days prior to their arrival in Egypt.

Hospitals
There are good hospitals in Cairo and Alexandria. However, they operate on a cash upfront basis and will not provide treatment on the production of foreign medical insurance plans. Keep all receipts and contact your insurance company to make a claim. Hospitals in Cairo include:

Anglo-American Hospital
3 Hadiqet El Zohreya Street, next to the Cairo Tower, Zamalik
Tel: 02-2735 6162
www.angloamericanhospital.com

As-Salam International Hospital
Corniche El Nile, Maadi
Tel: 02-2524 0066
www.assih.com

Al Salam Hospital
3 Shari Syria, Mohandessin
Tel: 02-3303 0502
www.alsalamhospital.org

Pharmacies
Pharmacies are usually open 10am–10pm and are staffed by competent professionals. Both locally made and imported medication is subsidised by the government and is inexpensive. Some medication requiring prescriptions abroad is sold over the counter in Egypt. Pharmacies that open 24 hours in Cairo include:

Ali & Ali Pharmacies
19 El Nasr St., El Gazaer Sq., El Borg Bldg., Maadi
Tel: 02-2754 3499/3500

Delmar & Attalla Pharmacies
79 26 July St, Boulaq Num. 3, Bulaq
Tel: 02-0219 9551

Elezaby Pharmacy
Has over 80 branches; check website for store locator and phone numbers;
www.elezabypharmacy.com.

I

Internet

Internet censorship and surveillance was severe under the rule of Hosni Mubarak, culminating in a total shutdown of the internet in Egypt during the 2011 Revolution, though it was restored following the ousting of Mubarak. If you don't want to use international roaming, a mobile and data sim is cheap, fast and your best bet in Egypt – available from phone shops from Etisalat, Vodafone and Orange. Not a lot of cafés have Wi-fi, as they are basically places for men

to drink Arabic coffee and smoke shisha pipes, but the bigger hotels and those popular with tourists do, and although it can be patchy, it is fast enough.

L

LGBTQ travellers

Although same-sex relationships are technically not a crime in Egypt, the charge of "debauchery" has been used to prosecute LGBTQ people. Any displays of affection between same-sex couples should be completely avoided in public and outwardly flirtatious behaviour is regarded as crass and immoral. However, foreign gay or lesbian couples should have no issues with requesting a double bed at most mid-range and top-end accommodation in the tourist areas.

M

Media

Radio
The Egyptian Radio and Television Union (ERTU) is the public broadcaster of Egypt, operated by the Egyptian government with dozens of radio stations from pop music to readings from the Qur'an. Most accessible for English speakers is Radio Cairo, 95.4 FM, for its mix of current music, news, sports, chat shows and podcasts. Nile FM, 104.2

Friendly face in Aswan.

FM, is a privately owned English-language radio station based in Cairo that plays English-language music hits and syndicated American and British current affairs and chat shows.

Television

Again, the state-owned Egyptian Radio and Television Union (ERTU) is the main broadcaster, and there are more than 10 stations, but these are rarely exciting. But it is the arrival of satellite television that has revolutionised viewing in Egypt, and satellite dishes now top many of Cairo's apartment blocks as well as rural houses. Egyptians spend a significant amount of time watching television – particularly during Ramadan when more than 50 extra TV series are especially made for broadcast. Most hotels, even quite modest ones, offer satellite TV, which usually includes channels for foreign films, kids' cartoons, syndicated American lifestyle and chat shows, and news and sport from CNN, BBC World or Al Jazeera.

Newspapers

In Cairo, all the major English, French, German and Italian daily newspapers are available at larger hotels and at newsstands in Zamalik and Maadi.

There are dozens of local publications – both in print and online. *Al-Ahram*, "The Pyramids", was established in 1875, making it the oldest newspaper in Egypt. It is still the most widely circulating daily newspaper. It also publishes two other Arabic-language editions – one geared to the Arab world and the other aimed at an international audience – as well as editions in English and French. In English, it is available online at http://english.ahram.org.eg.

The Daily News is another English option and is available both in print and online (www.dailynewsegypt.com). Online news portals in various languages include *Egypt Today* (www.egypttoday.com), which was launched in 2017 and covers local and international news and analysis, as well as cultural and lifestyle features. It also publishes a monthly magazine along with the corresponding *Business Today Egypt*. *CairoScene* (http://thecairoscene.me) is an informal website in English designed to appeal to fashionable Egyptians, tourists and foreign residents, and features gossipy news, but is best for listings for events, films, arts and culture, and travel news from around the country.

Money

Airport exchange

On arrival in Egypt, there are banks, bureau de changes and ATMs at the airports that are open 24 hours or to meet incoming flights. US dollars, euros and pounds sterling are the easiest to change (and change back at the end of your stay). Credit cards are accepted in most major hotels, but not always in shops and restaurants and certainly not at market stalls or by taxis. It is advisable to get some cash for smaller incidentals, meals and souvenirs from ATMs, which are widespread in the cities, but load up with cash before going somewhere remote like the oases in the Western Desert. How much you can withdraw each day depends on the limit set by your home bank, but it's usually somewhere around EGP2,000. Always keep small change for *baksheesh* (tips).

The currency is the Egyptian pound, divided into 100 piastres (pt), and is denoted variously as EGP, E£ or LE, which stands for Livre Égyptienne (French for Egyptian pound).

Denominations are as follows:
- notes in EGP: 200, 100, 50, 20, 10, 5.
- coins in EGP: 1 – note that most of the smaller piastre coins are being phased out.

Currently there are just over EGP 20 to the £1, EGP 18.5 to €1, and EGP 16.5 to the US$1.

Opening hours

Banks: Mon–Fri 8.30am–2pm, 9.30am–1.30pm during Ramadan. Closed Saturday, Sunday and public holidays.

Businesses: business hours are flexible. Few businesses function before 8am; many are open until 5pm, but some close in the afternoon and then reopen at 5pm.

Clinics: customarily open from 5pm to 8pm.

Government offices: 8am–2pm, closed Friday, Saturday and most holidays.

Shops: shop opening hours vary according to location and demand. In Cairo and the other major cities, shops generally open at 10am and can stay open until 8pm, but they close for a lengthy three-hour lunch. Muslim-owned shops may close all day on Friday, and Christian-owned shops all day on Sunday.

Khan El Khalili bazaar: open daily 10am–6pm or 7pm (later in summer and during Ramadan); most shops in the bazaar close from about midday to 3pm on Friday and many stalls are closed on Sunday.

Photography

Egypt is a photographer's paradise. Photography is forbidden in security zones, and a variety of rules pertain to Pharaonic monuments. In other areas photography is permitted for a fee. Charges for cameras run as high as EGP50, for video cameras up to EGP300. When it is permitted, flash photography is not allowed inside tombs and in museums.

Scholars and professional photographers working on projects

Egyptian money.

Eating the evening meal during Ramadan, Hurghada.

may apply to the Supreme Council for Antiquities for a special permit. Passes are not given out freely.

Photographing people requires a bit of consideration. Egyptians are constantly having cameras pushed in their faces, so be courteous, ask first and be prepared to pay if necessary.

Postal services

The Central Post Office at Midan al-Atabah in Cairo is open Saturday–Thursday 7am–7pm, Friday and public holidays 7am–noon. All other post offices are open daily 8.30am–3pm, except Friday. A post office locator can be found on Egypt Post's website: www.egyptpost.org. Post boxes, found on street corners and in front of post offices, are red for regular Egyptian mail, blue for overseas airmail letters and green for Cairo and express mail within Cairo.

Allow five days for airmail to Europe, 10 days to America. Mail sent from hotels seems to arrive quickest.

The major post offices, marked with the EMS sign, offer an international Express Mail Service (EMS; www.ems.post), which is more expensive but much faster. In addition to this there are various international courier services. Pick-ups can be arranged and office locations can be found on the websites:
DHL; www.dhlegypt.com
Federal Express; www.egyptexpress.com.eg
TNT; www.tnt.com

Public holidays

The following fixed national holidays in Egypt are celebrated across the country, when banks, government offices, schools and many businesses are closed.

Revolution Day 2011 and National Police Day 25 January
This double holiday celebrates both the day of the beginning of the Egyptian Revolution against President Mubarak in 2011, and the police's resistance against the British Army in 1952 during the final months of the colonial era.

Sinai Liberation Day 25 April
The day of the final withdrawal of the Israeli military from the Sinai in 1982.

Labour Day 1 May
Like Workers' Day in many other countries and a day off for all Egyptians.

30 June Day 30 June
Commemorates the June 2013 protests that saw President Morsi deposed by the military.

Revolution Day 23 July
Celebrates the revolution of 1952 against the monarchy, which led to the modern state of Egypt.

Armed Forces Day 6 October
Marks Egypt's first military victory in the Yom Kippur or October War against Israel, which lead to the liberation of the Sinai.

Muslim holidays

These are governed by the Muslim lunar calendar (see Calendars, page 312).

Feast of Breaking the Fast, 'Id al-Fitr, celebrates the end of Ramadan, the month of daytime fasting. During Ramadan, Muslims abstain from food, drink and sex during daylight hours. Business and social life, centring on the meal eaten after sunset, called iftar, becomes nocturnal and intense. 'Id al-Fitr, which is signalled by the appearance of the new moon, is a happy celebration with new clothes, gifts and a feast. It usually lasts for three days.

Feast of the Sacrifice, 'Id al-Adha, begins about 70 days after the end of Ramadan and commemorates Abraham's sacrifice of a sheep in place of his son. It is traditional to kill a sheep and share the meat with the extended family, neighbours and the poor. The festivities last for four days.

Other Muslim holidays include Ras al-Sana al-Higriya, the Islamic New Year, and Mawlid al-Nabi, the Prophet Muhammad's birthday.

Coptic holidays

Coptic Christmas lands on 7 January. Copts observe the birth of Christ on the same date as all other Orthodox churches except the Armenian. Prior to the feast they abstain from animal flesh and products for 43 days.

Coptic Easter ends the Coptic Lenten season. It is usually celebrated one week after Western Easter, when Coptic businesses are closed. Sham an-Nissim, or "Sniffing the Breeze", is celebrated on the Monday after Coptic Easter and is a real spring festival. Dating from Pharaonic times, It is marked by all Egyptians regardless of their religion. The tradition is for everyone to take a picnic out to the countryside or to an urban green space for the day.

R

Religion and religious services

Islam is the official religion of Egypt, but there is a large Coptic community and other Christian sects are represented in the country. There is also a small Jewish community. Islam is part of the Judaeo-Christian family of religions and was revealed to the Prophet Muhammad in what is now Saudi Arabia.

Islam

Islam has five major principles, known as "pillars", which form the foundation of the religion. The first principle is the belief that there is only one God and that the Prophet Muhammad is the messenger of God. The second is prayer, which should be performed five times every day. The third is almsgiving, and Muslims often donate a

☎ Telephone codes

Alexandria	03
Aswan	097
Asyut	088
Cairo	02
Hurghada	065
Ismailia	064
Luxor	095
Port Said	066
Sharm El Sheikh	069
Suez	062

percentage of their earnings to others. The fourth pillar is fasting during daylight hours throughout the holy month of Ramadan. The fifth pillar is the pilgrimage to Mecca, *haj*, which all Muslims hope to perform at least once. The pilgrimage is performed during the month of Dhu'l-Higga, which begins 70 days after the end of the Ramadan fast.

Coptic Orthodox

The Copts, who account for about 10 percent of the population, are a Christian sect, which separated from the Byzantine and Latin churches in AD 451 over a disagreement in religious doctrine. Copts founded the world's first monasteries, and the monastic tradition is an important part of the faith.

Religious observances

Non-Muslims should not enter mosques while prayers are in progress, and in mosques listed as antiquities they will not be asked an entrance fee, but the custodian will expect a tip. Muslims may enter any mosque free of charge. Non-Muslims should remove their shoes

St Paul's Coptic monastery.

before entering a mosque, and women should cover their hair.

Services

Visitors can attend any church service, and there are numerous services held all over Cairo, with times listed in the monthly *Egypt Today* magazine or in the weekend newspapers. The church of St Sergius and the Hanging Church in Coptic Cairo have the holy liturgy in Coptic and Arabic on Sunday from 6am to 8am. Even though you may not understand the words, the chanting is something quite special.

S

Shopping

There's plenty of opportunity to shop for souvenirs in Egypt in the souks, markets and specialist tourist shops. Haggling is a way of life in Egypt and vendors expect you to knock their initial prices down. The first price quoted can be as much as 10 times the worth of the piece. But more often than not, when you walk away complaining that their price is too high, the vendor will follow you, and if you stick with your maximum bid, most of the time they'll agree to it. Specialist items to look out for include papyrus pictures painted with traditional scenes from Ancient Egypt (although be aware most these days are banana leaf); carpets; gold (check the quality though); decorative lamps; ornaments made from onyx or alabaster; glassware and ceramics; arabesque-style boxes designed

with Islamic geometric patterns; cotton clothing and handmade leather slippers; Bedouin embroidery and jewellery; and authentic Egyptian cartouches (a kind of nameplate in hieroglyphic symbols hung as a pendant on a necklace). Cairo features a number of modern shopping malls featuring international brands where prices are fixed.

T

Telephones

Most five-star hotels offer a direct-dial service, but the costs are at a premium.

It is cheap to buy a SIM-card in Egypt, which can be used if your mobile phone is unblocked and you don't want to use international roaming. It is perhaps the cheapest way to call abroad and use data as a traveller. SIMs are available at phone shops from Etisalat, Vodafone and Orange, which are found at the airports and everywhere in all cities. Top-up cards can also be bought through your phone, or from these shops. In addition, scratch cards are available from small shops.

Time zones

Egypt observes Eastern European Time all year; (GMT + 2), which is exactly the same as Central Africa Time and South African Standard Time, and is collinear with neighbouring Libya and Sudan.

Tourist information

Egyptian Tourism Authority

Head office: Misr Travel Tower, 11 Abassya Square, Nasr City, tel: 02-3771 8921.

www.egypt.travel

Tourist offices: 5 Shari Adly, Downtown, tel: 02-2391 3454; Pyramids ticket office, Giza, tel: 02-3385 0259; Cairo International Airport, tel: 02-2291 4255; Ramses Railway Station, tel: 02-2276 4214.

New York

45 Rockefeller Plaza, New York, NY 10111, tel: 212-332 2570.

London

170 Piccadilly, W1J 9EJ, tel: 0207-493 5283.

Tour operators and travel agents

Abercrombie & Kent Egypt
2 Talaat Harb, 7th Floor, Downtown,
tel: 02-2394 7701
www.akdmc.com

Djed Egypt Travel
33 Shari Abd El Khalek Tharwat,
Downtown, tel: 02-2395 9124
www.djedegypt.com

Emo Tours Egypt
110 Shari El Ahram, next to Mercure
Cairo Le Sphinx Hotel, tel: 02-2347
1972
www.emotoursegypt.com

Misr Travel
1 Talaat Harb, Downtown, tel:
02-1244 7333
www.misrtravel.org

Soliman Travel
14 Ibn Bassam St, El Nozha,
Heliopolis, tel: 02-7370 6446
www.solimantravel.com

Travel Joy Egypt
3rd floor, 23 Shari Abd El Khalek
Tharwat, Downtown, tel: 011
28820106
www.traveljoyegypt.com

Visas and passports

All travellers entering Egypt must
have a passport valid for at least
six months and a valid visa. Visas
currently cost US$25, are valid
for a period of three consecutive months and can be used for
up to 30 days. For most visitors,
including nationals of the UK, the
European Union and the United
States, it is easiest and cheapest
to get a tourist visa at the point of
arrival. They can be obtained from
Cairo International Airport, Luxor
Airport, Aswan Airport, Hurghada
Airport, Sharm El Sheikh and
Alexandria Port. The fee can only
be paid in cash, but if you have currencies other than US dollars, bank
kiosks will exchange your money. It
is more time-consuming and costly
to acquire a visa in advance at an
Egyptian consulate abroad (see
page 314). Alternatively, you can
apply for an e-Visa at www.egypt
immigration.org.

Alexandria's souq.

Lost or stolen passports must be
reported to the police immediately. It
is a good idea to keep a photocopy of
your passport somewhere safe. New
passports can be issued in a matter
of hours at the consular office of
your embassy in Egypt but you will
require a copy of the police report
verifying the loss.

Extension of stay

Visas can be renewed at the
Mugama'a (Cairo's massive central
administrative building on Midan
at-Tahrir), generally after waiting
for a significant period of time. It
is inadvisable to overstay the initial
30 days as you will not be granted
entry in the future.

Websites

www.egypt.travel
Egyptian Tourism Authority.
http://sis.gov.eg
Information on Egypt from the
Egyptian State Information Service.
www.redsea-diving.info
Good information about the Red Sea
and diving.
http://thecairoscene.me
Cairo listings, new openings, restaurant and bar reviews.
www.egy.com
Modern history and architecture by
Samir Raafat.
www.guardians.net
Egyptology site run by the director of
the Supreme Council of Antiquities,
Zahi Hawass.
www.egyptair.com

The site for national carrier,
EgyptAir.
www.discoveringegypt.com
Egypt and Egyptology, especially
designed for school children.
www.ask-aladdin.com
Good general travel information and
also an agent for tours.
www.egyptimmigration.org
Website for Egyptian e-Visa
application.

Weights and measures

Egypt uses the metric system and
road signs (in both Arabic and
English) are denoted in kilometres.

What to bring

Be modest, be sensible and travel
light. Egypt is a conservative country, and it is disrespectful and an
affront to your hosts to wear clothing that is considered immodest.
Loose-fitting garments are appropriately modest and extremely practical in a hot climate. Both men and
women should keep their shoulders
and upper arms covered, and skirts
and shorts should at least cover the
knees. Away from the tourist areas,
it's advisable for men to wear trousers and women loose long trousers
and wrist-length tops. Alternatively,
a sarong or wrap is handy for
women to cover-up or use as a
headscarf. Swimwear should only be
worn on tourist beaches and hotel
pools; no topless or nude bathing is
permitted.

On the practical side, leave your
synthetics at home as they will prove
too hot in the summer and not warm
enough in winter. Lightweight and
quick-drying cotton is suitable for
all seasons, but bring a sweater or
fleece and light jacket for winter and
to cover up on cool summer nights.
Hats are vital to protect against heat
stroke, and so are sunglasses to
defend the eyes against the glare.
Bring stout, comfortable shoes: you
will be doing a lot of walking and
neither the streets nor the temple
floors are friendly to feet.

Almost everything you are likely to
need can be bought in Cairo, but may
be cheaper at home. Bring medica-
tions with you, as well as a basic
first-aid kit; antibiotics and remedies for diarrhoea may well come
in handy, too. If you have a favourite
sun lotion, toothpaste or shampoo,
bring it with you.

LANGUAGE

Standard Arabic is the official language of Egypt and the most widely written – it is taught in schools and is used for television, official government speeches, in the newspapers and so on. However, the most commonly spoken language is Egyptian Arabic. Locally it's called Masri or Masry, meaning simply "Egyptian". Masri is effectively a North African dialect of conventional Arabic; there is little variance and it can be understood by other Arab nations. To the untrained ear they will sound the same, and as a visitor, learning the differences is largely unnecessary.

Given that Egypt was a British colony for 70 years, most educated Egyptians learn English in school as well. If you stick to cities and tourist areas, you should comfortably be able to get by on English alone. But knowing a few words of the local language is polite, especially if you want to escape Egypt's well-established tourist trail.

PRONUNCIATION

Vowels

´ = glottal stop
a = a as in cat
aa = a as in RP English castle
e = e as in very
i = i as in if, stiff
ii = ee as in between
o = o as in boss
u = u as in RP put
uu = o as in fool

Consonants

All consonants are pronounced individually and as they normally are in English, with these exceptions (all emphatic consonants omitted):

kh = ch as in Scottish loch
sh = sh as in shut
gh = Arabic *ghayn*, usually described as resembling a (guttural) Parisian r
q = Arabic qaf, frequently pronounced in Cairo as a k or a glottal stop

GREETINGS

Hello, welcome *ahlan wa sahlan*
Good morning *sabáh-il-kheyr*
Good evening *masáal-kheyr*
Goodbye *mas-saláama*
What is your name? *íssmak eh?* **(to a male)**; *íssmik eh?* **(to a female)**
How are you? *izzáyak* **(to a male)**; *izzáyik* **(to a female)**
I am fine *kwayiss* **(M)**, *kwayíssa* **(F)**
Thank God *il-hamdo li-lah* (standard reply)
Often heard is "insha'Allah", which means "God willing". The standard reply to a casual "see you tomorrow", for instance, is "insha'Allah".
Do you speak English? *Betekkallem 'engelizi?* **(to a male)**, *betekkallemi 'engelizi* **(to a female)**
Please/thank you *minfadlak/ shukran*

Sign to Luxor Temple.

AT THE HOTEL

hotel *fúnduq*
room *ghorfa*
key *meftah*
bathroom *hammam*
towel *futa, manchafa*
I have reserved a room *ana hagazt oda*
How much does a room cost? *bi kam el-oda?*

SHOPPING

How much? *bekam?*
I want to pay for this *oreed an adfaa lehaza*
change/no change *fakka/mafiish fakka*
Where can I buy...? *fein mumken ashtari...?*
It's too expensive *ghali awi*

TRAVELLING

airport *matár*
plane *tayara*
bus *auto beas*
train *atre or kittar*

Packed teahouse in Cairo's Khan El Khalili Bazaar.

morning *is-sobh*
afternoon *bad id-dohr*
at night *belayl*
I/you *ana/enta*
he/she *huwwa/hiyya*
they/we *humma/ehna*

DAYS OF THE WEEK

Sunday *yowm al had*
Monday *yowm al-itnéyn*
Tuesday *yowm it-taláat*
Wednesday *yowm al-árba*
Thursday *yowm al-khamíis*
Friday *yowm ig-góma*
Saturday *yowm is-sabt*

MONTHS OF THE YEAR

January *yanáyer*
February *febráyer*
March *máris*
April *abreel*
May *mayuu*
June *yuunyuu*
July *ylílyuu*
August *aghustus*
September *sibtímbir*
October *októbir*
November *nofímbir*
December *disímbir*

boat *mérkeb*
car *arabiyya, sayára*
station *mahatta*
ticket *tazkara*
departure *zehab*
arrival *wussul*
delay *taakhear*
travel agent *wikalat safar*
When does the.... arrive? *emta wussul...*
When does the... leave? *emta qiyam...*
I want to go to... *ayez arrouh ella...*
Stop here please *wakeff hena men fadlak*
I need a ticket please *menfadlak aoreed tazkara*

chicken *dajaj*
fish *samak*
dessert *helu*
fruit *fakiha*
Can you recommend a restaurant? *hal youmken an torasheh mataam?*
May I have the bill please? *momken el-he-ssab men fadlak?*

SIGHTSEEING

visit *ziara*
open *maftuh*
closed *maqfoul*
ticket office *shubbak*
ticket *tazkara*
museum *mat-hhaf*
mosque *gamea*
May I visit the mosque? *mumken azur el-gamea?*
May I take a photo here? *mumken akhud surah hina?*

HEALTH

hospital *mustáshfa*
pharmacy *ssaydaliya*
doctor *doctur*
I'm feeling sick *ahsaor bel taab*
Where is the hospital? *Ayna hwa mustáshfa?*

EMERGENCIES

police *bolice/bishorta*
fire brigade *matafy/shurtat el-mataf*
I need help *ahtaju ila almusa'ada*
Can you call the police? *hal yumki-noka alitissal bishorta?*
Please call the doctor *etlob el-tabib men fadlak*
Call the ambulance *ettasel bel isaaf*

EATING OUT

restaurant *mataam*
breakfast *íftar*
lunch *ghada*
dinner *asha*
water *mayya*
juice *assir*
coffee *ahua*
tea *shay*
bread *aish*
salad *salata*
vegetables *khodar*
meat *lahma*

USEFUL WORDS

yes/no *aywa/laa'*
right *yemiin*
left *shemáal*
and/or *wa/walla*
big/little *kibiir/sughayyar*
good/bad *kwáyyis/mish kwáyyis*
here/there *hena/henáak*
hot/cold *sukhn/baarid*
many/few *kitiir/olayyel*
up/down *fo' (foq)/taht*
more/enough *kamáan/kefáya*
today *innahárda*
tomorrow *bokra*
yesterday *embáareh*

NUMBERS

1 *wáhid*
2 *itneyn*
3 *taláatah*
4 *arbá*
5 *khamsa*
6 *sitta*
7 *séha*
8 *tamánya*
9 *tíssah*
10 *áshara*
11 *hedásher*
12 *itnásher*
13 *talalásher*
14 *arbatasher*
15 *khamastásher*
16 *sitásher*
17 *sabatásher*
18 *tamantásher*
19 *tissatásher*
20 *ashríin*
30 *talatíin*
40 *arbaíin*
50 *khamsíin*
60 *sittíin*
70 *sabaíin*
80 *tamaníin*
90 *tissaíin*
100 *miiya, miit*

FURTHER READING

GENERAL

Alexandria: City of Memory, by Michael Haag. Illustrated with photographs, this is an engaging portrait of Alexandria during the first half of the 20th century when it was one of the liveliest and most cosmopolitan ports on the Mediterranean.

Apricots on the Nile: A Memoir with Recipes, by Colette Rossant. French-born Rossant is waiting out World War II among her father's Egyptian-Jewish relatives in Cairo, and by engaging with the cooks and servants in the kitchen, develops a love of the food. She evokes a good description of Cairo at the time.

A History of Egypt: From Earliest Times to the Present, by Jason Thompson. Thompson manages to cover and connect an impressive 5,000 years of Egyptian history in this single, weighty volume.

A Taste of Egypt: Home Cooking from the Middle East, by Dyna Eldaief. Egyptian-Australian food blogger Dyna Eldaief has a passion for Egyptian cooking that is equalled by her nostalgia for the country itself. Beautiful photographs of Egypt's people and markets place the recipes firmly in context.

Egypt Inside Out, by Trevor Naylor. Beautifully illustrated hard back (photographs by Doriana Dimitrova) that takes readers on a journey through Egypt, unearthing the essential qualities that make it just so special. From vast desert landscapes to the thronging streets of Cairo, Naylor's love letter to Egypt is irresistible.

Grand Hotels of Egypt: In the Golden Age of Travel, by Andrew Humphreys. A fascinating insight into the histories of Egypt's most iconic hotels, from the days of the earliest explorers. Hosting diplomats, military men, pioneers, artists, academics, archaeologists and socialites, these hotels provided bed, board and much more for major personalities from Winston Churchill to Agatha Christie and TE Lawrence.

Lifting the Veil: Two Centuries of Travellers, Traders and Tourists in Egypt, by Anthony Sattin. Stories about the first tourists, soldiers, fortune-seekers, tomb-raiders and empire-builders that travelled to Egypt, from Napoleon Bonaparte to the last British troops who departed Suez.

Manners and Customs of the Modern Egyptians, by Edward William Lane. First published in 1833, this two-volume book has been reprinted for astonishingly almost 190 years

⏏ Send us your thoughts

We do our best to ensure the information in our books is as accurate and up-to-date as possible. The books are updated on a regular basis using local contacts, who painstakingly add, amend and correct as required. However, some details (such as telephone numbers and opening times) are liable to change, and we are ultimately reliant on our readers to put us in the picture.

We welcome your feedback, especially your experience of using the book "on the road". Maybe you came across a great bar or new attraction we missed.

We will acknowledge all contributions, and we'll offer an Insight Guide to the best letters received.

Please write to us at:
Insight Guides
PO Box 7910
London SE1 1WE

Or email us at:
hello@insightguides.com

(last in 2016). Lane went to Egypt in 1825, and adopting the native customs, and with a good knowledge of Arabic, he mingled with the people; this is his account.

The Egyptians: A Radical Story, by Jack Shenker. Award-winning journalist Jack Shenker explores the wider context behind the Egyptian Revolution of 2011 that deposed Hosni Mubarak, revealing a surging public desire for democracy, sovereignty and social justice.

The Pharaoh's Shadow: Travels in Modern and Ancient Egypt, by Anthony Sattin. Also by Sattin, a British journalist and broadcaster. This is his memoir as he travels around Egypt visiting the archaeological sites and is a mix of history and travelogue.

The Voice of Egypt: Umm Kulthum, Arabic Song and Egyptian Society in the Twentieth Century, by Virginia Danielson. Chronicles the life of Umm Kulthum, the "voice of Egypt" and the most celebrated musical performer of the 20th century in the Arab world.

The White Nile and *The Blue Nile*, by Alan Moorehead. Originally written by Moorehead in 1960 and 1962 respectively, these books are ideally read consecutively and tell the story of the discovery of, and the events associated with, the Nile over 200 years. It starts with Richard Burton and John Hanning Speke setting out to find the source in 1858.

Women Travellers on the Nile: An Anthology of Travel Writing through the Centuries, by Deborah Manley. An all-female cast provide personal accounts of Egypt from 1779 through to 2006: Harriet Martineau, Florence Nightingale and Lucie Duff Gordon to name a few.

ANCIENT EGYPT

Egyptian Art, by Bill Manley. Richly illustrated tome tracing ancient Egyptian art, its motifs, its symbols and its legacy across some 3,000 years.

The Complete Gods and Goddesses of Ancient Egypt, by Richard H. Wilkinson. Lavishly illustrated with photographs and drawings, this text examines the evolution, worship and eventual decline of the numerous gods and goddesses of Ancient Egypt. Wilkinson is also author of *The Complete Temples of Ancient Egypt*.

The *Encyclopaedia of Ancient Egyptian Architecture*, by Arnold Dieter. This generously illustrated volume is the definitive reference on the diverse monuments built by the Ancient Egyptians across three millennia.

The Great Book of Ancient Egypt: In the Realm of the Pharaohs, by Zahi Hawass, an Egyptologist, archaeologist and former Minister of State for Antiquities Affairs. In this book, which is illustrated by hundreds of photographs, he explores the major archaeological sites and shares details of his personal adventures. When US President Barack Obama visited Egypt in 2009, Hawass was his guide.

The Rise and Fall of Ancient Egypt, by Toby Wilkinson. This tome gives a comprehensive documentation of the civilisation from 3000 BC to the reign of Cleopatra, the last active ruler of the Ptolemaic period, and covers the building of the pyramids and the conquest of Nubia.

The Story of Egypt: The Civilization that Shaped the World, by Joann Fletcher. Focuses on the history of Egypt from the earliest evidence of nomadic peoples, through its many dynasties of pharaohs, up until the annexation of the country by Rome. Professor Joann Fletcher also presented the *Immortal Egypt* TV series for the BBC.

King Tutankhamun: The Treasures of the Tomb, by Zahi Hawass. Also written by Hawass, this brilliantly illustrated book takes the reader through Tutankhamun's tomb, room by room, and in the order that it was discovered and excavated by Howard Carter in 1922.

FICTION

The Alexandria Quartet, by Lawrence Durrell. Published between 1957 and 1960, this quartet of novels – *Justine, Balthazar, Mountolive* and *Clea* – are stories of the trials and tribulations of a number of characters in Alexandria during World War II.

The Cairo House, by Samia Serageldin. This novel tells the story of a prominent Egyptian family's struggle to survive the turmoil of the post-World War II world in Cairo.

Death on the Nile, by Agatha Christie. This classic novel is about intrigue and murder on a Nile cruise and features the Belgian detective Hercule Poirot. The book was first published in 1937 and Christie wrote much of it from the Old Cataract Hotel in Aswan. The movie was made in 1978 and a remake is due in 2020; much of the filming for both is in Egypt.

The Forgotten Pharaoh, by David Adkins. This historical novel mixes fact with fiction, set during the 18th Dynasty under pharaohs Ahmose I, Hatshepsut, Thutmose III, Amenhotep III, Akhenaten and Tutankhamun. It's a "might-have-been" story about little-known Smenkhkare, the youngest son of Amenhotep III and brother to Akhenamun.

Our Horses in Egypt, by Rosalind Belben. The story of Philomena, an English hunting horse shipped to Egypt by the British army in World War I to become a military mount, and of Griselda, her former owner, who goes to Egypt in a bid to recover her.

The Quest, River God, The Seventh Scroll, Warlock, Pharaoh and *River God*, by Wilbur Smith. These six novels make up Smith's Ancient Egypt historical saga series and feature numerous characters from pharaohs to slaves.

Taxi, by Khaled Al Khamissi. Wonderful short stories based on conversations with taxi drivers in Cairo that give an inside view of the daily struggle to grind out a living on the streets.

The Cairo Trilogy, by Naguib Mahfouz. This accomplished trio of novels – named after streets in Cairo and written by Mahfouz, winner of the 1988 Novel Prize – follows three generations of the same family from 1917 to 1944. The family's fortunes are closely tied to those of a turbulent Egypt.

The Televangelist: A Novel, by Ibrahim Essa. Intriguing novel about Hatem el-Shenawi, TV star, celebrity and Islamic preacher. Hosting a popular call-in show, Hatem discusses different facets of Islam with a medley of different characters, allowing Essa to provide an insightful commentary on modern Islam and state media control, as well as on the relationship between Egypt and the West.

The Yacoubian Building, by Alaa al-Aswany. Superb evocative novel about the lives of several families sharing one apartment building in downtown Cairo; some live in squalor on its rooftop while others inhabit the faded glory of its apartments and offices.

CREDITS

INSIGHT GUIDE CREDITS

Distribution
UK, Ireland and Europe
Apa Publications (UK) Ltd;
sales@insightguides.com
United States and Canada
Ingram Publisher Services;
ips@ingramcontent.com
Australia and New Zealand
Woodslane; info@woodslane.com.au
Southeast Asia
Apa Publications (SN) Pte;
singaporeoffice@insightguides.com
Worldwide
Apa Publications (UK) Ltd;
sales@insightguides.com
Special Sales, Content Licensing and CoPublishing
Insight Guides can be purchased in bulk quantities at discounted prices. We can create special editions, personalised jackets and corporate imprints tailored to your needs.
sales@insightguides.com
www.insightguides.biz

Printed in China

All Rights Reserved
© 2020 Apa Digital (CH) AG and
Apa Publications (UK) Ltd

First Edition 1987
Seventh Edition 2020

Every effort has been made to provide accurate information in this publication, but changes are inevitable. The publisher cannot be responsible for any resulting loss, inconvenience or injury. We would appreciate it if readers would call our attention to any errors or outdated information. We also welcome your suggestions; please contact us at: hello@insightguides.com

www.insightguides.com

Editor: Helen Fanthorpe
Author: Lizzie Williams, Sylvie Franquet and Chris Bradley
Head of DTP and Pre-Press: Rebeka Davies
Managing Editor: Carine Tracanelli
Picture Editor: Tom Smyth
Cartography: original cartography Colourmap Scanning, updated by Carte

CONTRIBUTORS

This new edition was commissioned and copyedited by **Helen Fanthorpe** and comprehensively updated by **Lizzie Williams**. Originally from the UK, and now based in Cape Town, Lizzie has travelled in Africa and the Middle East for more than 25 years and has authored and contributed to more than 70 guide books. In Egypt, she's driven through Cairo's unfathomable traffic, camped in silence in the Western Desert, glided peacefully on the Nile by felucca and been awestruck by the magnificent tombs and temples. The book builds on the excellent work of previous authors, including **Sylvie Franquet, Chris Bradley, John Rodenbeck, Hisham Youssef, Jill Kamil, Max Rodenbeck, Elizabeth Maynard, William Lyster, Carina Campobasso, Alice Brinton** and **Cassandra Vivan**. This book was proofread and indexed by **Claire Rogers**.

ABOUT INSIGHT GUIDES

Insight Guides have more than 45 years' experience of publishing high-quality, visual travel guides. We produce 400 full-colour titles, in both print and digital form, covering more than 200 destinations across the globe, in a variety of formats to meet your different needs.

Insight Guides are written by local authors, whose expertise is evident in the extensive historical and cultural background features. Each destination is carefully researched by regional experts to ensure our guides provide the very latest information. All the reviews in **Insight Guides** are independent; we strive to maintain an impartial view. Our reviews are carefully selected to guide you to the best places to eat, go out and shop, so you can be confident that when we say a place is special, we really mean it.

Legend

City maps

	Freeway/Highway/Motorway
	Divided Highway
	Main Roads
	Minor Roads
	Pedestrian Roads
	Steps
	Footpath
	Railway
	Funicular Railway
	Cable Car
	Tunnel
	City Wall
	Important Building
	Built Up Area
	Other Land
	Transport Hub
	Park
	Pedestrian Area
	Bus Station
	Tourist Information
	Main Post Office
	Cathedral/Church
	Mosque
	Synagogue
	Statue/Monument
	Beach
	Airport

Regional maps

	Freeway/Highway/Motorway (with junction)
	Freeway/Highway/Motorway (under construction)
	Divided Highway
	Main Road
	Secondary Road
	Minor Road
	Track
	Footpath
	International Boundary
	State/Province Boundary
	National Park/Reserve
	Marine Park
	Ferry Route
	Marshland/Swamp
	Glacier Salt Lake
	Airport/Airfield
	Ancient Site
	Border Control
	Cable Car
	Castle/Castle Ruins
	Cave
	Chateau/Stately Home
	Church/Church Ruins
	Crater
	Lighthouse
	Mountain Peak
	Place of Interest
	Viewpoint

INDEX